HUERTA

A POLITICAL PORTRAIT

By

Michael C. Meyer

HUERTA

UNIVERSITY OF NEBRASKA PRESS • LINCOLN

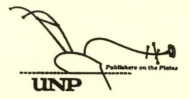

COPYRIGHT © 1972 BY THE UNIVERSITY OF NEBRASKA PRESS
ALL RIGHTS RESERVED
INTERNATIONAL STANDARD BOOK NUMBER 0-8032-0802-2
LIBRARY OF CONGRESS CATALOG CARD NUMBER 70-162343
MANUFACTURED IN THE UNITED STATES OF AMERICA

To My Parents and Their Grandchildren,
Scott, Debra, and Sharon

Contents

Preface

With all the interest that has focused on the Mexican Revolution in the last two decades and the immense body of literature resulting from that interest, no scholarly study of Victoriano Huerta and his regime based on archival research has been attempted in any language. The diplomacy of the Huerta presidency has been well covered from the Mexican, United States, and British points of view. The period has been circumscribed by excellent biographies of Francisco I. Madero on the one hand and monographs on the Convention of Aguascalientes on the other, but many aspects of the Huerta regime itself remain as enigmatic today as they have been for the last fifty years.

The problem of Mexican Revolutionary historiography is nicely synopsized by Victoriano Huerta's personal file in the Mexican Foreign Relations Archive. The label on the folder originally read "Huerta, Victoriano, Presidente Interino de México." Some well-meaning clerk, however, felt constrained to add the word *Usurpador*. The period from February, 1913, to July, 1914, is a critical era in the history of the early Mexican Revolution, but it does not even warrant a separate chapter in many of the general histories of the movement. In one study the reader is shuttled directly from "Madero" to the "Overthrow of Huerta," in another from "Madero" to "Carranza," and in still another

from "Francisco Madero" to the "Constitutionalist Revolution." The
most important set of published Revolutionary documents devotes
volumes to the *revolución maderista* and even more to the *revolución
constitucionalista* but not even a single volume to the *época huertista.*
It is as though the name itself is anathema and should, therefore, be
avoided.

The reasons for scholarly neglect of the Huerta regime are manifold.
The man himself was scarcely made of the moral fiber that inspires
the biographer hoping to examine the benevolent hero. But this
explanation alone is insufficient because other Mexican antiheroes,
Agustín de Iturbide, Antonio López de Santa Anna, and Porfirio
Díaz—none of whom will ever be remembered for their great humanity
or compassion—have been the subject of scholarly analyses. In the
case of Huerta another consideration is more significant. The commonly understood ideological posture of his regime has been regarded
as repugnant to the Revolutionary ethos and therefore, to many, not
worthy of serious academic pursuit. But this is precisely the aspect of
the administration most obviously needing systematic investigation.
Still more important is the series of technical obstacles standing in the
way of historical scholarship. There is no known public or private
Huerta archive. The few prominent persons still alive from that
chaotic period are old and reluctant to talk and, if they do, generally
choose to explain away their actions and dissociate themselves from
the regime as much as possible. Contemporary Mexican newspapers
were tightly censored and one is forced not only to use them with
extreme caution but to read between the lines in spite of the erroneous
conclusions which may be drawn.

Given these impediments and unwilling to compromise on the need
for primary research, I was forced to examine the private and public
archives of many persons, some on the fringe of power, whose careers
crossed that of Huerta at one time or another. This approach to
manuscript research made the process of reconstruction much more
tedious than would have been the case had I been able to consult one
or two consolidated collections under a common roof. But although the
process by necessity was drawn out over a long period of time, it did
carry with it certain dividends. The private collections most beneficial
were those of Bernardo Reyes, Samuel Espinosa de los Monteros,
Francisco I. Madero, Venustiano Carranza, Jenaro Amezcua, Francisco
León de la Barra, Silvestre Terrazas, and Albert Bacon Fall. The
number of government archives I believed basic was just as extensive.

In Mexico the records of the archives of the secretaría de gobernación and the Libros Copiadores de Madero were consulted in the Archivo General de la Nación. The diplomatic and consular records, as well as a large number of personal *expedientes* of Mexican officials, were used in the Archivo de la Secretaría de Relaciones Exteriores de México. The Archivo de la Defensa Nacional yielded some pertinent military records. From Washington I was able to secure microfilm copies of manuscripts from the Department of State, Department of Justice, Department of War, Adjutant General's Office, and the Wilson-Bryan Correspondence. And finally, the British Public Record Office made available a microfilm copy of the Embassy and Consular Archives pertaining to Mexico during the period of my interest.

The manuscript sources were complemented nicely by published primary documentation, most importantly the twenty-one volumes edited by the Comisión de Investigaciones Históricas de la Revolución Mexicana under the title of *Documentos Históricos de la Revolución Mexicana,* the *Diario de los Debates* of the Mexican Chamber of Deputies, the *Diario Oficial,* and a surprisingly large number of memoirs written by Huerta's cabinet officials. Numerous secondary works proved valuable as well and reference to them is found in the bibliographical essay.

Although the nature of the primary research trebled the projected time for completing the study, the process yielded much more than a simple store of information. The great diversity of opinion expressed in the governmental manuscripts of three countries, and by a number of prominent individuals often antagonistic to one another, helped to provide independent verification of several critical issues and hopefully helped to control personal prejudices so often nurtured by exposure to a single point of view. The research was disappointing only in one sense. I had hoped to locate private correspondence which would have enabled me to approach the subject with a different set of objectives. But Huerta's private papers, if they still exist, are not in the form of an archive; they possibly have been destroyed.

The nature of the documentation on the Huerta regime—a wealth and a sparsity at the same time—has led to a book which is neither a full-fledged biography nor an administrative history, but rather something in between, a political biography. The dearth of personal correspondence made it impossible to attempt a full biography. Huerta's unresolved inner conflicts must remain a mystery until some scholar, more enterprising, somewhat luckier, and perhaps differently prepared than I, uncovers a dusty box of letters or the draft of a memoir in some unknown Mexican attic. Utilizing the sources available, I have tried to re-create a public life which was molded by the force of events and which in turn shaped the configurations of a society in revolution. I have tried to probe, in so far as documentation, reason, and educated intuition permit, the motives for certain of Huerta's actions but have eschewed Freudian or neo-Freudian interpretation. Neither the data nor my own preparation permitted a venture into psychoanalytic history. My objectives are much more modest. I am interested specifically in the impression which Victoriano Huerta left on the course of his country's twentieth-century experience. More generally, by combining a descriptive narrative with an interpretive one, I hope to elucidate a critical juncture in Mexican Revolutionary history as well as the relationship of a man to his age.

Since the inception of this project some seven years ago I have sought and received assistance from many friends and colleagues. It is a pleasant task to offer thanks for their judgments and advice while at the same time reserving for myself full responsibility for any errors of fact or interpretation.

In 1960 William L. Sherman and Richard E. Greenleaf published a thumbnail reappraisal of Victoriano Huerta based on published materials. Not presuming their study to be a definitive biography, they continually pressed upon me over the years the need for a new study of Huerta and his administration drawn from archival research. Although both are now engaged in the rigors of sixteenth-century Spanish colonial paleography, they have allowed me to test pet theories on them and to solicit their counsel along the way.

Three of my former students, William L. Beezley, Anthony T. Bryan, and Mark T. Gilderhus, were working on related topics in the Mexican archives at the same time I was conducting my research. All of them made note of pertinent documentation that happened across their desks at the archives and graciously passed the information on to me. Similarly, on a subsequent research trip to Mexico City Ramón Ruiz and I were able to exchange both ideas and documentary citations while working at the Fundación Cultural de Condumex. In all of these cases archival material which I might well have missed because of irregularities in classification was brought to my attention.

I profited greatly from extended discussions with Professor Romeo Flores Caballero. His incisive commentaries caused me to reassess certain sections and, I believe, to improve them. Marvin Bernstein read a section of the manuscript with an unusually critical eye and saved me from some embarrassing errors. Trial balloons, perhaps not immediately recognized as such, were lofted from time to time in the presence of Edwin Lieuwen, Stanley R. Ross, Frederick M. Nunn, James W. Wilkie, Charles Hale, Roberto Esquenazi-Mayo, and Jack M. Sosin and their reactions mentally filed for future disposition.

Access to Mexican archival collections was greatly facilitated and guidance to their most profitable use provided through the kind cooperation of Guillermo Tardiff, Jesús Cabrera Muñoz Ledo, J. Ignacio Rubio Mañé, Manuel Saldaña, Josefina González de Arellano, Gustavo A. Pérez Trejo, Juan Luis Mutiozábal, and Antonio Pompa y Pompa. Especially helpful, Alicia Reyes and Eugenia Meyer secured photostatic copies of documents for me from the Capilla Alfonsina and Archivo Histórico de la Defensa Nacional. In both cases the contribution was major.

Finally, to that coterie of valiant wives without whom so many books would not have been written I must once again add Goldalee and for reasons too numerous to mention.

M. C. M.

Lincoln, Nebraska

List of Abbreviations

ABFC   Albert Bacon Fall Collection, Papers from the Senate Office Files of Senator Albert Bacon Fall Relating to Mexican Affairs, Huntington Library, San Marino, California

AEM   Archivo Espinosa de los Monteros, Mexico City

AGN/LCM   Archivo General de la Nación, Libros Copiadores de Madero, Mexico City

AGN/RSG   Archivo General de la Nación, Ramo de la Secretaría de Gobernación, Mexico City

AGO   Records of the Adjutant General's Office, National Archives, Washington, D. C.

AHDN   Archivo Histórico de la Defensa Nacional, Mexico City

AM   Archivo de don Francisco I. Madero, Museo Nacional de Antropología e Historia, Mexico City

APBR   Archivo Particular Bernardo Reyes, Mexico City

AREM   Archivo General de la Secretaría de Relaciones Exteriores de México, Mexico City

Burnside Reports   War Department and General and Special Staff,
                       Military Intelligence Division, Reports of
                       Captain W. A. Burnside, Washington, D. C.
Condumex/AC   Fundación Cultural de Condumex, Archivo
                       Carranza, Mexico City
Condumex/AJA   Fundación Cultural de Condumex, Archivo Par-
                       ticular del General Jenaro Amezcua, Mexico
                       City
Condumex/FLB   Fundación Cultural de Condumex, Corres-
                       pondencia Personal y Oficial de Francisco
                       León de la Barra como Embajador de México
                       y Presidente de la República, Mexico City
DHRM   *Documentos Históricos de la Revolución
                       Mexicana,* edited by Isidro Fabela and the
                       Comisión de Investigaciones Históricas de la
                       Revolución Mexicana, Mexico City
F.O.   Great Britain, Foreign Office, Public Record
                       Office, Embassy and Consular Files, London.
RDJ   Records of the Department of Justice, National
                       Archives, Washington, D. C.
RDS   Records of the Department of State Relating to
                       the Internal Affairs of Mexico, 1910-29, Micro-
                       film Publication, Microcopy No. 274, Wash-
                       ington, D. C.
STC   Silvestre Terrazas Collection, Correspondence
                       and Papers, Bancroft Library, University of
                       California, Berkeley
Wilson-Bryan   Correspondence of Secretary of State William
  Correspondence   Jennings Bryan with President Woodrow Wil-
                       son, 1913-15, National Archives, Washington,
                       D. C.

HUERTA

CHAPTER 1

The Formative Years

IN THE EARLY SUMMER OF 1869 a military convoy slowly wound its way through the treacherous mountains of Michoacán on its way south to Mexico City. It was the rainy season and the normally placid mountain streams became torrents each afternoon. The corn in the terraced farms was only beginning to come up. It would not be harvested for several months. General Donato Guerra, a young cavalry officer who had earned his reputation and his military rank fighting against the French during the recent War of the Intervention, preferred the saddle to the uncomfortable command wagon, but he

1

was behind in his paperwork and for a week resigned himself to sitting in the wagon dictating military reports to his recently acquired secretary, a boy who had just celebrated his fifteenth birthday. In the evenings, in the more convivial atmosphere of the campfire, the general inquired about young Victoriano Huerta's background, and, with the information he had already obtained from the boy's father, was able to piece together a life hardly different from that of tens of thousands of other nineteenth-century rural Mexicans.

Late in the evening of March 23, 1854, a midwife had been summoned to a weather-beaten adobe shack in the town of Colotlán, a village of some 2,200 people, in extreme northern Jalisco. Within the hour a son was born to the Huichol Indian wife of a young mestizo. The following Sunday the local parish priest celebrated a mass and christened the infant Victoriano.

Victoriano Huerta's father farmed an unirrigated plot of land on the outskirts of Colotlán. In many ways he was better off than he would have been as a peón on one of the surrounding haciendas; he enjoyed a modicum of personal freedom. The green chile, corn, and beans which he cultivated provided the family with some of the basic staples but did not allow them to buy other daily necessities. Life for the Huerta family was not good but they accepted it as preordained.

Victoriano spent his first years playing barefoot on the mud streets and along the bank of the Río Colotlán with other Huichol and Teca Indian children. Even as a young child he looked much more like his Indian mother than his mestizo father. In all likelihood *huichichil* was his first language; at least he learned it simultaneously with Spanish.

Unlike many of his neighbors, when his son reached school age, Victoriano's father insisted that he attend classes regularly rather than work at his side in the fields. The young boy in return compiled a good academic record in the poor rural school run by the priest who had christened him.[1] On weekends he brought home a few extra centavos by shining shoes in the village plaza, but as *guaraches* were the common footwear, this enterprise was scarcely profitable. Sometime in his early teens, he read, by chance, in the *Monitor Republicano* an official advertisement listing the necessary qualifications for admission to the Colegio Militar de Chapultepec. He confided to his

1. José T. Meléndez, *Historia de la Revolución Mexicana* (Mexico: Talleres Gráficos de la Nación, 1938), p. 149.

father that he would like to go to Mexico City and follow a military career—a desire that must have seemed sheer fantasy to them both.

But in May, 1869, General Guerra's convoy rode into the center of the town; the commanding officer asked the crowd which had quickly gathered around the troops if there was anyone present who could read and write. Young Victoriano volunteered and, after a cursory examination and a brief chat with the elder Huerta, Guerra took him on as his personal secretary and aide. The general, also a native of Jalisco, was impressed with the unsophisticated intelligence of his new assistant and decided to use his considerable influence in the capital to work for Victoriano's admission to the Colegio Militar. With the intercession of President Benito Juárez himself, General Guerra was able to arrange for Huerta's eventual entrance into the military academy. The chance contact with General Guerra also reaped benefits for Victoriano's father back in Colotlán. For several years after the boy left for Mexico City, the elder Huerta was hired as a stablemaster by General Guerra's personal friend Colonel Miguel Ahumada, and thus was able to escape the dreary life of a rural nineteenth-century Jaliscience.[2]

Huerta did quite well for himself in his five-year cadetship at the Colegio Militar. Although handicapped by his mediocre primary training, as he gained confidence he was able to hold his own in competition with classmates who, destined for a life of privilege, had attended some of the best private schools in the republic. His

2. Data on Victoriano Huerta's early years is extremely sparce and much of what does exist is contradictory. The best single source is George Jay Rausch, Jr., "The Early Career of Victoriano Huerta," *The Americas* 21 (October 1964): 136-45, taken largely from his "Victoriano Huerta: A Political Biography" (Ph.D. diss., University of Illinois, 1960), pp. 1-18. Additional information can be gleaned from a number of articles: Rubén Salido Orcillo, "El Coronel Ahumada y Huerta," *Excélsior*, April 5, 1954, p. 6; Alberto Morales Jiménez, "Gentle del Cuartelazo: Victoriano Huerta," *El Nacional*, September 25, 1943, pp. 3, 7; Hernán Rosales, "Huerta: Los Azares de su Destino," *Todo* 254 (July 21, 1938): 40-41, 62; and Louis Simonds, "Victoriano Huerta, A Sketch from Life," *Atlantic Monthly* 113 (June 1914): 721-32. Finally, several books contain information on Huerta's early years: William L. Sherman and Richard E. Greenleaf, *Victoriano Huerta: A Reappraisal* (Mexico: Mexico City College Press, 1960), pp. 89-94; José Juan Tablada, *Historia de la Campaña de la División del Norte* (Mexico: Imprenta del Gobierno Federal, 1913), pp. 85-87; and Nemesio García Naranjo, *Memorias de Nemesio García Naranjo*, 10 vols. (Monterrey: Talleres de "El Porvenir," n.d.), 7:13. García Naranjo relates that on one occasion shortly after Huerta's admission to the Colegio Militar, Presidente Benito Juárez met him in the patio of the school and admonished him "de los indios que se educan como usted, la patria espera mucho," *Memorias*, 7:13.

analytical skills were solid but scarcely brilliant. Once having been exposed to the full array of subjects required of a Mexican cadet, he developed a special interest in scientific classes, especially mathematics and astronomy, and he consistently excelled in these subjects. While Huerta was in the academy, a new course of study was introduced by the director, General Francisco de Paula Troncoso. Qualified students were allowed to pursue a special course preparing them for eventual assignment on a newly contemplated army General Staff. The first three students admitted to the program, and the first three to complete all of the requirements, were Joaquín Beltrán, Angel García Peña (both of whom subsequently would serve Porfirio Díaz and Francisco I. Madero with distinction), and Victoriano Huerta. Upon graduation in 1877, Huerta received his commission as a second lieutenant in the Corps of Engineers[3] and immediately was chosen to participate in a supplementary training program in Germany. The sudden death of his father, however, left Victoriano the head of the family. Since his mother was completely dependent upon him for support, he requested that he be relieved of the foreign assignment, and the request was honored.[4] Several months later, however, his mother died as well and he was granted twenty-five days leave to attend to family matters.[5]

No reminiscences of the young cadet's personal life at the college have been passed down—no amorous adventure, no scrapes with the law, not even a scuffle with a fellow student. One can but speculate that appreciating his good fortune at having escaped the barren existence of his childhood, he dedicated himself to succeeding in his studies. But imbued as he was with the traditions and psychology of rural, Indian Mexico, the transition could not have been an easy one. On the other hand, the alternatives were all disconcerting and Huerta quickly made himself comfortable in the mold of a junior army officer.

The prerevolutionary military career of Victoriano Huerta coincided almost exactly with the thirty-four-year dictatorship of General Porfirio Díaz. As a federal army officer pledged to support the national government in Mexico City, Victoriano became an agent, and an

3. Victoriano Huerta, Empleos y Fechas en que los Obtuvo, Correspondencia y Historia de la Secretaría de la Defensa Nacional, Cancelados, Archivo Histórico de la Defensa Nacional, Mexico City, Expediente XI/111/1-104 (hereafter cited as AHDN with appropriate information).

4. "A key to the Sanguinary Temperament of Victoriano Huerta," *Current Opinion* 56 (January 1914):20.

5. Victoriano Huerta, Conceptos de los Jefes a cuyas Ordenes ha Servido, AHDN, Cancelados, Exp. XI/111/1-104.

effective one, of the system of enforced peace which has become almost synonomous with the Díaz regime. In spite of his special training at the Colegio Militar, Huerta's first assignment was not to work on the gradually maturing plans for the new General Staff; rather he was ordered to head a small team of army engineers which was charged with constructing and repairing military fortifications in the states of Veracruz and Puebla.[6] Two years later he engaged in combat for the first time when he was sent briefly into Sinaloa and Tepic to participate in a series of pacification campaigns that typify the first Díaz administration's attempt to consolidate power.[7] Huerta played no major role in the engagements of 1878 and 1879. It was at this time, however, that he chanced to meet a young colonel whose career would be intertwined with his own for the next thirty-four years. The young military commander, also serving in the pacification, was Bernardo Reyes.

In 1879 President Díaz determined that the blueprints for the organizational structure of the new General Staff were not being drafted with suitable dispatch and ordered his secretary of war to expedite the preparations. A selected number of junior and senior officers were summoned to the capital and asked to submit plans for consideration. Because of Huerta's educational preparation he was among those chosen to participate. Once the various drafts were studied and modified, the decision fell to the president himself. Díaz chose Huerta's plan for the organization of the General Staff and authorized his promotion to captain.[8]

One of the first tasks the newly organized General Staff set for itself was the preparation of a detailed military map of the republic.

6. Huerta's military service record, including promotions and special honors, has been compiled from his army personnel files and is included as Appendix A, pp. 233-234.

7. It has been conjectured that Huerta saw his first military action at the battle of Tecoac in December, 1876, when Porfirio Díaz defeated the Lerdistas and made good his bid for power. There is no documentary evidence to support this contention, however. See Victoriano Huerta, Campañas y Acciones de Guerra, AHDN, Cancelados, Exp. XI/111/1-104.

8. Substantial information on this period in Huerta's life can be found in an unpublished article prepared for the State Department by Edwin Emerson, a war correspondent in Mexico City: "Victoriano Huerta," Records of the Department of State Relating to the Internal Affairs of Mexico, 1910-29, National Archives Microfilm Publication, Microcopy No. 274, File No. 812.00/7929 (hereafter cited as RDS with appropriate information). Supplementary data are in Manuel Doblado, *El Presidente Huerta y su Gobierno* (Mexico: Imprenta de Antonio Enríquez, 1913), pp. 94-102; and García Naranjo, *Memorias*, 6:282.

The job was undertaken by the Comisión Geográfico Exploradora and Huerta was assigned to the commission headquarters first in Puebla and later in Jalapa, Veracruz. For the next nine years he supervised geographic and geodetic studies, cataloging of flora and fauna, mineralogical exploration, land surveying projects, and, most importantly, the cartographic endeavors ordered by the General Staff. These assignments carried him to almost every state and territory in the republic.[9] By 1890, when he was recalled to Mexico City and received a permanent appointment on the General Staff, he had been promoted twice and held the rank of colonel.

During the late 1880s Huerta married Emilia Aguila. His bride, a well-educated and talented Veracruzan, came from a *criollo* family which had accumulated some wealth in the first half of the nineteenth century but had lost a good portion of it during the period of the French intervention. Throughout Huerta's career Doña Emilia remained in the background but was a continual source of strength to her husband.[10]

Huerta's military career changed drastically in character in October, 1893, when he was pulled off his desk job and sent into the field. The change was occasioned by a serious rebellion in the state of Guerrero.[11] In April, 1893, the governor of the state, Francisco Arce, a hand-picked Díaz politician, completed his third term in office and, in good Porfirian fashion was "elected" to a fourth term. The commander of the federal forces in the state, General Canuto Neri, recognizing the massive popular discontent with the state political machine, decided to lead a rebellion against the incumbent governor. Although General Neri wrote immediately to Díaz indicating that his revolt was entirely local in character, and in no way should be considered an act of insubordination against the federal government, the president was far from convinced. Díaz amassed a huge federal war machine under the command of General José B. Cueto to punish the defecting officer. Colonel Huerta was placed in charge of the Third Infantry Battalion and arrived in the state in late October, 1893. Although the federal forces had no trouble in quelling Canuto Neri's movement, Victoriano Huerta became involved in the first controversy of his public career.

9. Victoriano Huerta, Corporaciones en que ha Servido, AHDN, Cancelados, Exp. XI/111/1-104.

10. "Victoriano Huerta," RDS, 812.00/7929; Rausch, "Victoriano Huerta," p. 8.

11. This rebel movement is analyzed in detail in Vicente Fuentes Díaz, *La Revolución de 1910 en el Estado de Guerrero* (Mexico: Nacional Impresora, Fresno 30, 1960), pp. 18-25.

When Canuto Neri surrendered to General Cueto's federal troops, the acting governor of the state, Mariano Ortiz de Montellano, declared an amnesty for all rebels who would lay down their arms. Several weeks later in the town of Mezcala, Huerta ordered the execution of a number of captured rebels who had every reason to believe that they were covered by the amnesty declaration. When some of the Mexico City press criticized the seemingly unnecessary execution of Neri's followers, Huerta responded predictably that he was simply following orders.[12] Although neither Huerta's specific orders from the Department of War nor any private communications from General Cueto have ever been uncovered, all indirect evidence suggests that Huerta exceeded his authority in no way. Not only was he never called to answer for the executions but in November, 1895, he received an appointment as commander of government forces in Chilpancingo, a post which he held for almost two years. The hard-line approach had apparently redounded to his military credit and the lesson would not be lost. From this point forward he became increasingly authoritarian and found it exceedingly difficult to accept any criticism.

The last two and a half years of the nineteenth century found the rapidly rising officer in Mexico City in charge of the General Staff's topographical and astronomical departments. Late in 1900, however, he was again removed from his desk job and placed into the field, this time in the position of Indian fighter in support of the Pax Porfiriana. Huerta left for the state of Sonora in December in command of an infantry battalion sent to subdue the rebellion of Yaqui Indians, a tribe which had been at war with the Mexican government for almost three and a half centuries.

During the early years of the Díaz regime the Yaquis had bitterly resisted the government's policy of land despoliation. A tenuous armistice was reached in 1887 but it soon gave way to a long series of military encounters between the tribe and the federal government. Under the leadership of Juan Maldonado (Tetabiate), Yaqui guerrilla fighters determined that to preserve their independence they would have to drive interlopers from their lands; the government of Don Porfirio was just as adamant in its insistence that national interests could not be served so long as autonomous and militant groups were allowed to operate freely within the confines of the Mexican republic. The Yaquis held the government to a virtual standoff for almost ten

12. Francisco Bulnes, *El Verdadero Díaz y la Revolución* (Mexico: Editora Nacional, 1960), pp. 60-61.

years, although they were driven back deep into the Bacatete
Mountains. In May, 1897, the Yaquis were forced to sue for peace but
Tetabiate accepted the Paz de Ortiz most reluctantly. Two years later
the Yaquis were in arms again, this time more determined than ever.
Victoriano Huerta's Sonoran assignment coincided with a major
federal offensive. The government would give no quarter on this
occasion.

During the winter of 1901-2 some of the fiercest battles of the Yaqui
campaigns occurred and the tribe was put on the run. By spring it
was obvious that the Yaqui resistance had been spent. Tetabiate held
out until July, when he was killed by a federal detachment under the
command of Major Loreto Villa. The punishment for resistance to the
dictates of Mexico City was harsh with rebel and peaceful farmer
suffering alike. According to a plan devised by Colonel Angel García
Peña (one of Huerta's former classmates at the Colegio Militar), hundreds of Yaquis—men, women, and children—were sold into slavery to
work on the henequen plantations far away in Yucatán. Scores of
others were imprisoned and a good percentage of those fortunate
enough to escape capture sought the sanctuary of the Arizona border
in voluntary expatriation.[13]

Huerta's role in the Yaqui campaigns was not of great importance.
He did participate in the strategy sessions and commanded troops in
the field on at least several occasions. But a seemingly more immediate threat to the Díaz regime during the spring of 1901 prompted his
recall to Mexico City, and he did not take part in the ultimate Yaqui
defeat. The state of Guerrero was in open rebellion once again and
Huerta, because of his familiarity with the region, was chosen to command the government forces.

Conditions in Guerrero did not improve with the suppression of
Canuto Neri's revolt. The governors appointed to succeed Francisco
Arce were no more ready to deal with the inadequacies of rural
Mexico as the twentieth century approached than their predecessors
had been since the time of independence. The new opposition leader
was Rafael del Castillo Calderón, who, in 1901, decided to run for the
governorship in opposition to the Díaz-picked machine candidate.
When the official candidate won the obviously rigged election,
Castillo Calderón decided to resist the imposition by force.[14]

13. For a good account of the Yaqui wars see Claudio Dabdoub, *Historia de
el Valle del Yaqui* (Mexico: Librería de Manuel Porrua, 1964), pp. 138-58.
14. Fuentes Díaz, *La Revolución en Guerrero*, pp. 25-33, 44-47.

On Huerta's return to the capital he found that his old friend Bernardo Reyes had become minister of war. The two men conferred briefly and Reyes dispatched Huerta to Guerrero to treat with the rebels. Huerta arrived in the state on April 14 and in his first detailed dispatch back to the war ministry predicted that suppression of the rebellion would be difficult. The rebels were broken down into twenty or thirty different groups and had taken to the mountains to harass his troops.[15] Huerta quickly discovered that he could not count on the local populace to help him. "When these people tell you that someone has gone to the north," he wrote to Reyes, "you must look for him in the south, or east, or west . . . but they are so tricky that you better not discount the north."[16] For the next five months Huerta waged a relentless campaign in the state. Towns were burned, hostages were held, and noncombatants were terrorized. After only a month Huerta had gained the reputation of being a blood thirsty animal.[17] He was especially harsh on any follower of Castillo Calderón who had participated in the movement of Canuto Neri eight years earlier.[18] These rebels were considered incorrigible and, when captured, a number were executed without ceremony. The Department of War again showed itself less concerned with Huerta's methods than with his results. As the news filtered back to Mexico City that the federal troops had gained the upper hand, Secretary of War Reyes authorized a temporary brigadier generalship for his commander in Guerrero.[19] The appointment went into effect on May 27, 1901. Several weeks later Huerta offered amnesty to those rebels still in the field. By June 24, he was able to report to his superior in Mexico City that some sixty rebels had surrendered; but he also had to admit that the four most important leaders of the movement—Castillo Calderón, Anselmo Bello, Manuel Vásquez, and Genaro Ramírez—refused to consider seriously the amnesty offer. Huerta did not believe that these four would ever surrender, but if they did, he wrote Reyes, "too bad for them."[20]

By late July the rebellion was practically quelled although much

15. Huerta to Reyes, April 24, 1901, Archivo Particular de Bernardo Reyes, Cartas, 1901 (hereafter cited as APBR with appropriate information).

16. Huerta to Reyes, May 4, 1901, APBR, Cartas, 1901.

17. Huerta to Reyes, May 16, 1901, APBR, Cartas, 1901.

18. Huerta to Reyes, May 28, 1901, APBR, Cartas, 1901.

19. Victoriano Huerta, Emplos y Fechas en que los Obtuvo, Hoja Dos, AHDN, Cancelados, Exp. XI/111/104-1.

20. ". . . no se presentarán nunca, y si lo hacen peor para ellos" (Huerta to Reyes, June 24, 1901, APBR, Cartas, 1901).

of the leadership had escaped capture by fleeing the state. Huerta undoubtedly would have been recalled to Mexico City in August had not rampant rumors begun to circulate that the fugitive Castillo Calderón was plotting an even larger revolution directed not against the state government in Guerrero but against Porfirio Díaz himself.[21] A month of investigation convinced the brigadier general that the rumors of the new revolt were exaggerated and that even if Castillo Calderón entertained such a scheme it was doomed to failure from the outset. Huerta then requested that he be allowed to return to Mexico City because of a private family matter.[22]

Shortly after his marriage to Emilia Aguila, Huerta had purchased a small four-room house in Colonia San Rafael in Mexico City. Once the mortgage was cleared he offered the house as collateral on a personal loan. Through some misunderstanding on the terms of repayment, the holder of the note threatened to evict Señora Huerta while her husband was on assignment in Guerrero.[23] Reyes, convinced that

21. Huerta to Reyes, August 4, 1901, APBR, Cartas, 1901.
22. Huerta's action in the Castillo Calderón rebellion is significant historiographically because it furnished the pro-Revolutionary historians with their first ammunition for anti-Huerta vituperations. Not content with the justifiable condemnation of Huerta for showing his enemies no quarter and for overplaying his hand shamelessly, these historians used his activities in Guerrero in 1901 to begin creating a historical ogre. With no evidence, Huerta is charged with having kicked one of his soldiers to death during the campaign because the soldier sat down on the side of the road. Huerta's explanation was simply: "My soldiers don't get tired" (See Alejandro Sánchez Castro, "La Revolución de Castillo Calderón," in Fidel Franco, *Eusebio S. Almonte: Poeta Mártir Guerrerense* [Mexico: I.C.D., 1947], pp. 29-34). The documentation concerning the campaigns, never before examined, treats this incident. Two soldiers did sit down on the side of the road during a rest period and hid themselves when the column moved out. They then deserted the unit and fled to the mountains with their arms and ammunition. When captured Huerta asked Secretary of War Reyes how they should be punished. Reyes replied that they should be court-martialed and, if found guilty, they should be given the death penalty. See Huerta to Reyes, May 4, 1901, APBR, Cartas, 1901; Reyes to Huerta, May 11, 1901, APBR, Telegrams, 1901. Although the disposition of the case is not contained in the correspondence, there is little doubt that the offending parties were found guilty and executed. The original falsification of Sánchez Castro was picked up with additional embellishments and repeated twenty-two years later in Fuentes Díaz, *La Revolución en Guerrero*, pp. 25-33, 44-74. Other historians have pointed out that Huerta struck up his sinister acquaintance with Aureliano Urrutia during the Guerrero campaigns; since both men had Indian blood, the pair were portrayed as Huitzilopochtli and Huichilobos, to whom the Aztecs offered human sacrifices. See, for example, Rubén Salido Orcillo, "Huerta y el Ejécito Federal," *Excélsior,* June 5, 1959, pp. 6, 9.
23. Huerta to Reyes, August 22, 1901, APBR, Cartas, 1901.

the rebellion in Guerrero had been extinguished anyway, honored Huerta's request. Upon his return to the capital during the first week of September, Huerta confronted his creditor immediately. There is little question but that the new stars he sported on his dress uniform added substance to the logic of his arguments. The issue was resolved in Huerta's favor and the family was allowed to remain in the house.

Huerta's reprieve from the hardships of campaign was short-lived. Less than a month after his return to Mexico City Secretary of War Reyes called him in for consultation and then ordered him back into the field—this time to quell an uprising of the Maya Indians in the Yucatán Peninsula. His conduct on this campaign would serve to cement further his personal relationship with Reyes.

The Mayas in the south, much as the Yaquis in the north, had long lists of grievances against the regime in Mexico City. Recalcitrant from the moment of the initial Spanish contact in the sixteenth century, they still maintained enough will and strength 350 years later to practically drive their white oppressors out of Yucatán. Periods of peace were more notable than periods of conflict during the early years of the Díaz regime but tensions mounted in the late 1890s when the president awarded two large lumber companies, La Compañía Agrícola and La Compañía Colonizadora, immense tracts of forest land without regard to the rights of the Indians occupying the areas. By early 1900 railroad crews preparing a new roadbed from Peto to Ascencion Bay on the East coast had to be defended against possible Indian attack by federal batallions and Yucatecan National Guard units (Nacionales). Within a few months full scale war had erupted in Yucatán.[24] Although the government scored an impressive victory at Chan Santa Cruz in May, the Mayas simply broke up into small bands and continued to harass the federal troops and railroad workers.

Huerta's orders, received in October, 1901, named him second in command to General José María de la Vega, a naval commander given army rank for this particular campaign. The orders charged Huerta with the task of supporting de la Vega's military maneuvers and supervising the completion of the railroad line between Chan Santa Cruz and Vigía Chico on Ascencion Bay. Shortly after his arrival in Yucatán Huerta became utterly appalled with the conduct of the campaigns. He kept his displeasure to himself for about four months, satisfied merely to observe and analyze the reasons for the stalled

24. Nelson Reed, *The Caste War of Yucatán* (Stanford, Calif.: Stanford University Press, 1964), pp. 232-43.

federal operations. He noted that the morale of the soldiers was dangerously low, supply lines were inadequate, and even the uniforms were inappropriate for the hot humid climate in which the troops were expected to operate efficiently. In the swampy areas of the peninsula the heavy military boots quickly became covered with thick mud which when dry was almost impossible to remove. Steel helmets scarcely served a useful function in the jungle. The soldiers carried much useless equipment with them wherever they went. On March 4 Huerta decided to jump the normal chain of command and directed a long letter to Secretary of War Reyes, specifying at the outset that since he was not in full command the communiqué should be considered unofficial and confidential.[25] He informed his superior in the War Department that many of the troops operating in the southern war zone should be withdrawn and replaced with two crack battalions. The large number of troops already there, he continued, constituted more of a liability than an asset because of their poor attitude and the inability to keep them properly provisioned. "It would be better to have fewer troops, but good ones, than a large number inadequate for the necessary operations."[26] The replacements he requested should be fitted out properly for the tropics:

> They should be supplied only with light khaki uniforms, caps, shoes and a duffle bag containing a mess kit, blanket, hammock, raincoat, and a machete with a leather sheath. The caps preferably should be of heavy khaki and the shoes should be *guaraches;* the machetes should definitely have leather sheaths because the troops injure themselves on march with the metal scabbards they now have.[27]

If the War Department saw fit to follow his advice, Huerta gave assurances that he would bring the campaigns to a successful conclusion within a matter of months. Secretary Reyes did not rebuff Huerta for circumventing General de la Vega and communicating directly with the department and, in fact, took his recommendations under advisement. Emboldened by the response Huerta wrote again to Reyes before the month was out and on this occasion directly impugned the competence of de la Vega:

25. ". . . no me dirijo a la personalidad del Ministro de Guerra sino al entendido del General Bernardo Reyes . . ." (Huerta to Reyes, March 4, 1902, APBR, Letters, 1901 [sic]).

26. Ibid.

27. Ibid.

Quite by accident I found out that the General-in-Chief [de la Vega] is currently carrying out an expedition and I am somewhat annoyed. If, unfortunately, he should become ill or if something else should happen I would have great difficulty rendering effective assistance which I know is my duty. I have not even been informed of the route of his expedition.[28]

Reyes pondered Huerta's advice and recommendations for a month and decided finally that he was correct in his assessments. By early May the troops which Reyes had requested had been authorized and, more importantly, the War Department recalled General de la Vega to Mexico City—Huerta was placed in full command of the Maya campaigns.[29] Once having received command Huerta decided to change the campaign strategy completely. Until this time the federal army had conducted conventional maneuvers—marching along a fixed line to an enemy stronghold and engaging him in battle. After the defeat of the Mayas in Chan Santa Cruz, however, the enemy adopted guerrilla tactics and conventional warfare was scarcely practical. Like other military commanders in the twentieth century, Huerta articulated his problems and proposed solutions as follows:

The old methods are no longer of value . . . . Today . . . our troops only control the ground they stand on and therefore it is necessary, in my judgment, to adopt another, more carefully conceived means of exploration that has as its purpose reducing the enemy to obedience or finishing him off. Let me tell you that I think the Indians—or at least many of them—have not submitted to the government because we haven't forced them to. The reason for this is our deficient method of attack that consists simply of engaging those we encounter along a fixed line. The enemy, now understanding this, realize that merely by moving one or two kilometers away from the line of march they will be outside the line of attack.

For this reason, General, I find it necessary that in the future we concentrate on zones, not lines, taking care that the explored zones remained secured by a small number of troops so that the enemy does not return to occupy them.[30]

Huerta's strategy, "search, seize and secure," worked. Throughout the summer, new zones were brought under effective federal control and, as a consequence, the immense territory once occupied by the

28. Huerta to Reyes, March 31, 1902, APBR, Letters, 1901 *[sic]*.
29. Huerta to Reyes, May 20, 1902, APBR, Letters, 1901 *[sic]*.
30. Ibid.

Mayas was consistently reduced. By the early fall dispatches to the war ministry expressed more concern with the progress of the railroad than with the Indian menace.[31] In October Huerta was able to report that the area was pacified. The final defeat of the Mayas did not occur in a single battle. As they were pushed further and further from their homes and their fields they simply recognized the futility of their effort and gave up what had been a gallant fight.

Huerta's reward upon return to Mexico City after twelve months in Yucatán was a permanent brigadier generalship, the Military Merit Decoration,[32] and appointment as a justice on the Mexican Military Supreme Court.[33] But Huerta returned from the Maya campaigns in bad health. He had developed a cataract condition on his eyes which would plague him for the rest of his life. After a month's leave of absence which he spent with his wife and family in Puebla, Huerta took up residence once again in the capital and began to cultivate his close personal and professional relationship with Secretary of War Bernardo Reyes. Reyes had established an enviable record as governor of Nuevo León and, as a loyal supporter of the Díaz regime, had been given the secretariat of war in 1900 on the death of General Felipe Berriozabal. By the time Huerta returned from the Maya campaigns, Reyes had presented himself as a serious candidate for the vice-presidential nomination in the 1904 general elections. The development of Reyismo in 1903 did not signify any incipient revolutionary movement. To the contrary, Reyismo nurtured itself from within the system and drew its strength largely from loyal Porfirists

31. Huerta to Reyes, August 31, 1902, APBR, Letters, 1901 [*sic*]; Huerta to Reyes, September 3, 1902, APBR, Letters, 1901 [*sic*].

32. Victoriano Huerta, Premios y Recompensas, AHDN, Cancelados, Exp. XI/111/104-1.

33. It has been suggested that Huerta falsified military reports to the secretary of war, exaggerating his own role in subduing the Mayas; therefore his promotion to brigadier general was unjustified. See Juan Sánchez Azcona, *Apuntes para la Historia de la Revolución Mexicana* (Mexico: Biblioteca del Instituto Nacional de Estudios Históricos de la Revolución Mexicana, 1961), pp. 347-50. Pro-Huerta sources disagree and argue that his contributions to the Maya campaigns were indeed significant. See, for example, Doblado, *El Presidente Huerta*, pp. 100-101. More importantly, however, accounts which by no means can be considered eulogistic or even sympathetic concur that his military maneuvers in the south were well conceived, well executed, and contributed substantially to the defeat of the Mayas. Héctor R. Olea, "El Indio Victoriano," *El Nacional,* February 17, 1955, p. 11; Manuel García Purón, *México y sus Gobernantes: Biografías* (Mexico: Librería de Manuel Porrua, 1964), p. 217; Meléndez, *Historia de la Revolución,* p. 149; Miguel Angel Peral, *Diccionario Biográfico Mexicana,* 2 vols. (Mexico: Editorial P.A.C., 1944), 1:397.

who saw in Reyes an opportunity for liberalization and reform well within the established order.[34] Reyes's followers, and most especially his son Rodolfo, gradually began stepping on toes and incurred the antipathy of the *científicos*, Díaz's brain trust and his most ardent body of support. The leader of the científico clique, José Ives Limantour, Díaz's competent minister of the treasury, had political ambitions of his own and used his influence with the president in an attempt to nip the Reyista movement in the bud.

Victoriano Huerta was a staunch adherent of General Reyes's vice-presidential ambitions. Finding in Reyes a talented and energetic military man who could possibly rejuvenate the rapidly aging regime, he began to attend the weekly strategy sessions in the house of Don Angel Reyes in the Mexico City district of Mixcoac.[35] Bernardo sought to repay Huerta's support by having him appointed as undersecretary of war, but before the appointment could pass through all of the proper channels Reyes found himself caught in Limantour's científico vise and was forced to resign his cabinet position and abandon his vice-presidential campaign. Reyes's resignation marked a major victory for the científicos; Limantour was able to use his powers of persuasion with the president to insure that his choice, Ramón Corral, would be accepted as the vice-presidential candidate. Huerta, fully devoted to the Reyista cause by this time, reportedly approached Reyes and suggested that the time might be ripe for instigating a military coup against the Díaz dictatorship.[36] Reyes would have no part of it. He returned to his home state of Nuevo León and, as a result, Huerta's appointment as undersecretary was never ratified.[37]

General Huerta remained in Mexico City for almost a year after Reyes's first political demise. In 1907, as he completed his thirtieth

34. An excellent discussion of Reyismo can be found in Anthony T. Bryan, "Mexican Politics in Transition, 1900-1913: The Role of General Bernardo Reyes," (Ph.D. diss., University of Nebraska, 1969), passim.

35. Joaquín Piña, "Triunfo y Calvario del Presidente Huerta," *Así* 275 (March 23, 1946): 48; Meléndez, *Historia de la Revolución*, p. 149.

36. Oswaldo Sánchez, "Para los Depositarios de la Verdad Histórica: D. Victoriano Huerta, Cuartelacista por Temperamento," *El Nacional*, June 25, 1930, pp. 3, 7; Juan Andreu Almazán, "Memorias del General Juan Andreu Almazán," *El Universal*, November 24, 1957, pp. 1, 23.

37. The Reyista interpretation of these events of 1903 can be found in Rodolfo Reyes, *De Mi Vida: Memorias Políticas*, 2 vols. (Madrid: Biblioteca Nueva, 1929-30), 1:25-29. A much more balanced, but nevertheless sympathetic treatment is contained in Victor Eberhardt Niemeyer, "The Public Career of General Bernardo Reyes," (Ph.D. diss., University of Texas, 1958), pp. 148-162.

year of active military service, he requested an indefinite leave of absence for reasons of health, and once it was approved, he moved north to Monterrey, Nuevo León, where Reyes had again assumed the state governorship.[38] For the next two and a half years he worked as a practicing engineer and on several occasions received handsome state contracts for street paving from his old patron and political ally.[39]

The year 1909 was an intensely political year in Nuevo León as in the remainder of Mexico. In the spring a group of mildly anti-Díaz Reyistas formed the Partido Democrático to urge once again that Bernardo Reyes be accepted as Díaz's vice-presidential candidate in the 1910 elections. As the dictator vacillated, the party became more militant and began directing much of its propaganda toward the army in an attempt to entice support.[40] Huerta again attached himself to the Reyes camp in Monterrey, but neither he nor any of the other members of the Partido Democrático could convince the governor to openly solicit the vice-presidential office. It has been suggested that Reyes was afraid to oppose Díaz who was already leaning toward the renomination of Ramón Corral as his vice-president. It seems more likely, however, that Reyes wanted to avoid an open split within official circles because a new and much more serious threat to the political *status quo* had appeared in the person of Francisco I. Madero.

First achieving national prominence in 1908 with the publication of a political treatise entitled *La Sucesión Presidencial en 1910,* Madero became a candidate for the presidency in 1909 and embarked upon a vigorous campaign tour of the entire country. Although Madero attracted large crowds and seemed to be well received wherever he went, Díaz was more concerned with the inroads which the Reyistas were making in the army.[41] Reyes was popular with the military, especially the second echelon of career officers, and although he had not committed himself enthusiastically to the movement being waged

---

38. Victoriano Huerta, Licencias, AHDN, Cancelados, Exp. XI/111/104-1; and Huerta, Corporaciones en que ha Servido, AHDN, Cancelados, Exp. XI/111/104-1.

39. Huerta's memoirs, probably written by journalist Joaquín Piña, indicate that on one occasion a misappropriation of some 18,000 pesos occurred on one of the paving contracts and that this incident caused a temporary breach between Huerta and Reyes. Because of the apocryphal nature of the memoirs, and the lack of corroborating evidence, no definite conclusion can be drawn. See [Joaquín Piña?] *Memorias de Victoriano Huerta* (Mexico: Ediciones Vertice, 1957), p. 10.

40. Al C. Gral. Bernardo Reyes, May 23, 1909, Archivo Espinosa de los Monteros, IV, fol. 49a (hereafter cited as AEM with appropriate information).

41. Club Central Reyista (Memorandum), AEM, IV, fol. 86, June 8, 1909.

in his name, he did constitute a genuine threat. Díaz responded by harassing all political activities of the Partido Democrático, by removing sympathetic army officers from areas in which they enjoyed support, and even depriving Reyista deputies of their seats in the Congress. But the movement continued to grow. Unwilling to take any chances, the president thought it best to get Reyes out of the country. On November 5, 1909, the general from Nuevo León tacitly agreed to political exile by accepting Díaz's request that he undertake a military study mission in Europe.[42]

Francisco Madero's fortunes improved as those of Bernardo Reyes declined. In late 1909 and early 1910 he was able to pick up support from groups who previously had been leaning toward Reyes. Madero set April 15, 1910, as the date for his national Anti-reelectionist Convention. The meeting was well attended with delegates present from almost every Mexican state. In the afternoon of April 15, acting on a motion from Abraham González, the president of the Anti-reelectionist club in Chihuahua City, the convention nominated Madero as their presidential candidate in the upcoming presidential elections. The following day Francisco Vásquez Gómez was selected the vice-presidential candidate. On April 17, the convention adjourned with the delegates promising to return to their home states to campaign for the national ticket.[43]

The presidential campaign for the 1910 elections lasted for about a month and a half. In May as the tempo accelerated, so did Díaz's harassment of the opposition. Rallies were dispersed, Anti-reelectionist leaders and pro-Madero journalists were arrested, and finally in June Madero himself was imprisoned on the trumped up charges of plotting revolution and harboring a fugitive from justice. Madero was still in jail the day that the ballots for president were cast. To no one's surprise Porfirio Díaz and Ramón Corral were declared elected for a new six-year term. Not long after the final votes were tabulated, Madero released on bond but confined to the environs of the city of San Luis Potosí, decided to effect an escape. Disguised as a mechanic, he eluded his guards and secretly boarded a northbound train which

42. Bryan, "Mexican Politics in Transition," 250-51.
43. The campaign and election of 1910 can best be traced in the two standard English language biographies of Francisco Madero: Stanley R. Ross, *Francisco I. Madero: Apostle of Mexican Democracy* (New York: Columbia University Press, 1955), pp. 80-112, and Charles Curtis Cumberland, *Mexican Revolution: Genesis under Madero* (Austin: University of Texas Press, 1952), pp. 101-18.

eventually carried him to the international bridge at Laredo and the sanctuary of the United States.

When Madero made his decision to escape to the United States, he had already determined that Díaz could be unseated only by revolution. All legal means had been exhausted and, if one accepted that the dictator had to go, use of force remained the only option. From San Antonio, Texas, Madero issued a manifesto dated October 5, the last day he was in San Luis Potosí, calling for a general insurrection to begin on November 20, 1910. The Mexican masses would respond favorably and would initiate their revolutionary struggle under the banner of this Plan de San Luis Potosí.

Victoriano Huerta was little more than a spectator in the hectic political events of the summer and fall of 1910. Shortly after Bernardo Reyes was dispatched to Europe, Huerta returned to Mexico City. For six months he remained in a state of semi-inactivity, teaching private classes in mathematics to supplement the small army pension he was drawing. With his own choice for the presidency eliminated, he did not participate in the electoral campaign of 1910. His life, however, as that of tens of thousands of other Mexicans, was severely jolted on November 20, the opening day of Madero's revolution. Huerta immediately applied for active duty and was welcomed back into the federal army.

CHAPTER 2

The Revolution

THE INITIAL RESPONSE TO MADERO'S CALL for a general uprising on
November 20, 1910, must have been reassuring to the leadership of
the contemplated movement. Isolated pockets of rebellion sprang up
in many quarters of the nation on the stipulated day. By the end of
the month, however, Díaz's federal army and the rurales seemingly
had turned the tide against the rebels except in the state of Chihuahua,
where Pascual Orozco, Jr., a self-trained *guerrillero* from the small
town of San Isidro, had the government on the run. In December, as
the rebel movement was crushed in most of the other states, Orozco's

Chihuahua revolt continued to grow. By the end of the year he had augmented the size of his force to over one thousand men, had scored a number of victories over the Díaz army, and was planning an attack on Ciudad Juárez on the United States border.[1]

As the revolt moved into its third and fourth months groups of southern rebels initially defeated by the federals began to take heart from promising developments in the north and set out to reorganize themselves. By early April the states of Zacatecas, Durango, Veracruz, and Puebla were under siege but the most immediate southern threat emanated from Guerrero and Morelos, where the Zapata brothers and the Figueroa brothers scored an impressive series of victories. During the first week of April Victoriano Huerta received his orders as commander of the federal forces in Guerrero.

The War Department initially made plans to place ten thousand men at Huerta's disposal but pressing demands in other sections of the republic, as well as problems of recruitment, dictated that the federal force be limited to a fraction of that size. When Huerta left the capital in the middle of April he had only six hundred men under his command. When the troops arrived at Cuernavaca, they were informed that Zapata had captured the nearby town of Cuautla and was preparing to march on Cuernavaca. The expected attack did not materialize for several weeks and in the interim Secretary of War Manuel González Cosío recalled Huerta to Mexico City for consultation.[2] Ciudad Juárez had fallen to Pascual Orozco and Pancho Villa in early May and Díaz's military position had become untenable. Reviewing the military situation with his leading officers, Díaz decided that the time had come to tender his resignation. Early in the morning of May 25, 1911, the president prepared his statement of abdication; Congress accepted it on the afternoon of the same day. Fearing that an attempt might be made on his life on his way to exile, Díaz decided to travel to Veracruz with an armed escort. Huerta was chosen to command the convoy which escorted the dictator to the port city.[3] The train carrying Díaz and his family left Mexico City

1. See Michael C. Meyer, *Mexican Rebel: Pascual Orozco and the Mexican Revolution, 1910-1915* (Lincoln: University of Nebraska Press, 1967), pp. 19-25.
2. "Victoriano Huerta," RDS, 812.00/7929.
3. Peter Calvert, in a recent study of Anglo-American rivalry in Mexico during the early years of the Revolution, has uncovered documentation which reveals that the English colony in Mexico City was particularly fearful that some harm might come to Díaz during his escape to the coast. Several Englishmen, including oilman Lord Cowdray, First Secretary Thomas Beaumont Hohler, and E. N.

early on the morning of the twenty-sixth. No incidents occurred until the train reached Estación de Tepeyahualco. At that point a small party of rebels stopped the train and Huerta was forced to engage them. He succeeded in dispersing the group and the convoy reached Veracruz without further incident.

The peace treaty, according to which Díaz agreed to resign the presidency (the Treaty of Ciudad Juárez), provided that Francisco León de la Barra, the secretary of foreign relations, would serve as interim president until elections could be convoked. In the months that followed Mexico was torn by turmoil. It took fully three months before the chaos resulting from half a year of constant warfare began to yield to some semblance of order. But while Interim President de la Barra and Francisco Madero were gradually pacifying most of the country, the state of Morelos under the leadership of Emiliano Zapata was preparing to renew hostilities.

Madero's relationship with Zapata began auspiciously enough. When Madero made his triumphal entrance into Mexico City on June 7, 1911, Zapata was there to greet him and received a promise that Madero would visit him in his native Morelos within a short time. True to his word Madero conducted his tour of the state in the middle of the month, and while in Cuernavaca, agreed with Zapata on terms for demobilizing the twenty-five hundred rebel troops under arms. The demobilization began almost immediately but the hacendados of the state, fearing that Zapata was going to retain some measure of military control, argued that the mustering out was not proceeding with suitable speed and that Zapata was planning to rebel.[4] President de la Barra, believing the Morelos landowners and the alarmist reports of the Mexico City press, decided to take matters into his own hands and ordered General Victoriano Huerta back into the state to enforce the demobilization orders. If the disarming of the Zapatistas could not be effected peacefully, Huerta, at his own discretion, was to use force.

Huerta arrived in Cuernavaca with about a thousand men on August 10. Meanwhile Madero informed the interim president that

Brown, president of the National Railways, helped plan the exodus. See *The Mexican Revolution, 1910-1914: The Diplomacy of Anglo-American Conflict* (Cambridge: Cambridge University Press, 1968), pp. 72-73.

4. The local political situation in Morelos in the summer of 1911 is analyzed skillfully in John Womack, Jr., *Zapata and the Mexican Revolution* (New York: Alfred A. Knopf, 1969), pp. 97-103.

the only thing this action would accomplish would be to increase Zapata's mistrust of the national government.[5] At the same time Zapata predictably demanded that the troops be withdrawn and admonished Secretary of Gobernación Alberto García Granados, "I won't be responsible for the blood that is going to flow if the federal forces remain."[6] The blood did begin to flow on August 11 when one of Huerta's columns was ambushed by a party of Zapatistas north of Cuernavaca.[7]

Madero saw in the new movement of federal troops into Morelos the possibility of repeated incidents which would constitute a very real danger to the tenuous peace which existed throughout the country. Without de la Barra's permission he set out for a conference with Zapata and once having established telegraphic communications with the rebel leader, pleaded with the interim president to revoke Huerta's orders. He indicated at the same time that he had already met with Huerta and that the two men were apparently on excellent terms.[8] The meeting was attended by Edwin Emerson, a war correspondent assigned to Huerta's headquarters to cover the Morelos campaign. Emerson later revealed that Huerta agreed not to initiate any hostilities until Madero had an opportunity to meet with Zapata at the rebel headquarters in Cuautla.[9] President de la Barra also yielded slightly and on August 17 ordered Huerta to suspend operations for a period of forty-eight hours. Zapata was far from satisfied, however, and wrote to de la Barra demanding that all federal troops be withdrawn from the state. If this were done, he assured the interim president,

---

5. Madero to de la Barra, August 15, 1911, Correspondencia Personal y Oficial de Francisco León de la Barra como Embajador de México y Presidente de la República, Adquisición X, Cartas del Sr. don Francisco Madero Dirigidos a Sr. don Francisco León de la Barra, Centro de Estudios de Historia de México, Fundación Cultural de Condumex (hereafter cited as Condumex/FLB with appropriate information).

6. Zapata to Ministro de Gobernación, August 12, 1911, cited in Isidro Fabela, ed., *Documentos Históricos de la Revolución Mexicana*, 21 vols. (Mexico: Fondo de Cultura Económica and Editorial Jus, 1960-71), 6:48-49 (hereafter cited as DHRM with appropriate information).

7. Womack suggests (*Zapata,* p. 111) that the ambushing party was led by Genoveo de la O and that Zapata had not ordered the encounter.

8. Madero to de la Barra, August 14, 1911, cited in Alfredo Alvarez, ed., *Madero y su Obra: Documentos para la Historia* (Mexico: Talleres Gráficos de la Nación, 1935), pp. 9-10.

9. "Victoriano Huerta," RDS, 812.00/7929.

he could restore peace within twenty-four hours.[10] The president did not even consider the proposal seriously. He apparently believed that complete demobilization of the Zapatistas could be effected within the forty-eight hour period of grace; when it was not, he reaffirmed Huerta's earlier orders.

Huerta remained in Cuernavaca for two days but as soon as the forty-eight-hour period expired on August 19, he began to march on Yautepec, a short distance from the Zapatista stronghold at Cuautla. By this time he had received reinforcements, federal regulars and several companies of rurales (organized by Ambrosio Figueroa), bringing his total strength up to 3,000 troops. When the march to Yautepec began the Zapatistas had already reached an accord with Madero; the demobilization was proceeding according to plan. The self-appointed negotiator, upon learning of the federal advance, was beside himself. He again sent urgent dispatches to the president pleading that Huerta be withdrawn and also released statements to the press (very likely designed to mollify Zapata) indicating that Huerta's movements had not been approved by the government and that the federal commander was acting on his own initiative. Huerta, more than a little annoyed, on August 22 prepared a special press release explaining his own actions. After stating that groups of bandits had been raising havoc in the state (a charge that Madero contended was exaggerated), he summarized his position:

> The president of the republic judged indispensable that a part of the army, under my command, operate in this region to provide guarantees for the sane portion of the population, for the humble worker and the powerful industrialist alike, so that everybody can continue working . . . for the general good.
> . . . the mission that I am in charge of is not one of war or extermination but rather one of peace. I will exhaust all means of resolving this sorrowful situation, resorting to persuasion and indulgence with the object of curing the social wounds opened by the tremendous fight which had just ended.
> I come here not with the unsheathed sword of the avenger, but with an extended hand and with the desire to bring together all of the good citizens here. I believe that I can count on all men

10. Zapata to de la Barra, August 17, 1911, Archivo Particular del General Jenaro Amezcua sobre la Revolución Zapatista, Adquisición VIII, Carpeta 1, Centro de Estudios de Historia de Mexico, Fundación Cultural de Condumex (hereafter cited as Condumex/AJA with appropriate information).

of good will because peace will be of benefit to the entire
country . . . .

These are the instructions which I have received from the
president of the republic, and these are also my own ideas on
how to proceed, in spite of all of the slander cast about recently
by those restless souls interested in making it appear that the
interests of the public are in some way different from the mission of the army.[11]

Huerta marched into Yautepec on August 23, the Zapatistas aban-
doning the town without a fight. Later the same day the federal
general began his march on Cuautla. In a hurried telegram to the
president, Huerta made what assuredly must have been one of the
most injudicious prophecies of the entire Revolution. Once we reach
Cuautla, he promised de la Barra, "Zapata and his followers will
never again dare to oppose the desires of the government of the
nation."[12] Madero returned to Mexico City on the twenty-fourth in
full realization that his peace mission had been a failure. By the end
of the month full scale war had erupted between the federals and
Zapatistas—Emiliano Zapata would not lay down his arms again for
years.[13]

Throughout September Huerta pursued the Zapatistas without
inflicting a single serious defeat on them. Unable to cope with the
guerrilla tactics of the enemy, Huerta decided to utilize the tactic of
zones of conflict that he had developed in Yucatán. With this in
mind he prepared a plan to establish federal outposts in the seven
most important towns of the state: Cuernavaca, Yautepec, Cuautla,
Morelos, Jonacatepec, Jojutla de Juárez, and Tetecala.[14] By early
October all of these towns were in federal hands but Zapata, much
more adept at guerrilla warfare than the Maya Indians, was still on
the loose and, in fact, had assumed the offensive in some portions
of the state. On October 24 the Morelos rebel led an assault of several
thousand men on Milpa Alta on the border between the state of
Morelos and the Federal District. Madero jumped at the opportunity
to decry Huerta's incompetence and used his influence in Mexico

11. Telegrama Especial para *La Actualidad*, August 22, 1911, *DHRM*, 6:74-75.
12. Huerta to de la Barra, August 22, 1911, Condumex/FLB, Cartas Dirigidas
a Francisco León da la Barra, 1863-1825 [sic].
13. Madero's role in the peace negotiation in August, 1911, can be traced in
some detail in Ross, *Madero*, pp. 188-202; Cumberland, *Mexican Revolution*, pp.
172-84; and Womack, *Zapata*, pp. 111-20.
14. *El Heraldo Mexicano*, September 28, 1911.

City to have him removed from his command.[15] A few days later Madero wrote to the federal general explaining the reasons for his hostility. After charging Huerta with having deceived him, Madero added:

> When I was in Cuautla concluding negotiations with Zapata, you continued advancing on Yautepec and approaching Cuautla without having received explicit orders from the president of the republic nor the undersecretary of war . . . . From the moment that I left on my mission of peace, although in an extraofficial capacity, you knew perfectly well the true nature of my endeavor and if you had been inspired with the same patriotic sentiment, you would have worked with me and not frustrated my plans like you did . . . . Take note of the fact that the undersecretary of war is asking for your absolute resignation from the army.[16]

The Morelos campaign had involved Huerta in the first serious controversy of his public career. Madero was justifiably furious but was not sure whether to direct his vehemence against de la Barra or against his field commander in Morelos. He chose to do both but saved his harshest remarks for Huerta. Huerta's press releases during the entire controversy implied that he had really come to Morelos with an olive branch in hand.[17] The implication is clearly fallacious. On the other hand Madero simply had his facts wrong. He was not apprised of each order and counterorder which Huerta received from the ministry of war and on several key occasions believed that Huerta had exceeded his authority when the federal commander was acting in compliance with the letter—indeed the spirit—of his orders from the secretary.[18] As de la Barra subsequently told Congress, Huerta had precise and specific instructions to pursue the Zapatistas vigorously if they did not submit to federal authorities immediately.[19] The

---

15. A number of sources have concluded that Huerta was at the point of defeating Zapata when Madero had him recalled to Mexico City. See for example, Ricardo García Granados, *Historia de México Desde la Restauración de la República en 1867 Hasta la Caída de Huerta*, 2 vols. (Mexico: Editorial Jus, 1956), 2:203; José Fernández Rojas, *La Revolución Mexicana: de Porfirio Díaz a Victoriano Huerta, 1910-1913* (Mexico: Editores F. P. Rojas y Cía., 1913), p. 12.

16. Madero to Huerta, October 31, 1911, *DHRM*, 6:218-20.

17. See, for example, *El Heraldo Mexicano*, September 28, 1911.

18. Madero, for example, believed that Huerta marched on Yautepec without orders. The president assured him, however, that this was not the case. Madero to de la Barra, August 18, 1911, Condumex/AJA, Carpeta 1; and de la Barra to Madero, August 20, 1911, Condumex/AJA, Carpeta 1.

19. De la Barra to H. Congreso, 1911, Condumex/FLB, Documentos Diversos.

antipathy generated between Madero and Huerta during the late summer and autumn of 1911 very definitely had its roots in the failure of the peace mission. The schism was inflamed, however, as the problems encountered in the military campaigns became intertwined with those of the political campaign which was unfolding simultaneously.

The 1911 presidential campaign got underway in July with the foundation of a new political party, the Progressive Constitutional party which replaced Madero's old Anti-reelectionist party. The national convention was held in late August and Madero won the first spot on the ticket by acclamation. Debate over the vice-presidential nomination, however, was intense. Ultimately, the new party chose Madero's personal favorite, José María Pino Suárez, a lawyer from Yucatán as his running mate.

The political opposition to the forces of the revolution came from an unexpected quarter. In early June General Bernardo Reyes returned to Mexico from his military study mission in Europe. Reyes had been ordered to return by Limantour before the dictatorship collapsed but he arrived too late to take the field against the insurgents. Shortly after landing at Veracruz, Reyes made his way to Mexico City, held a conference with Madero, and pledged not to present himself as an opposition candidate. In return Madero promised, upon his own election, to appoint Reyes secretary of war. In the course of the next six weeks, however, supporters of the ex-Porfirist general began to press upon him the desirability and the necessity of opposing Madero in the forthcoming elections. Madero's own supporters were displeased with their leader for having compromised with one of the symbols of the old regime; they even founded a Club Antirreyista to harass the general. By the end of July Reyes had made his decision to break with Madero and run against him.

Madero was dismayed with Reyes's change of mind. But he was an avowed democrat and was not about to use pressure to try to eliminate Reyes from the race. On the other hand Madero and his close body of advisors did fear that should Reyes lose the election he might precipitate a military revolt against the victorious party. Because Victoriano Huerta had supported Reyes in 1903 and again in 1909, Madero was suspicious of him almost from the outset of the Morelos campaigns.[20] As the peace negotiations with Zapata broke

20. Discurso Pronunciado por don Francisco Madero en el Kiusko de la Plaza Central . . . de Cuautla, Morelos, 18 de Agosto de 1911, Condumex/AJA, Carpeta 1.

down Madero became convinced that Huerta was working under the secret orders of Reyes, who, he reasoned, wanted the peace mission to fail.[21] On August 19, Madero publicly charged Huerta, in *El Imparcial,* with collaborating with Reyes to thwart the peace efforts. Huerta vigorously denied the charge and countered in his own news release: "The line of conduct that I, as Chief of Federal Troops in Morelos, have followed, is today, and has always been, in direct accord with my superiors; for that reason I find it necessary to protest against Mr. Madero's statements."[22] Samuel Espinosa de los Monteros, the president of the Club Central del Partido Reyista, also denied the charges publicly.[23] Madero, remained unconvinced. Several days later he severely castigated de la Barra for allowing the Reyista movement to run rampant in the country. Madero, seeing a vast Reyista conspiracy in Mexico during the late summer and early fall of 1911, held the Reyistas accountable for almost all of Mexico's ills. After explaining his position to the interim president he expressed his concern:

> With a blind faith in the loyalty of the army, you forget that it is not against you that they are thinking of rising up but against me. . . . Also, surrounded by I don't know what influences, you unconsciously congratulate Reyes in his work. To give you just the most salient example I'll refer to your sending Huerta to Morelos. This general is well known everywhere for his Reyista past. You have seen the indignant way in which he treated me in Cuernavaca; in spite of having instructions to work with me, he not only refused but also mocked me. In addition, all of his actions have been undertaken to provoke hostilities, not to calm them . . . .[24]

In the same letter Madero went so far as to allege that Huerta had offered a Mexico City newspaper, *El Hijo del Ahuizote,* an eight thousand peso bribe to support the Reyista cause in the presidential elections. The evidence does not bear out any of Madero's charges. Neither the interim president nor the secretary of war ever repudiated Huerta's conduct or gave any indication that his actions were not in compliance with the orders that he had received. The presence of federal troops in Morelos undoubtedly was the major factor which caused the failure of the peace mission; however, the allegation that

21. Madero to de la Barra, August 19, 1911, Condumex/AJA, Carpeta 1.
22. Telegrama Especial para *La Actualidad,* August 20, 1911, *DHRM,* 6:62-63.
23. Editorial dispatch, AEM, II, fol. 7, no date.
24. Madero to de la Barra, August 25, 1911, *DHRM,* 6:86-91.

Huerta's actions were part of a nationwide Reyista conspiracy is simply unfounded.

In September, 1911, the presidential campaign became quite heated. Early in the month at a Reyista rally in Mexico City, a group of Madero supporters, in spite of their leader's benign expressions and without his knowledge or approval, attacked Reyes physically. The Reyista convention was held ten days later and the delegates petitioned the Congress to postpone the elections because of the unfair treatment afforded their candidate. Both Madero and the majority of the Congress opposed the postponement, however, and when the request was denied, Reyes withdrew from the race and went into a self-imposed exile in San Antonio, Texas. The election took place without further incident on October 1, 1911, and, with only a few minor opposition candidates in the race, the ticket of Madero and Pino Suárez carried the day. The new president and vice-president were sworn into office on November 6.

When Madero assumed the presidential office, Emiliano Zapata was again threatening rebellion in Morelos and followers of Bernardo Reyes were urging a similar course of action from their seat of exile in the United States. Madero, believing that Huerta could not be trusted, in one of his first orders to his new secretary of war, José González Salas, demanded that the general be removed from the army.[25] Upon hearing of his imminent retirement Huerta wrote a long letter to Madero explaining pathetically his role in the Zapatista campaigns. It was addressed coldly and almost irreverently to *Muy Señor Mío:*

> As commanding general of the troops which I had the honor of commanding for the eleven weeks that I remained in that state, and with the unconditional approval of the president of the republic and the secretary of war, I did no more than fight successfully the rebels that I found, open the schools, try to reestablish police service, and reinstitute rail services.[26]

Several days later Madero's order was modified and Huerta was allowed to remain in the army but was placed in a state of semi-inactivity. Although no concrete evidence regarding the modification is available, it seems likely that it reflected a change of mind rather than one of heart. Needing the support of the army during the

25. *El Imparcial,* November 9, 1911.
26. Huerta to Madero, October 28, 1911, Condumex/AJA, Carpeta 1.

difficult period of transition, Madero's body of advisors must have convinced him that Huerta's premature retirement at best could be impolitic and at worst could drive him into the extending arms of Bernardo Reyes in San Antonio. Huerta accepted the partial reconciliation with less than full enthusiasm. On November 11 at an official banquet given in honor of the new president, Huerta toasted Madero but could not hide his fundamental contempt in his short speech which chastized the president for his suspicions: "Mr. Madero, you were wrong in doubting the army. Doubt is the greatest insult you can hurl at an honorable and loyal army . . . . The constituted government can count unconditionally on the army."[27] Some not too astute political observers interpreted Huerta's protestation of loyalty as an event of major significance.[28] Madero, himself, was far from convinced, however, and even when a series of military revolts struck out against the new government he was content to allow Huerta to remain in Mexico City rather than take the field.

The Zapatistas in Morelos were the first to break out in open rebellion. Zapata's demands, essentially agrarian in nature, were formalized in the Plan de Ayala less than a month after Madero came to office. Claiming that his followers were the true heirs to the Plan de San Luis Potosí, Zapata called for the immediate occupation of hacienda lands by the peons. Madero abandoned the conciliatory policy which he had shown during de la Barra's interim presidency and instead adopted a firm attitude. The armed conflict began late in November and quickly spread to the neighboring states of Guerrero, Tlaxcala, Puebla, and Mexico. Arnoldo Caso López and Federico Morales, the first federal commanders sent into Morelos, did not pursue the campaign vigorously enough for the president[29] and were replaced in January, 1912, by General Juvencio Robles. For the next six months Robles conducted a devastating campaign in the state but was unable to check the rebellion.[30]

27. Gustavo Casasola, ed., *Historia Gráfica de la Revolución Mexicana,* 4 vols. (Mexico: Editorial F. Trillas, 1965), 1:422.

28. Herriberto Barrón to Madero, November 18, 1911, *DHRM,* 6:304.

29. Madero to General Ambrosio Figueroa (governor of Morelos), December 9, 1911, *DHRM,* 6:395-96.

30. The Zapatista campaigns can best be followed in Gildardo Magaña, *Emiliano Zapata y el Agrarismo en México,* 5 vols. (Mexico: Editorial Ruta, 1951-52), 2: passim. Additional information is contained in Sergio Valverde, *Apuntes para la Historia de la Revolución y de la Política del Estado de Morelos* (Mexico: n.p., 1933); and Porfirio Palacios, *Emiliano Zapata: Datos Biográficos-Históricos* (Mexico: Libro Mex Editores, 1960), pp. 69-87.

At approximately the same time that Zapata initiated his movement in the south, a second military revolt was launched in the north by General Bernardo Reyes. Reyes began gathering followers around him in San Antonio in the fall of 1911 and set December 1 as the date for his movement. In the middle of November, however, he was arrested in Laredo on charges of violating United States neutrality legislation. Released on bond, he continued preparations as though nothing had occurred. During the third week of November leaflets were distributed to the Mexican army soliciting support for the contemplated insurrection.[31] Madero was concerned and sent a personal agent, Francisco Naranjo, to the United States in order to collect all pertinent data on Reyes's activities.[32]

In many ways the contemplated movement of Bernardo Reyes was potentially a much more serious threat to the Madero government than was the movement of Zapata. Reyes still enjoyed a good deal of support with the Mexican army and any major defection of army personnel could mark the difference between success and failure. As Madero began to scan his officer slate for someone to place in charge of the federal troops to be dispersed to the north, he realized that he faced a problem. Victoriano Huerta, because of his close ties with the Reyistas in the past, was not even considered seriously. General Aureliano Blanquet, who was still in charge of government forces fighting Jesús Salgado in Guerrero, was also of questionable loyalty. Finally, Madero decided to place the military operations in the hands of a revolutionary general who was not a career officer and who had no previous contacts with the former secretary of war. He chose General Pascual Orozco, who recently had been named commander of the rurales in Sinaloa. But on November 20, 1911, Madero ordered him to return to Mexico City so that he could take charge of the northern operations.[33] Orozco arrived in Chihuahua on about December 1 and several days later received a telegram from the president indicating that Reyes was expected to move his rebellion into that state shortly.[34] Reyes did cross into Mexico in the middle of the month but found practically no support from the masses whom he

31. *El Heraldo Mexicano,* November 21, 1911.
32. Madero to Señores Consules de San Antonio, Laredo, Eagle Pass . . . November 24, 1911, Archivo General de la Nación, Libros Copiadores de Madero, I, fol. 13 (hereafter cited as AGN/LCM).
33. Sec. de Gobernación to Governor Banderas (Sinaloa), November 20, 1911, Archivo General de la Nación, Ramo de la Secretaría de Gobernación, Leg. 21, Exp. 4 (hereafter cited as AGN/RSG).
34. Madero to Orozco, December 4, 1911, AGN/LCM, I, fol. 37.

hoped would rally to his banner. Realizing that his movement was bound to fail, he surrendered to a small detachment of rurales at the small town of Linares, Nuevo León, on December 25. He immediately sent the following dispatch to General Gerónimo Treviño, commander of the Third Military Zone: "I called upon the army, I called upon the people and none responded. This attitude I regard as a protest, and I am resolved not to continue this war against the government. I place myself at your disposition." [35]

Treviño sent Reyes first to Monterrey and subsequently to Mexico City where he was placed in the Prisión Militar de Santiago Tlaltelolco.[36] President Madero played his political cards perfectly on this occasion. Had he dispatched a large force to the north under the command of either Huerta or Blanquet, it is quite possible that a major army defection would have ensued and seriously threatened his government. Huerta undoubtedly viewed the Reyista insurrection and its premature collapse with more than mild interest from his semi-retirement in Mexico City. Reyes had been his political favorite for a full decade and although there is some evidence to suggest that Reyes expected Huerta to come to his aid,[37] there was little he could do with no troops directly under his command. But Madero was wrong in evaluating the significance of Reyes's surrender. In letter after letter he wrote to friends and politicians that the collapse of the Reyes movement marked a major turning point in his administration.[38] Even as he was forming his optimistic appraisal, however, new revolutionary forces were at work seeking to undermine the girders of his political support.

At the same time that Bernardo Reyes launched his revolt from the United States, Emilio Vásquez Gómez initiated an independent movement against the federal government from Chihauhua. Charging

35. *San Antonio Express,* December 26, 1911; *Diario del Hogar,* December 25, 1911.

36. *El País,* December 29, 1911. The abortive Reyes rebellion is best covered in Victor Niemeyer, "Frustrated Invasion: The Revolutionary Attempt of General Bernardo Reyes from San Antonio in 1911," *Southwestern Historical Quarterly* 67 (July 1963-June 1964): 213-25; and Bryan, "Mexican Politics in Transition," pp. 310-34.

37. Miguel Alessio Robles, "Los Documentos y los Hechos Reales, Verdaderos y Irreprochables ante la Historia," in Bernardo Mena Brito, ed., *Carranza: Sus Amigos, sus Enemigos* (Mexico: Ediciones Botas, 1935), p. 279.

38. Madero to de la Barra, January 8, 1912, AGN/LCM, I, Fols. 163-64; Madero to Eleuterio Margain, January 9, 1912, AGN/LCM, I, fol. 174; Madero to Manuel Mestre Ghigliazza, January 10, 1912, AGN/LCM, I, fols. 199-200.

that he and his brother, Francisco Vásquez Gómez, had been unfairly treated in the presidential election (Francisco had wanted the vice-presidency), he gained some supporters for his movement in late November. A series of small Vasquista insurrections broke out in Chihuahua in December but the federal forces were able to keep them in check. By January the movement had assumed more serious proportions and Madero sent in his work horse General Pascual Orozco to take charge. On January 31 the rebels captured Ciudad Juárez, looting stores and saloons and burning a number of buildings.[39] Orozco and his troops arrived on the outskirts of the city three days later. Realizing that he still enjoyed a good deal of popularity with the northern rebels because of the leadership which he had provided during the anti-Díaz movement, Orozco in his new role as federal general arranged to speak to the rebels before initiating hostilities. His appeal for national unity was convincing, and he persuaded the army troops who had joined the movement to lay down their arms without firing a shot. Madero was elated. Even though Zapata was still in revolt in the south, two northern rebellions had been nipped in the bud without the use of regular army officers. But the most serious anti-Madero rebellion had not yet occurred. On March 3, 1912, Pascual Orozco, the government defender, withdrew allegiance from Madero and formally declared himself in revolt.

The causes of the Orozquista insurrection were multiple. There was a good deal of personal antipathy between Madero and Orozco dating from the fight against the Díaz dictatorship. In addition, Orozco believed that although Madero had never indicated any profound desire to implement a program of social reform, he had veered away even from the promises of political reform delineated in the Plan de San Luis Potosí. Finally, conservative interests in the state of Chihuahua began to cultivate the northern guerrilla fighter and convinced him that he alone, because of his great prestige, could bring some order to the country which had experienced nothing but chaos since November 20, 1910.[40]

Madero had been warned for months and by many disparate sources

---

39. *El Paso Morning Times*, February 1, 1912.
40. The root causes of Orozquismo are developed in depth in Meyer, *Mexican Rebel*, pp. 53-66. An English translation of the Plan Orozquista is contained in the same work, pp. 138-47. A copy of the original plan is preserved in AEM, II, following fol. 26.

that Orozco could not be trusted,[41] but the president's faith seemed to be vindicated when his controversial general put down the Vasquista revolt in Ciudad Juárez. Orozco's own revolution came as a complete shock to Madero and for a time in early March he even considered recalling Huerta to head up the new federal campaign—a proposal seemingly vetoed by the secretary of war, José González Salas. Once González Salas began to receive military dispatches from Chihuahua, he recognized the full significance of the new movement and, not trusting Huerta, persuaded Madero to release him from the cabinet so that he could take the field personally.[42] But the secretary of war had little experience in the field, having spent most of his military career instructing swimming and swordsmanship at the Colegio Militar.

The Orozquista revolt, unlike the various anti-Madero rebellions which preceeded it, had a definite plan of military strategy. By March 6, Orozco's forces numbered eight thousand men, and he had developed a blueprint for a gigantic southward thrust and the eventual capture of Mexico City. Two weeks later all of Chihuahua was in rebel hands and the march to Mexico City was underway. The government counteroffensive began on March 8, when General González Salas left the capital commanding some two thousand men. After several preliminary sorties, the major encounter occurred on March 23 at Rellano, close to the Chihuahua-Durango border. Orozco's troops, utilizing a variety of unconventional tactics, soundly defeated the government forces. General González Salas, fearful of being publicly rebuked upon his return to Mexico City, took his own life shortly after the battle.[43]

41. Enrique Llorente to Madero, January 31, 1912, Archivo General de la Secretaría de Relaciones Exteriores de México, L-E 817, Tomo 208 (hereafter cited as AREM); Ross (special agent) to Secretary of State, November 22, 1911, RDS 812.00/2645; M. A. Esteva to Secretaría de Relaciones Exteriores, October 19, 1911, *DHRM*, 6:178-80; Madero to Aureliano González, December 13, 1911, AGN/LCM, I, fol. 60.

42. Major Adolfo Ramírez to González Salas, March 6, 1912, AHDN, XI/481.5/68, fol. 8; Protestación de González Salas, March 8, 1912, AGN/RSG, Leg. 18, Exp. 10.

43. The official federal army account of the battle of Rellano was prepared by one of González Salas's fellow officers, General Joaquín Téllez. It is found in AHDN, XI/481.5/68, Vol. I, fol. 28, May 1, 1912, and fol. 493, April 12, 1912. The account of the United States military attaché is contained in "General González Salas' Military Expedition in Chihuahua, March 26, 1912," War Department and General and Special Staff, Military Intelligence Division, File 5761, Reports of Captain Burnside, 1912-1913 (hereafter cited as Burnside Reports with appropriate information).

The crushing federal defeat at Rellano and the resulting panic in Mexico City provided the proper set of circumstances for bringing Victoriano Huerta out of his five-month state of inactivity. Upon hearing of the federal setback and the suicide of González Salas, Madero immediately convoked an emergency cabinet meeting. The session was heated, with the president voicing the major opposition to investing Huerta with the new command. Most of the cabinet, led by newly appointed Secretary of War General Angel García Peña and Secretary of Foreign Relations Manuel Calero, favored naming Huerta to head the federal forces.[44] García Peña was given the major voice. He had been the head of the Comisión Geográfica during the period in which Huerta performed his cartographic services and was therefore well acquainted with his personal and professional qualifications. García Peña slowly convinced Madero of Huerta's tactical and strategical expertise and the president agreed to the appointment, albeit somewhat reluctantly. The commission was dated April 1, 1912.[45] When Huerta was informed of the cabinet decision he accepted only with the qualification that he not be encumbered in any way in making the preparations for the next campaign. The arrangements were all to be left up to him. He clearly wanted to avoid any situation which would entail controversial chain of command decisions such as those which had characterized his military efforts against Emiliano Zapata the previous fall. Madero, however, was not to be without his own independent sources of information; his brother Emilio received an appointment as commander of the Fourth Brigade of Irregulars to be attached to Huerta's Division of the North and his other brother, Raul, was already in the field.

Huerta undertook his preparations with all deliberate care. Volunteer contingents were mustered into the army in a number of states but the main striking force was readied in Mexico City. A medical team, a group of engineers, and a corps of communication technicians were added to his forces. Huerta ordered a few small units north to join troops still in the field during the first week in April, but the main body of federal troops left the capital with him, on April 10. Before departing the general submitted his battle plans to a full meeting of the cabinet and they were accepted without

44. See Manuel Calero, *Un Decenio de Política Mexicana* (New York: Middleditch Co., 1920), p. 131.
45. Victoriano Huerta, Campañas y Acciones de Guerra, AHDN, Cancelados, Exp. XI/111/104-1.

modification.[46] Establishing his permanent headquarters in Torreón, he announced a fifteen day amnesty for all Orozquistas who would surrender unconditionally and turn over their arms to the nearest government authority. Only a small unit of rebel railroad workers accepted the offer. But the surrender of enemy troops was not the main purpose of the amnesty declaration, nor was it a sign of federal weakness, fear, or even good will. Rather the amnesty was a calculated military ploy. On March 14, 1912, the United States Congress had passed a joint resolution approving an arms embargo against any American country in which conditions of domestic violence existed.[47] The same day that the resolution was approved, President William Howard Taft specified Mexico as meeting the requirement and prohibited all future shipments of arms and ammunition. The embargo hit the Orozquistas hard because their control of the north gave them access to the United States border. Huerta knew that time was on his side, that the rebels weakened daily as they expended their backlog of ammunition in indecisive minor encounters, and that his own troops needed additional training.

On April 18, six days after his arrival in Torreón, Huerta wrote a long letter to the president indicating that the federal troops who had participated in the first series of campaigns against the Orozquistas were poorly organized, had insufficient equipment, and were suffering from low morale. The volunteer brigades which had converged on Torreón to bolster the federal effort (those of Pancho Villa, Emilio Madero, and Eugenio Aguirre Benavides) needed additional training. To remedy the defects, Huerta undertook a complete reorganization of his División del Norte. Understaffed companies were combined to bring the units up to full fighting strength. Additional cannon and other military supplies were requested from Mexico City. A network of fortifications, including walled entrenchments, were prepared in Torreón. The general hastened to assure his commander in chief that although the fortifications probably would not be needed, he preferred preventive to corrective action. In addition, the work was not going to

46. Madero to Ignacio Rivero, July 11, 1912, AGN/LCM, II, fol. 450.
47. U. S., Department of State, *Papers Relating to the Foreign Relations of the United States, 1912* (Washington, D. C.: Government Printing Office, 1919), p. 745. The Madero government had various lobbyists in the United States urging the Congress to adopt the measure and believed them to be responsible for the final enactment of the measure. See Madero to Samuel Willis Scott, March 25, 1912, *DHRM*, 7:244-45; and Madero to William Lloyd Simpson, March 25, 1912, *DHRM*, 7:245-46.

cost the government a cent because the municipal president of
Torreón, Alberto L. Guajardo, agreed to provide prison labor for the
trench work and battlements.[48]

The period of calculated delay was not without other serious
problems. Because of the lack of adequate sanitation facilities in
Torreón, hundreds of troops contracted typhoid fever in the middle of
the month and, for a time, threatened to disrupt the entire northern
campaign.[49] The medical corps checked the outbreak in late April but
at approximately the same time a group of four hundred volunteers
mutinied against their officers in Torreón and declared that they would
not fight against the Orozquistas under any circumstances. Huerta was
forced to call in a body of loyal troops to disarm the mutineers and
after subduing them sent them back to Mexico City under guard. The
loss was not of great significance, however, as the volunteer brigades
and reinforcements from other areas brought his total federal force to
over eight thousand men by late April.[50] He also had at his disposal
fifty-four of the best artillery pieces in Mexico. His greatest liability
by the first of May was very limited wagon and pack transportation.
As a consequence, he would have to conduct his campaigns close to the
railroad line.[51]

Huerta dispatched probing expeditions during the first week of
May and by May 12 had engaged and defeated a large force of
Orozquistas at Estación Conejos on the Central Railroad. A much
more significant encounter occurred two weeks later, by sheer chance
at the same site where Orozco had defeated González Salas the
previous March. Huerta decided to march on Rellano shortly after
the engagement at Conejos. He made the advance and the advance
made him a hero. The second battle of Rellano began early in the
afternoon of May 22 and lasted well into the night. Huerta's delaying
tactics and his reorganization of the federal forces paid immediate
dividends. The Orozquista troops, handicapped by lack of adequate
ammunition, were unable to withstand the superior federal artillery
fire. Huerta dispatched his first battle report to the secretary of war
the following morning:

48. Huerta to Madero, April 18, 1912, *DHRM,* 7:320-23.
49. H. A. Cummins, British vice-consul, Gómez Palacio, to Francis Stronge,
British ambassador, Mexico City, April 20, 1912, Great Britain, Public Record
Office, Foreign Office Records, F.O. 115/1684, 91 (hereafter cited as F.O. with
appropriate information).
50. Military notes, April 23, 1912, Burnside Reports.
51. General situation, May 4, 1912, Burnside Reports, May 4, 1912.

The division under my command began its fight against the rebel positions in the mountains of Rellano yesterday at 3:30 P.M. The battle has now lasted twenty hours and we are continuing to fight. When I finish [this engagement] I will have the honor of reporting to you, Mr. Minister, that the enemy positions have been taken by our troops . . . I believe that with the movements we are carrying out, we will be able to seize their positions before the day is out.[52]

Huerta's assessment of the battle situation proved correct. In the middle of the afternoon of the same day he was able to report: "Our troops have just succeeded in taking the last and most important enemy position. Rellano is in our hands." [53] The rebels suffered about six hundred and fifty casualties, over six times as many as did the government troops. In addition Huerta captured nine rebel field pieces and most of the enemy's horses. Huerta immediately sent a telegram to Orozco demanding his surrender but the rebel general answered that he would die rather than give up.

The second battle of Rellano was, without question, the turning point in the federal offensive against the Orozquistas. Madero was elated; the same day that the president received the news he began to include mention of it in his official correspondence. Maderista officials exchanged telegrams congratulating one another on their good fortune.[54] Huerta also had reason to rejoice. Seven months earlier his career ostensibly had reached its end. Now he was a national military hero who had saved Mexico City and the country from the Orozquista onslaught. He had cultivated many new military friendships. The Mexico City press glorified and exaggerated his exploits and even Emilio Madero wrote to his brother from the field recommending that Huerta be promoted to division general.[55]

The optimism generated by the federal victory over the Orozquistas proved somewhat premature and irresponsible. Orozco was not yet vanquished. During the last week of May and into early June Huerta pushed the Orozquistas steadily northward but, as the federal commander explained to the president, the pursuit was greatly

52. Huerta to Secretaría de Guerra y Marina, May 23, 1912, AHDN, XI/481.5/68, vol. I, fol. 68.

53. Huerta to Secretaría de Guerra y Marina, May 23, 1912, AHDN, XI/481.5/68, vol. I, fol. 71.

54. Madero to Nicolás Cámara Vales, May 23, 1912, AGN/LCM, II, fol. 193; Manuel Cuesta to Félix A. Sommerfield, May 23, 1912, *DHRM,* 7:401.

55. Emilio Madero to Francisco Madero, May 30, 1912, *DHRM,* 7:424-25.

impeded because the rebels mined railroad lines and bridges and destroyed other communication facilities as they retreated;[56] and the federal army had to move along the railroad. Madero was not interested in excuses. Somewhat naively he dispatched a messenger to Huerta's camp "to insist that Huerta undertake a movement to cut off the enemy's retreat." [57] Madero did not specify just how this feat was to be accomplished, however. If this infeasible and unsolicited advice from the civilian president were not enough to raise military eyebrows, Madero also began meddling in the day to day operations of the campaign. On one occasion, for example, General Aureliano Blanquet, Huerta's second in command, had ordered that his men not be permitted to take any *soldaderas* along with them on the march because he believed the women would slow the troops down. Madero ordered that Blanquet issue a countermand.[58] Worse yet from the generals' point of view was the fact that on occasion the president complained to junior officers in the field that he was unhappy with the movements being carried out by their seniors.[59] Madero confirmed his displeasure by failing to act on several recommendations which he received to promote Huerta to division general and by denying many recommendations for promotion which Huerta made for his troops in the field. In still another slap at Huerta the president authorized a pay increase for the rurales attached to Huerta's command but made no effort to increase the salary of Huerta's regular forces.[60]

A week and a half after the battle of Rellano an incident occurred in Ciudad Jiménez which brought Huerta into even more direct conflict with the president. Several of Pancho Villa's officers appropriated an expensive Arabian mare from a local horsebreeder who had imported it from Spain. Villa decided to keep the animal for himself whereupon the owner complained to Huerta asking that it be returned. Huerta ordered Villa to return the animal, and when the commander of the volunteer brigade refused the direct order, Huerta accused him of insubordination in the time of war and issued orders for his

56. Huerta to Madero, July 2, 1912, AREM, L-E 735.
57. Madero to Jacinto Treviño, Columna Expedicionaria del Gral. Huerta, June 5, 1912, AGN/LCM, II, fol. 280.
58. Madero to Blanquet, June 5, 1912, AGN/LCM, II, fol. 272.
59. Madero to Major Luis G. Garfías, June 5, 1912, AGN/LCM, II, fol. 281.
60. Leonardo Reyes to Pagador del Cuerpo, July 13, 1912, AGN/RSG, Cuerpos Rurales de la Federación, Leg. 639.

summary execution.[61] Only the timely intervention of Emilio Madero, Raul Madero, and Colonel Rubio Navarte prevented the execution of the order. Placing Villa under their personal custody, the Madero brothers wrote to the president explaining the incident and received instructions to send Villa to Mexico City under guard so that the case could be reviewed. Although Villa was interned briefly in the Federal District Penitentiary, Huerta considered Madero's action a direct violation of his promise not to intervene in any way with the conduct of the northern campaign.[62] When, shortly thereafter, some misguided patriot from Mexico City sent Huerta's troops a large shipment of lapel buttons bearing Madero's picture, the general had them destroyed proclaiming angrily that the campaign was not fought for one man but for the republic.[63]

By the middle of June Huerta felt himself completely hamstrung by his commander in chief and began writing letters to friends spelling out his frustrations. One of these letters, written to Emetrio de la Garza, Jr., a lawyer and former congressman from Coahuila, somehow got back to Madero. The president, apparently taken aback, immediately sent a detailed missive to his commander in the field. After indicating that his confidence in Huerta was clearly attested to by having placed over seven thousand men under his command, and after having denied that his brothers were placed in the field to spy on Huerta, the president continued:

> We [the secretary of war and I] have agreed that it is not suitable after the first battle, to approve many promotions, but we feel that when the campaigns are completed, which will be when you occupy Chihuahua or completely destroy the enemy in battle, then we can approve promotions . . . I am aware of the general

61. Huerta had little confidence in the volunteer brigades, the irregular forces, and their respective commanders. Villa held the rank of honorary general and Huerta had been baiting him for weeks by referring to him as "mi general honorario." See Clarence C. Clendenen, *Blood on the Border: The United States Army and the Mexican Irregulars* (New York: Macmillan Co., 1969), p. 135.

62. Villa's interpretation of the incident is told in his "memoirs." Martín Luis Guzmán, *Memorias de Pancho Villa* (Mexico: Compañía General de Ediciones, 1960), pp. 142-50. Villa's defense was undertaken by Adrián Aguirre Benavides, who pointed out that the horse had been taken from Marcos Russek Ramírez, the owner of a local mercantile store in Ciudad Jiménez and a man who had provided the Orozquistas with supplies. The implication was clear. Since Russek had collaborated with the enemy, the theft was justifiable. See Francisco R. Almada, *La Revolución en el Estado de Chihuahua*, 2 vols. (Mexico: Biblioteca del Instituto de Estudios Históricos de la Revolución Mexicana, 1964), 1:341-43.

63. Campaign in Chihuahua, July 24, 1912, Burnside Reports.

interests of the republic and see the need for a quick end to the campaign . . . I understand very well that there are many problems which impede your advance. . . . the advice I give is designed for the purpose of making the battles more decisive. . . .

I hope you erase from your mind the fears you have about me . . . and rest assured that the great services you have rendered are esteemed not only by me but by the entire nation . . . . You can be sure that in due time you will have that high distinction [division general] . . . . My only desire is that you try to be more decisive in the battles which you are undertaking; and for that purpose I am going to send you more troops. We are making an effort to send you some two thousand additional men. . . .

My dear General, you can be sure that envy and pride will never find fertile ground in my heart. I believe that you have served the fatherland well and that you enjoy the esteem and confidence of my fellow citizens.[64]

Without question Madero was sincere. He had hoped that the battle at Rellano would spell the end of the Orozquista insurrection, and when it did not he feared that the federal offensive would degenerate into an endless and futile pursuit of semi-independent guerrilla bands much the same as had the Zapatista campaigns in Morelos. The accouterments of war had all been provided but complete victory had been denied. Madero was impatient. Huerta and his fellow officers, on the other hand, saw the meddling hand of a civilian president who had no appreciation of military exigencies and who was rapidly destroying the morale which the general's staff had hoped to capitalize upon after the federal success at Rellano. Huerta felt himself for the second time placed in a position in which Madero brought into question his professional competence. The president's energetic assertions, he believed deeply, did not stem from the requisite knowledge of the day to day operations. The conflict was a classic example of the civilian and military at odds with one another. The personal enmity generated on this occasion, much more obvious in the federal commander than in the president, would never abate.

The military campaigns following Orozco's defeat at Rellano proved indicisive. In early June Huerta was forced to abandon his pursuit temporarily because of a supply problem, but once the matter was

64. Madero to Huerta, June 22, 1912, Archivo de don Francisco T. Madero, Instituto Nacional de Antropología e Historia (microfilm copy), copybook 20, fols. 50-55 (hereafter cited as AM with appropriate information).

resolved he set the rebels running again.[65] Early in June Orozco decided to make a stand near Bachimba, a small town on the Mexican-Central Railroad not far south of Chihuahua City. As had been the case at Rellano six weeks earlier, the superior federal artillery power was too much for the rebels who were low on ammunition. Orozco ordered another retreat to the state capital. Huerta, in a marvelously picaresque gesture, placed the president's brother Raul and his volunteer brigade in charge of sealing off Orozco's retreat. But the rebel chief destroyed the railroad tracks and burned the bridges behind him as he moved north and not even Raul Madero could effect the desired mission.[66]

Shortly after his defeat at Bachimba, Pascual Orozco decided to spare Chihuahua City the horrors of a full-scale engagement with the federals and withdrew his troops allowing General Huerta to enter the city unopposed on July 7. In a great public ceremony Huerta turned the civil government of the state over to the constitutional governor, Abraham González, but almost immediately the governor and the federal commander became involved in a heated dispute.[67] González favored stern punishment for all the citizens of his state who had aided the rebels. Huerta, on the other hand, realizing that in many cases cooperation with the Orozquistas had not been voluntary and believing that severe retribution could cause more problems than it resolved, urged a more moderate course of action. González wrote to Madero explaining his hard line but surprisingly the president supported Huerta on the punitive issue. He advised González to overlook the errors of the masses and to punish only the instigators and principal leaders of the movement. Even these he felt should be dealt with gently. "If it is possible to pardon all of them, then this would be even better. In this manner you would attract the unanimous sympathy of

65. *El País,* June 5 and June 9, 1912.

66. Railroad Mines, July 24, 1912, Burnside Reports.

67. González had been elected governor with Madero's support in August, 1911, following the overthrow of Porfirio Díaz. When Madero set up his new cabinet in November, he chose González to head the ministry of gobernación, whereupon the governor asked his state legislature to appoint an interim governor in his place. When the Orozquista insurrection broke out in Chihuahua in March, 1912, González asked Madero to be relieved of his cabinet duties so that he could resume his gubernatorial functions. For a careful analysis of his career see William H. Beezley, "Revolutionary Governor: Abraham González and the Mexican Revolution in Chihuahua, 1909-1913" (Ph.D. diss., University of Nebraska, 1968).

the citizens of the state." [68] Madero's support of Huerta's position was accidental and did not signify any healing of the breach. To the contrary, the president's relationship with the commander of the División del Norte deteriorated still more once Chihuahua City was in federal hands. The governor informed Madero that the moneyed interests of the state who had supported the Orozquistas (the Terrazas-Creel clique) also had begun to cultivate Huerta as soon as the general arrived in the city. Madero immediately rebuked Huerta indicating that he was fully aware of the conservative machinations. [69] A few days later the president recalled Huerta to Mexico City for consultation. The general arrived in the capital on July 28; significantly Secretary of War García Peña met him at the station, not the president.

Madero wanted to evaluate Huerta's loyalty himself. He held several private conferences with his commander and apparently was convinced because a few weeks later he authorized Huerta's promotion to division general. [70] After a month's rest in the capital, Huerta returned to the north. Neither the tenuous rapprochment nor the promotion served to assuage him and once having resumed command of his troops he realized that nothing had really changed. The rumors of Huerta's compact with the Chihuahua oligarchy picked up in intensity and filtered back to Mexico City with greater frequency. The press ventured that only the question of Huerta's possible assumption of the provisional presidency separated the northern científicos and the federal commander. González was certain of the imminence of Huerta's defection; and Huerta was just as certain that the situation in Chihuahua could never be resolved as long as González occupied the governorship. The general was convinced that only González's removal would bring Chihuahua back into the federal fold. [71]

By early September the Orozquista army had broken up into groups of semi-independent guerrilla bands which harassed federal outposts mercilessly. Although the press played down the importance of these attacks, Madero, receiving reports from the ministry of war, must have realized that the military situation in Chihuahua in the fall and winter

68. Madero to González, July 20, 1912, AM, copybook 20, fols. 153-54.
69. Madero to Huerta, July 20, 1912, AM, copybook 20, fols. 151-52.
70. Victoriano Huerta, Empleos y Fechas en que los Obtuvo, AHDN, Cancelados, Exp. XI/111/104-1.
71. Rafael L. Hernández to Madero, August 29, 1912, *DHRM,* 8:101-3.

of 1912 was not unlike that in Morelos.[72] Huerta, being a keen student of military strategy and having experienced previously the hit-and-run tactics of the Maya Indians and the Zapatistas, realized that the Mexican army was not equipped to engage in antiguerrilla operations; certainly this factor, as well as his possible ideological attachments to the prerevolutionary days, created the paradoxical situation in which the military leader was calling for a political settlement and the civilian president for a military victory.

With the military situation deteriorating and the rumors intensifying, Madero appeared immobilized by doubt. He found his opportunity to break the stalemate and recall Huerta when the federal commander revealed in a dispatch that his chronic eye condition was beginning to bother him again. Madero ordered him to return once more to the capital but shrewdly did not formally remove him from his command while he was still in the north. Huerta arrived in Mexico City in the middle of October and made plans to enter the private sanatorium of Dr. Aureliano Urrutia for an operation to remove the cataracts. While Huerta was recuperating from the delicate surgery, Madero announced that "at his own request" Huerta had been permanently relieved of his command. In a press interview which Huerta held about a month later he revealed that Madero had subsequently offered him a post in Europe. Huerta did not reject the offer outright but asked that it be delayed because he was still convalescing.[73]

Whether or not the rumors of Huerta's plans to defect to the Orozquistas are valid, Madero was certainly justified in removing him from his command. He had been deceived by federal army officers in the past and Huerta's loyalty at this time was certainly open to question. The general, on the other hand, saw only that he had been removed from command by Francisco Madero and denied the possibility of victory over the enemy twice in one year. As he sat in the capital in the winter of 1912-13, Huerta must have received some satisfaction upon learning that the rebel spark in the north was not extinguished but by early 1913 had once again assumed serious

72. Fernando Trucy Aubert to Victoriano Huerta, September 14, 1912, AHDN, XI/481.5/68, fol. 162; José de la Cruz Sánchez to Huerta, September 1912, AHDN, XI/481.5/68, fol. 168; Síntesis de los Expedientes de la Revolución Mexicana Correspondiente a los Expedientes de Chihuahua, October 1912, AHDN, XI/481.5/201, fols. 8-10.

73. *El País,* January 25, 1913.

proportions.[74]

President Madero's political fortunes in the fall of 1912 received still another challenge when in October another antigovernment rebellion, totally unconnected with either the Zapatistas in the south or the Orozquistas in the north, was launched in the state of Veracruz. The leadership of the October, 1912, insurrection fell on Félix Díaz, the nephew of the former dictator. This revolt, perhaps more than any of the others, was motivated by opportunism rather than by ideological considerations.[75] The Plan Felicista consisted of vague vituperations aginst the incumbent regime and strong appeals for support from the armed forces.[76] Díaz especially hoped to attract Commodore Manuel Azueta, commander of the Mexican navy stationed in Veracruz, and General José M. Hernández, head of the Veracruz prison of San Juan de Ulúa. Neither of these officers rose to the cause, however.

Madero placed all available government troops in the hands of General Joaquín Beltrán and sent him toward the coast. For a week, the newspapers in the capital brazenly predicted that Beltrán was about to defect with his three thousand armed men, but Beltrán and the army remained loyal. On October 25 he attacked the port city, found it poorly defended, and after several hours of fighting put down the rebellion and captured its leader. Félix Díaz was hurriedly tried by court-martial, found guilty, and sentenced to death; but the sentence was suspended by the president of the Mexican Supreme Court, Francisco S. Carbajal. Félix Díaz, as Bernardo Reyes before him, was taken to Mexico City and incarcerated.[77]

If Madero's faith in the army was reinforced by the suppression of the Felicista uprising, his good will was undeserved. In the winter of 1912-13 still another army intrigue of gigantic proportions was brewing in Mexico City. Madero would not only lose the presidency as it unfolded, but would lose his life as well.

74. Antonio Rábago to Secretaría de Guerra, January 11, 1913, AHDN, XI/481.5/69, t. I, fols. 29-60; Rábago to Secretaría de Guerra, February 3, 1913, AHDN, XI/481.5/69, t. I, fols. 108-18.

75. The militarist nature of the Felicista revolt is suggested in Edwin Lieuwen, *Mexican Militarism: The Political Rise and Fall of the Revolutionary Army* (Albuquerque: University of New Mexico Press, 1968), pp. 15-16.

76. The Plan Felicista is reproduced in Casasola, *Historia Gráfica*, 1:502.

77. The abortive rebellion and trial of Félix Díaz is examined in detail in Fernández Rojas, *De Díaz a Huerta*, pp. 221-96.

CHAPTER 3

The Ten Tragic Days

THE ARMY COUP WHICH BEGAN in Mexico City early in the morning of Sunday, February 9, 1913, was not nearly as spontaneous as it must have seemed to the startled citizens of the capital who woke to the sound of artillery fire. The movement had been in the planning stages for nearly four months. The intrigue began in Havana, Cuba, the previous October. Two army officers, Generals Manuel Mondragón and Gregorio Ruiz, and one civilian, Cecilio Ocón, disillusioned with what had happened in Mexico since the overthrow of the old dictator, began to conspire. As they analyzed the series of

45

unsuccessful anti-Madero revolts which had occurred thus far, they must have realized that the decisive focal point which none of the rebels had been able to touch was the capital of the country. They reasoned that an army coup originating in Mexico City could quickly seize the executive power and thereby expect at least some allegiance from the outlying areas. The three conspirators returned to Mexico in late October, shortly after the defeat of Félix Díaz in Veracruz, and quickly added several prominent and disgruntled Felicistas and Reyistas to their number: Luis Licéaga, Miguel Othón de Mendizabal, Rafael de Zayas Enríquez, Samuel Espinosa de los Monteros, and Rodolfo Reyes. By bribing guards the would-be rebels gained access to Bernardo Reyes in the Military Prison of Santiago Tlaltelolco and Félix Díaz in the Federal District Penitentiary. Both generals were apprised of the preliminary plans and took part in subsequent planning.

Bernardo Reyes suggested that contact be established with Victoriano Huerta. Huerta's relationship with Madero by this time was well known in the inner circles of the army and Reyes believed that he would be a natural and exceedingly valuable recruit. From his prison cell Reyes ordered Zayas Enríquez to feel the general out. Zayas, in turn dispatched two confidants, Joaquín Clausell and Fernando Gil, to open negotiations. Huerta was in the sanatorium of Dr. Aureliano Urrutia recovering from his recent surgery when the agents reached him and initiated discussions. In a general way he was apprised of the plans and his support solicited. The leadership of the proposed movement must have been surprised when Huerta turned them down. Clausell and Gil reported back that although Huerta agreed that Madero should be replaced, he felt that the time was inopportune and categorically refused to participate. From that time on, Huerta was eliminated as a potential ally.

Almost without exception the pro-Revolutionary school of Mexican historians has argued that Huerta had reached a compact of some kind with the conspirators prior to the outbreak of the Decena Trágica, offering as proof, his disillusionment with Madero before February 9, 1913, and his actions during the Ten Tragic Days. However, overwhelming evidence from the participants themselves proves conclusively that General Huerta refused the rebel offer of alliance and only subsequent events made him change his mind.[1]

1. The statement of Samuel Espinosa de las Monteros can be found in José Valadés, "La Espera en las Puertas de Santiago," *La Prensa* (San Antonio, Texas),

Huerta's decision not to join the conspirators had nothing to do with any loyalty to President Madero. His refusal was prompted simply by his own desire to lead. Although contacted early by the representatives of Félix Díaz and Bernardo Reyes, Huerta, as an invited participant, would have been placed in a position of following the orders of others rather than molding the rebel movement and the subsequent government to his own liking. In the months that followed, he did not inform the government of the incipient movement, however. He was clearly biding his time.

The tempo quickened in January, 1913, as all semblance of law and order broke down in the republic. Zapata and Orozco were still uncontained and a number of other small, uncoordinated anti-Madero movements broke out in Durango, Jalisco, San Luis Potosí, Tlaxcala, Michoacán, and Puebla.[2] As rebellion broke out all over the country, haciendas were attacked, prominent persons were kidnaped, railroads were destroyed, and communications were interrupted. The army was helpless to quell the uprisings and, one by one, officers in the capital were won over to the contemplated coup. Manuel Mondragón, more than any other single individual, was responsible for attracting the recruits.[3] Throughout January secret meetings were held in the house of General Mariano Ruiz; and in one of the meetings held late in the month, General Mondragón submitted his plans for seizing control to the assembled group.[4] Although a number of previous plans had been rejected as impractical, Mondragón's ideas were

December 4, 1932. Cecilio Ocón's corroboration is contained in Isaac Díaz Araiza, "Preliminares Revolucionarios," *Hoy* 353 (November 27, 1943): 22-23, 81; Félix Díaz gives the same account in José C. Valadés, "Habla Félix: La Decena Trágica," *Hoy* 316 (March 13, 1943): 30-31; Zayas Enríquez concurs in Rafael de Zayas Enríquez, *The Case of Mexico and the Policy of President Wilson* (New York: Albert and Charles Boni, 1914), p. 62; Manuel Mondragón indicates the same, in a letter to Félix Díaz, by stating that Huerta's revolt was a separate movement. Manuel Mondragón to Félix Díaz, June 26, 1913, *DHRM*, 1:92-95. Even the British embassy was apprised that Huerta had been approached early and had declined the invitation to participate. Hohler to Grey, September 24, 1913, F.O. 115/1741, fols. 289-90.

2. Theodore Hamm to Secretary of State, January 15, 1913, RDS, 812.00/5872; M. B. Kirk to Secretary of State, January 22, 1913, RDS, 812.00/5862; Wilbert Bonny to Secretary of State, January 14, 1913, RDS, 812.00/5866; Henry Lane Wilson to Secretary of State, January 16, 1913, RDS, 812.00/5877; Thomas B. Edwards to Secretary of State, January 16, 1913, RDS, 812.00/5878.

3. Manuel Mondragón to Félix Díaz, June 26, 1913, *DHRM*, 1:92-95.

4. Emigdio S. Paniagua, *El Combate de la Ciudadela Narrado por un Extranjero* (Mexico: Tipografia Artística, 1913), pp. 20-22.

accepted and after several changes in dates, February 9 was selected as the target time.

Between 3:00 A.M. and 5:00 A.M. on the scheduled day, General Manuel Mondragón called at the Escuela Militar de Aspirantes in the Mexico City district of Tlalpan and the artillery barracks of Tacubaya. The groundwork had been carefully laid; over three hundred students from the school and about four hundred men from the first and fifth artillery regiments readied themselves hurriedly and placed themselves under Mondragón's command. Dividing his striking force into two groups, the general directed one body of troops, consisting mainly of cadets, to the National Palace and led the other personally, first to the Prison Militar de Santiago Tlaltelolco and then to the penitentiary of the Federal District, setting free both Bernardo Reyes and Félix Díaz. General Lauro Villar, commander of the loyal troops stationed at the National Palace, was awakened in his home early in the morning and told that the palace had fallen to a group of rebels. He immediately organized a unit of sixty troops from the twenty-fourth Battalion, penetrated the National Palace from a side door, and easily disarmed the cadets. The palace was thus recaptured even before the president knew that it had fallen.

In the meantime Bernardo Reyes and Manuel Mondragón began their march across the city to join the cadets and, believing that the National Palace was under rebel control, approached the complex of buildings unaware of the rapid change. The plan was to have Reyes proclaim his provisional presidency from the presidential office itself. As the rebel troops neared the front entrance of the National Palace, General Villar ordered his soldiers to open fire; General Reyes was felled by the first machine gun blast and after a ten minute exchange of fire the rebels were forced to retreat westward across the city. Mondragón and Díaz immediately decided to move upon a secondary target, the arsenal of the Ciudadela. The Ciudadela, about a mile and a half from the *zócalo*, was secured after a brief skirmish and would serve the rebels as their headquarters for the next ten days. As a result arms and ammunition would be no problem.[5]

5. The military engagements of the Decena Trágica can be followed in Francisco Vela González, "La Quincena Trágica de 1913," *Historia Mexicana* 12 (January-March 1963): 440-53; Gonzalo N. Espinosa et al., *La Decena Roja* (Mexico: n.p., 1913); Alfredo Aragón, *El Desarme del Ejército Federal por la Revolución de 1913* (Paris: n.p., 1915). A skillful weaving together of the military and political events of the period is found in Ross, *Madero*, pp. 276-311.

Later on the morning of February 9, Secretary of War Angel García Peña informed Francisco Madero of the events which had already transpired. The president decided to go to the National Palace escorted by a group of cadets from the Colegio Militar and a small presidential guard. General Victoriano Huerta, inactive for a period of almost five months, met the presidential convoy on the way to the National Palace and offered his services to the government.[6] At one point the convoy came under fire and the president was forced to take refuge in a nearby building. At this juncture Huerta admonished Madero to return to Chapultepec Castle, arguing that the president of the country should not expose himself in this manner.[7] Madero refused and simply asked Huerta to accompany them the rest of the way. Upon their arrival, finding that General Villar had been wounded during the first encounter, the president, clutching at straws, named Huerta as interim commander of the loyal troops.[8] The cabinet subsequently confirmed the appointment.

Shortly after Huerta assumed command of the government troops an order was issued for the execution of a captured rebel general, Gregorio Ruiz. Conservative sources generally attribute the order to the president while the pro-Revolutionary school cast the blame on Huerta.[9] It is certain that Huerta saw to it that the order was implemented. While the data are inconclusive enough to warrant any definitive determination, the incident nevertheless is significant because it marked the end of an era in which leaders of opposition factions

6. Huerta had informed the government at the time of his "retirement" that he would be willing to serve again if he were needed. Huerta to Secretaría de Guerra y Marina, December 24, 1912, AHDN, Exp. XI/111/104-1.

7. Huerta's advice to Madero is recorded by Federico González Garza, the governor of the Federal District at the time and a member of the presidential convoy. See his *La Revolución Mexicana: Mi Contribución Político-Literaria* (Mexico: A. del Bosque Impresor, 1936), pp. 397-99. See also Robert H. Murray, "Huerta and the Two Wilsons," *Harper's Weekly* 62 (April 8, 1916): 365.

8. Victoriano Huerta, Cargos y Comisiones, AHDN, Cancelados, Exp. XI/111/104-1.

9. The argument that Huerta wanted Ruiz silenced because the latter knew of his previous agreement with the rebel forces obviously is not valid. Ruiz undoubtedly knew that Huerta had been approached but he also knew that Huerta had refused to participate. The two sets of opinion concerning the issuance of the order can be traced in García Granados, *Historia de México*, 2:355, and José Mancisidor, *Historia de la Revolución Mexicana* (Mexico: Libro Mex Editores, 1959), p. 188; two other accounts record that Madero's cabinet issued the order. See Fernández Rojas, *De Díaz a Huerta*, p. 321, and Daniel Gutiérrez Santos, *Historia Militar de México, 1876-1914* (Mexico: Ediciones Ateneo, 1955), pp. 132-33. Stanley Ross did not find the evidence on either side conclusive (*Madero*, p. 287).

were treated with indulgence and foreshadowed a period of political assassination for crimes often no more serious than an imprudent utterance or a suspected alliance with a potentially hostile force.

The choice of Huerta to command the federal troops can only be explained in terms of desperation. The president twice had removed Huerta from important command positions because of his questionable loyalty and his inability to achieve complete military victory over an enemy availing itself of guerrilla warfare. But on February 9 Madero was forced to act quickly. Huerta had offered his services to the government and his old classmate, Secretary of War García Peña offered no objections. In addition, he was the most prestigious officer with combat experience in Mexico City who had not already defected to the rebel side. Perhaps Madero reasoned that he had been hasty in his previous assessment of Huerta's competence and fidelity but, more importantly, his options were severely circumscribed by the peculiar set of circumstances in which he found himself. Madero might have felt that shunning Huerta's offer could have pushed him immediately into the enemy camp. If, on the other hand, he was loyal, he could help ensure the loyalty of a number of very questionable military contingents. Madero himself was not sure that he had made the correct decision but in face of severe criticism from many friends, family, and supporters, he refused to change his mind.[10]

For the next several days military units stationed in and around Mexico City chose sides. By February 11 both the government troops commanded by Huerta and the rebels commanded by Díaz and Mondragón received numerous reinforcements. In the week that followed citizens of the capital received their first practical lessons in the destruction and violence that had characterized the Revolution in the remainder of the country since November, 1910. Foreign nationals by the thousands sought refuge in the various embassies. The downtown business district and even some adjacent residential areas became battlegrounds. Huerta threw corps of rurales against the Ciudadela in an attempt to dislodge the Felicistas but the rebels repulsed each assault. Artillery fire from both sides reduced public buildings and private residences to heaps of rubble. As commercial

10. Venustiano Carranza, the governor of Coahuila, believing that Huerta was censoring all telegraphic communications, went so far as to dispatch a special agent Francisco J. Múgica to Mexico City to warn Madero that Huerta was not loyal. See Miguel Alessio Robles, "Los Documentos y los Hechos Reales, Verdaderos, y Irreprochables ante la Historia," in Mena Brito, *Carranza*, p. 281.

establishments were forced to close their doors, consumer goods became scarce and prices skyrocketed. The streets of the capital were strewn with burning cars, abandoned field pieces, and runaway horses. All normal traffic in the heart of the city came to a halt as public transportation and communication facilities were almost totally interrupted.[11] Mobs sacked the leading metropolitan newspaper buildings and the owners were forced to suspend publication. On one occasion in the middle of the week a barrage of federal artillery fire opened a breach in one of the walls of Belem prison and hundreds of prisoners escaped.

Throughout the week Mexico City was complete chaos. Looters broke the windows of stores and helped themselves to the wares with complete impunity. Civilian casualties mounted into the hundreds;[12] corpses were piled high and turned into pyres in the interests of sanitation. But neither side gained a clear military advantage. To Madero's exhortation for greater military force, Huerta replied that although destruction of the Ciudadela was within the realm of possibility, it would also entail devastation of a large section of the city. The outcome was not to be decided on the field of battle at any rate; rather a political settlement would be worked out as a result of the intercession of the foreign diplomatic corps in general and the United States Ambassador Henry Lane Wilson in particular.

For months prior to the outbreak of the Decena Trágica, Ambassador Wilson had been predicting the collapse of the Madero government in his messages to the secretary of state. On February 9, the first day of the battle, the Felicistas sent an emissary to entice Wilson to urge Madero's resignation in order to avoid bloodshed.[13] Although the ambassador was sympathetic to the rebel cause and hostile to the incumbent regime, he demurred for the moment. Two days later he determined to take action and asked the state department for far-reaching discretionary powers:

11. Not even the Mexican Foreign Office received its regular dispatches during the Decena Trágica. The communiques sent during the period were received in bulk on February 24. Various Dispatches of Mexican Consuls, February 9 to February 18, 1913, AREM, L-E 683, fols. 15-54.

12. Henry Lane Wilson's statement that eight thousand people were killed is a gross exaggeration. The casualty figure may have reached one thousand. U. S., Senate, Committee on Foreign Relations, *Investigation of Mexican Affairs*, 2 vols. (Washington, D. C.: Government Printing Office, 1919-20), 2:2260 (hereafter cited as *Fall Committee Hearings*).

13. Henry Lane Wilson to Philander C. Knox, February 9, 1913, RDS, 812.00/6058.

In view of the serious and possibly prolonged fighting between the federal and revolutionary forces now taking place in the heart of a modern capital city, a warfare which is violating the rules of civilized combat and entailing untold loss of life and destruction of noncombatant property and depriving of any guarantees of protection the twenty-five thousand resident foreigners, I am convinced that the Government of the United States, in the interest of humanity and in the discharge of its political obligations, should send hither instructions of a firm, drastic and perhaps menacing character to be transmitted personally to the Government of President Madero, and to the leaders of the revolutionary movement.

If I were in possession of instructions of this character or clothed with general powers in the name of the President, I might possibly be able to induce a cessation of hostilities and the initiation of negotiations having for their object definite pacific arrangements.[14]

Although President Taft and Secretary of State Philander C. Knox had asked the ambassador for his candid assessment, neither was convinced of the desirability or the efficacy of giving Wilson such a free hand. They argued that if such representations were disregarded by either the Madero government or the rebels, the United States, in order to give substance to its demands, would be forced to intervene militarily. They felt it more advisable for Wilson to instruct all foreigners to seek places of safety away from the zone of combat.[15] The department's response did not discourage the ambassador, however. The same day that he received the rebuff, he reported to the state department that in the company of Paul von Hintze, the German minister, and Bernardo Cólogan y Cólogan, the Spanish minister, he had called upon President Madero, protested against the continuance of hostilities in the city, complained of the loss of American property, and indicated the great concern of the president of the United States.[16] The same afternoon, the three ministers, joined by the British minister, Francis Stronge, traveled to the Ciudadela and made similar representations to Félix Díaz. Although not armed with a carte blanche from the state department, Wilson's protests were quite strong. Not

14. Wilson to Knox, February 11, 1913, RDS, 812.00/6092.
15. Knox to Wilson, February 12, 1913, RDS, 812.00/6092.
16. Wilson to Knox, February 12, 1913, RDS, 812.00/6122; Henry Lane Wilson, *Diplomatic Episodes in Mexico, Belgium, and Chile* (New York: Doubleday Page, 1927), pp. 257-58.

called upon by the secretary of state to answer for this action, Ambassador Wilson was encouraged to assume a still tougher stance.

Early in the morning of February 15 Wilson invited the British, German, and Spanish ministers to the American embassy to discuss the crisis in Mexico City. On Wilson's initiative, the assembled ministers decided to request Madero's resignation. Wilson reported the meeting as follows:

> We then considered the question of making direct representations to Madero relating to his resignation to save further bloodshed and *possible international complications.* The opinion of the assembled colleagues was unanimous and clear that we should at once, even without instructions, take this action to terminate the intolerable situation, the idea being that the Executive Power should be turned over to Congress. The Spanish Minister was designated to bear to the President our joint views.[17]

Cólogan y Cólogan's recollections of the same meeting are contained in a confidential statement prepared by the diplomat a year later. A typed copy of the memoir is housed in the Mexican Foreign Relations Archive:

> I was woken at one in the morning on Saturday the fifteenth, called by the [American] ambassador. I was driven [to the embassy] mysteriously in a car with its lights turned off. The commander of the patrol of the soldiers who was accompaning us (and who I didn't recognize) told me that four people had just been shot . . . . In the embassy I met the German and English ministers. Mr. Wilson, nervous, pale, and with exotic gestures, told us for the hundredth time that Madero was crazy, a fool, a lunatic who could and should be declared incompetent to sit in the office. This situation in the capital is intolerable. "I will put order," *[sic]* he told us hitting the table . . . . "Madero is inevitably lost and his fall is a question of hours, depending now only on an agreement that is being negotiated between Huerta . . . and Félix Díaz. The time has come for letting him know that only his resignation can save him, and I propose that it be the Spanish minister . . . who communicates this to him."[18]

17. Wilson to Knox, February 15, 1913, RDS, 812.00/6175. Emphasis added.
18. Confidential statement of B. J. de Cólogan, August 2, 1914, AREM, L-E 1579, sec. 2, Exp. 56.

Stronge's account corroborates the details of the early morning meeting:

> At about half past ten at night two motor cars came over from the American Embassy bearing a request that I should go there at once. They had been fired at on the way, and one of them had been struck in several places. I, at once started off . . . . After a long delay the Spanish and German Ministers made their appearance. Mr. Wilson then told us that he had called us together as he thought the time had come for us to take some further action . . . . We discussed the matter until nearly three in the morning, and finally decided that Mr. Cólogan, the Spanish Minister, should go to the Palace as soon as it could be arranged, and after making an appeal to the President's feelings of patriotism should suggest to him as a private hint from himself and his colleagues of the United States, Germany, and England that his resignation could simplify the situation and lead the way to peace. The exact wording we left to the Spanish Minister in whose tact we had every confidence.[19]

Cólogan y Cólogan carried out the mission later the same day. Madero was infuriated. As soon as the minister left the National Palace he drafted a vigorous protest to President Taft indicating that at Wilson's instigation the ministers had threatened him with military intervention should he not resign. Taft responded that the Mexican chief executive must have misunderstood Wilson's representations and indicated that no armed intervention was imminent.[20] But Madero had not misunderstood anything. In his dispatch to the department Wilson had not spelled out what he meant by "possible international complications." Taft either had not seen the telegram or having seen it assumed that since Wilson's request for a free hand had been denied, the ambassador would not have dared to commit United States fighting forces in Mexico. The assumption was, of course, incorrect. For all practical purposes Wilson had conducted himself exactly as if his request for plenary powers had not been denied.

Madero's position was made still more untenable by the action of a group of Mexican congressmen. On February 15 thirty senators, most of whom were Felicistas, met in the Senate chambers. On a motion by José Diego Fernández the group voted twenty-seven to

---

19. Memorandum of Francis Stronge, F.O. 115/1738, fols. 57-72.
20. Taft to Madero, February 16, 1913, RDS, 812.00/6219A.

three to send delegates to the president and demand his resignation. The senatorial commission arrived at the National Palace just as Cólogan y Cólogan was leaving. The president refused to talk to them directly but their message was conveyed by Ernesto Madero, who met with them briefly. The following day a circular, signed by eighty-nine Mexican deputies, was distributed on the streets of the capital. The congressmen were extremely critical of the Senate resolution and asked all loyal Mexicans to unite around the president.[21]

Throughout the first eight days of the tragic ten, Victoriano Huerta remained on the brink. His sympathy lay with the Felicistas and yet he was commanding the federal troops. Twice he met with representatives of Félix Díaz but on neither occasion was any agreement reached. Huerta wanted the Madero government to fall but he was concerned that he might not be given a prominent position in either the peace negotiations or the interim government that would follow. As a result, he procrastinated. The military operations which he directed were designed to prolong a stalemate. While the federal forces were operating from an advantageous position of strength, their offensive maneuvers were calculated simply to keep the rebels off balance, not to inflict decisive defeat. During one brief period of armistice, the federal commander turned his head while the rebels replenished their provisions in the Ciudadela. When General Aureliano Blanquet arrived on the outskirts of Mexico City with reinforcements on February 14, Huerta ordered him to remain where he was rather than to enter the battle.

Huerta must have been encouraged by the political events of February 15. Henry Lane Wilson informed him of the representations made by the diplomatic corps and of the senatorial mission led by Joaquín Pimentel and Guillermo Obregón to the National Palace. When apprised by the American ambassador that federal batteries in the immediate vicinity of the embassy were endangering "not only the property and records of the United States . . . but also many men, women, and children," Huerta agreed immediately to remove the controversial gun emplacements.[22] His final agreement with the Felicistas was probably sealed in the evening of February 16. Huerta had made plans to visit with Henry Lane Wilson that day but late in the evening sent a messenger to the American ambassador to report

21. Al Pueblo Mexicano, February 16, 1913, AM, Roll 17.
22. Wilson to Huerta, February 15, 1913, RDS, 812.00/6840; Huerta to Wilson, February 15, 1913, RDS, 812.00/6840.

that it was impossible for him to keep the appointment. The messenger also related that Huerta "expected to take steps tonight towards terminating the situation." [23] The following day the ambassador was able to provide a little bit more information: "General Huerta has just sent his messenger to me again to say that I may anticipate some action which will retire Madero from power at any moment and that plans are fully matured, the purpose of the delay being to avoid any violence or bloodshed." [24]

The plans agreed upon by Huerta and Díaz were almost handed their *coup de grâce* on the evening of February 17. Gustavo Madero, who for days had been urging the president to remove Huerta from his command position, decided to take matters into his own hands. The president's brother was informed by Jesús Urueta that Huerta and Díaz had held a conference in the house of Enrique Cepeda. Unable to convince President Madero of the imminent danger, Gustavo arrested Huerta in his own office. The president was informed of the arrest early in the morning of the eighteenth and immediately ordered Gustavo to bring the general before him. Madero questioned Huerta at length but was apparently convinced by the general's predictions of victory and protestations of loyalty. He ordered that Huerta be released, personally returned Huerta's side arm, and berated his brother for his impulsive action.[25]

On the morning of February 18 General Huerta marched his troops in front of the National Palace where the President reviewed them from the balcony. After the brief parade the general summoned a number of senators to his office and they informed him that a majority of the senate continued to favor Madero's resignation. Huerta then invited Minister of War García Peña and General Aureliano Blanquet into the same office and had the senators repeat their resolution for the benefit of his military associates. Next he arranged for the group to meet with the president to request again, as they had three days earlier, that Madero tender his resignation. Madero's answer was terse: "I will never resign. The people have elected me, and I will die, if necessary, in the fulfillment of my obligation." About three hours later Madero, meeting with some of his ministers in an executive conference room in the National Palace, found himself

23. Wilson to Knox, February 16, 1913, RDS, 812.00/6186.
24. Wilson to Knox, February 17, 1913, RDS, 812.00/6225.
25. Ross, *Madero*, pp. 304-5; Bernardo Mena Brito, *Felipe Angeles, Federal* (Mexico: Publicaciones Herrería, 1936), pp. 63-66.

accosted by Lieutenant Colonel Teodoro Jiménez Riveroll, Major Rafael Izquierdo, and a small escort of soldiers from General Aureliano Blanquet's Twenty-ninth Battalion. Riveroll informed the president that he was under arrest, on orders of Generals Huerta and Blanquet. Several of the president's aides decided to resist and in the ensuing exchange of shots, Riveroll and Izquierdo, as well as Marcos Hernández, one of the president's aides and confidants, were killed.[26]

During the melee Madero managed to escape from the room and ran into the patio of the National Palace trying to muster some support among loyal troops. Instead, he ran into the arms of General Aureliano Blanquet, who admonished: "You are my prisoner." The president responded, "You are a traitor," to which the general simply reaffirmed, "You are my prisoner." Within thirty minutes the vice-president and most of the cabinet had been taken prisoner as well. Gustavo Madero, the president's brother, was lunching with Victoriano Huerta at the Gambrinus restaurant when the arrests took place. Shortly before 2:00 P.M. Huerta excused himself and telephoned the National Palace to confirm that the scheduled events had indeed occurred. A few minutes later a squad of soldiers entered the restaurant and arrested Gustavo, who was still sitting at the table. Within the hour the huge bells at the cathedral tolled that the fighting was over.

The exact terms of Huerta's agreement with the Felicistas have never been revealed. The negotiations must have been difficult; although both men agreed on the overthrow of Madero, they both desired the presidency. But Díaz needed Huerta more than Huerta needed Díaz. Madero's commander held most of the trump cards. Not only did he possess a greatly superior military force but he could also offer the possibility of arresting the president and thus toppling the government with a single easy stroke. It is possible that Félix Díaz, as his biographer Luis Licéaga contends, never agreed to Madero's

26. Many anti-Madero historians have contended unconvincingly that Riveroll was shot by Madero himself but this interpretation appears to be a complete fabrication. Federico González Garza, an eyewitness, maintains that Gustavo Garmendia, a member of the president's staff, fired the shot that felled Riveroll; see his *La Revolución Mexicana*, p. 406. The hectic events of February 18 can be traced in Sánchez Azcona, *Apuntes*, pp. 373-77; Calixto Maldonado R., ed., *Los Asesinatos de los Señores Madero y Pino Suárez* (Mexico: n.p., 1922), pp. 51-53; Ross, *Madero*, pp. 305-10; and Paniagua, *El Combate de la Ciudadela*, pp. 68-72.

arrest.[27] He could have left the details up to Huerta.[28] The means of effecting the overthrow, however, were less significant than establishing a working rapport. Although no documentary evidence exists it is obvious that the set of circumstances that Huerta assessed toward the middle of the Decena Trágica was quite different from the options that had presented themselves the previous October when he was first approached by the rebel leadership. By the second week in February the military coup was a genuine reality, not merely a blueprint for action. The unexpected death of Bernardo Reyes left a political vacuum which Huerta could hope to fill. In addition, as subsequent events clearly demonstrate, Félix Díaz eliminated one of Huerta's earlier concerns by assuring him a major voice in the establishment of a new government. Finally, by February 15, Huerta was pretty well convinced, and with good reason, that he enjoyed considerable personal support not only from the federal army and many of the rebel rank and file, but from a majority of the Senate and from the most influential members of the diplomatic corps as well. It was a better than average bet that he could beat Díaz in the race for the presidency. Any remaining modicum of loyalty to Madero was overwhelmed by the complex of circumstances laden with political opportunity.[29]

Once the president, the vice-president, and the cabinet were taken prisoner, Huerta sent a dispatch to the United States ambassador. The message was designed to secure United States support for the plans which the general already had in mind for the organization of a new government.

> HIS EXCELLENCY, THE AMERICAN AMBASSADOR:
> The president of the republic and his ministers are now in my power at the National Palace as prisoners. I trust that Your Excellency will interpret this act of mine as the most patriotic manifestation of a man who had no other ambition than to serve his country. I beg Your Excellency to accept this act as one which has no further object than to restore peace in the republic and to

27. Luis Licéaga, *Félix Díaz* (Mexico: Editorial Jus, 1958), p. 213.

28. José C. Valadés, one of the few historians to offer intelligent conjecture on the negotiations, maintains that Díaz gave full command to Huerta for the moment. See his *Historia General de la Revolución Mexicana,* 5 vols. (Mexico: Manuel Quesada Brandi, Editores, 1963-65), 2:269-71.

29. An excellent file of newspaper clippings on the Decena Trágica is found in AREM, L-E 754, Leg. 4, fols. 1-124.

insure the interests of its children and those of foreigners who have brought us so many benefits.

I offer Your Excellency my greeting and with the greatest respect I beg you bring the contents of this note to the attention of His Excellency President Taft.

I also beg of you to convey this information to the various diplomatic missions in this city.

If Your Excellency would honor me by sending this information to the rebels at Ciudadela, I would see in this action a further motive of gratitude from the people of this Republic and myself towards you and the always glorious people of the United States.

V. HUERTA[30]

Henry Lane Wilson transmitted the information to the secretary of state with obvious relief.[31] He also responded directly to Huerta suggesting that in view of the chaotic conditions prevailing in the capital and throughout the republic, Huerta should place himself and the federal army at the disposition of the Mexican Congress.[32] Huerta had something else in mind, however. At four o'clock in the afternoon hastily prepared flyers were distributed on the streets of the capital indicating that Huerta had assumed executive functions. While not actually naming himself provisional president he had arrogated the duties of the office. The flyer, reproduced the following day in the newspapers, read:

In view of the very difficult circumstances through which the nation, and in the last days, the capital of the republic have labored, and in view of what may be considered a state of anarchy resulting from the incapable government of Mr. Madero, I hereby assume executive powers. Until the Congress of the union meets and makes determinations on the present situation, I shall hold Francisco I. Madero and the members of his cabinet, prisoners in the National Palace. Once the matter is resolved every effort will be made to unite all minds in this historic moment. We must all work together to reestablish the peace which for the entire nation is a matter of life or death.

Issued in the Executive Palace, February 18, 1913.

The General Military Commander in Charge of the Executive Power.

V. HUERTA[33]

30. Huerta to Wilson, February 18, 1913, RDS, 812.00/6840.
31. Wilson to Knox, February 18, 1913, RDS, 812.00/6244.
32. Wilson to Huerta, February 18, 1913, RDS, 812.00/6840.
33. *El País,* February 19, 1913.

Huerta's assumption of executive functions had not been previously cleared with the Felicistas and the publication of the flyer ushered in a brief period of profound concern that the hostilities would begin anew. Among the most apprehensive was Henry Lane Wilson, who, on his own initiative, invited Díaz and Huerta to the American embassy for the purpose of negotiating a settlement. The meeting took place at 9:30 P.M. on the eighteenth, and after more than three hours of discussion, during which each of the principals threatened to walk out, a compromise was reached. The major point of contention revolved on the provisional presidency. Díaz favored the appointment of Licenciado Luis Méndez, a lawyer who had taken no part in the rebellion. Huerta, on the other hand, believed that since the responsibility for the maintenance of law and order rested largely with him, he should have the full authority of the office. Henry Lane Wilson supported Huerta and gradually badgered Díaz into submission.[34] The Pact of the Ciudadela (or Pact of the Embassy) provided for Victoriano Huerta to assume the provisional presidency within seventy-two hours. The cabinet, heavily Felicista, included Francisco León de la Barra as minister of foreign affairs, Toribio Esquivel Obregón as minster of finance, General Manuel Mondragón as minister of war, and Rodolfo Reyes, the son of the slain general, as minister of justice. Any changes in the cabinet were to be agreed upon by both parties. Finally, Díaz himself declined any position in the cabinet so that he could begin campaigning for the presidency in the next scheduled elections. Although the pact did not stipulate any date for these elections, it was commonly understood that they would be held within a few months. Also understood, but not explicitly stated, was the fact that Huerta was to support Díaz in these elections.[35]

The American ambassador was pleased with the outcome. A number of years after the event he testified about the pact before a Senate committee. His testimony indicates that he had no better appreciation of Mexico in 1920 than he did in February, 1913:

> These generals [Huerta and Díaz] came to the Embassy one hour after the receipt of the request. They remained in the embassy four hours, during which time a vast crowd surrounded the building, anxiously waiting for the decision. There were three

34. Luis Licéaga (*Félix Díaz*, pp. 214-15) contends that the American ambassador threatened military intervention if Díaz refused to accept Huerta.

35. The Pact of the Ciudadela has been translated by the author, and is included in its entirety as Appendix B, pp. 235-236.

actual breaks but by persuasion and threat they were finally brought to agree and signed an agreement . . . . This was deposited in the embassy safe; and the news was given out from the embassy veranda to the assembled crowds, and that night a crowd estimated to have been over 50,000 filled the streets of Mexico giving thanks to the American government for having made peace in Mexico.[36]

After the meeting Huerta and Díaz prepared their first joint public statement to be released the following morning. The pronouncement summarized the spirit of the Pact de la Ciudadela without spelling out any of the details:

> The unbearable and perilous situation through which the capital of the republic has passed has prompted the army, represented by the undersigned, to unite in a sentiment of fraternity to achieve the salvation of the country; in consequence of that action, the nation can now rest in peace. All the liberties compatible with order are guaranteed under the responsibility of the undersigned officers who henceforth assume command and the reins of government so far as is necessary to afford protection to nationals and foreigners, promising that within seventy-two hours the legal situation will have been duly organized.
>
> The army exhorts the citizens, on whom it relies, to continue in the noble attitude of respect and moderation which they have hitherto observed; it also invites all revolutionary factions to unite for the purpose of consolidating national peace.
> MEXICO. February 18, 1913
>
> FÉLIX DÍAZ
V. HUERTA[37]

Seeking to cloak their military venture with a semblance of legality, Huerta and Díaz saw the procurement of Madero's resignation as their first order of business. On the morning of February 19 a group of congressmen visited Madero and Pino Suárez urging them to formally relinquish their offices. A representative of Huerta, General Juvencio Robles, called on the captives with the same message. The president and vice-president, realizing that they had little choice, agreed to resign with the following conditions: (1) the incumbent governors of all of the states would be allowed to continue in office;

36. Testimony of Henry Lane Wilson, *Fall Committee Hearings*, 2:2263.
37. Mexico, Congress, *Diario Oficial* (Mexico: Imprenta del Gobierno Federal, 1913), 124:407.

(2) Madero's supporters would not be molested in any way by the new regime; and (3) Madero, Pino Suárez, General Felipe Angeles and their respective families would be accompanied to Veracruz on their way into exile by the Japanese and Chilean ministers. By noon Huerta had accepted the terms and the prisoners were preparing their letter of resignation.

Huerta wanted a special evening session of the Congress to consider the resignations and the Congress obliged. Debate on the resignations lasted for slightly over an hour. The fight against accepting the letters was led by Deputy Francisco Escudero from the state of Jalisco. He argued that the Congress was acting under direct military pressure and that rather than accept the resignations the Congress should vote to dissolve itself.[38] Many loyal Maderista congressmen believed that failure to accept the resignations could endanger the lives of the president and vice-president. When their votes were coupled with the anti-Madero factions, the motion for accepting Madero's resignation passed 123 to 5 and the motion for accepting Pino Suárez's passed 120 to 8.[39]

As soon as the resignations were accepted, the presidency, as stipulated by Article 81 of the Constitution of 1857, devolved upon the secretary of foreign relations, Pedro Lascuráin. The new president was sworn into office at 10:24 P.M. His first official act as president was to name General Victoriano Huerta as secretary of gobernación (interior); his second and last act was to submit his own resignation.[40] The resignation, previously agreed upon by Huerta, Díaz, and Lascuráin, was accepted by the Congress at 11:20 P.M.[41] Lascuráin had served as president of the republic for fifty-six minutes.

In the absence of a vice-president and a secretary of foreign relations, the Mexican presidency passed constitutionally to the secretary

38. Andrés Molina Enríquez, *La Revolución Agraria de México,* 5 vols. (Mexico: Talleres Gráficos del Museo Nacional de Arqueología, Historia y Etnografía, 1933-37), 5:130.

39. Those voting against accepting Madero's resignation were Francisco Escudero, Luis Manuel Rojas, Leopoldo Hurtado y Espinosa, Alfredo Ortega, and Alfonso Alarcón.

40. Mexico, Congress, *Diario de los Debates de la Cámara de Diputados del Congreso de los Estados Unidos Mexicanos: XXVI Legislatura* (Mexico: Imprenta de la Cámara de Diputados, 1922), no. 29, pp. 13-14; *Diario Oficial,* February 20, 1913.

41. Even Henry Lane Wilson knew the procedure to be employed. He reported the exact nature of what would occur before the meeting of the Congress. Wilson to Knox, February 19, 1913, RDS, 812.00/6271.

of gobernación. Huerta was observing the proceedings from a doorway in the congressional chamber. Shortly before midnight a delegation was sent to summon him and accompany him to the platform at the head of the room for the purpose of being sworn in. Clad in a black tuxedo, the fifty-eight-year-old general repeated the oath of office:

> I swear, without any reservation, to uphold and enforce the political Constitution of the United Mexican states with its amendments, the Laws of the Reform, and the other laws which emanate from the Constitution. I will loyally and patriotically discharge the duties of interim president of the republic which, through the rule of law, I am asked to fulfill, concerning myself above all with the well being and prosperity of the nation.[42]

The ceremony, in effect, was the funeral service for Madero-style democracy, and when it ended, Mexico had its third president that day.

42. Armando de María y Campos, "Renuncia de Lascuráin y Protesta de Huerta," *A.B.C.* 64 (November 22, 1952): 39.

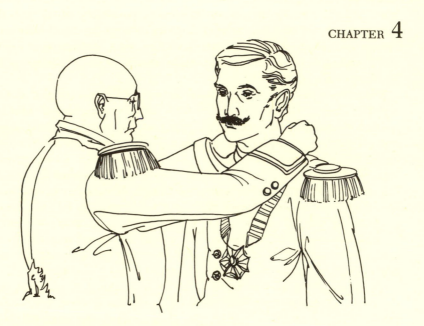

CHAPTER 4

Establishing the New Government

WHEN VICTORIANO HUERTA assumed the presidency, he was faced not only with all of the organizational problems inherent in the establishment of any new government, but also with a set of special difficulties resulting from the peculiar avenue by which he ascended to that office. While the army was expected to pledge its support, the attitude of the state governors, many of whom were staunch Maderistas, was seriously in question. It was possible that the legality of the political charade perpetrated before the Congress on the evening of February 18 might be challenged in the courts or elsewhere and, if it were,

Mexico's foreign posture would be seriously jeopardized. Recognition from the various foreign heads of state might even be delayed. Then again, the alliance of Huerta and the federal army with the Felicistas was a tenuous one, evoked for the specific purpose of overthrowing Madero and Pino Suárez; having accomplished its objective, it could easily disintegrate and thus induce dissolution of the new government from within. Finally, the most disquieting possibility of all was that one or more of the revolutionary factions at arms intermittently since November, 1910, might initiate hostilities even before the regime could entrench itself firmly and make manifest its positions on the burning issues of the day.

When he arrived at the National Palace on the morning of February 19, Huerta, keenly aware of the political realities of Mexican revolutionary politics, had a good deal on his mind. Convinced he was of sufficient stature, he approached the job eagerly. Within a week the ambiguous and problematic circumstances which greeted him on this first day had clarified themselves somewhat. Although the general political situation remained fluid, Huerta did have a number of specific answers which dictated the direction in which the new government was to move. Little did he realize, however, the extent to which, throughout his tenure, he would be forced to react to external circumstances rather than assuming the initiative on his own and delineating an original course of action.

On the morning of the nineteenth the populace of the capital read the morning newspapers not with righteous indignation but with a profound sense of relief.[1] With the guns hushed, the work of cleaning up and rebuilding could begin. Red Cross units and teams of volunteers gathered up the bloated and decaying corpses and tried their best to make identifications from what remained. Those who could not be identified were loaded on carts and transported to vacant fields for mass burials. Sanitation workers scoured the streets and attacked a ten-day back load of garbage, while electricians began to repair broken wires dangling dangerously from their poles. Children couped up during the fighting sallied from front doors and shopkeepers posted signs announcing that they were again open for business as usual. The huge public square in front of the National Palace

---

1. Even staunch supporters of the deposed president agree that there was no general sense of outrage. See, for example, Luis Lara Pardo, *Matchs de Dictadores* (Mexico: A. P. Márquez, 1942), p. 148.

was cleared of debris and a shiny military parade, replete with drum and bugle corps, intimated the return of happier days.

Federal generals, as expected, began to pledge support of the new government at once. The first three to send telegrams of congratulations to the new president were Generals Antonio Rábago, Luis Medina Barrón, and Fernando Trucy Aubert.[2] Their declarations of loyalty were a good omen and foreshadowed the prompt submission of most of the federal army. Several revolutionary army commanders, including Zapatistas Jesús (Tuerto) Morales, Simón Beltrán, and Joaquín Miranda, followed their example within a few days.[3] The community of Mexican civil servants, a group not remembered for its zealous dedication to office, dutifully accepted the new regime.

The new cabinet, as provided for in the Pact of the Ciudadela, was sworn into office in the early afternoon of February 20. Only one ministerial designate refused to accept his appointment. Díaz and Huerta had agreed upon David de la Fuente for the post of secretary of communications. De la Fuente was an Orozquista officer and both Huerta and Díaz believed that his appointment to a cabinet position would help ensure Orozco's submission to the new government. Although Orozco did send the new president a telegram of congratulations, he was not yet ready to pledge support; as a result, de la Fuente declined the portfolio of communications.[4] Huerta wisely determined to leave the office vacant for the time being and, in consultation with Díaz, selected Rafael Vásquez as undersecretary of communications. Significantly, the Congress accepted the entire cabinet without serious question or debate.[5]

Once the cabinet was duly installed, Huerta directed two of his new secretaries to begin work on matters which were uppermost on his mind. Secretary of Foreign Relations Francisco León de la Barra was asked to prepare immediately autograph letters soliciting recognition from foreign heads of state. The president directed the new secretary of interior, Alberto García Granados, to draft an amnesty law designed to encourage all rebel bands to lay down their arms and

2. Rábago to Huerta, *Diario Oficial*, February 19, 1913; Medina Barrón to Huerta, *Diario Oficial*, February 19, 1913; Trucy Aubert to Huerta, *Diario Oficial*, February 19, 1913.

3. Womack, *Zapata*, p. 162.

4. *El Imparcial*, February 21, 1913. Once Orozco submitted to the new government, de la Fuente accepted the post and was sworn into office on March 12, 1913.

5. *Diario de los Debates*, February 28, 1913.

thus contribute to the consolidation of peace throughout the republic. León de la Barra must have hired a team of talented calligraphers because the elaborate handwritten letters were ready for Huerta's signature the same evening. Without detailing the intricacies of the change in government that had occurred, the letters read as follows:

> Division General, Victoriano Huerta, Interim Constitutional President of the United Mexican States, to His Excellency ——— President of the Republic of ———
> GREAT AND GOOD FRIEND:
> Through the rule of law, and by reason of the Congress having accepted the resignations presented by the president and vice-president of the republic, on this day, by virtue of my position as secretary of the interior, I have been called upon to exercise the interim presidency of the United Mexican States.
> I have the honor of communicating to Your Excellency how I have taken possession of the above mentioned post and, at the same time I am pleased to express to you that in the exercise of my functions I will place special emphasis on consolidating and extending the bonds of friendship between our two countries.
> Assuming that Your Excellency embraces the same desire, it is my pleasure to present my sincere best wishes for the prosperity of your nation and for the personal well being of Your Excellency to whom I extend sentiments of highest esteem.
> Your loyal and good friend,
V. HUERTA.[6]
>
> 19 February 1913

Secretary of the Interior García Granados also discharged his assignment immediately. The amnesty law gave complete immunity for political crimes to all those rebels who would lay down their arms within fifteen days. The leaders of the various bands were asked to present themselves to the nearest state governor or *jefe político* as soon as possible so that they would be covered by the law.[7] Ambassador Wilson also decided to lend a hand and sent a circular telegram to all United States consuls in Mexico instructing them to do everything possible to bring about a general acceptance of the Huerta regime.[8]

By the late afternoon and early evening of his first day in office

6. Cartas Autógrafas, AREM, Huerta, Victoriano, Presidente Interino (Usurpador) de México, L-E 1579, Exp. III/311.2 "913."
7. *Diario de los Debates,* March 1, 1913.
8. Wilson to Knox, February 21, 1913, RDS 812.00/6319.

President Huerta had already begun to receive protestations of
loyalty from some of the state governors. Although most of the governors during the Decena Trágica had promised Madero unswerving
loyalty, one by one they allied themselves with the new regime.[9]
The only cause for alarm on February 19 was the attitude assumed
by the governor and legislature of the state of Coahuila. Governor
Venustiano Carranza challenged the legitimacy of Huerta's accession
to the interim presidency. Charging that the Senate had no right to
designate an interim president, Carranza exhorted his own legislature
to adopt an appropriate resolution upholding "legal principles and
the interests of the country."[10] The legislature needed little prompting and the same day passed a resolution withdrawing recognition of
the regime and authorizing the governor extraordinary powers in the
military sphere.[11] Although Carranza issued a circular telegram to all
of the state governors urging them to follow his example, he encountered no immediate enthusiasm.[12]

Carranza picked a bad point to attack and, in addition, misrepresented the issue of Huerta's assumption of the presidency. The Senate
had not designated him as interim president of the nation. Rather,
the Chamber of Deputies had confirmed first his appointment as Secretary of gobernación and, secondly, his constitutional accession to
the presidency from that post. To be sure the political maneuvering
constituted a blatant mockery of the spirit of the law but the technicalities had all been met.[13]

9. The attitude of the governors during the battle in Mexico City can be traced
in a series of dispatches catalogued in *DHRM*, 9:88-109. The *volte-face* is
apparent as one peruses the correspondence from the governors to Secretary of
Gobernación Alberto García Granados in the *Diario Oficial*, February 19, 20, 25,
and 27, 1913.

10. Carranza to H. Congreso del Estado, February 19, 1913, *DHRM*, 4:29.

11. The decree is reproduced in Manuel González Ramírez, ed., *Fuentes para la
Historia de la Revolución Mexicana*, vol. 1, *Planes Políticos y Otros Documentos*
(Mexico: Fondo de Cultura Económica, 1954), 134.

12. Circular Expedida por Venustiano Carranza, February 19, 1913, *DHRM*,
1:3-4.

13. Felipe Tena Ramírez, the dean of the Mexican constitutional lawyers and
by no means an adherent of Victoriano Huerta, concludes that "the constitutional
formalities were impeccably observed . . . therefore the government of Huerta
was not born of usurpation. The jurist who desires to make a determination with
precision must emphasize the facts, rigorously exact from the formal point of view,
even if in his moral and historical judgment he considers this [government] the
most disgraceful example of treason in our history" (Felipe Tena Ramírez,
Derecho Constitucional de México [Mexico: Editorial Porrua, 1955], p. 73). Tena
Ramírez is challenged, but not very convincingly, in a thesis submitted to the law

For all practical purposes the question of legality was settled two days later when Huerta received an official letter of congratulation from the Mexican Supreme Court. The court offered to cooperate fully with the new government in its noble and patriotic task, thus implying not only its moral approbation but also sympathetic decisions in any case contesting the legality of the new regime. The new president thus had every reason to be sanguine about the first few days of transition. Although it was still too early to expect the countries of the world to commit themselves on the crucial matter of recognition, most of the other uncertainties had been clarified in the best interests of the regime. Only Carranza's bellicose posture in the north marred Huerta's auspicious initiation to the presidential office and there were some grounds for optimism even here. On February 21, two days after he had withdrawn recognition, Carranza decided to dispatch two agents, Eliseo Arredondo, a congressman in the national legislature, and Rafael Arizpe y Ramos, a professional engineer, to Mexico City for the purpose of opening negotiations. At the same time the governor expressed his hope that the outstanding problems could be satisfactorily resolved. Of equal significance, the telegram from Carranza introducing the delegation was addressed to Señor Victoriano Huerta, Presidente de la República.[14] But all of the good signs served for naught. On the evening of February 21 an event occurred which drastically altered the political course of the new regime.

Francisco I. Madero and José María Pino Suárez had been held as prisoners in the National Palace since February 18, the day of their arrest. The original plans to send them by train to Veracruz for subsequent European exile were cancelled when Huerta was informed that a group of Maderistas in the port city, led by General José Refugio Velasco, planned to intercept the train, rescue the prisoners, and sponsor an attempted come back. Huerta was uncertain of what to do and went so far as to ask Henry Lane Wilson if it would be better "to send the ex-president out of the country or place him in

---

faculty of the Universidad Nacional Autónoma de México in 1952: Arturo Amaya Morán, *Examen Histórico-Jurídico del Gobierno de Huerta* (Mexico: Universidad Nacional Autónoma de México, 1952). Amaya Morán argues that the Constitution did not explicitly give the interim president (Lascuráin) the power of appointing a secretary of gobernación and then resigning. Thus, upon his resignation, the presidency should have passed to Manuel Vásquez Tagle, the minister of justice and next in line.

14. Carranza to Huerta, February 22, 1913, *DHRM*, 4:33-34.

a lunatic asylum." Wilson's coldly clinical reply was that Huerta "ought to do that which was best for the peace of the country." [15] Secretary of State Knox was incensed that the American ambassador should have even ventured an opinion on the sarcastic question and cautioned him that the consultation gave him a certain degree of moral responsibility in the matter. Knox further admonished: "It goes without saying that cruel treatment of the ex-president would injure in the eyes of the world the reputation of Mexican civilization and this Government earnestly hopes to hear of no such treatment and hopes to hear that he has been dealt with in a manner consistent with peace and humanity." [16]

The United States Department of State was not alone in expressing fear concerning the well-being of the captured chief executive. Prominent government officials throughout the world indicated their alarm. The Cuban ambassador in Mexico City, Manuel Márquez Sterling, was convinced that Madero and Pino Suárez would never get out of the country alive and informed as many persons of his fears as possible. [17] The apprehensions indeed had some substance because early in the morning of February 19 Gustavo Madero had been cruelly murdered while in federal custody. Although few serious contemporary analysts held Huerta directly responsible, the type of protection afforded federal prisoners justifiably was called into question.

At noon on February 21, Huerta held his first cabinet meeting during which the ministers discussed the disposition of Madero and Pino Suárez. They decided that neither exile nor commital to a lunatic asylum were desirable alternatives; rather the former-president and vice-president were to stand trial for political crimes. Because the government would need time to prepare its case and because security arrangements at the National Palace were poor, the prisoners were to be transferred to the Federal District Penitentiary for safekeeping. The following night, during the transfer, they were both murdered. The government explanation of what happened appeared in all of the newspapers the next day: A group of Maderistas attacked the convoy escorting the prisoners, attempted to free them, and during the gun fight which ensued both Madero and Pino Suárez were killed. [18] This version found few believers. The Spanish ambassador

15. Wilson to Knox, February 19, 1913, RDS, 812.00/6271.
16. Knox to Wilson, February 20, 1913, RDS, 812.00/6271.
17. Manuel Márquez Sterling, *Los Ultimos Días del Presidente Madero: Mi Gestión Diplomática en México* (Havana: Imprenta el Siglo, 1917), pp. 548-52.
18. See, for example, *El País*, February 23, 1913. A detailed account of the

ventured that he knew of nobody who took the official account seriously.[19] The British ambassador advised his superior in London that "the story of an attempted rescue is an invention." [20]

The assassination of the former president and vice-president has given rise to an entire series of historical myths. Not only are the questions of ultimate and immediate responsibility misrepresented, but even the accounts of how the assassinations occurred are riddled with inaccuracies.[21] But careful use of testimony collected during an investigation of the assassinations in September and October, 1915, makes possible a reasonably accurate reconstruction of what occurred on the evening of February 22.[22] When the evidence collected during the investigation is combined with isolated documentation in a number of other accounts, it is possible not only to reconstruct the events of the evening but also to offer some reasoned judgments on the matter of guilt.

On the afternoon of February 22, Frank Doughty, an English citizen who owned a car rental service in Mexico City (the Garage Inglés), received a request by telephone to reserve a car for Señor Ignacio de la Torre y Mier. The client, a wealthy hacendado, had rented cars from Doughty in the past to drive to his Hacienda de San Nicolás Peralta and had always preferred convertible models. On this occasion, however, he specified that he wanted a closed car.[23] At about 6:30 in the evening, Francisco A. Alanís, one of Torre y Mier's employees, called at the rental agency on Avenida Juárez, near the

---

official version is contained in the de la Barra archive. See Informe sobre la Muerte de los Señores Francisco I. Madero y Lic. José María Pino Suárez, March 28, 1913, Condumex/FLB, Notas Oficiales, Nombramientos, y Renuncias, 1913-20.

19. Confidential Statement, B. J. Cólogan, August 2, 1914, AREM, L-E 1579, sec. 2, Exp. 56. Henry Lane Wilson did inform his superior in Washington that he was disposed to accept the government version but subsequently changed his mind. Wilson to Knox, February 24, 1913, RDS, 812.00/6353; and Wilson to Bryan, March 12, 1913, RDS, 812.00/6840.

20. Francis Stronge to Sir Edward Grey, February 26, 1913, F.O. 115/1738, fol. 7.

21. The best factual account of the assassinations, but by no means free of error, is Maldonado R., *Los Asesinatos*, pp. 10-15. The most palpable interpretive essay is that of Valadés, *Historia de la Revolución*, 2:322-53.

22. The testimony is available in *DHRM*, 9:237-342. The investigation, ordered shortly after the overthrow of Huerta by Ing. Alfredo Robles Domínguez, the new governor of the Federal District, was conducted by Luis Amieva, chief of Mexican Special Services.

23. Testimony of Frank Doughty, September 7, 1914, *DHRM*, 9:243-44. Doughty informed the British embassy of the matter and his testimony was forwarded to the Foreign Office in London. See Thomas Hohler to Grey, September 30, 1913, F.O. 115/1742, fols. 245-47.

Alameda, and picked out a fifty-five horsepower Peerless touring car. He had orders from his employer to deliver the car to Major Francisco Cárdenas, an officer of the Seventh Corps of Rurales and a man who had visited the Torre y Mier hacienda many times.[24] Doughty dispatched Ricardo Hernández as driver and Genaro Rodríguez as driver's aide. Alanís asked the men to drive the one mile to the central gate of the National Palace, park in front of the main door, and wait for Major Cárdenas as long as necessary.[25]

At approximately the same time, in another section of the city, nineteen-year-old Ricardo Romero, the private chauffeur of Señor Alberto Murphy, was asked by his employer to prepare his car, a new Protos sedan. When the car was ready Murphy directed Romero to place himself at the total disposition of Cecilio Ocón, a Mexico City businessman, one of the original planners of the Felicista uprising, and a guest in the Murphy home. Ocón directed Romero to the National Palace. As the car entered the main gate it passed a parked Peerless with two men sitting in the front seat. Ocón spoke briefly to Major Cárdenas and General Aureliano Blanquet inside the National Palace, returned to his car, and asked the driver to take him to the home of Félix Díaz; after a short conference at the Díaz residence, Romero was ordered to drive to the secretariat of war where Ocón held another brief conference. On the return trip to the National Palace, he stopped once again at the house of Félix Díaz.[26]

In still another corner of the city, at the Barracks of the Zapadores, Corporal Rafael Pimienta was summoned by his superior officer and told that General Blanquet wished to see him at the Comandancia Militar of the National Palace. With no indication of what the conference was about, Pimienta presented himself at the general's office. Blanquet informed the corporal that he had been chosen for a very delicate mission and ordered him to place himself under the command of Major Francisco Cárdenas. Cárdenas was waiting for Pimienta when he left Blanquet's office and ordered him to return to his barracks, pick up his rifle and ammunition, and report back to the National Palace as soon as possible.[27]

Ricardo Hernández and Genaro Rodríguez had been parked in front

24. Testimony of F. A. Alanís, September 14, 1914, *DHRM*, 9:260.
25. Testimony of Ricardo Hoyos [Hernández], September 8, 1914, *DHRM*, 9:246; Testimony of Genaro Rodríguez, September 9, 1914, *DHRM*, 9:250-51. The correct name of the first witness here cited was Ricardo Hernández. He changed his name to Ricardo Hoyos after the assassinations fearing that he would easily be traced and killed by the assassins.
26. Testimony of Ricardo Romero, September 10, 1914, *DHRM*, 9:253.
27. Declaration of Rafael Pimienta, May 4, 1921, *DHRM*, 9:323.

of the National Palace for almost four hours when they saw the Protos with Ocón inside enter the palace grounds for the second time. At approximately the same time a lone soldier strolled past the main gate with a Mauser rifle slung on his shoulder. A few minutes later the two men in the Peerless were approached by Francisco Cárdenas who directed Hernández to drive into the patio and park behind the Protos. Both Hernández and Rodríguez recognized Romero as the driver of the other car. After a few minutes delay Major Cárdenas, Cecilio Ocón, and several guards ushered Madero and Pino Suárez into the patio. Although both beleaguered former magistrates must have been desperate, neither expressed any real concern; the hectic months in office and long days in prison seemingly had given them the power to anesthetize themselves to danger. Cárdenas ordered Madero into the Protos and Pino Suárez into the Peerless, while Ocón directed Romero to place himself at the disposition of Major Cárdenas. The army personnel divided themselves up between the two cars. Cárdenas and Corporal Francisco Ugalde flanked Madero in the back seat of the Protos, while Captain Agustín Figueres and Corporal Rafael Pimienta accompanied Pino Suárez in the back seat of the Peerless.

As the two cars pulled away, Cecilio Ocón went up to the office of General Blanquet to tell him that the plans were proceeding according to schedule. Blanquet then telephoned Colonel Luis Ballesteros, the director of the penitentiary, and told him, "I'm sending you two dangerous little doves my friend. Put them in a couple of good cells and take care of them." Fifteen minutes later he called again to say, "It won't be long now. Be careful." [28]

The Protos took the lead on the drive to the penitentiary via Calle Lecumberri. Hernández followed it at a close distance. The two cars, with a total of nine men inside, made their way through the city at normal speed, finally reaching the main door of the penitentiary shortly after 11:00 P.M. Cárdenas stepped out of the lead car and spoke to Román Rojas, the chief jailer who was waiting at the front gate, and then got back into the car. The jailer jumped on the running board of the lead car and directed the drivers to continue around two corners to the east wall of the prison where the back door was located. When the cars had come to a stop, the lights high on the walls of the prison were turned off, obviously by some prearranged

28. The content of the telephone calls was related by Cipriano Núñez, a telephone operator at the penitentiary. See Salvador Martínez Mancera, "Madero y Pino Suárez Iban a Ser Inhumados en la Peni," *Universal Gráfico,* February 23, 1938.

signal. Major Cárdenas ordered the former president to step out of the car; once Madero was clear of the vehicle Cárdenas removed his side arm, a .38-caliber Smith and Wesson revolver, and after hurling a sobriquet questioning the prisoner's masculinity, shot the helpless man through the neck from behind. Madero fell to the sidewalk without uttering a word. At almost the same time Captain Figueres and Corporal Pimienta ordered Pino Suárez out of his vehicle. Either Figueres or Pimienta fired the shots which killed the vice-president.[29] As both bodies lay prostrate on the pavement, several additional rounds were pumped into them. With the drivers of the two vehicles still in their seats, Cárdenas ordered his subordinates to fire a number of shots into each car. Although windows and headlights shattered, the occupants were fortunate to escape any injury.[30]

Immediately after the two shootings, Cárdenas ordered Hernández and Rodríguez in the Peerless to take Pimienta and Figueres to a downtown location and leave them off. Before the soldiers got out of the car in the heart of the city they threatened the witnesses with death should they reveal any of what they had seen. Meanwhile at the penitentiary, Ricardo Romero drove Major Cárdenas, his two remaining associates, and the jailer around to the front door of the prison where they were joined by two additional employees from inside. Cárdenas ordered Romero to drive the jailers back to the scene of the crime where the bodies were placed into the car and transported back to the central gate. At that point they were dragged out by the feet, wrapped into two coarse grey serapes, and taken inside. The chauffeur then drove the three soldiers who had accompanied him earlier back to the National Palace and, after having received a warning similar to that given Hernández and Rodríguez, returned to the Murphy residence. Romero immediately was summoned by his employer and, after having related the entire episode, was assured by Murphy that his silence would be well rewarded.[31]

29. Pimienta subsequently was tried for the murder of Pino Suárez and was acquitted. He, of course, claimed that Figueres fired the shots which killed the vice-president, and the state was unable to prove the case against him. Neither the two drivers, nor the driver's aide, were able to offer conclusive evidence on this point. After examining a wealth of evidence, Calixto Maldonado R. (*Los Asesinatos*, pp. 366-72) concludes that the evidence against Pimienta was very strong.

30. Testimony of Hoyos, *DHRM*, 9:247; Testimony of Rodríguez, *DHRM*, 9:250-51; Testimony of Romero, *DHRM*, 9:255-56; Hohler to Grey, F.O. 115/1742, fols. 245-47.

31. Testimony of Romero, *DHRM*, 9:257.

The foregoing account of the assassinations, based largely on the testimony of the two drivers and the driver's aide, is as accurate a reconstruction as is possible given the nature of the evidence available. The three testimonies differ in minor details (such as the rank of some of the accompanying soldiers and the seating arrangements in the cars), but they are in agreement on the basic facts. In addition, the part of the testimonies concerning what occurred after the cars arrived at the prison is corroborated in large measure by four other eyewitness accounts: three jailers and one of the participants, Rafael Pimienta.[32] The minor inconsistencies in the individual testimonies would be of importance to the historian seeking a more detailed account, or to a jury deliberating on the guilt or innocence of the principals, but for the purpose of a general reconstruction they are not of great significance.

This account of the assassinations, first of all conclusively disproves the official version of what happened on the night of February 22. It also disproves a number of other fallacious interpretations of the assassinations: that Cecilio Ocón led a simulated attack on the convoy; that the prisoners were transferred to the penitentiary on the morning of February 22 and subsequently lined up against the prison wall and shot; that they were both tortured before being killed; that the murders took place within the prison walls; that the assassinations occurred in the National Palace and the bodies were subsequently taken to the penitentiary and dumped out; that a mysterious General Venegas shot the two prisoners; and that President Huerta was present during the assassinations.[33]

If one attempts to determine the ultimate responsibility for the murders, even most of the better accounts degenerate into a series of unsubstantiated platitudes. The reconstruction of the narrative, however, at least suggests that in addition to the persons actually

32. Declaration of Enrique Ramírez, February 19, 1916, *DHRM*, 9:306-7; Declaration of Nicolás Ramírez, February 22, 1916, *DHRM*, 9:307-9; Declaration of Moisés R. Díaz, February 29, 1916, *DHRM*, 9:309-14; Licéaga, *Félix Díaz*, p. 235; and Declaration of Rafael Pimienta, May 4, 1921, *DHRM*, 9:323-27.

33. For a small sampling of the various unfounded versions see Diego Arenas Guzmán, *Del Maderismo a los Tratados de Teoluyucan* (Mexico: Talleres Gráficos de la Nación, 1955), p. 114; Rafael Martínez and Eduardo Guerra, *Madero: Su Vida, su Obra* (Monterrey: n.p., 1914), pp. 44-46; Espinosa et al., *La Decena Roja*, pp. 126-27; Memorandum of W. H. Field, Group F, Papers from the Senate Office Files of Senator Albert Bacon Fall Relating to Mexican Affairs, Albert Bacon Fall Collection, University of New Mexico (hereafter cited as ABFC). Accounts which accept the official version include Zayas Enríquez, *The Case of Mexico*, pp. 125-31; and G. Núñez del Prado, *Revolución de México: La Decena Trágica* (Barcelona: F. Granados y Co., 1914?), pp. 270-87.

present when the shots were fired, Cecilio Ocón, General Aureliano Blanquet, and Luis Ballesteros were intimately involved in the assassinations. Unless one accepts the unlikely possibility that Francisco Cárdenas acted completely on his own, he must conclude that Ocón, Blanquet, and Ballesteros had previously agreed with Cárdenas on plans for effecting the crime. The participation of Félix Díaz is denied by Luis Licéaga, his most careful, albeit very sympathetic biographer.[34] The only existing evidence which implicates Díaz (and it is entirely omitted by Licéaga) is the testimony of Ricardo Romero that Ocón visited the Díaz home twice in the late afternoon and early evening of February 22. Although this testimony, when coupled with the past relationship of Ocón and Díaz, directs some understandable suspicion at the nephew of the former dictator, by itself it scarcely warrants the epithet murderer.

Another favorite target for responsibility in the assassination is United States Ambassador Henry Lane Wilson. Wilson has been charged, without a semblance of proof, with having planned and directed the two murders.[35] It is clear that the American ambassador meddled shamelessly in Mexico's internal affairs and that his opposition to the Madero government was responsible, at least in part, for the collapse of that regime. For a time he even claimed to accept the official version of the assassination. Interpreting his mission in Mexico simply as the protector of United States economic interests, he was the stereotype ambassador of the age of dollar diplomacy. Much of the indignation expressed against him is understandable—even justifiable—but the charges that he authored the assassination plot are simply without foundation.[36] To the contrary Wilson, on orders from

34. Licéaga, *Félix Díaz*, pp. 233-35.

35. See, for example, José Luis Melgarejo Vivanco, *Breve Historia de Veracruz* (Xalapa, Universidad Veracruzana, 1960), p. 198; Benito R. Blancas, *Ensayo Histórico Sobre la Revolución Mexicana* (Mexico: Talleres de Publicaciones Mexicanas, S.C.L., 1963), p. 18; Louis M. Teitelbaum, *Woodrow Wilson and the Mexican Revolution (1913-1916)* (New York: Exposition Press, 1967), pp. 19-20, 41; Daniel Moreno, *Los Hombres de la Revolución* (Mexico: Libro Mex Editores, 1960), p. 104. Wilson's complicity in the assassinations is strongly implied, but not specifically charged, in Lara Pardo, *Matchs de Dictadores*, p. 137; Ramón Prida, *La Culpa de Lane Wilson, Embajador en la Tragedia Mexicana de 1913* (Mexico: Ediciones Botas, 1962), p. 112; and M. S. Alperovich and B. T. Rudenko, *La Revolución Mexicana de 1910-1917 y la Política de los Estados Unidos* (Mexico: Fondo de Cultura Popular, 1966), pp. 148-54.

36. Placing Wilson in perspective, but by no means excusing his actions, are Lowell L. Blaisdell, "Henry Lane Wilson and the Overthrow of Madero," *Southwestern Social Science Quarterly* 43 (September 1962): 126-35; and John P. Harrison, "Henry Lane Wilson, el Trágico de la Decena," *Historia Mexicana* 6 (January-March 1957): 374-405.

the Department of State, and in the company of German Minister von Hintze, urged Huerta (although not strongly) that all precautions be taken to guarantee the lives of the former president and vice-president.[37]

But more important, what was the role of President Victoriano Huerta? Huerta's alleged complicity in the assassinations is presented as an established fact in literally hundreds of historical accounts. In the large majority of cases the only proof offered is a possible motive: he heard that Madero, if released, would attempt a come back and, whether successful or not, would disrupt Huerta's own plans for perpetuating himself in office. The motive is deemed so overpowering in itself that the conclusion invariably drawn is that Huerta ordered the assassination.[38] The more carefully conceived chronicles realize that motivation alone is insufficient to impute guilt and proffer two bits of "evidence": the confession of Francisco Cárdenas and the cabinet meeting of February 21, 1913.

When Huerta was overthrown in July, 1914, Francisco Cárdenas joined a rebellion which Pascual Orozco pronounced against the new interim government of Francisco S. Carbajal. The movement, doomed

37. Wilson's own defense is obviously suspect; his own claim to having urged Huerta to protect the prisoners, however, is verified by the German and English ambassadors. Wilson's account is contained in his *Diplomatic Episodes*, p. 283. See also Stronge to Grey, February 25, 1913, F.O. 115/1738, fols. 3-4; Stronge to Grey, March 1, 1913, F.O. 115/1738, fols. 191-92; Von Hintze to Wilson, January 8, 1916, in *Diplomatic Episodes*, pp. 344-48.

38. A bibliographical enterprise of major proportions would be required to cite even most of the works alleging Huerta's guilt on the grounds of motive or on no grounds at all. For a sample covering a broad chronological period one can consult the following: José Vasconcelos, *Breve Historia de México*, 3rd ed. (Mexico: Ediciones Botas, 1937), p. 544; Rosendo Salazar, *Del Militarismo al Civilismo en Nuestra Revolución* (Mexico: Libro Mex Editores, 1958), pp. 229-30; Roberto Blanco Moheno, *Crónica de la Revolución Mexicana: De la Decena Trágica a los Campos de Celaya* (Mexico: Libro Mex Editores, 1958), pp. 156-59; Jesús Silva Herzog, *Breve Historia de la Revolución Mexicana*, 2 vols. (Mexico: Fondo de Cultura Económica, 1960), 1:302; Luis Bello Hidalgo, *Antropología de la Revolución: De Porfirio Díaz a Gustavo Díaz Ordaz* (Mexico: B. Costa-Amic, Editor, 1966), p. 73; García Purón, *México y sus Gobernantes*, p. 214; Emilio Portes Gil, *Autobiografía de la Revolución Mexicana* (Mexico: Instituto Mexicano de Cultura, 1964), p. 126; Ignacio G. Suárez, *Carranza: Forjador del México Actual* (Mexico: B. Costa-Amic, Editor, 1965), pp. 25-26; Francisco Ramírez Plancarte, *La Ciudad de México Durante la Revolución Constitucionalista*, 2nd ed. (Mexico: Ediciones Botas, 1941), p. 43; Juan Sánchez Azcona, *La Etapa Maderista de la Revolución* (Mexico: Biblioteca del Instituto Nacional de Estudios Históricos de la Revolución Mexicana, 1960), p. 79; Armando de María y Campos, "El Asesinato de Madero y Pino Suárez," *A.B.C.* 67 (December 13, 1952): 30-33; Baltasar Dromundo, *Emiliano Zapata* (Mexico: Imprenta Mundial, 1934), p. 85; José Luis Melgarejo Vivanco, *Breve Historia*, p. 198.

to failure from the outset, lasted for only a month.[39] While Orozco moved north seeking the security of the United States border, Cárdenas moved south and took refuge in Guatemala. For several months he earned his livelihood as a muleteer, but unable to resist the temptation of occasionally bragging of his exploits, he was called to the attention of the Guatemalan government and eventually arrested by order of Manuel Estrada Cabrera, the Guatemalan dictator. In June, 1915, thinking that he was about to be extradited, Cárdenas made a detailed confession in which he claimed that he had received direct orders from Victoriano Huerta to murder Madero and Pino Suárez.

Cárdenas's confession, invariably accepted at face value by the pro-Revolutionary school of Mexican historians, must be qualified and placed in perspective. No historical account has ever mentioned, for example, that between February, 1913, and June, 1915, Cárdenas made three separate detailed statements concerning the assassinations. These statements not only contradicted one another but also were at odds with what is known of the facts. Shortly after the assassinations, Cárdenas, parroting the official version, swore under oath that the convoy under his command was attacked by a group of armed men and the two prisoners were killed in the gunfight which ensued.[40] A few months later Cárdenas consented to a long interview with Guillermo Mellado, a newspaper man, during the course of which he repudiated the official account and indicated that General Mondragón first ordered him to assassinate Madero and Pino Suárez. After having brought the prisoners down to the patio where the cars were located, he continued, the former president protested so vigorously and raised such a commotion that he felt compelled to return to Mondragón's office for a reaffirmation of the instructions. While in the office he chanced to meet Victoriano Huerta who assured him: "What must be done, must be done." Reassured, Cárdenas had his men lead the two prisoners into one of the stables located in the National Palace. The executions occurred in the stable and the bodies were subsequently picked out of the hay, loaded into the two cars, and taken to the penitentiary.[41]

The third statement, and the only one ever cited, contradicts not only his other two statements, but also the testimony of Frank

39. For a brief account of this movement see Meyer, *Mexican Rebel*, pp. 115-17.
40. Statement of Francisco Cárdenas, *DHRM*, 9:315-16.
41. Guillermo M. Mellado, *Crímenes del Huertismo* (Mexico: n.p., 1914), pp. 27-31. This account is reproduced in Meléndez, *Historia de la Revolución*, 1:182-85.

Doughty, Alberto Murphy, Ricardo Romero, Ricardo Hernández, and Genaro Rodríguez. In the declaration made while Cárdenas was in a Guatemalan city jail, he contended that he was first ordered to assassinate Madero by General Aureliano Blanquet. After having received additional inspiration from Manuel Mondragón, Félix Díaz, and Cecilio Ocón, and before having gone to pick up the prisoners in their rooms, he asked to speak to Victoriano Huerta. The president affirmed that the two men had to die. Cárdenas then went to the home of Ignacio de la Torre y Mier where, with Rafael Pimienta, he picked up the two cars used during the assassinations. The prisoners were subsequently taken to the back side of the penitentiary where Cecilio Ocón led a feigned assault and Cárdenas, following the orders of his superiors, carried out the murders.[42]

The statements of Francisco Cárdenas, far from proving Huerta's complicity, indicate only that the major, in addition to being an assassin, was an inveterate liar. It is possible, of course, that the alleged order from Huerta is one of the few truthful statements in the June declaration but, on the other hand, it is also possible that Cárdenas was simply trying to ingratiate himself with the Constitutionalists and gain a pardon by handing them a bigger fish. At best the Cárdenas confession must be viewed as extremely suspect.[43]

42. The confession was published in the *El Paso Morning Times,* June 16, 1915. It is reproduced in Maldonado R., *Los Asesinatos,* pp. 123-26, with the incorrect date of June 6, 1913.

43. Cárdenas was never extradited because Estrada Cabrera, a dictator in many ways ideologically akin to Porfirio Díaz, would never come to an agreement with the Carranza regime. Released from prison shortly after his confession, Cárdenas lived comfortably in Guatemala City for the next five years, occasionally plotting anti-Carranza revolutions with other disgruntled Mexican exiles in the country. With the overthrow of Estrada Cabrera in 1920 and the election of Obregón in Mexico, extradition proceedings were again initiated and Cárdenas was again arrested, this time on a charge of having ordered an assault on a man who was competing for the favors of a young woman whom Cárdenas was seeing regularly. Released on bond at the time when the extradition proceedings were about to be completed, he tried to escape to Costa Rica but was captured by the Guatemalan army. As he was being escorted into Guatemala City, he produced a small revolver which he had hidden on his person and shot himself in the head. His anti-Carranza activities can be traced in AREM, L-E 798, Leg. 26. His amorous escapades, his second arrest, release, and capture were covered extensively in the Guatemalan press. See *El Diario de Centro América,* November 29, 1920, November 30, 1920, and December 1, 1920; *Excélsior, Diario Independiente de la Tarde,* November 29, 1920; *Diario Nuevo,* November 29, 1920, and November 30, 1920. Additional information on Cárdenas's activities in Guatemala is contained in [Rafael Martínez], "La Verdad en la Muerte de Fcs. I. Madero," *Excélsior,* February 22, 1927; Alfonso Taracena, "Las Revelaciones del Asesino de Madero," *Excélsior,* September 18, 1930; and Agustín Haró y T., "Guatemala Vengó a Madero y a Pino Suárez," *Crisol* 36 (December 1931): 410-14.

In addition to the confession of Cárdenas, a number of historians offer the cabinet meeting of February 21 as evidence of Huerta's guilt. The reconstruction of this meeting varies somewhat from one account to another but generally one of two stories emerges: Huerta informed the cabinet that Madero and Pino Suárez had to be killed and the cabinet gave its approval; or one or another of the cabinet members (Rodolfo Reyes is the favorite choice) voiced the opinion that the two former magistrates should be murdered and the president and the other cabinet ministers concurred.[44] The cabinet ministers present at the meeting have denied categorically in their published memoirs that any plan to kill Madero and Pino Suárez was submitted or that any such agreement was reached.[45] They are in very close agreement concerning what did occur. Secretary of Foreign Relations Francisco León de la Barra initiated discussion of the former president and vice-president by questioning the legality of holding them prisoner without filing specific charges against them. Huerta explained that the original arrest was a military act not requiring legal formalities, but agreed that since the government now had been legally constituted, the situation had changed. The cabinet and the president were in accord that Secretary of Justice Rodolfo Reyes should proceed immediately to prepare formal charges. Specific possibilities raised included the order given by Madero for the execution, without trial, of General Gregorio Ruiz on the first day of the Decena Trágica and the shooting of Jiménez Riveroll and Rafael Izquierdo on February 18, the day of the arrests. When the discussion was completed, Huerta announced that the prisoners would be transferred to the penitentiary where security was much tighter. All of the ministers and the president agreed that the disposition of the case should be handled with the greatest respect for legal technicalities because the entire world would be scrutinizing Mexico's actions on this matter.

While it is not surprising that the Huertista cabinet should deny having participated in any discussion, much less a decision, to murder

44. See Edmundo González-Blanco, *Carranza y la Revolución de México* (Madrid: Imprenta Helénica, 1916), p. 525; Martínez and Guerra, *Madero*, p. 43; González Garza, *La Revolución Mexicana*, p. 413; Alberto J. Pani, *Mi Contribución al Nuevo Régimen, 1910-1933* (Mexico: Editorial Cultura, 1936), pp. 180-81; Alfredo Breceda, *México Revolucionario, 1913-1917*, 2 vols. (Madrid: n.p., 1920), 1:314.

45. Toribio Esquivel Obregón, *Mi Labor en Servicio de México* (Mexico: Ediciones Botas, 1934), pp. 84-98; Jorge Vera Estañol, *La Revolución Mexicana* (Mexico: Editorial Porrua, 1957), pp. 95-109; Reyes, *De Mi Vida*, 2:90-155; and Armando de María y Campos, "Los Ministros de Huerta Explican su Actuación," *A.B.C.* 66 (December 6, 1952): 44-47.

Madero and Pino Suárez, and although their desire to exculpate themselves must be considered, the force of logic is nevertheless on the side of the ministers. The cabinet consisted of four lawyers, three engineers, and one general—not a group of common thugs. Several members enjoyed international reputations in their fields and all were widely respected in the country. To infer that this body of eight of the best-educated, most-talented, and highly respected political leaders in the country, all of whom had enviable records of public service, should have unanimously agreed on murder, not only defies reason but also embraces a conspiracy theory of enormous proportions. Although the murders were not the work of a single deranged assassin acting completely on his own, neither were they the result of a compact signed by the president in conjunction with his cabinet.[46]

The Cárdenas confession and the spurious accounts of the cabinet meeting of February 21 have been used for decades as proof of Huerta's guilt. Debunking them, however, by no means proves Huerta's innocence. The fact that the accredited diplomatic representatives of the United States, Great Britain, and Germany all believed Huerta unjustly charged with the assassinations likewise cannot be offered as proof of innocence.[47] Huerta may very well have issued the orders for the assassinations and there is some circumstantial evidence—quite apart from the two generally accepted evidences of guilt—that raises serious questions. Huerta's first two political appointments once he assumed his new office, for example, were critical ones for anyone contemplating the murder of Madero and Pino Suárez. On February 21 the president announced the appointment of Luis Ballesteros as director of the Federal District Penitentiary. From the careful reconstruction of the events of February 22, the complicity of the new director appears self-evident. Also on February 21 Huerta handpicked a new chief inspector of police for the Federal District, Celso E. Acosta.[48] Placing men of unquestionable trust in these two key posts the day before the assassinations may not

46. Stanley Ross apparently placed no credence in the allegations that the cabinet, in conjunction with Huerta, agreed to eliminate Madero and Pino Suárez. In his brief account of the meeting he makes no reference to this version (*Madero*, p. 326). Charles Cumberland concludes that the "accusation has not been substantiated sufficiently to warrant serious considerations" (*Mexican Revolution*, p. 241 n. 50).

47. Grey to Stronge, March 1, 1913, F.O. 115/1738, fols. 191-92; Testimony of Henry Lane Wilson, *Fall Committee Hearings*, 2:2273.

48. Alberto Garza to Secretaría de Gobernación, February 21, 1913, AGN/RSG, Varios.

have been a mere coincidence. Equally damaging is the fact that the two men directly responsible for the murders, Francisco Cárdenas and Rafael Pimienta, received rapid promotions in their military rank following the assassinations.

It is possible that in time new documentation will be uncovered to shed still more light on Huerta's role in the assassination of Madero and Pino Suárez.[49] Although the evidence available at present precludes positive determination, the circumstantial evidence at least implies the new president's complicity. If he did not order the murders, certainly he could have taken special precautions to protect the former magistrates. But the more familiar one becomes with the nature of the evidence, the more he becomes aware that the data simply do not warrant a conclusive determination. Huerta's guilt remains circumstantial and should not be presented as incontrovertible.[50]

The assassination most assuredly changed the course of Mexican history. Prior to the evening of February 22 Huerta had every reason to be pleased with the transitional progress of the new administration. Venustiano Carranza was not nearly as implacable as his apologists have painted him. In addition, Secretary of State Knox wrote to Henry Lane Wilson on February 21 that the United States government considered the Huerta government to be legally established and recognition was under careful consideration.[51] But the news released in the morning papers on February 23 changed a good deal. While there was no outcry of moral indignation in Mexico City, hope of a prompt reconciliation with the Carrancistas in the north and early recognition from the United States was lost.

49. A potentially valuable source, the personal diary of Francisco Cárdenas, is located in the Guatemalan Foreign Ministry Archives, housed in the Archivo General de Centroamérica. Cárdenas was carrying the diary when he was arrested by the Guatemalan army in 1920. During a research trip to Guatemala in July, 1970, I was informed by the foreign ministry that the diary, although fifty years old, is still considered to be classified and therefore is not available to researchers.

50. A good reconstruction of the assassinations is contained in William Weber Johnson, *Heroic Mexico: The Violent Emergence of a Modern Nation* (Garden City, New York: Doubleday and Co., 1968), pp. 119-25. Although Johnson does not use the Cárdenas confession critically, nor does he develop how it differs substantively from other testimony, his conclusions concerning Huerta's guilt are properly cautious.

51. Knox to Wilson, February 21, 1913, RDS, 812.00/6325A.

CHAPTER 5

War on the Military Front

By the end of February, 1913, scarcely a week after the assassinations, Huerta and his cabinet had recognized that pacification of the countryside was their number one priority. Protestations of loyalty had been received almost immediately from Governors José Portillo y Rojas of Jalisco, Rafael Cepeda of San Luis Potosí, Francisco Barrientos y Barrientos of Puebla, Manuel Mestre Ghigliazza of Tabasco, J. T. Alamillo of Colima, and Antonio P. Rivera of Veracruz, and although many more were to follow shortly, Venustiano Carranza, in spite of encouraging reports from his two negotiators in Mexico

City,[1] decided to bring all talks to a halt and to prepare the state of Coahuila for war. He informed President Taft of the decision on February 26[2] and withdrew fifty thousand pesos from the banks of Saltillo for military expenditures. President Huerta immediately demanded to know why the money had been withdrawn; Carranza replied brazenly that he was in no way accountable to the new regime.[3]

Governor Carranza's decision to pronounce against the government in Mexico City after having sent personal agents to the capital ostensibly to negotiate a rapprochement was not simply the result of his moral outrage at the news of the assassinations.[4] For a week after Huerta's assumption of power the First Chief left his options open. He needed time to test the revolutionary winds, and his peace commissions, although ostensibly negotiating in good faith, bought him this time. With only a small military force at his disposal in his home state and with little reason to expect a massive defection of federals to his banner, an immediate revolt would have been as suicidal as those which Bernardo Reyes and Félix Díaz launched against Madero. But the assassinations were significant. Carranza reasoned that they could possibly have tipped the delicate balance in his favor. By March 1, 1913, all hope of reconciliation had been lost. A few days later the Carrancista headquarters issued a formal statement withdrawing recognition of the government.[5]

1. Rafael F. Arizpe and Eliseo Arredondo to Carranza, February 26, 1913, ABFC, Group T.
2. Carranza to Taft, February 26, 1913, cited in Secretaría de Relaciones Exteriores, *Labor Internacional de la Revolución Mexicana* (Mexico: Imprenta de la Secretaría de Gobernación, n.d.), p. 21.
3. Huerta to Carranza, March 1, 1913, ABFC, Group T.
4. This thesis is developed convincingly, if not entirely originally, in Kenneth J. Grieb, "The Causes of the Carranza Rebellion: A Reinterpretation," *The Americas* 25 (July 1968): 25-32. Grieb concludes that the rebellion was motivated by a desire for power rather than by revolutionary idealism. For a similar interpretation see Alfonso Junco, "Carranza ante Huerta," in Mena Brito, *Carranza*, pp. 386-96; and Lara Pardo, *Matchs de Dictadores*, pp. 169-78. In an interesting analysis of Carranza's motivation, Gildardo Magaña (*Emiliano Zapata*, 3:76-77) contends that the commission was sent to Mexico City to determine the true facts concerning Madero's resignation and Huerta's assumption of power. He did not want to revolt until his suspicions were confirmed.
5. Se Desconoce al General Victoriano Huerta, Presidente Usurpador, y a Cualquier Otro que Provenga del Cuartelazo de Febrero, Agua Prieta, March 6, 1913, Archivo Carranza, Documentos Pertenecientes al Archivo del Primer Jefe del Ejército Constitucionalista y Presidente de México, don Venustiano Carranza, Fundación Cultural de Condumex (hereafter cited as Condumex/AC with appropriate information).

Carranza found his first body of allies in the state of Sonora. The governor, José María Maytorena, a lukewarm Maderista at best, was not disposed to follow the example of Carranza but considerable pressure was brought to bear upon him by anti-Huerta elements in the state led by Alvaro Obregón, Plutarco Elías Calles, Benjamín Gil, and Salvador Alvarado. By the end of the month Governor Maytorena, not wanting to make the decision himself, asked his state legislature for a six-month leave of absence; his successor, General Ignacio L. Pesqueira, succumbed to the demands of Obregón's supporters and allied himself with the Carrancistas.[6] The state legislature made the decision official on March 5 by passing a decree withdrawing recognition of the federal government.[7]

Three weeks after Sonora defected, a third northern state Chihuahua followed suit. The last Maderist governor of Chihuahua, Abraham González, was arrested shortly after Huerta seized power and the governorship was turned over to General Antonio Rábago, a career soldier completely loyal to the new president. Although the state technically remained in the federal fold, by the end of March Pancho Villa had assumed military leadership of a formidable insurrection in Chihuahua. The alliance of Villa with Carranza and Obregón was sealed in the middle of the month and the pronouncement of defection was issued formally on March 28, 1913.[8]

Carranza was pleased with the support he garnered in Sonora and Chihuahua but he knew that it was insufficient. In order to publicize his movement and entice additional converts, on March 26 he promulgated the Plan de Guadalupe. Charging Huerta with treason, but saying nothing of the assassinations, the plan withdrew recognition of the federal government and also all state governments which continued to support Huerta thirty days after the date of the pronouncement. It named Venustiano Carranza "First Chief of the Constitutionalist Army" and provided that he, or someone designated by him, would occupy the interim presidency once Huerta was defeated and Mexico City was occupied. The plan was purely political in nature

6. Alvaro Obregón, *Ocho Mil Kilómetros en Campaña* (Mexico: Fondo de Cultura Económica, 1960), pp. 28-32.

7. Decreto del Congreso del Estado de Sonora por el que se Desconoce a Victoriano Huerta, March 5, 1913, cited in González Ramírez, *Fuentes para la Historia*, pp. 135-36.

8. Chihuahua Denuncia los Espureos de Huerta y Rábago, March 28, 1913, Silvestre Terrazas Collection, Correspondence and Papers, Bancroft Library, University of California, Berkeley (hereafter cited as STC with appropriate information).

and embodied absolutely no program of social reform.[9] A few weeks later Carranza hosted a conference of northern rebels in the town of Monclova. Representatives of the Sonora and Chihuahua movements (Roberto V. Pesqueira, Adolfo de la Huerta, and Samuel Navarro) met with the First Chief and his aide Alfredo Breceda to iron out differences and formalize the alliance. After three days of negotiation —some of it difficult—the delegates agreed to endorse the Plan de Guadalupe and fight to the end. Roberto Pesqueira was to be dispatched to the United States to secure Washington's recognition of belligerency.[10]

The initial response of the Huerta government to the revolt in the north was to begin a purge of state governors whose loyalty was in any way suspect. Although most of the governors in the republic had sworn allegiance to Huerta by the beginning of March, many had been Maderistas with no place else to turn. Fearful that they might begin to ally with the Constitutionalists in the north, Huerta began replacing them one by one in late February and early March with military men of unquestionable fidelity. The first three to be replaced, all accused of Constitutionalist sympathies, were Rafael Cepeda of San Luis Potosí, Alberto Fuentes D. of Aguascalientes, and Felipe Riveros of Sinaloa. The policy backfired. By removing state governors on the slightest of pretext, Huerta inadvertently drove them and their supporters into the arms of the opposition.

At approximately the same time Huerta undertook efforts to gain the allegiance of two important revolutionary generals who had large contingents of fighting men under their control—Pascual Orozco in the north and Emiliano Zapata in the south. At the end of February Huerta sent three commissioners—Ricardo García Granados, Antonio Herrejón López, and Esteban Maqueos Castellanos—to negotiate with Orozco and to determine his conditions for recognition of the new regime. The conference was held at Villa Ahumada, a small town on the Mexican-Central Railroad between Chihuahua City and Ciudad Juárez. Orozco laid down five conditions: his own soldiers were to be paid up to date from the federal treasury; federal pensions were to be established for the widows and orphans of those killed in the

9. The Plan de Guadalupe is reproduced in Felipe Tena Ramírez, *Leyes Fundamentales de México, 1808-1957* (Mexico: Editorial Porrua, 1957), pp. 744-45; and in González Ramírez, *Fuentes para la Historia*, pp. 137-39.
10. Acta de la Convención de Monclova, April 18, 1913, *DHRM*, 4:67-69.

anti-Madero campaigns; meaningful agrarian reform laws were to be enacted immediately; the government was to pay the debts contracted by the Orozquistas for supplies; and, finally, Orozco's soldiers were to be employed as rurales. Orozco's submission was considered vital and, as a result, Huerta agreed to all of the demands.[11] A week later Orozco informed the government that if his men were supplied with additional arms and ammunition he could supply between three and four thousand seasoned troops for duty in either Sonora or Coahuila.[12]

Negotiations between the Huerta regime and the Zapatistas in Morelos did not progress nearly as well even though some individual southern commanders had sworn allegiance during the first week. The day after Huerta came to the presidency the Zapatistas made their position graphically manifest by attacking the town of Tlalpan in the Federal District itself. A week later Zapata notified his subordinates in the field that the Huerta government intended to use negotiations as a guise for capturing and executing the leadership of the southern movement.[13] Huerta, not easily discouraged, dispatched Pascual Orozco, the father of the Chihuahua general, as a peace commissioner to treat with Zapata. Armed with letters of introduction from the president and from his son, Pascual Orozco, Jr., the elder Orozco suggested that the Zapatistas accept terms similar to those which the Orozquistas had already agreed upon as the price for their submission.[14] Zapata rejected the suggestion angrily, charged Huerta and the federal army with having betrayed the Revolution, and arrested the commissioners of the federal government. Although the rebels from Morelos never formally allied themselves with the Constitutionalists in the north, Huerta was forced to turn his troops toward Morelos as well as toward the northern tier of Mexican states.[15]

At the outbreak of the Constitutionalist revolution the federal army (regulars and irregulars) probably numbered between forty-five thou-

---

11. Meyer, *Mexican Rebel*, pp. 96-99; [Jan Leander De Bekker], *De Como Vino Huerta y Como se Fué: Apuntes para la Historia de un Régimen Militar* (Mexico: Librería General, 1914), p. 257.

12. Maqueos C. [Castellanos] to Manuel Mondragón, March 8, 1913, AHDN, Exp. XI/481.5/68, vol. 2, fols. 253-54.

13. Zapata to Genovevo de la O., February 27, 1913, quoted in Palacios, *Emiliano Zapata*, p. 96.

14. Huerta to Orozco, March 22, 1913, Condumex/AJA, Carpeta 2.

15. The Orozco peace mission is treated in Meyer, *Mexican Rebel*, pp. 100-102.

sand and fifty thousand.[16] Because the ministry of war was making plans to conduct three major campaigns in the north and one in the south, as well as to maintain strong contingency units throughout the republic, Secretary of War Mondragón announced in early March that he hoped to increase the size of the army to eighty thousand by the end of April. Recruitment efforts met with scant success, however, and in late April President Huerta decided to increase the daily salary of the Mexican soldier from 1.00 to 1.50 pesos a day.[17] Even with the new inducement few recruits were attracted and the desired goal of eighty thousand was not reached.

The contemplated military struggle also stimulated a major program of army reorganization. Although responsibility for the reorganization rested properly with the secretary of war, Huerta, much more at home with military matters than anything else, assumed the responsibility himself. After three weeks of work he announced the results of his efforts. The Mexican army was divided into ten new divisions, each under the command of a general officer. The four most critical new units were the Yaqui Division (Torín, Sonora) under the command of General José María Mier, the Division of the North (Chihuahua City) under General Antonio Rábago, the Brazos Division (Monterrey) under General Emiliano Lojero, and the Division of the Federal District (Mexico City) under General Aureliano Blanquet.[18] Huerta envisioned greater military efficiency in the struggle against the rebels as a direct result of this new organization.

16. Secretary of War Manuel Mondragón claimed in March that the army numbered sixty-one thousand (*El País,* March 10, 1913). Several months later General Félix Díaz claimed that the strength of the federal forces was seventy thousand. Both of these figures are grossly inflated, however. Mexican field commanders were notorious for padding their rolls and not reporting deaths and defections to the ministry of war. In this way they were able to pocket the salaries of nonexistent soldiers and sell extra uniforms and supplies received from Mexico City. Captain Burnside's estimate of twenty thousand to twenty-five thousand fighting men in June seems quite low. See Summary of Military Events from May 28 to June 30, 1913, Burnside Reports, June 10, 1913. In April the Department of State reported the figure to be twenty-eight thousand, but again this would appear to be a low estimate. See Memorandum of Fred Morris Dearing, April 16, 1913, RDS, 812.00/8070.

17. *El País,* April 22, 1913.

18. The other six divisions were the Peninsular Division (Mérida) under Fernando Trucy Aubert, the Division of the East (Puebla) under Samuel García Cuellar, the Division of the South (Iguala) under Juan A. Hernández, the Central Division (León) under Rómulo Cuellar, the Division of the West (Guadalajara) under Joaquín Téllez, and the Division of Nazas (Torreón) under Ignacio Bravo (*El País,* March 22, 1913).

On April 1, the president appeared before a joint session of Congress to present his first formal national policy address. Because of the physical impairment to his eyes he made only a few introductory remarks himself and then had an aide read the presidential speech. Perhaps taking his cue from Henry Lane Wilson, he tried to minimize the importance of the Constitutionalist revolution, hoping thus to gain United States support:

> The relations with the states of the republic for the most part are cordial because those governors who were not sympathetic with the provisional government resigned their posts and the respective legislatures are naming persons in accord [with the government]. One must take note, however, of the lamentable exception in the states of Coahuila and Sonora whose public officials are displaying themselves in open rebellion. . . . It is certain that the government will be able to reestablish its full authority over all sections of those states.[19]

But other parts of the presidential address impugned the calculated statement of optimism. The president announced, as a *fait accompli,* his program of reorganization for the armed forces; and, in an emotional outburst after the speech had been read, Huerta proclaimed, "I guarantee to the republic with my own life, that the chief executive of the union, seconded by the other powers which constitute the government, will reestablish peace, *cost what it may.*" The impromptu remark was received with enthusiastic applause and with shouts of "Viva el General Huerta! Bravo!"[20]

Pacification, however, proved much more elusive on the field of battle than on the podium in front of Congress. By the end of March Alvaro Obregón had scored two impressive victories in Sonora. The border city of Nogales had fallen to his Constitutionalist troops on March 14, and Cananea was captured a week and a half later. By the end of the month rebel troop strength in the northwest approached eight thousand whereas the government could count on only one-fourth that number.[21] In the middle of April Obregón captured Naco, his second border city, while his fellow officer Benjamin Gil was taking the town of Álamos.[22]

19. *Diario de los Debates,* April 1, 1913.
20. Ibid.
21. William Fearon, acting British vice-consul, Guaymas, to Stronge, March 30, 1913, F.O. 115/1738, fols. 330-32.
22. De la Cueva, consul, Naco, to Secretaría de Relaciones Exteriores, April 15, 1913, AREM, L-E 771, Leg. 1.

The rebel movement in Chihuahua followed a similar pattern. By the time Pancho Villa arrived in the state in early March, Manuel Chao, Tomás Urbina, Rosalío Hernández, and Toribio Ortega were up in arms against the new regime.[23] Before the month was out, however, Villa, never content with occupying a subordinate position, was clearly in command. During April he scored a series of victories over government troops at Camargo, Hidalgo del Parral, and Ciudad Guerrero, and a month later was threatening the large and well-equipped federal garrison of General Salvador Mercado in Chihuahua City, the state capital.

If the Constitutionalist revolution began auspiciously in Sonora and Chihuahua, the First Chief found the going much rougher in his own home state. On March 7 in his first engagement, a skirmish with federals at the Hacienda de Anhelo, General Trucy Aubert forced Carranza to order a hasty retreat. Two weeks later the First Chief was more decisively defeated and lost over four hundred casualties and prisoners in an attack on Saltillo, the capital of Coahuila.[24] The patterns established in the spring continued into the early summer. The federal government was able to stall the Constitutionalists in northeast Mexico but the rebel movement continued to grow in the northwest and north central parts of the country.

Had Huerta been able to direct his total army against the Constitutionalists in the three northern states, and against the Zapatistas in Morelos, it is possible that great strides could have been made toward pacification in the late spring. But as summer approached isolated rebel sparks began to proliferate in thirteen other states. One of the earliest of the minor rebellions broke out in the state of Tabasco where an old Maderista Isidro Cortés won the support of Pedro C. Colorado and Aurelio Sosa Torres and declared the state in open revolt. Within a matter of weeks the movement was seconded in neighboring Chiapas. The rebel leadership in Veracruz was assumed by Candido Aguilar and in Michoacán by Miguel Silva, an ex-Maderist governor, and Gertrudis Sánchez. The Arrieta brothers (Domingo and Mariano) in Durango and the Figueroa brothers (Ambrosio and Francisco) in Guerrero pronounced against Huerta and by May were leading troublesome movements. In addition, Martín Espinosa in Tepic, Rafael Buelna in Colima, Jesús Agustín Castro and Emilio P. Nafarrete in

23. Almada, *La Revolución en Chihuahua*, 2:24-25.
24. General H. Casso López to Secretaría de Guerra, March 24, 1913, AHDN, Exp. XI/481.5/26.

Tamaulipas, all declared that they could not support the government in Mexico City and called their followers to arms. While Pánfilo Natera headed a small movement in Zacatecas, a formidable insurrection was initiated in San Luis Potosí by two rebels who would subsequently become famous in the Revolution—Eulalio Gutiérrez and Saturnino Cedillo. And finally Carrancistas Lucio Blanco and Antonio I. Villarreal were dispatched to Nuevo León and Obregonista Ramón F. Iturbe to Sinaloa to get the movement underway in those two federal entities.

The relationship between these isolated movements and the Carrancista command headquarters has never been studied. The insurrections are generally labeled Constitutionalist (and in a few cases even Zapatista) but coordination was, for the most part, minimal. The physical distance of the local rebel movements from the Constitutionalist strongholds generally dictated the amount of overt cooperation. Carranza had his hands full trying to make one movement out of his three-pronged attack in the north and could not have been expected to offer much more than moral support to the isolated pockets of rebellion throughout the republic. Liaison even with the Zapatistas in Morelos was practically nonexistent, and on several occasions the Constitutionalists expressed concern about the possibility of the Zapatistas selling out to Huerta.[25] But from the government point of view the question of Constitutionalist affiliation was little more than academic. Each time that a new outbreak was reported, troops had to be dispatched, supplies provided, and payrolls met. And, as efforts were directed toward quelling the local uprisings, the Carrancista and Zapatista movements were given additional time to mature.

Huerta did not initially place all of his confidence in the military. In the spring of 1913 several attempts were made to negotiate outstanding differences with the rebels. These efforts were initiated in the middle of March when the president decreed a new sweeping amnesty law for those revolutionaries who would lay down their arms. To follow up the decree, Dr. José S. Sáenz, a personal friend of Secretary of Communications David de la Fuente, was sent to Sonora for the purpose of convincing Obregón and his staff to lay down their arms and talk.[26] The mission was a complete failure. The govern-

25. J. F. Urquidi to Roberto V. Pesqueira, April 30, 1914, Condumex/AC, Telegramas de Chihuahua a Diferentes Personas.
26. Rafael Martínez Carrillo to Secretaría de Relaciones Exteriores, March 29, 1913, AREM, L-E 771, Leg. 1.

ment's first negotiator at Carranza's headquarters, Rafael Cepeda, accomplished no more and his successor to the peace table, Luis F. Saldaña, fared even worse. Not only was he informed by Carranza that there was nothing to discuss, but he was thrown into jail for his trouble.[27] To blunt the public outcry against the arrest of a negotiator who came with white flag in hand, the Constitutionalist headquarters subsequently decreed that all government peace commissioners were to be immediately imprisoned when captured.[28] Future Huertista envoys would know what to expect.

After Emiliano Zapata's first rebuff at government overtures in Morelos, Huerta actually intensified his peace efforts in that southern state. Vague promises for agrarian reform were made but to no avail. In fact, in the summer Zapata ordered the execution of the elder Pascual Orozco, Huerta's prime peace negotiator in the state whom Zapata had arrested previously.

With virtually no hope of persuading either the Constitutionalists or the Zapatistas to lay down their arms through negotiation, and with isolated movements increasing throughout the republic, Huerta launched his first major offensive in the late spring and summer of 1913. In the middle of April the government placed the Zapatista campaigns in the hands of General Juvencio Robles, a career officer whose reputation for needless military excess rivalled that of the president himself. When Robles left the capital he was accompanied by several leading Zapatista defectors, including Jesús (Tuerto) Morales. His orders specified that he was to assume the military governorship of the state and, when the Morelos legislature refused to be swayed by the presidential decree, Robles simply arrested Governor Benito Tajonar and the recalcitrant legislators and shipped them off to the Mexico City penitentiary for safekeeping. The arrest of the state deputies and the governor touched off a heated debate in the national Congress with Deputy Juan Sarabia from San Luis Potosí leading the attack on the administration's blatant violation of state sovereignty.[29] But Huerta was not moved to change his ways. In fact he quickly pledged full government support to the new military governor of Morelos.

Zapata responded by attacking and capturing the town of Jonaca-

27. Ricardo S. Bravo, consul, Eagle Pass, to Secretaría de Relaciones Exteriores, May 22, 1913, AREM, L-E 767, Leg. 2.
28. Circular No. 1, Teniente Coronel Treviño, April 23, 1913, Condumex/AC.
29. *Diario de los Debates,* April 19, 1913.

tepec from the federal General Higinio Aguilar. Aguilar himself was taken prisoner and, after being pardoned by Zapata (for propaganda purposes), for a short time toyed with the idea of joining the rebel cause.[30] In spite of the presence of General Robles's strong column of federal troops, the movement in Morelos continued to grow. By late May Zapatista lieutenants were operating almost freely in the adjacent state of Guerrero and would shortly move into Puebla as well. General Robles lived up to his reputation as he conducted a devastating type of campaign. Pueblos suspected of harboring "bandits" were razed, hostages were taken and sometimes executed, and thousands were herded into resettlement camps which were little more than concentration camps. The Zapatistas too were grossly guilty of intimidation and irresponsible terrorism. As a consequence, the Morelos campaigns turned out to be among the fiercest ever experienced in the Mexican Revolution. As the summer passed, Robles could do no better than control the larger towns. Zapata was clearly the master of rural Morelos.

In early September, Huerta recalled General Robles to Mexico City and relieved him of his command. His successor, General Adolfo Jiménez Castro, who also carried the title of military governor, would fare no better. Huerta's own experience during the Maya campaigns of Yucatán had taught him something of the difficulties of guerrilla warfare but he could devise no military technique equal to the demands of countering the hit-and-run tactics of the Zapatistas.[31]

President Huerta's northern offensive began on May 9, when General Pascual Orozco, Jr., was given twelve hundred men with orders to move north, engage the enemy where he found them, and finally to reinforce Salvador Mercado's federal garrison in Chihuahua City. A week after Orozco left the capital, Carranza, in a singularly intemperate gesture, announced that a decree proclaimed fifty-one years earlier by Benito Juárez, providing for the summary execution of captured enemy soldiers, was again in effect.[32] More convinced than ever that all moral virtue resided in his followers, Carranza believed that the decree would hasten the Constitutionalist victory. Although

30. Womack, *Zapata*, p. 167. When Aguilar returned to Mexico City in late May he defended himself of ·charges of treason by indicating that he had made conciliatory statements only to save his life and those of his men.

31. The Morelos campaigns are skillfully developed in Womack, *Zapata*, pp. 164-76.

32. The Ley Juárez of January 25, 1862 had been decreed at the time of the Veracruz intervention by French, English, and Spanish troops.

individual Constitutionalist commanders were given discretionary powers concerning implementation, the First Chief's desires were amply clear. The decree was made applicable, not only to enemy soldiers, but also to "all those who, in an official or unofficial manner, have recognized or helped, or who in the future recognize or help, the so-called government of General Victoriano Huerta." [33] The decree was extremely significant for it presaged that the rebels in the north planned to give no quarter—nor did they expect any. With the tone of war thus set, both sides abused civilians, rationalized executions, and demonstrated little concern for property rights. As Edward Bell noted acrimoniously, "It must have puzzled the devil to know which side to favor, their ethics being undistinguishable." [34]

Orozco's northern campaign went well. By early July he had won successive victories at Jaral Grande, Estación Dolores, Ortíz, Jiménez, and Bachimba. Follow-up victories at Ciudad Camargo and Santa Rosalía secured Chihuahua temporarily for the government and gave the regime in Mexico City its first cause for genuine optimism since the outbreak of the Constitutionalist revolution almost five months earlier. [35] The general buoyancy generated by Orozco's summer campaign proved rather premature, however. The territory through which his troops passed was by no means secure. As his army moved north, the rebels simply fell in behind and began recapturing the areas temporarily denied them. On June 18, with Orozco camped at Torreón, Villista General Tomás Urbina took a coveted prize. The important city of Durango fell to him when federal defenders and volunteer contingents broke ranks and deserted. During the battle for control of the city one English citizen was killed and several Americans injured. Once the federals withdrew and the rebels entered the city complete chaos ensued. The British vice-consul described the aftermath:

> The town was then given over to be sacked, and the scenes that ensued were appalling. All the rebels were provided with dynamite bombs with which they blew up doors, etc. Every store in town was sacked, irrespective of nationality and four blocks in the Calle Principal, the business section, were burned.
>
> Most of the ladies of the town took refuge either with the

33. Arturo M. Elías, consular inspector, San Antonio, to Secretaría de Relaciones Exteriores, May 20, 1913, transmitting text of decree of May 14, AREM, L-E 786.
34. Edward Bell, *the Political Shame of Mexico* (New York: McBride, Nast, and Co., 1914), p. 352.
35. Orozco to General Jefe de la División del Norte, August 26-27, 1913, AHDN, Exp. XI/481.5/69, vol. II, fols. 399-401.

Archbishop or with me (I have 82 women and children in the house now). The volunteers were hunted and shot like rats, and rape and looting were the order of the day and night. How we escaped I can hardly tell. I sat at the door all night and succeeded in stalling off no less than ten different parties who wished to search and loot. . . .

Yesterday some order was restored, and we visited the General [Urbina] and arranged that he would pardon the remainder of the volunteers on condition of their surrendering and giving up their arms, if any. The condition of the town is simply lamentable. Every store has been literally gutted and you could not buy anything for its weight in gold. Fortunately, I had laid in supplies for three months against the siege, so I am able to feed the unfortunates who are my guests.

I went to see Urbina and requested him to investigate and punish the murderers who were identified . . . but I must say that he . . . was most insolent and discourteous. He positively refused to make any investigation whatsoever, and stated that foreigners must take their chance with the rest. It is lamentable to think that the prestige of an Englishman has fallen so low that a cold-blooded murder is treated as a jest, but so it is, at any rate here.[36]

The fall of Durango brought home the potent realities of the military campaigns in the north, and Huerta responded by implementing his "peace—cost what it may" philosophy. The famous statement has been interpreted since its initial exposition as a license for all type of federal debauchery on and off the field of battle. Without denying that Huerta's federal army was guilty of scandalous disregard for noncombatant interests during the protracted struggle, and acknowledging that military malfeasance generally went unpunished, still the statement has been misinterpreted for years. To Huerta "peace—cost what it may" meant that he intended to pacify the country—that he intended to defeat the Constitutionalists and the Zapatistas—even if in doing so he found it necessary to convert Mexico into the most completely militarist state in the world. And he came close to doing just that.

In the summer and fall of 1913 the area of Mexico under federal

36. W. W. Graham to Stronge, June 22, 1913, F.O. 115/1740, fols. 136-37. The description of the British vice-consul is confirmed by the report of the American consul. Copy of Telegram from American consul at Durango, June 21, 1913, F.O. 115/1740, fols. 245-46; Hamm to Bryan, June 21, 1913, RDS, 812.00/7919.

control was gradually converted into one huge military base.[37] Factories and stores not related to the war effort were forbidden by law to keep open on Sundays so that civilian employees could be given military instruction. The railroads, when in operation, carried military personnel and hardware almost to the complete exclusion of civilian traffic and freight. Artillery pieces, military supplies, uniforms, soldiers, and horses preempted the rolling stock to such a degree that food staples and other daily necessities had to be transported into the cities by other means, most often by hundreds of *cargadores.* The railroad stations in Mexico City especially were military embarkation posts and little else.[38] The government installed new equipment for rifling and boring gun barrels at the National Arms Factory, constructed a modern sulphuric acid plant at the National Powder Factory, and ordered a new furnace for forging large artillery pieces at the National Artillery Workshops.[39] Scarcely a week passed without some military parade or show of the latest equipment. The president seldom missed the opportunity to participate personally in military ceremonies and availed himself of the occasions to sport his favorite dress uniform, replete with ribbons covering the left side of his jacket and medals draped from his neck.

The commanders of local barracks in the Mexico City area never knew when the president might leave his desk and stop by unannounced for an immediate tour of inspection. Military decorations, including the coveted Cross of Military Merit, were passed out in wholesale lots to old cronies.[40] Whenever possible Huerta conducted the ceremonies personally and posed for pictures with the newly decorated officer. Not even the paramilitary Mexico City police force satisfied his craving for absolutist military organization; it was transformed into a regular army regiment comprised of two battalions and placed under the command of a regular army infantry officer.[41] The mounted police were similarly attached to a cavalry regiment.[42]

37. The extent of Huerta's militarization is traced in Michael C. Meyer, "The Militarization of Mexico, 1913-1914," *The Americas* 27 (January 1971): 293-306.

38. Aragón, *El Desarme del Ejército,* p. 56.

39. Decree 446, ministry of war and marine, August 14, 1913, F.O. 115/1741, fols. 203-7.

40. Secretary Mondragón authorized Huerta's own Cross of Military Merit in April. Mondragón to Huerta, April 18, 1913, AHDN, Exp. XI/111/104-1.

41. Samuel García Cuellar to Secretaría de Estado y del Despacho de Gobernación, April 1, 1913, AGN/RSG, Policía, Gobierno del Distrito, 1912-13.

42. *Diario de los Debates,* September 16, 1913.

By the winter of 1913-14 the Mexico City police force had been augmented by some one thousand men.[43]

The Mexican educational system felt the full impact of the militarization in late summer as school after school found its governing regulations changed to provide for the mandatory wearing of military uniforms and training in the military arts and sciences. The professional schools in Mexico City were the first to capitulate and were followed shortly by most of the secondary and primary schools. Not to be outdone by these overt manifestations of patriotism in the nation's capital, General Joaquín Maass, the military governor of Puebla, ordered nine hundred wooden rifles for distribution among the primary school children in his state. All official school ceremonies would demonstrate the proper martial sprit.[44] At approximately the same time the president let it be known that he would view with favor any decision of government employees to request uniforms and military instruction. As could have been expected, the civilian personnel of the war ministry were the first to fall into line. With almost clocklike precision other ministries followed suit as did the nation's telegraph workers, primary school teachers, and a variety of other blue- and white-collar workers.

Militarization of the provinces was never as complete as that of the Federal District but the military presence was still abundantly evident. The population of a village could double or triple overnight as a large unit moved in. Because there was little or no advance warning, a stay of two or three days could deplete stores of food, supplies, and other basic necessities, thus aggravating other outrages of war. When the troops pulled out the villages were often on the verge of starvation. The receipts which a local merchant might receive as a commander emptied his store were scarcely worth the paper they were printed on. Complaints flooded the offices of state officials but the military governors—hand-picked by the president and given absolute powers—were seldom sympathetic. But, village resistance was almost nonexistent. The surrounding countryside was often decorated with bodies of captured enemy soldiers stripped below the waist, hanging from trees and telephone posts. The lessons were not lost on those who might harbor notions of resistance.

The presidential office in Mexico City issued thousands of orders and counterorders. New military awards were created to compensate

43. *El Independiente*, February 24, 1914.
44. *El Independiente*, September 12, 1913.

favorites. Huerta, considering himself much more apt in military matters than either his secretary of war or his general staff, did his own work down to the most minute details of projected military organization. The president's office formulated policy, devised strategical blueprints, and even participated in tactical decisions of small units. Huerta was thus guilty of precisely the same thing that he accused Madero of during his campaigns against the Orozquistas the previous year.

When the staff from the defense ministry presented military proposals for congressional approval, they invariably prefaced their presentations by indicating that the plan had been passed down by the president.[45] Time after time Huerta decreed increases in troop strength. Age limits for military service were forgotten. By October, 1913, the president had authorized 150,000 troops.[46] Three and a half months later he raised the figure to 200,000.[47] Actual troop strength never reached authorized levels but Huerta utilized every imaginable means to replace casualties and deserters and simultaneously increase the size of his fighting force. Small pay raises were attempted but invariably failed to attract large numbers.[48] Each state was assigned a specific quota apportioned on the basis of population. The military governors were not in the least scrupulous about how they attempted to meet their requirements but they always seemed to come up short.

The most notorious recruitment technique was the *leva,* a system of forced conscription which was directed almost exclusively at the poor and uneducated masses. The *leva* had been used and abused many times in the past but never as extensively as during the summer and fall of 1913. In May, Huerta confided to Henry Lane Wilson that "recruitment" was proceeding at the rate of eight hundred soldiers per day.[49] Almost all of these were obtained through the *leva.* During the summer and fall of 1913 tens of thousands of illiterate men were picked up off the streets in the slum barrios of the large cities and in the rich agricultural belt of the Central Valley, inducted into the

45. *Diario de los Debates,* April 30, 1913; ibid., May 13, 1913; Huerta to Aureliano Blanquet, August 14, 1913, F.O. 115/1741, fols. 203-7.

46. *Diario Oficial,* October 27, 1913, p. 637.

47. Carden to Grey, February 6, 1914, F.O. 115/1789, fol. 90.

48. In July, 1913, the daily pay (in Mexican currency) for the lower ranks was: privates, $1.50; corporals, $1.75; second sergeants, $2.00; and first sergeants, $2.25. Although uniforms and equipment were provided by the government, subsistence was not. See Summary of Military Events, July 8-15, Burnside Reports, July 15, 1913.

49. Wilson, *Diplomatic Episodes,* p. 302.

army, and sent out into the field without being allowed first to return
to their homes. Anyone suspected of disloyalty was a natural target,[50]
as were vagabonds wandering unsuspectingly into a strange village.
Such was the fear of being picked up that it was not unusual for
many streets in the capital to become deserted after dark.[51] On
several occasions over a thousand men were dragooned in Mexico
City in a single day.[52] The crowds coming out of a bullfight, a movie,
or a cantina closing its doors for the night were favorite targets.

Wives and families learned to accept the *leva* stoically because
they had no choice, but influential employers, robbed of their labor
force from one day to the next, complained bitterly to the government.[53] Criminals in jail on minor offenses were held just long enough
to be sent out with the next *cuerda*.[54] When criticized for throwing
prisoners into the ranks, the government responded weakly that it had
adopted no such general policy—determinations were made on the
merits of individual cases.[55] Edith O'Shaughnessy was not exaggerating
much when, after a friend complained to her about her servants being
dragooned, she noted in her memoirs that "posting a letter may mean,
literally, going to the cannon's mouth."[56]

To meet the growing demand for officers (some of doubtful loyalty
were placed on inactive status), Huerta authorized young cadets
from the Tlalpan military academy to assume officer status and be
assigned to regular units before their training was completed. Regi-
mental commanders were also given discretionary powers to appoint
cadets from within the ranks.[57] When these two methods proved
unequal to the steadily growing demand, the National Preparatory
School in Mexico City was converted into a new military academy[58]

50. Even the pro-Huerta press admitted that enemies of the regime were made
subject to the *leva*. See *El Independiente,* August 15, 1913.

51. Ramírez Plancarte, *La Ciudad de México,* p. 52.

52. John Lind to Bryan, November 5, 1913, RDS, 812.00/9568; Vera Estañol,
La Revolución Mexicana, p. 351.

53. W. D. Howe, director, International Banking Corp., to Secretaría de
Gobernación, November 13, 1913, AGN/RSG, Asuntos Varios, Diversas
Secretarías, Gobierno del Distrito . . . , 1913-14.

54. Lara Pardo, *Matchs de Dictadores,* p. 153.

55. General Comandante Militar de México to Secretaría de Gobernación,
May 8, 1914; Secretaría de Guerra y Marina to Secretaría de Gobernación, May
30, 1914, AGN/RSG, Asuntos Varios, Diversas Secretarías, Gobierno del Distrito
. . . , 1913-14.

56. Edith O'Shaughnessy, *A Diplomat's Wife in Mexico* (New York: Harper
and Brothers, 1916), p. 67.

57. Summary of Military Events, July 8-15, Burnside Reports, July 15, 1913.

58. *Diario Oficial,* September 4, 1913.

and the Colegio Militar was completely reorganized into three separate schools: the Escuela Militar Preparatoria to train junior officers; the Escuela Militar Profesional to provide more advanced training in the field of specialty; and the Escuela Superior de Guerra to furnish officers for the General Staff.[59] The National Naval Academy received orders to admit more cadets and promptly complied. But it took time before results could be realized from most of these measures and Huerta began passing out military emoluments, even generalships, to friends and supporters with no military experience whatsoever.[60] Military organization charts quite specifically designated the required time in rank for promotions, but Huerta had his Congress amend the regulations to permit more rapid advancement as a reward for distinguished service or simply "para mejorar el servicio de campaña."[61] As a practical matter promotions were won, not on the battlefield, but by the intercession of influential friends in the capital. Changes of rank occurred so rapidly in the summer and fall that not even war ministry personnel could keep the records up to date. In the three-month period between June and September, 1913, the number of generalships in the Mexican army rose from 128 to 182 and other high-ranking offices from 888 to 1,081.[62] In the spring of 1914 Congress authorized a new rank, general of the army. Huerta, of course, was given the rank immediately.[63] And in the most bizarre display of all the cabinet ministers were given general rank (the minister of foreign relations a division generalship and the others brigadier generalships) and asked to wear uniforms.

The effects of Huerta's recruitment and promotion policies were disastrous. The quality of his fighting force declined markedly. The lack of training meant no *esprit de corps,* no discipline, and high desertion rates. On several occasions entire units of recruits turned themselves over to the enemy without even firing a shot. Officers could not trust men on outpost duty, when in close proximity of the enemy, for fear of desertions with any arms and ammunition they might be carrying.[64] The soldiers of the federal army had no more

59. *Diario de los Debates,* September 16, 1913.
60. Calero, *Un Decenio de Política Mexicana,* p. 139.
61. *Diario de los Debates,* September 16, 1913.
62. Ibid.
63. El Congreso de los Estados Unidos Mexicanos Decreta . . . , AHDN, Exp. XI/iii/104-1.
64. Memorandum of Lieutenant Colonel Gage, British military attaché, January 23, 1914, F.O. 115/1789, fol. 10.

notion of what they were fighting for than did the revolutionaries, so graphically stereotyped by Mariano Azuela's Demetrio Macías in *Los de Abajo*. But in many ways the situation in the federal army was even worse because the ranks were filled with men who were there only because they would be shot if they refused the conscription order. Where notions of nationalism were still so primitive the leadership of the country could not possibly appeal with *dulce et docorum est pro patria mori*.

When the untrained troops did engage the enemy they expended ammunition at such fantastic rates that the demand could not be met. [65] The inspector general of the army, at Huerta's request, finally ordered that troops be sent into battle with a bandoleer of fifty cartridges rather than with a hundred as was the case previously.[66] Only in the most extraordinary of cases was rapid fire to be authorized at all.

Corruption in the officer ranks reached new heights, extreme even for Mexico, by the time-honored method of keeping dead soldiers on the lists. It was not without good reason that many officers believed that soldiers were worth more dead than alive. Looting and pillage following the capture of a town became the order of the day, and the officers in charge invariably received their fair share. Entire shipments of military supplies were sold to the highest bidder with the booty going into the pockets of those in command.[67] On a number of occasions military equipment was sold in wholesale lots to the rebels. Military justice on the campaign trail was, by common consent, scandalously corrupt.

The professional officer corps, of course, resented the civilians who became generals overnight. Whenever the opportunity presented itself, they would inform interested bystanders that they had won their rank during the *época porfirista*. But the professional officer corps did not always fail to profit from the examples of their new colleagues. Many of the older senior officers trafficked in illicit military equipment and uniforms as well. A few were reprimanded but the large majority were not. Speaking of the extent to which corruption pervaded the army, one United States observer noted in

65. See, for example, F. Aruz Romo to Comandante Jefe de Esta Inspección, June 3, 1914, AGN/RSG 4° Cuerpo, Armamento y Municiones.
66. El General Inspector to Comandante del 4° Cuerpo Rural, April 21, 1914, AGN/RSG, Armas, 1913; Rafael Serrano to Coronel Inspector de los Cuerpos Rurales, November 3, 1913, AGN/RSG, 4° Cuerpo, Armamento y Municiones.
67. *El Independiente*, August 19, 1913.

July that one of the most hopeless features of the military situation was that the officers had every incentive to prolong it, not to end it.[68]

Not all of Huerta's military build-up went into the regular army. With considerable foresight the president envisioned that a select corps of aviators could increase the efficiency of his ground forces. In April, 1913, he sent a team of fifty junior officers to France where they studied at the Bleriot Aviation School. At the same time the government contracted for twenty Bleriot airplanes which were added to four eighty-horsepower Duperdussins already in government possession.[69] When the aviators returned to Mexico in October, they were given sufficient time to become familiar with their new aircraft and then attached to regular combat units. The air wing began reconnaissance activities in the winter of 1913-14 (similar to that of the great European conflict a few months later) and by February, 1914, even made several bombing raids against the enemy in the north.[70]

In a more conventional move Huerta reorganized the rurales. Not long after coming to office the president decided to move the rurales temporarily from the jurisdiction of the secretary of gobernación to the control of the war ministry, hoping thereby to make them conform to established disciplinary standards.[71] In July he authorized an expansion of ten thousand men, and, realizing that other recruitment efforts had fallen conspicuously short of their goals, he tried to propagandize them as an elitest corps. The recruit could enlist for a relatively short period of time (six months); his daily pay would be $2.05, considerably higher than a regular army recruit; and when he left the service he could take his horse and all of his equipment, except his arms and ammunition, with him.[72] The newly organized corps of rurales would be made up of four squadrons, each numbering

68. Memoranda on Affairs in Mexico, prepared by William B. Hale, July 9, 1913, RDS, 812.00/8203. The most consistent and persuasive accounts of military corruption concern the activities of Secretary of War Mondragón. Apparently he accepted large bribes when letting contracts for military supplies. See, for example, Ernest Gruening, *Mexico and its Heritage* (New York: D. Appleton-Century Co., 1934), p. 306.

69. Summary of Military Events, October 16-22, 1913, Burnside Reports, October 22, 1913.

70. *El Independiente*, February 8, 1914. The bombing must certainly be one of the first times in history that aircraft was used in actual combat operations.

71. Report of Captain W. A. Burnside, May 21, 1913, RDS, 812.00/7575.

72. Secretaría de Estado y del Despacho de Gobernación to Inspector General de los Cuerpos Rurales, July 9, 1913, AGN/RSG, Gobernadores de Estados, Asuntos Varios.

one hundred to one hundred and fifty men. The ultimate goal was twenty corps, or a total of between eight thousand and ten thousand men.[73] The old units, redesignated as Cuerpos Exploradores, were assigned to regular army duty in August and, for all practical purposes, ceased to exist as a unique military entity.

At approximately the same time new auxiliary forces, attached to the new rurales, were organized in outlying areas threatened by the rebels. The decree providing for the establishment of the auxiliaries stipulated that they were to be recruited from among the rural laboring force on a hacienda and would be provided with arms and ammunition by the federal government. The new troops would not wear uniforms but simply an identification badge. Minimum size for the new contingents was set at fifty men, but if a single hacendado could not provide that many, he was encouraged to band together with his neighbors to form a fifty-man group. Finally, in time of emergency the auxiliaries would work in concert with the nearest detachment of rurales.[74] The hacendados responded with enthusiasm and assured the government that with proper assistance they would be able to maintain half a million men ready to serve the nation whenever needed.[75]

In general the augmentation and reorganization of the new rurales proceeded with greater speed than did the plans to increase the size of the regular army or organize the auxiliaries. The inspector general of rurales, Carlos Rincón Gallardo, through a series of carefully considered disciplinary innovations, was able to cut down somewhat on desertion rates and other manifestations of bad military conduct that had plagued the corps for years.[76] But there is little evidence that their fighting efficiency was improved greatly.

Although the presidential office concerned itself daily with problems of recruitment, military reorganization, morale, staffing the officer corps, and bolstering special types of fighting units, no military matter was deemed of greater importance than the acquisition of arms and ammunition. Because the arms embargo enacted by the United States Congress in March, 1912, remained in effect, Huerta

73. *Diario de los Debates,* September 16, 1913.
74. Secretaría de Estado y del Despacho de Gobernación, July 7, 1913, AGN/RSG, Decretos, 1913.
75. *El Independiente,* September 5, 1913.
76. These directives are described in Paul J. Vanderwood, "The Rurales: A Study of Mexico's Rural Police Force" (Ph.D. diss., University of Texas, 1969), passim.

found it necessary to devise other means of securing ordnance. At
first he relied on stopgap measures. In the summer of 1913 the
government confiscated all firearms and ammunition from the nation's
pawnbrokers,[77] and military commanders in the states were allowed to
"requisition" arms and ammunition they found in private hands.[78]
Huerta even asked the United States to return the arms of federal
soldiers who had interned themselves voluntarily in the United States
after battles along the border.[79] But these palliatives scarcely satisfied
the always increasing demands of the federal army. The capacities
of the National Arms Factory and the National Cartridge Factory
were increased steadily throughout the summer, as even the women
were conscripted to work in them, but by fall demand still outran
supply.[80] As soon as Huerta realized that much of his ordnance would
have to be secured from the outside world, he began dispatching
teams of purchasing agents to Europe and placed orders for over
forty million rifle ball-cartridges and tens of thousands of rifles in
England, France, Germany, Belgium, and Spain.[81] The Far East
looked promising as well and Huerta negotiated successfully for
seventy thousand rifles from the Mitsui Company of Japan, one of
the largest ordnance manufacturers in the world at the time.[82] By
October some of the rifles had been delivered but orders for 145
million rounds of ammunition were still outstanding.[83]

As varied as the sources might have been, they were still insufficient, and in the late summer of 1913 Huerta sent teams of smugglers
to the United States to find means of circumventing the embargo
restrictions and establishing a more or less regular supply route from
the north. These agents worked effectively on the eastern seaboard
where they purchased supplies for consignment to Havana, Cuba,

77. Stronge to Grey, July 26, 1913, F.O. 115/1741, fol. 64.
78. Stronge to Grey, Enclosure of Vice-Consul Sanford, Monterrey, March 10,
1913, F.O. 115/1738, fol. 261.
79. Pedro Gama y Uriguen, consul, Marfa, Texas, to Secretaría de Relaciones
Exteriores, April 7, 1913, AREM, L-E 757, Leg. 3.
80. *Diario de los Debates*, September 16, 1913.
81. De Lama to Secretaría de Relaciones Exteriores, March 18, 1914, AREM,
L-E 783, Leg. 1; Departmento de Artillería to Secretaría de Relaciones Exteriores,
October 7, 1913, AREM, L-E 759, Leg. 9.
82. Arms, Ammunition, and Equipment, Mexican Army, September 13, 1913,
Burnside Reports; Thomas Summons, consul general, Yokohama, to Bryan,
November 19, 1913, RDS, 812.00/9845; Guthery, Minister, Tokyo, to Bryan,
December 1, 1913, RDS, 812.00/10129.
83. Summary of Military Events, October 16-22, 1913, Burnside Reports,
October 22, 1913.

then arranging for their transshipment to Mexico. They also oper-
ated quite freely in New Orleans, where private boat captains were
always ready, for a handsome commission, to smuggle arms and ammunition out of the Louisiana docks and carry them across the Gulf
to Tampico and Veracruz. Finally, Huerta's smugglers moved into
the border states of the Southwest where they illegally purchased
arms shipments from small merchants and carried them into Mexico,
often through the Constitutionalist lines, to federally controlled strongholds in the south.[84] All of Huerta's methods of acquiring arms, both
legal and illegal, did not satisfy the need, and arms shortages conditioned strategical plans for the winter of 1913-14.

Given all the time and energy Huerta spent on reorganizational
schemes and the acquisition of men and supplies, the results were
hardly exemplary. Many of the reforms, especially those which increased the size of the fighting force, did more harm than good. It
was a grossly inefficient army which Huerta sent north to engage the
enemy in the fall of 1913. The federals still moved in large units,
always along the railroads which were easy prey to small teams of
rebel saboteurs. Desertion rates, although cut somewhat, were still
embarrassingly high; the officer corps was still shoddy, and the lo-
gistical problems were far from overcome.

After the capture of Durango in the early summer, Constitutionalist
strategy called for an assault on Torreón, the cotton capital of Mexico,
to be followed by a concerted drive on Chihuahua City. If these key
cities fell, north central and northwest Mexico would be firmly under
rebel control. Venustiano Carranza, after having been driven out of
his headquarters at Monclova, decided to lead the drive on Torreón
himself. The Torreón garrison, recently reinforced by three thousand
fresh troops, was ready.[85] Benjamín Argumedo, an experienced Orozquista field commander, defeated the First Chief and forced him to
take refuge in Durango. Carranza spent several weeks there and then
made the decision to move his headquarters to Sonora, the most
secure state in the north. The northeast campaigns were consigned
to General Pablo González, and on August 9 Carranza began a three-
week trek through federal lines to Hermosillo, Sonora.

The Constitutionalist headquarters still gave Torreón top military

84. The activities of the smugglers are examined in greater detail in Michael
C. Meyer, "The Arms of the *Ypiranga*," *Hispanic American Historical Review* 50
(August 1970): 543-56.
85. Summary of Military Events, July 15-22, 1913, Burnside Reports, July 22,
1913.

priority and entrusted the job of taking the city to Pancho Villa.
During the last week of September Villa amassed a huge force, all
mounted and well supplied, and began the drive. Federal reinforcements under the command of General Trucy Aubert were dispatched
but Villa arrived first. The battle for control of the city began at
3:00 A.M. on October 1 and by nine o'clock in the evening Villa had
forced a federal surrender, taking one hundred and twenty prisoners
and capturing a huge supply of ordnance, including sixteen valuable
pieces of artillery. [86] The brigandage of the next week was worse than
that which accompanied the capture of Durango three months earlier;
many captured federal officers were executed in compliance with the
letter and spirit of the decree of January 25, 1862.[87]

Huerta was stunned by the defeat of his army in Torreón. His
manifold reforms were not paying the expected dividends. Felipe
Alvírez, the commander in charge of the defense of the city, was
killed during the battle but Huerta, wanting a scapegoat, ordered a
court-martial to try General Eutiquio Munguía, the second in command and the officer who ordered the evacuation. In his own defense
Munguía testified that his troops were terribly demoralized after the
death of General Alvírez, that he was hopelessly outnumbered, and,
most importantly, that his troops had little military experience or
training. The members of the military tribunal evaded their charge
and rather than render a verdict of guilty or innocent declared that
they simply could not offer a judgment.[88] Perhaps Huerta was dis-
satisfied with the outcome but the trial did nevertheless serve a useful
purpose. It put his field commanders on notice that the president
would not accept lightly either retreat or surrender.

Villa began his march on Chihuahua City late in October taking
over five thousand troops from Torreón with him. On November 1
he asked General Salvador Mercado for the surrender of the city and,
on being refused, readied his army for the assault. The attack began
four days later but Mercado's federal garrison, reinforced by Pascual
Orozco's irregular troops, lacerated the enemy lines and drove the
attackers off after six hours of uninterrupted fighting. Rather than
return to Torreón Villa opted to continue north and lay seige to the
important border point of Ciudad Juárez. The surprise attack was

86. Summary of Military Events, October 9-16, 1913, Burnside Reports, October
16, 1913.
87. Guzmán, *Memorias de Pancho Villa*, p. 202.
88. Casasola, *Historia Gráfica*, 2:635.

effected on the morning of November 15 and by noon the city had fallen.[89] When the news of Villa's victory reached the capital of the state, Orozco wanted to move north immediately to engage the Villistas. Mercado, however, vacillated long enough to give the rebels time to recuperate from their long march. By the time Orozco was given permission to dispatch his troops, Villa was ready. The engagement took place at the scorched desert town of Tierra Blanca, some twenty miles to the south of the El Paso–Ciudad Juárez complex. Orozco's irregulars, led by José Inés Salazar, had the best of the first day as his superior artillery power ripped the enemy lines some two thousand yards away. But on the second day Villa's cavalry effected a neat flanking maneuver and the Orozquistas, fearing complete encirclement, began to evacuate their well-fortified positions. With the federals in a state of disarray Villa opened a shrapnel attack and Salazar ordered a retreat which soon turned into a rout. The Orozquistas who fell into enemy hands were all executed on the spot.[90] Carranza sent Villa a prompt and well-deserved telegram of congratulations for his brilliant conduct of the campaign.[91]

It was a bedraggled and demoralized Orozquista army that marched back into Chihuahua on November 25 but disillusionment quickly gave way to anger when Mercado announced that he planned to evacuate the state capital without a fight. The decision threw the city into panic. Villa's reputation for turning his head while his troops pillaged and sacked had already become legendary and the Chihuahuan merchants implored General Mercado to accept the challenge and take the field.[92] But Mercado was not inclined to change his mind and he withdrew the federal garrison, as scheduled, on November 29,[93] retiring northeast to Ojinaga on the Texas border. Villa took

89. Edwards, consul, Ciudad Juárez, to Bryan, November 15, 1913, RDS, 812.00/749; *El Paso Morning Times,* November 15, 1913.

90. The battle of Tierra Blanca is detailed in the memoirs of Villa's American artillery officer I. Thord Grey. See his *Gringo Rebel* (Coral Gables, Fla.: University of Miami Press, 1960), pp. 36-46. Villa's own account is found in Guzmán, *Memorias de Pancho Villa,* pp. 230-37.

91. Carranza to Villa, November 27, 1913, *DHRM,* 1:155.

92. C. Eugenio Pasquel, administrador del timbre, Chihuahua, to Secretaría de Guerra y Marina, AHDN, Exp. XI/481.5/70, vol. I, fols. 4-5; Arturo M. Elías to Secretaría de Guerra y Marina, December 17, 1913, AHDN, Exp. XI/481.5/69, vol. III, fols. 583-89.

93. Letcher to Secretary of State, November 30, 1914, RDS, 812.00/10054; Evacuación de Chihuahua por Fuerzas Federales, December 17, 1913, AHDN, Exp. XI/481.5/5, 69, vol. III, fols. 583-89; and various dispatches in AREM, L-E 774, Leg. 11.

the city unopposed a few days later and for all practical purposes the
the state of Chihuahua was in rebel hands.[94]

With the capture of Chihuahua the Constitutionalists had spread
themselves a little thin. The size of their combined force was insufficient to hold securely the huge mass of land between the United
States border on the north and the city of Torreón on the south. On
December 9 the federal general José Refugio Velasco recaptured
Torreón from Calixto Contreras and the Arrieta brothers and thus
temporarily neutralized the loss of Chihuahua City. But as the new
year approached President Huerta's military position was becoming
more and more untenable. His federal army had not given a good
account of itself on the field of battle. Zapata could not be contained
in Morelos; the number of isolated rebellions throughout the republic
continued to mount; and the three Constitutionalist armies in the
north were mobilizing themselves for a gigantic southern thrust which
would have as its objective the capture of Mexico City. But most significantly, by early 1914, both Huerta and his enemies had convinced
themselves that the war could end only with the complete military
defeat of their antagonist.

94. The federals were driven out of Ojinaga on January 10, 1914 with a good
percentage of the army, including General Mercado, taking refuge across the
border in the United States. The Ojinaga episode is described by war correspondent John Reed in his *Insurgent Mexico* (New York: International Publishers,
1969), pp. 1-8. For an analysis of federal difficulties surrounding the evacuation
of Chihuahua and subsequently in Ojinaga, see Meyer, *Mexican Rebel*, pp. 105-9.
A good contemporary account is found in Monterrey's *El Noticiero*, January 7,
1914.

CHAPTER 6

War on the Diplomatic Front

I<small>N</small> <small>LATE</small> F<small>EBRUARY</small> and early March, 1913, as the sides were being chosen for a new series of military campaigns and as the antagonists were preparing themselves for a protracted struggle, skirmishes in a second war, on the diplomatic front, were beginning to unfold simultaneously. In these engagements Victoriano Huerta found an ally in the American ambassador Henry Lane Wilson and a formidable enemy residing in the White House in Washington.[1]

1. The diplomatic struggle between Woodrow Wilson and Victoriano Huerta has been carefully studied primarily from the point of view of United States policy in Kenneth J. Grieb, *The United States and Huerta* (Lincoln: University of Nebraska Press, 1969).

When Francisco Madero and José María Pino Suárez were assassinated, President William Howard Taft had less than two weeks remaining in his presidential term. He decided to leave the delicate question of recognition to his successor, Woodrow Wilson. Huerta sent President Wilson a letter of congratulations upon his inauguration on March 4; the only response was an acknowledgment of receipt addressed not to President Huerta but to General Huerta.

A week after the inauguration ceremonies in Washington, Ambassador Wilson sent the new president a 213-page report summarizing, interpreting, and justifying his own participation in the events of February, 1913. After presenting the "facts," he made a cautious plea for recognition, arguing that "there can be no doubt as to the legal constitution of the present provisional government in conformity with the precedents and the Mexican Constitution." [2] He pointed out that since the United States had recognized the interim government of Francisco León de la Barra, after the overthrow of Porfirio Díaz, "the provisional government of Huerta is entitled to the same acceptance." But not wanting to push the new chief executive too far or too fast, he tempered the request by indicating that recognition should be predicated upon Huerta's ability to restore peace throughout the republic.[3] For the next month Henry Lane Wilson tried to convince the State Department that the United States now had a friend in the Mexican presidential chair and that the incipient revolt in northern Mexico was of little consequence. The Huerta administration, he reported repeatedly, had a firm grip on the country. The consular reports from the north, however, clearly belied the ambassador's contentions and the new secretary of state William Jennings Bryan, the leader of the Democratic party for a decade and a half, wisely placed more confidence in the dispatches sent to Washington from the zone of conflict than from the secondhand accounts of the chief diplomatic representative in Mexico City.

As the month of March drew to a close Huerta saw himself caught in a vicious political circle. United States recognition, he felt, could not be expected until the country was pacified and the rebellious states brought under effective governmental control. But the hostile attitude of the United States toward his government encouraged and abetted the Constitutionalists and the Zapatistas in their defiance of Mexico City. Huerta clung wistfully to the belief that pacification

2. H. L. Wilson to Bryan, March 12, 1913, RDS, 812.00/6840.
3. Ibid.

was his number one priority and that once achieved, recognition from the United States—and perhaps even the residual benefits of foreign loans—would logically follow. In this reasoning he failed entirely to take cognizance of the moralistic political creed of his opponent in the White House.

Woodrow Wilson, the former Princeton professor, with an abiding faith both in the philosophy and *modus operandi* of the democratic state, was ill prepared to treat with the Mexican Revolution. Knowing little of the complicated background of the conflict, Wilson believed that the needs and aspirations of the Mexican people were but a stark reflection of those of the United States populace north of the dividing line. This oversimplification, more palatable to notions of Wilsonian idealism than the truth, shaped his response to the Huerta regime. Huerta was a symbol of all that was wrong with Latin America. He had come to power, not through the ballot box, but by forcefully ejecting a legally constituted government. This was an affront to Wilson's ethics. He recognized correctly that the government account of the assassination of Madero and Pino Suárez was simply a euphemism for murder, but, without good evidence, he jumped to the conclusion that Huerta personally authored the tragedy of February 22.

On March 11, scarcely yet comfortable in the presidential chair, Wilson issued a press release which portended not only a significant change in the Mexican policy of the United States but also a new policy of diplomatic recognition. After calling for a new era of cooperation with Latin America, Wilson intoned: "We can have no sympathy with those who seize the power of government to advance their own personal interests or ambition."[4] As the general declaration subsequently evolved, constitutional legitimacy was to be scrutinized and, in addition, a moral judgment made before recognition was extended.[5] Huerta was morally unacceptable and, as a consequence, nonrecognition of the regime became a *sine qua non* of Wilsonian foreign policy.

Neither Huerta nor even Henry Lane Wilson really conceived of such a drastic change in United States recognition policy. The Mexican president continued to believe that recognition would flow from pacification; the ambassador advised, in addition, that the new United

4. Samuel Flagg Bemis, *The Latin American Policy of the United States: An Historical Interpretation* (New York: W. W. Norton Co., 1967), p. 175.

5. Howard F. Cline, *The United States and Mexico* (New York: Atheneum, 1963), pp. 141-43.

States president was holding out for concessions and set to work on gaining favorable resolution of a series of outstanding diplomatic entanglements.[6] Huerta yielded to the ambassador's request on almost every count but resolution of these impasses mattered not at all. In the month of May the American president confided privately to a friend, "I will not recognize a government of butchers." [7]

Other nations refused to follow Wilson's lead. In early March recognition came from three Latin American countries: Peru, El Salvador, and Guatemala. More importantly, the State Department was informed on March 13 by British Foreign Secretary Sir Edward Grey, that His Majesty's government would extend recognition as soon as it had received an autograph letter from the Mexican president.[8] The letter was received and recognition granted before the month was out.[9] British acceptance of the regime carried with it diplomatic dividends; twenty-three other European, Latin American, and Asian countries shortly followed the British lead. By early summer Huerta had been recognized, in succession, by France, China, Spain, Austria-Hungary, Colombia, Montenegro, Germany, Honduras, Italy, Ecuador, Japan, Holland, Uruguay, Monaco, Bulgaria, Turkey, Costa Rica, Denmark, Haiti, Portugal, Bolivia, Switzerland, and Russia. By the end of the summer, Belgium, Norway, and Serbia had been added to the list and Mexico had regular diplomatic relations with 75 percent of those countries with which it normally maintained relations.[10]

As recognition from foreign heads of state accumulated, the American business community, in the United States as well as in Mexico, fearing an unfavorable competitive position and possible economic reprisals, began to muster their forces for a show of strength. The

6. H. L. Wilson to Bryan, March 14, 1913, RDS, 812.00/6849. The specific cases in point included the Chamizal controversy, the Colorado River and Imperial Valley case, the long drawn out Tlahualilo case, the specific claims cases, and the general damage claims growing out of the Revolution. For the ambassador's account see his *Diplomatic Episodes,* pp. 296-97. Huerta's position on the Chamizal case is outlined in Sheldon B. Liss, *A Century of Disagreement: The Chamizal Controversy, 1864-1964* (Washington, D. C.: University Press, 1965), pp. 42-46.

7. Arthur S. Link, *Woodrow Wilson and the Progressive Era, 1910-1917* (New York: Harper and Row, 1963), p. 109.

8. Grey to Bryan, March 13, 1913, F.O. 115/1738, fol. 94.

9. British recognition of Huerta is treated in detail in Calvert, *The Mexican Revolution,* pp. 131-66 and William S. Coker, "United States-British Diplomacy over Mexico, 1913" (Ph.D. diss., University of Oklahoma, 1965), pp. 16-29.

10. The holdouts, following the United States position, included Argentina, Brazil, Chile, Cuba, Santo Domingo, Panama, Venezuela, Persia, and Greece. See *Diario de los Debates,* September 6, 1913.

Wilson administration received telegrams from mine owners, oil interests, bankers, and presidents of large corporations urging recognition. Kansas City attorney Delbert J. Haff drafted a proposal for four of the largest and most influential United States investors in Mexico: the Southern Pacific Railroad; Phelps, Dodge and Company (copper); Greene Cananea Consolidated Copper Company; and Edward L. Doheny's Mexican Petroleum Company. The proposal, presented to the State Department on May 6 by Julius Kruttschnitt, president of the board of directors of the Southern Pacific, called for a cessation of hostilities by the contending parties in Mexico; the recognition of Huerta by the United States; and the agreement by Huerta to hold a free election prior to October 26, 1913, a date that had already been established.[11] It is not inconceivable that the Kruttschnitt plan would have been favorably received in Mexico City, but the First Chief of the Constitutionalists could never have accepted the idea of an election held under Huerta's auspices. But it really didn't matter because President Wilson was not prepared to authorize even temporary recognition in return for promises of an early and free election.

Undaunted by the rejection of their proposal, and failing to recognize that the days of dollar diplomacy were quickly receding into the past, the Kruttschnitt clique made a second more modest proposal a few weeks later. On this occasion Edward Brush and S. W. Ecoles, representing the businessmen, met with the president and, without insisting that Huerta be recognized, urged the government to use its good offices to mediate the dispute in Mexico and promise to recognize the president who would be chosen in an early election. The second Kruttschnitt plan caught Secretary Bryan's fancy and he advised the American president to accept it:

> The suggestion they make is a new one and it strikes me favorably . . . . Instead of asking for recognition of Huerta they suggest that Huerta be notified that this Government will recognize a constitutional president . . . . If you make an appointment for any time tomorrow, I would like to go over the matter with you. This seems to me to offer a way out.[12]

11. Arthur S. Link, *La Política de los Estados Unidos en América Latina, 1913-1916* (Mexico: Fondo de Cultura Económica, 1960), pp. 44-45; Harrison, "Henry Lane Wilson," p. 376.

12. Bryan to Wilson, May 27, 1913, Correspondence of Secretary of State William Jennings Bryan with President Woodrow Wilson, 1913-15, National Archives (hereafter cited as Wilson-Bryan Correspondence).

President Wilson agreed that the plan had possibilities but rather than meeting with his secretary of state the next day, he informed him that he would take the matter up "at an early date." [13] Not without reason the president believed that he needed time to familiarize himself with the intricacies of the Mexican situation, and because he had little confidence in the reports of Ambassador Henry Lane Wilson, he had already sent the first of a number of personal agents to Mexico to provide him with an "unbiased" assessment. William Bayard Hale, a former clergyman, journalist, and personal friend of the president, arrived in Mexico City in early June and announced to the press that he was preparing an article for a magazine. By the time his first detailed dispatch reached Washington the president had already prepared a set of instructions for Henry Lane Wilson based largely on the second Kruttschnitt proposal. The American ambassador was informed that the United States would use its good offices to mediate the disputes if Huerta gave assurances of early elections, honored his promise not to present himself as a candidate in these elections, and guaranteed an absolute amnesty.[14] The State Department informed the embassy, however, that the information at this point was confidential and was not to be passed on to the Mexicans. But Hale's report of June 15 was so damning that Wilson decided that the ambassador could not be trusted and decided to shelve the proposal temporarily.

After interviewing members of the diplomatic corps (including Henry Lane Wilson), a select group from the American colony, and many prominent Mexicans, Hale described for the president the Decena Trágica, the assassinations of Madero and Pino Suárez, and concluded with an interpretation of the complicity of the American ambassador:

> . . . the movement against Madero was a conspiracy and not a popular revolution—a *cuartelazo*, a military coup, the plot of a few and not the uprising of an outraged people; the betrayal

13. Wilson to Bryan, May 28, 1913, Wilson-Bryan Correspondence.

14. Bryan to H. L. Wilson, June 13, 1913, RDS, 812.00/7743. Arthur Link suggests that the statement "reveals a puzzling misconception on Wilson's part regarding Huerta's position. Huerta had never promised that he would not be a candidate" (*Wilson and the Progressive Era*, p. 113 n. 12). Although Link is technically correct, it is not unlikely that Wilson, as many political analysts of the day, interpreted the Pact of the Embassy as Huerta's disclaimer. Hale's message of June 15 reaffirmed that Huerta had promised to support Félix Díaz for the presidency.

of the President by his generals was mercenary treachery and was not in the slightest degree a response to the sentiments of the nation, or even of the city . . . . There was not a moment during the *decena trágica* when it would not have been possible to end the distressing situation and put a stop to this unnecessary bloodshed by stern warning from the American Embassy to the traitorous army officers that the United States would countenance no methods but peaceful constitutional ones and recognize no government set up by force. President Madero was not betrayed and arrested by his officers until it had been ascertained that the American Ambassador had no objection to the performance. The plan for the immediate setting of a military dictatorship would never have been formed except in the American Embassy, under the patronage of the American Ambassador, and with his promise of his Government's prompt recognition. Madero would never have been assassinated had the American Ambassador made it thoroughly understood that the plot must stop short of murder.

It cannot be but a source of grief that what is probably the most dramatic story in which an American diplomatic officer has been involved, should be a story of sympathy with treason, perfidy and assassination in an assault on constitutional government.

And it is particularly unfortunate that this should have taken place in a leading country of Latin America, where, if we have any moral work to do, it is to discourage violence and uphold law.[15]

The president himself would not have written the report any differently had he gone to Mexico City. It confirmed everything that he suspected and appealed to everything he believed. It also added still another ingredient to the diplomatic potpourri. Because of Henry Lane Wilson's complicity, any cooperation with the Huerta regime would, in a sense, sanction United States participation in the overthrow of a duly constituted government and undermine the moral posture which the president wished to assume.[16] In addition, Hale confided that Huerta was in much deeper trouble than the press had reported. The policy that Wilson had initiated therefore was sound. Significantly Hale concluded by suggesting that Wilson be removed from the ambassadorship.[17]

By the time the Hale report arrived in Washington, Henry Lane

15. Confidential Report of William Bayard Hale for President Wilson, June 15, 1913, RDS, 812.00/7798 1/2.
16. Blaisdell, "Henry Lane Wilson," p. 135.
17. Confidential Report of Hale, June 15, 1913, RDS, 812.00/7798 1/2.

Wilson had pulled out all of the stops in urging immediate recognition. Anti-Americanism, he ventured, was deep-seated and continuing to grow. The resident nationals of those countries which had extended recognition, especially the British, were moving into business areas which had been an American preserve until this time and their diplomatic representatives were actively assisting them. Necessary transactions between the American embassy and the Mexican government were made intolerably difficult and the rebels were justifiably encouraged by the posture of the United States.[18] With more audacity than prudence the ambassador then declared: "At the risk of being considered intrusive and insistent I must again urge upon the President that on the highest grounds of policy . . . we should without further delay, following the example of all governments accredited here but two, accord official recognition to the present provisional government."[19] Edith O'Shaughnessy, the wife of the American chargé, noted in her delightful memoir of diplomatic life in the Mexican capital that the British "can't understand our not protecting American lives and interests. Their policy here is purely commercial, while ours, Alas! has come to be political."[20]

Henry Lane Wilson's days in Mexico were numbered. After receiving the Hale report, the president informed Secretary Bryan that he hoped he would consider the advisability of recalling the ambassador.[21] But Bryan needed little prompting. A second long report from Hale, charging Wilson with malfeasance and improper use of his influence,[22] convinced the Latin American desk at the State Department of the necessity for his recall.[23] The order was issued in the middle of July and a few days after arriving in the United States, the ambassador had a conference with the president. Subsequently in his memoirs he recalled that President Wilson demonstrated

> a certain inflexibility of preconceived views which rendered discussion and a faithful presentation of the situation difficult. He impressed me as being under the influence of opinions other than those which I had been reporting to the department and

18. H. L. Wilson to Bryan, May 15, 1913, RDS, 812.00/7562; H. L. Wilson to Bryan, June 9, 1913, RDS, 812.00/7743.

19. H. L. Wilson to Bryan, June 9, 1913, RDS, 812.00/7743.

20. O'Shaughnessy, *A Diplomat's Wife in Mexico,* p. 22.

21. Wilson to Bryan, July 3, 1913, Wilson-Bryan Correspondence.

22. Memoranda on Affairs in Mexico, prepared by William B. Hale, July 9, 1913, RDS, 812.00/8203.

23. John Basset Moore to Bryan, July 14, 1913, RDS, 812.00/8378.

as having perhaps a different version of the events which occurred in Mexico . . . . The President's questions suggested a
lack of knowledge of the psychology and facts of the situation
in Mexico.[24]

The president was not impressed with Wilson's performance and
not amused by the apologia which he felt constrained to make before
the Senate Foreign Relations Committee a few days later. In the
middle of August Secretary Bryan informed Wilson that the president
would be pleased to accept his resignation.[25] The ambassador, of
course, had no alternative but to comply. With Wilson's forced resignation, the jurists in the State Department decided that rather than
replace the ambassador, an act which in itself would constitute recognition, Nelson O'Shaughnessy, the second secretary, should be made
chargé d'affaires and be left in charge of the embassy. O'Shaughnessy's assessments of the Mexican situation would be weighed
against those of new presidential agent John Lind—a Hearst journalist, a former governor of Minnesota, a Democratic stalwart, and a
long-time friend of Secretary Bryan.

Throughout the first five months of his difficulties with the United
States, Huerta exercised amazing restraint, less out of affection for
his northern neighbor than in the hope of some reconciliation. In
May he complained to Washington that the Constitutionalists were
recruiting on United States soil but refused to press further when he
received a noncommittal reply.[26] As the months wore on and Wilson
became increasingly obdurate, Huerta, his ministers, and the Mexico
City populace grew more and more short-tempered. Diplomatic notes
became harsh; Huerta began to complain openly, and many of his
followers began to demonstrate their displeasure. As early as the
middle of May a group of Mexico City women organized a boycott
of United States products. Posters in the public schools encouraged
students to rally around the government in defiance of the "imperialist
ambition of strong peoples."[27] And in July Mexican students, no
doubt prompted in part by a series of incendiary articles in the pro-
government press, staged an angry anti-American demonstration. The
crowds, with derisive placards, marched through the streets howling

24. Wilson, *Diplomatic Episodes,* p. 313.
25. Ibid., pp. 318-20.
26. J. B. Moore to Señor A. Algara R. de Terrenos, May 9, 1913, AREM, L-E
771. Leg. 1, fol. 112.
27. Frederick C. Turner, "Anti-Americanism in Mexico, 1910-1913," *Hispanic
American Historical Review* 47 (November 1967):512.

"Mueran los gringos!"[28] Government emissaries throughout the republic, in an obvious attempt to capitalize on the anti-American feeling, exaggerated the possibility of war with the United States and at the same time encouraged young Mexican men to volunteer for military instruction.[29]

The arrival of John Lind in Mexico early in August did nothing to soothe the malaise. As his personal "advisor to the American Embassy," the president had chosen a man with no diplomatic experience, no knowledge of Spanish, and precious little understanding of the Mexican people. Yet Lind was entrusted with the delicate mission of securing Huerta's agreement to a plan basically the same as the second Kruittschnitt proposal. Lind met briefly in Veracruz with Admiral Frank F. Fletcher, William Bayard Hale, and United States consular agent William W. Canada, before setting off for the capital. His arrival coincided with a great anti-American demonstration in front of the National Palace. On the morning of August 14, pleading that he was on a peace mission, Lind laid a four-point proposal before Secretary of Foreign Relations Federico Gamboa: (1) an immediate cessation of fighting to be accompanied by a general armistice; (2) promise of a free and early election in which all parties would participate; (3) Huerta's assurance not to be a candidate in these elections; and (4) the agreement of all concerned to abide by the results of these elections.[30]

Huerta's response was predictable. Demonstrably unhappy that a special confidential agent should have been sent from the United States rather than a regular accredited diplomat, he instructed Gamboa to inform Lind that negotiations could not proceed until recognition was afforded. Gamboa informed Lind that the Mexican government could not even consider the four points which President Wilson proposed. On his own he added that it was strange that Lind was on a peace mission when a state of war did not exist between the two countries.[31] Huerta then ordered that the exchange of notes be made public in an attempt to garner support from nationalist elements. Lind was unprepared for the rebuke and countered with a series of

28. *Mexican Herald,* July 12, 1913.

29. Turner, "Anti-Americanism in Mexico," pp. 512-13.

30. George M. Stephenson, *John Lind of Minnesota* (Minneapolis: University of Minnesota Press, 1935), pp. 216-17.

31. Gamboa to Lind, August 16, 1913, AREM, Copias y Notas Relativas a la Desocupación de Veracruz por los Americanos, III/252 (73:72)/353 (hereafter cited as AREM, Desocupación, with appropriate information).

threats. Since Huerta was not the true choice of the Mexican people, he informed Gamboa, the United States would never recognize the regime. If Huerta persisted in his rejection of President Wilson's proposals, the American president might well direct Congress to authorize the sale of arms to the Constitutionalists and perhaps even extend to them the status of belligerents. The warnings fell on deaf ears and a few days later Lind, clearing his plan first with the White House, decided to change his tactics. If Huerta would agree to hold early elections and not present himself as a candidate, President Wilson would use his influence to help secure a Mexican loan in the United States. Huerta fairly blustered. Annoyed by Lind's repeated intimations that Huerta did not represent the Mexican people, Gamboa recounted for him the extent of Mexican territory under federal control and sarcastically suggested that the rebellion in the north was at least in part attributable to the attitude of the government he represented. Further, he gave Lind a brief lesson in Mexican constitutional law, indicating that the Constitution of 1857 prohibited Huerta from running for office in the next elections, and finally he informed the confidential agent that Mexican national dignity would not be bribed by the promise of a loan.[32]

As clear as the rebuke was, Lind seized upon Gamboa's instruction in constitutional law as evidence of having secured a great diplomatic victory. Before departing for Veracruz he notified Secretary Bryan that the outstanding problems were nearing resolution. Huerta was not planning to run. Even the secretary of state considered that the Lind mission had been a success and congratulated the presidential envoy on his good work.[33]

But Huerta had yielded absolutely nothing. He had not agreed to step down. He had not agreed to speed up the elections. He had not agreed to any general armistice, and, most importantly, he had not given any indication that he would not be a candidate in the presidential elections. Lind's ignorance of Mexican political practices betrayed him. The fact that the Constitution of 1857 stipulated that a provisional president could not succeed himself as constitutional president had meaning only when the constitution was in effect. In periods of suspension or abeyance, it simply did not apply, and Mexican history gave ample exemplifications of just such contingencies. If Huerta

32. The exchange of notes is found in the *Diario Oficial*, August 29, 1913. See also Casasola, *Historia Gráfica*, 2:617-19.
33. Bryan to Lind, August 29, 1913, RDS, 812.00/8593.

wanted to remain in office he could either delay the elections or suspend the constitution, or both.

Huerta still wanted a reconciliation with the United States but was
not about to accept one totally on Wilson's terms. He took heart in
the fact that the American public was far from unanimous in their
support of Wilson's policy. A number of congressmen and senators,
some from the president's own party, and even members of Wilson's
cabinet (most notably Secretary of War Lindley M. Garrison) had
urged recognition as had some of the traditional allies of the United
States in Europe. The large majority of the American colony in
Mexico supported Huerta and made their position manifest back
home. In early September the Mexican president decided to send
distinguished career diplomat Manuel Zamacona to Washington, much
in the same capacity as Lind had come to Mexico.[34] At the same time,
to create the proper atmosphere, he directed Secretary of Gobernación
Manuel Urrutia to send a circular telegram to the governors of all
the states urging them to do everything in their power to protect the
interests of foreign nationals residing in their territory.[35] Nelson
O'Shaughnessy believed that Zamacona should be received unoffi-
cially by the secretary of state but Lind, perhaps annoyed because
he had been bypassed, reported that the visit was merely a delaying
tactic of the Huerta regime.[36] Accepting Lind's analysis Bryan decided not to receive Zamacona at all and the mission failed.

When Huerta gave his second formal address to Congress on September 16, 1913, he showed restraint in his evaluation of the United
States-Mexican controversy. The strained relations, he declared to
the membership of both houses, had caused anxious moments and
needless suffering and had hindered the pacification efforts of his
government. But he held out hope that the difficulties would soon
be resolved; however, he could not go into detail because of the
delicacy of the relations.[37]

The diplomatic correspondence for the fall of 1913 indicates that

34. Huerta had already sent Francisco León de la Barra secretly to the United
States on a reconciliation mission. De la Barra spoke at length with Boaz W.
Long, the chief of the State Department's Division of Latin American Affairs but
the mission came to nought. De la Barra to Secretaría de Relaciones Exteriores,
August 26, 1913, Condumex/FLB, Correspondencia Interesante, Actividades
Alemanas.

35. Telegrama Circular a los Gobernadores de los Estados, *Diario Oficial*,
September 10, 1913.

36. O'Shaughnessy to Bryan, September 1, 1913, RDS, 812.00/8648; Lind to
Bryan, September 4, 1913, RDS, 812.00/8671.

37. *Diario de los Debates*, September 16, 1913.

no meaningful negotiations between the contending parties were being conducted at the time of the presidential address. To the contrary, relations worsened with the passage of each week. When the new British minister, Sir Lionel Carden, arrived in Mexico City in early October, Wilson realized that his many attempts to obtain British support for his Mexican policy had failed. Carden had long since given evidence of his staunch support of the Huerta regime. Meanwhile, Lind sat in hot, humid Veracruz for the next four months sending back increasingly pessimistic, bellicose, and inaccurate reports, often laded with anti-Catholic and anti-Indian slurs. Not understanding in the least how Huerta could possibly have rejected the generous terms he had proposed, he wrote to Bryan in September that the Mexicans simply have no political standards. "They seem more like children than men—The only motive I can discover in their political action is appetite and vanity . . . . Their talk about pride is all rot." [38] As it became increasingly obvious that his mission to Mexico had failed, he saw only two possible courses of action for the United States to follow. The White House could establish a close relationship with the Constitutionalists in the north or could consider actual military intervention. Lind's own preference, as he became more and more anxious to return to the cool Minnesota lake country, was the latter. In the middle of November he suggested that the United States should "take possession of Mexico and administer the affairs of the country substantially as done in Cuba until such time as it may appear prudent to turn the government over to the Mexicans." [39] Although President Wilson threatened Huerta publicly with intervention in the late fall, and began, massing troops along the border, he preferred a more moderate course and decided, at least for the time, to place his stock in cultivating better relations with the Constitutionalists.

The White House had opened negotiations with the Constitutionalists in the early summer, when Reginald del Valle, another of Wilson's team of special emissaries, had been sent to northern Mexico to enter into talks with Venustiano Carranza. [40] After having completed this

---

38. Lind to Bryan, September 19, 1913, Wilson-Bryan Correspondence.

39. Lind to Bryan, November 15, 1913, RDS, 812.00/9760. Chargé Nelson O'Shaughnessy had been urging a similar course of action for several months. See O'Shaughnessy to Bryan, August 28, 1913, RDS, 812.00/8608.

40. Senator Albert Bacon Fall from New Mexico charged that del Valle was a paid attorney for the Maderistas and therefore was not likely to send back unbiased reports. Albert Bacon Fall, *Affairs in Mexico* (Washington: Government Printing Office, 1914), p. 5.

mission, he was to carry out a similar endeavor at the Zapatista head-quarters in Morelos. A Californian of Mexican parentage and a former member of the California state legislature, del Valle had an advantage over Hale and Lind as he at least spoke the language; it was presumed that he also was equipped with at least a modicum of appreciation for Mexican history and culture. But his complete lack of diplomatic experience and tact was his undoing. The reports which he sent back to the State Department bore little resemblance to the political realities of the day. The only thing that Secretary Bryan was able to glean from them was that the Constitutionalists were uncompromising and that del Valle, after a brief interview with the First Chief in Piedras Negras, was not favorably impressed with him.[41] Apparently Carranza was not impressed with del Valle either because after the brief parley at Piedras Negras the First Chief broke off the talks.[42] Demonstrating an amazing lack of tact, even for an inexperienced diplomat, del Valle traveled to Mexico City and agreed to a public press interview; although he was on a secret mission for the president, he outlined in general terms his aims.[43] Even William Bayard Hale, not distinguished either for his sensitivity or discrimination, was offended by del Valle's public statements and complained to the secretary of state. Bryan had no choice but to recall him immediately, thus canceling the mission to Morelos.

Wilson's next envoy to the northern rebels, Dr. Henry Allen Tupper, carried no credentials from the State Department whatsoever.[44] A representative of the International Peace Forum, he had on his own tried to serve as an intermediary between the department and the Constitutionalists earlier in the year but since del Valle had been

41. Bryan to Wilson, June 25, 1913, Wilson-Bryan Correspondence.
42. Carranza had been forewarned not to trust del Valle because of the possibility that he did not really possess State Department authorization and because he was an instrument of *científico* interests. Manuel Pérez Romero to Carranza, June 11, 1913, *DHRM*, 1:69-70; Pérez Romero to Carranza, June 15, 1913, *DHRM*, 1:72-73.
43. *El Diario*, July 7, 1913.
44. The contention of Louis Teitelbaum (*Wilson and the Mexican Revolution*, pp. 58-60) that his uncle William Teitelbaum served as a Wilsonian agent to the Carrancista headquarters in August, 1913 (between the del Valle and Tupper missions) is little more than conjecture based on a photograph which pictures Teitelbaum with several Constitutionalist notables including Pablo González, Isidro Fabela, and Ricardo Suárez Gamboa. Even if Teitelbaum did serve in such a capacity, the historiographical significance of the mission is negligible because of the total absence of records indicating how his reports might have influenced the principals.

chosen, his services were rejected. When he made himself available again in October, Secretary Bryan seized the opportunity.[45] Bryan instructed the new unofficial envoy to find out what he could of the Constitutionalists, their aims and desires, and report back his findings.[46] At the end of October, Tupper held a long conference with Carranza in Nogales in which the First Chief predictably gave assurances that his forces would soon drive Huerta from power. He confided to Tupper, and Tupper advised the department, that the Constitutionalists wished to come to an accord with Washington, but only under certain prescribed conditions.[47] Bryan reported back that he could receive no proposition officially, but urged the agent to find out any information he could.[48] Carranza was made to understand that Washington would have to assume any initiative and that the Constitutionalists should just be patient. At this point the First Chief closed off any further discussions.

Although there is no evidence detailing what Venustiano Carranza was about to propose, it appears certain that he would have insisted upon at least three points. For months he had been urging his own confidential agents in the United States to do everything possible to secure legislation permitting the Constitutionalists to legally import arms and ammunition.[49] He informed Tupper of this particular desire in one of his early communiqués to him.[50] But as the Constitutionalists in the north continued to score impressive victories on the field of battle, his diplomatic aims became more ambitious—he also wanted

45. Tupper's credibility as a disinterested advisor was brought into serious question several years later when he was accused by Edward L. Doheny, president of the Mexican Petroleum Co., as having been on Carranza's payroll. A few weeks after Huerta's overthrow Doheny wrote a check to the Mexican government, presumably in payment of taxes, for $3,466.86 (U.S.) The check was endorsed over to Tupper who cashed it in New York City on August 19, 1915. See Testimony of Edward L. Doheny, *Fall Committee Hearings*, 1:292.

46. Morris Sheppard to Bryan, October 3, 1913, RDS, 812.00/9064; Bryan to Sheppard, October 4, 1913, RDS, 812.00/9064.

47. Tupper to Bryan, November 1, 1913, RDS, 812.00/9499.

48. Bryan to Tupper, November 2, 1913, RDS, 812.00/9499.

49. See, for example, Carranza to F. González Gante, May 1, 1913, *DHRM*, 1:25-26; and Manuel Pérez Romero to Carranza, October 10, 1913, *DHRM*, 1:135. Carranza maintained an entire team of agents in the United States throughout his fight against Huerta. In addition to those treated throughout the text some of the most active included Juan Urquidi in Washington, Francisco Urquidi in New York, Rafael E. Muzquiz in El Paso, José Lozano Pérez in Naco, Ives Lelevier in Douglas, Guillermo N. Seguín in Eagle Pass, and Enrique V. Anaya in Nogales. See Letcher to Carranza, April 23, 1914, AREM, L-E 1579, Leg. 5.

50. Carranza to Tupper, October 31, 1913, AREM, L-E, 861, Leg. 5.

full recognition of his belligerency.[51] And finally, as subsequent events demonstrate, he was not at all willing to pawn the sovereignty of his movement in any way to secure these ends.

A week after the negotiations with Tupper broke down, the State Department ordered William Bayard Hale to Nogales for a series of more official talks with Carranza. Washington was now ready to assume the initiative and had something concrete to propose—a joint United States-Constitutionalist effort to rid Mexico of Victoriano Huerta. Hale informed the First Chief that President Wilson was ready to permit the introduction of arms, would grant belligerent status, and would even intervene militarily in Carranza's behalf! All that the president wanted in return was guarantees for American lives and property and full assurance that immediately upon Huerta's resignation a proper provisional government would be established and free elections would be held. Both Wilson and Bryan were distressed when an offer, they obviously considered helpful and generous —even altruistic—was rejected. Carranza and his advisors informed Hale that no provisional government would be set up with any remnants of the Huerta regime; they had no intention of letting up the fight until they had captured Mexico City and destroyed the elements that Huerta represented.[52] The presence of United States troops on Mexican soil, even to fight Huerta, would be countenanced in no way. Carranza further warned President Wilson that he did not recognize the right of any power to intervene in the domestic affairs of the Mexican republic. Armed intervention, therefore, was deemed "inadmissible upon any grounds or upon any pretext."[53] Hale was instructed not only to pass this information on to the White House but was admonished to make it emphatic.[54]

Secretary Bryan reported back that the president was "deeply disturbed by the impression he gets from your last telegram . . . . He would not be willing, even indirectly, to assist them if they took so narrow and selfish a view. It would show that they do not understand the Constitutional process."[55] Carranza did, of course, understand the Constitutional process. What he did not understand was the missionary impulse which conditioned Wilson's under-

51. Hale to Bryan, November 2, 1913, RDS, 812.00/9506.
52. Hale to Bryan, November 14, 1913, RDS, 812.00/9735.
53. Hale to Bryan, November 14, 1913, RDS, 812.00/9738; Francisco Serrano to Inspección de Consulados, *DHRM*, 14:394-95.
54. Hale to Bryan, November 14, 1913, RDS, 812.00/9738.
55. Bryan to Hale, November 16, 1913, RDS, 812.00/9759.

standing of it. In response to one of John Lind's many entreaties to be more vigorous in support of the northern rebels, Bryan was forced to answer that their attitude makes it impossible to help them.[56]

Carranza, however, knew exactly what he was doing. For several months the regime in Mexico City had been propagandizing that the commander of the northern rebels desired United States intervention in the country to help his cause.[57] Carranza could not allow Huerta to preempt nationalist sentiment, and therefore he was forced by circumstances to take the bellicose stand which he did. In addition, the First Chief was encouraged by the military victories which his forces were enjoying, and finally, he did not want to be obligated to the United States in any way once his revolution swept him to power.

The breakdown of the Nogales conference bought Huerta and his government a little extra time. The diplomatic war reached an impasse in the late fall of 1913 and, for the time being, the outstanding issues between Huerta and the rebels were to be fought out on the mountains and deserts of northern Mexico rather than on Washington desk tops. But Woodrow Wilson, in spite of Carranza's rejoinders, drew closer and closer to the Constitutionalists. Customs inspectors along the border turned their heads increasingly while rebel agents smuggled arms and ammunition into Mexico.[58] At the end of the year several rebel commanders were invited to dine aboard the U.S.S. Pittsburgh off the Sinaloa coast. They were welcomed with a sixteen-gun salute as they boarded.[59] Experienced Huerta diplomat Francisco León de la Barra realized that a rapprochment with the United States was no longer possible and had already begun to urge much closer ties with Great Britain in an attempt to neutralize the hostility of Washington.[60]

Both Huerta and Carranza had hoped for more from the United States but, for different reasons, neither was able to yield to the

56. Bryan to Lind, December 13, 1913, RDS, 812.00/10152.
57. Miguel Díaz Lombardo to Carranza, May 13, 1913, *DHRM*, 1:42-43.
58. Failure to enforce the embargo in certain convenient areas was by no means an accident. It had been proposed by Hale and the Carrancista agent Roberto V. Pesqueira as preferable to lifting the embargo which would entitle Huerta to an easy supply of United States arms as well. See Pesqueira to Carranza, December 30, 1913, *DHRM*, 1:184-85. Huerta was fully apprised of the extent of Constitutionalist arms smuggling. See, for example, William A. Ross to Huerta, April 4, 1913, AREM, L-E 754, Leg. 3.
59. Grieb, *The United States and Huerta*, p. 64.
60. De la Barra to José Limantour, September 23, 1913, Condumex/FLB, Viaje de Washington a México del Sr. de la Barra, . . . 1911-29.

demands of President Wilson. Both must have been a little relieved in the fall of 1913 that Washington had not yet taken a definite stand in support of the other. But Carranza knew that he had considerably less to worry about on this score than did Huerta. As the new year approached, Carranza sensed that time was on his side. Huerta had been unable to pacify the country as he had repeatedly promised. Not only did he have an untractable government to contend with north of the Río Grande, but even the Mexican populace and their elected representatives in the capital had become restless and increasingly recalcitrant. The domestic political and financial crises which Huerta faced during his first nine months in office were, in large measure, a by-product of the armed insurrection and the diplomatic hostility of the United States. They warrant separate consideration.

CHAPTER 7

The Man and the Dictatorship

FOR A COMPLEX SET OF REASONS growing out of the nature of the Mexican Revolution, Victoriano Huerta has been singled out for censure and abuse perhaps unparalleled in twentieth-century Latin American history. He has been scrutinized through Revolutionary prisms which, by their very nature, cannot help but distort. A different view, however, does not necessitate an apologia.

A generation of polemicists have exhausted the vocabulary of invective and virulence in their denunciations of the dictator, picturing not a man but a grotesque caricature. Huerta's debauchery has been likened to that of Caesar Borgia and his philosophy of life to the worst in Machiavelli.[1] His unbridled use of force is branded as an inheritance from the Huichol Indians, "that savage race of butchers."[2] Like a villain from a Shakespearean tragedy, Huerta has been portrayed as happily walking through the streets of Mexico City delighting in the wailing of widows and orphans.[3] He has been dubbed "the Supreme Pontiff of Infamy,"[4] an admirer of bloody orgies.[5] Relapsing atavistically to his Huichol roots, he allegedly once personally cut out the tongue of a particularly articulate critic.[6] But by far the most prevalent charge hurled against him, in literally hundreds of accounts, is that he was an alcoholic and a dope addict.[7] He supposedly conducted the affairs of state in a constant stupor and, in the evenings, between generous helpings of alcohol and marijuana, amused himself with every imaginable type of psychopathic aberration. Without delving into the tendentious character of Mexican Revolutionary historiography, suffice it to say that these fanciful caricatures provide little useful insight into the nature of the man.[8]

Victoriano Huerta, at the age of fifty-nine, was robust and in good health except for his chronic eye problem but was ill prepared by formal training, experience, and temperament for the high political office which he assumed in February, 1913. With much more faith in the logic of force than in the art of persuasion, he was too much the warrior to be at all successful as a statesman. Throughout his career he had demonstrated a keen intelligence, but certainly not a polished intellect. Not only is it impossible to picture him fretting over a metaphysical abstraction, but he openly ridiculed those who

1. Calero, *Un Decenio de Política Mexicana*, p. 125; Aragón, *El Desarme del Ejército*, p. 29.

2. Antonio Manero, *Por el Honor y por la Gloria* (Mexico: Imprenta T. Escalante, 1916), p. 43.

3. González-Blanco, *Carranza y la Revolución*, p. 527.

4. Martínez and Guerra, *Madero*, p. 27.

5. Sandalio Mejía Castelán, "El Verdadero Huerta," *Excélsior*, August 30, 1951, pp. 6, 12.

6. *El Caústico* (Jalapa), August 5, 1914; *La Voz de Sonora* (Hermosillo), April 10, 1914.

7. It is scarcely worthwhile to attempt any listing of works alleging Huerta's drunkenness and dope addiction. A conservative estimate would suggest that at least three-quarters of the works which mention Huerta's name echo one or both of these charges.

8. An interpretive essay on the problems of Revolutionary historiography relevant to the defamation of Huerta's character is found in Michael C. Meyer, "Perspectives on Mexican Revolutionary Historiography," *New Mexico Historical Review* 44 (April 1969):167-80.

did. Very much the self-made man of action, Huerta was a strict disciplinarian, with a domineering personality and great confidence in his own ability. Impetuous and inordinately egotistical, he found it exceedingly difficult to admit an error or alter a course of action once he had made a decision.

Scarcely of exemplary moral fiber, he was not above the use of bribery or deceit in the day to day operations of government. Yet, surrounded by peculation and graft of every imaginable variety, he apparently did not seek to enrich himself.[9] After his ouster in July, 1914, he was forced to live frugally in his Spanish exile, and a year later, at the time of his death, his wife had probated only a very small estate.

Not even Huerta's worst enemies denied either his resourcefulness or his initiative—they simply used pejorative synonyms to describe them. He had the ability to recognize talented men and attract them to his side, but few could work with him for very long. Those persons who were closely acquainted with him did not find the dissolute brute that historians have subsequently painted. To the contrary he is often described as witty and charming in social settings, a man who cultivated warm friendships.[10] On the other hand, when the business of state was at issue he was stern, impatient, and easily moved to angry outbursts. For example by the fall of 1913 the mere mention of John Lind's name would send him into a rage. Disagreement with him was tantamount to incompetence and he seldom forgave an abuse of confidence.

Even in the presidency, Huerta was modest in his dress. He disliked pomp and display, especially the occasions which required that he wear black frock coat and silk hat, and in the many pictures taken at formal state receptions, he appears bored and uncomfortable with many of the official duties that the presidential chair demanded. At the same time he was not awed by public speaking. While not a polished orator, he expressed himself with facility and occasionally even turned an eloquent phrase and evoked an original image. But

9. It has been suggested that two of Huerta's sons, Victoriano, Jr., and Jorge, used their father's influence for profiteering. While there is no substantive reason to doubt the charge, it is difficult to document with any degree of accuracy. See Johnson, *Heroic Mexico,* p. 131. The charge that Huerta himself pilfered the treasury of millions of pesos immediately prior to his resignation is without basis in fact. The charge is voiced by Juan Gualberto Amaya, *Venustiano Carranza: Caudillo Constitucionalista* (Mexico: n.p., 1947), pp. 132-33.

10. See, for example, Stronge to Grey, August 20, 1913, F.O. 115/1741, fols. 246-47; O'Shaughnessy, A *Diplomat's Wife in Mexico,* p. 244.

in conversation he often lapsed into profanity. From all indications he led a proper married life and was a good father to his eleven children—at least no evidence of personal scandal has ever been brought to light. Unlike his predecessors in the presidential office, Huerta refused to move into the palatial official residence, preferring to remain in his modest family home in Colonia San Rafael, where he could enjoy the instantaneous camaraderie of a street vendor or other neighborhood employee. When the affairs of government demanded formal entertaining, the presidential residence on Calle Liverpool would be used with Doña Emilia personally supervising the preparations. Perhaps to compensate for his country bumpkin reputation, the parties that the Huertas offered were lavish. For example in October, 1913, at a particularly critical political juncture, the cabinet was treated to:

> Huître Casino
> Consommé Brunoise Royale
> Suprême Barbue à L'Espagnole
> Vol-au-Vent à L'Estrasbourg
> Tournedos aux Cèpes
> Dinde Roti Crèsson
> Asperges Sauce Mousseline
> Gâteaux Bavarois Vanille
> Glace à la Pistache
> Café, Thé[11]

On weekends he liked to escape with his wife and a few of the children to another small house he purchased in Popotla, a short distance from the capital. He called this weekend cottage his División del Norte and there, on a Saturday or Sunday afternoon, removed from the vicissitudes of high office and French cuisine, Doña Emilia would prepare his favorite *puerco con chiles pasado* or *enchiladas con mole*. Occasionally a special cabinet meeting would be held in Popotla,[12] but Huerta discouraged carrying on state business there, as he used the solitary retreat to rejuvenate himself for the following week. He evidenced little taste for music or art but might consume one or two books (a history or biography) on a quiet weekend.

Stories of Huerta's physical bravery were as widespread as they were apocryphal and were circulated by friend and foe alike. Some whispered that his delicate eye surgery in the fall of 1912 was, at

11. *El Independiente*, October 2, 1913.
12. Ibid., October 6, 1913.

Huerta's insistence, performed without benefit of an anesthetic. Others found more daring, and at the same time more amusing, the tale that the barber who shaved him everyday with a freshly stropped razor was the brother of a man whom he personally had condemned to death by firing squad. Coupled with his eleven children, what better evidence of his *machismo!*

Like many persons of his day, Huerta was amazed by the arrival of the motor car in Mexico City and took a childish delight in having a chauffeur drive him through the streets of the metropolis. He was often out on a ride when he should have been in the presidential office, and, on occasion, foreign diplomats and cabinet ministers with important business waited fretfully in the presidential antechamber while their chauffeurs or aides scouted the streets in search of him. Certainly during his frequent automobile tours of the city the president must have pondered the military advantages that would accrue from the proper use of the internal combustion engine.

There is no evidence that Huerta was addicted to marijuana but it is not unlikely that he smoked it occasionally. One can simply dismiss the charges of dope addiction as pro-Constitutionalist propaganda, part of the attempt to discredit the enemy in Mexico City. On the other hand there is ample evidence that Huerta drank heavily. His drinking habits began during the 1880s when, on military campaign, he began to fortify himself with generous amounts of pulque and tequila. With age and position, his tastes became more epicurean, and by the time he became president he preferred a good cognac. Mrs. Edith O'Shaughnessy reported, with tongue in cheek, that once in office Huerta believed that the only two foreigners really worth knowing in Mexico were Hennessy and Martell.[13] It was not at all unusual for him to consume an entire bottle at an evening's outing at El Globo or El Colón, two of his favorite restaurants. But those who knew him personally in 1913 and 1914, freely admitting that he drank to excess and suggesting that perhaps he had a pathological need for alcohol, add nevertheless, that they never saw him drunk.[14] Similarly, those who worked closely with him, while criticizing him on many grounds, do not even imply that his drinking habits interfered with his daily work schedule.

13. O'Shaughnessy, *A Diplomat's Wife in Mexico*, p. 48.
14. A summary of contemporary opinion on Huerta's drinking habits is contained in García Naranjo, *Memorias*, 7:103. See also Joaquín Piña, "Triunfo y Calvario," p. 48.

Huerta was not the type of drinker who disappears for a few days on a bout. Seeking solace in the bottle, he would drink to excess, generally with old military cronies, and rather than become irritable or pugnacious, would sit for hours glibly exchanging uncouth jokes, reminiscences, and anecdotes about the trauma of military campaigning. Tales of military conquests shared the limelight with those of the boudoir. The commonly accepted evidences of alcoholic deterioration —disturbances of the memory, inability to concentrate, neglect of family, and loss of pride in personal appearances—are all absent and prompt one to conclude that the years of imbibing had not yet taken their toll.

Huerta believed that his government had but one prime responsibility—the restoration of order. Because pacification became his personal crusade, the rule of law was sacrificed to it and the regime initiated a dictatorship that in many ways was even more excessive than that of Porfirio Díaz. Since criticism was tantamount to treason, neither scruples nor compassion hindered Huerta in the effort to concentrate all power in his own hands. With increasing power he became increasingly imperious. But the personalization of power was not, as so often implied, for purposes of self-gratification. Huerta may have had only a scant appreciation of what Mexico really needed in the second decade of the twentieth century but he was convinced that nothing could be accomplished until pacification was effected. And in the name of pacification he consistently refused to allow any broad participation in the conduct of public affairs.

Like all effective dictators, Huerta fully appreciated the value of a controlled press and initiated a policy of censorship soon after coming to office. The largest and most influential dailies in the country supported him, and, in fact, the Association of Metropolitan Dailies sent Carranza a telegram early in the administration urging him to end his rebellion.[15] During the first months, a few small papers in the capital adopted a frankly hostile attitude. Huerta allowed them to operate, but anyone currying official favor was not likely to be seen carrying one of these papers under his arm. As the inability of the regime to suppress the rebellion in the north became patently obvious, Huerta became more and more sensitive to criticism and served notice on the opposition press to support him or face the consequences. He did not try to hide the fact that he was censoring the press and, in fact, admitted it freely to the American chargé.[16] It was

15. Mario Rojas Avendaño, "El Periodismo," in *México: 50 Años de Revolución*, vol. 4, *La Cultura* (Mexico: Fondo de Cultura Económica, 1962), p. 624.
16. Testimony of Nelson O'Shaughnessy, *Fall Committee Hearings*, 2:2708.

not necessary to pass legislation making it a criminal offense to offend the dignity of public officials. Those editors who did not fall into line were simply forced, without ceremony, to close their doors.

The larger and more important dailies were handled in a slightly different manner. Although generally sympathetic to the regime, an occasional editor would sometimes venture a critical opinion. Rather than close down the entire operation, the secretary of gobernación would simply appoint a more obsequious man in his place.[17] Newspapers in financial trouble such as *El Diario* and *El Imparcial* were offered government subsidies and on accepting them, of course, compromised their journalistic independence.[18] José Elguero's *El País* did not require a subsidy but with a few exceptions supported the dictator throughout the entire period, as did *El Independiente* and *El Diario del Hogar*.[19] In the north, in order to offset the influence of the pro-Constitutionalist *El Paso del Norte*, Huerta agreed to a heavy subsidy for Manuel Alvarado's *El Eco de la Frontera*, published in Ciudad Juárez, and a smaller subsidy for *La Nueva Era*, published in Nogales.[20] Criticism of the government by *El Regional* in Guadalajara was resolved by arresting the director, Guillermo Enríquez Simoní.[21] Antonio Ortiz Gordova, editor of *El Correo de Jalisco*, met a similar fate.[22] *La Opinión* and *La Union* of Veracruz as well as *La Voz de Juárez* were forced to cease publication altogether.

Curtailing criticism, however, was only one aspect of the government's censorship policy. Equally important was the careful management of news, especially from the battle zones. Ostensibly to keep public morale high, the Mexican citizenry, especially in the capital, received reports from the front which bore only the slightest resemblance to the facts. Sizes of opposing contingents were shamefully misrepresented, evidences of government heroism covered up

17. For example, Secretary of Gobernación Urrutia replaced the managing editor of *El Independiente,* Adolfo Rodríguez, with Carlos Díaz Dufoo, a well-known científico. Adolfo Rodríguez Illera to Secretaría de Gobernación, August 1, 1914, AGN/RSG, Asuntos Varios, Diversas Secretarías, Gobierno del Distrito . . . 1913-14.

18. F. L. Day, International News Service, to Business Manager, *El Diario,* May 6, 1914, and June 9, 1914, AGN/RSG, Imprenta del Gobierno, 1914; Subdirector, *El Imparcial,* to Director, *El Diario,* June 2, 1913, AGN/RSG, ibid.

19. Unlike the other major dailies, *El Diario del Hogar's* support of Huerta did not attribute all of Mexico's current difficulties to former president Francisco Madero. Rather, the United States was considered to be the culprit.

20. M. E. Diebold, Inspector, El Paso, to Secretaría de Gobernación, July 25, 1913, AREM, L-E 714, H/513 910-20/1, Leg. 6, fol. 35.

21. Taracena, *La Verdadera Revolución,* 2:147.

22. *El Independiente,* October 10, 1913.

obvious manifestations of incompetence and cowardice, and indeed, defeats were represented as victories. Battlefield excesses of the enemy (and there were many) received full coverage whereas those of the government (and there were also many) were suppressed.[23] When Huerta wanted to keep news out of the papers altogether he was generally able to do so. The serious diplomatic encounter with the United States at Tampico, for example, was withheld from the press until the time of the invasion of Veracruz.

Huerta was somewhat less successful in his attempt to woo the foreign press to his cause. The regime extended invitations for formal receptions to journalists from the United States and Europe with surprising regularity. The newsmen who accepted were feted at gala banquets and the president quite naturally used these opportunities to propagandize his regime.[24] But more often than not it was the rebels in the north and south who captivated the foreign journalists' imagination. Except for a few leading newspapers in the great financial centers of the world, Huerta did not enjoy a particularly favorable international press.

Press censorship alone could not effect all of the ends of the authoritarian state. With the propaganda resources of the state mobilized, the government employed a vast network of secret agents and spies to report on the activities of potential and real enemies, both within and outside of the country.[25] Roughnecks in police or army uniforms broke into houses and hotel rooms without warrants, usually in the early hours of the morning, to drag critics off to jail. The regime was implacable with all those who voiced criticism and in the fall of 1913 the jail cells in Mexico City and the state capitals quickly filled with persons whose only crime was disagreement, publicly espoused or privately confessed.[26] Visiting foreign dignitaries who might utter an intemperate statement, such as the modernist Peruvian poet José Santos Chocano, were ordered to leave the country immediately.[27]

23. Newspaper coverage of the war was so inaccurate as to make it almost useless as a historical source. One does much better to consult consular and military dispatches, and even these must be used with caution.

24. Casasola, *Historia Gráfica*, 2:684-85.

25. M. Carrillo to Secretaría de Guerra y Marina, May 20, 1913, AGN/RSG, Inspección General de Policia.

26. See, for example, Blas Rodríguez to Secretaría de Gobernación, December 10, 1913, AGN/RSG, Asuntos Varios, Diversas Secretarías, Gobierno del Distrito . . . 1913-14, which discusses the arrest of an individual simply for criticizing the *leva*.

27. Manuel B. Trens, "México en 1913," *El Nacional*, October 24, 1957.

Not even those who exiled themselves voluntarily were free from the prying eyes of the regime. A team of secret agents, including a number of United States citizens, were employed north of the Río Grande to penetrate Constitutionalist organizations and keep the government informed of troublemakers. The reports were forwarded to the secretary of foreign relations through regular consular channels.[28] Mexican consuls in the United States were able to intercept an amazing number of Carrancista telegrams and forward their contents to the secretary of foreign relations.[29]

Without question the most reprehensible aspect of the dictatorship was the unbridled use of assassination as a political weapon. Although proof implicating Huerta directly to the assassinations is nonexistent, or at best inconclusive, there seems little doubt that the assassins were carrying out orders and implementing directives from persons high within the administration—possibly in some cases even from Huerta himself. Certainly Huerta could have checked the practice by diligently prosecuting those directly responsible.

The first in a series of politically significant murders was the assassination of Abraham González, the governor of Chihuahua and minister of gobernación during the Madero presidency. Refusing to recognize the new regime, González was arrested by Huerta's orders on February 22, 1913, and forced to resign his governorship. Fear for his life prompted several of his business associates and personal acquaintances to call for United States intervention.[30] The United States government was unprepared to intervene in the matter, however, and Huerta promptly issued an extradition order to Chihuahua so that González could be legally transferred to Mexico City. On March 6, Antonio Rábago, the interim governor of Chihuahua appointed to replace González, turned the prisoner over to a military escort comprised of Lieutenant Colonel Benjamín Camarena, Captain Hernando Limón, and Lieutenant Federico Revilla.[31] The train, with

28. One of the most active of these was Paul Mason, an ex-Orozquista gunrunner. Mason turned out to be a double agent, accepting money from both Huerta and Carranza. See Arturo M. Elías to Secretaría de Relaciones Exteriores, May 23, 1913, AREM, L-E 785, Leg. 5.

29. Telegramas Carrancistas Durante el Movimiento Revolucionario, 1913-14, AREM, L-E 760, Leg. 2.

30. J. F. Fallansbee to Albert Bacon Fall, February 26, 1913, ABFC, Group F; Price McKinney to William Howard Taft, February 26, 1913, RDS, 812.00/6397.

31. When subsequently tried by the Constitutionalists for complicity in the assassination, Rábago maintained that he knew of no orders from Huerta indicating that González was to be killed. See Almada, *La Revolución en Chihuahua*, 2:19-20.

the entourage on board, left Chihuahua City shortly before midnight bound for Mexico City but was ordered to stop several hours south of the state capital (between Bachimba and Mápula). Camarena ordered González off the train and had him shot on the spot.[32] A shallow grave was prepared where he fell.[33] The official explanation was no more imaginative than that offered several weeks earlier at the time of the assassination of Madero and Pino Suárez: A group of rebels attacked the train and González was caught in the cross fire.[34] The news of the murder, once made public, contributed to a premature crystalization of the opposition in the north, drawing to the Constitutionalist cause many who were still resisting the undertow of war and greatly lessening any chance for a reconciliation.[35]

More shocking yet was the celebrated case of Belisario Domínguez, a senator from the state of Chiapas and an outspoken critic of the regime. Throughout the late spring and summer of 1913, Senator Domínguez had criticized Huerta and his advisors for their utter disregard for the rights and principles that Mexicans held dear. On one occasion in a closed session of the Senate, where Secretary of Foreign Relations Francisco León de la Barra had presented the official explanation for the nonrecognition policy of the United States, Domínguez caustically retorted: "How can the United States recognize the Government stained with the blood of President Madero and Vice-

32. The widely circulated story that González was thrown under the wheels of the train has no basis in fact.

33. The most careful analysis of the assassination, based upon both primary and secondary evidence is found in Beezley, "Revolutionary Governor," pp. 223-37. Also detailed is Francisco R. Almada, *Vida, Proceso y Muerte de Abraham González* (Mexico: Biblioteca del Instituto Nacional de Estudios Históricos de la Revolución Mexicana, 1967), pp. 143-63. Beezley suggests that Camarena might have ordered the assassination on his own with the purpose of currying Huerta's favor. He also indicates that in a meeting with Huerta, Captain Limón received the impression that the president at least hinted that *ley fuga* might well be invoked in this case. Less dispassionate assessments, including the oft-aired contention that González was thrown under the wheels of the train on Huerta's orders, can be traced in Jesús Romero Flores, *Del Porfirismo a la Revolución Constitucionalista* (Mexico: Libro Mex Editores, 1960), p. 255; Pedro González-Blanco, *De Porfirio Díaz a Carranza* (Madrid: Imprenta Helénica, 1916), pp. 119-20; Martínez and Guerra, *Madero*, p. 46; Alberto Calzadíaz Barrera, *Hechos Reales de la Revolución*, 2 vols. (Chihuahua: Editorial Occidental, 1959-60), 1:102. Guillermo Mellado, who reconstructed the details of the assassination from the testimony of an unidentified witness, maintains that Huerta subsequently paid Camarena 600,000 pesos for a job well done (*Crímenes*, pp. 51-52).

34. Almada, *Abraham González*, pp. 149-50.

35. One year after the assassination, the Constitutionalists were in control of Chihuahua and Provisional Governor Manuel Chao declared March 7, the date of González's death, a legal state holiday. *El Legalista* (Hidalgo del Parral), February 25, 1914.

President Pino Suárez?"[36] Despite warnings from friends and colleagues in the Senate, Domínguez persisted in his courageous attacks. He viewed any suggestion of compromise with the regime as the basest blasphemy. Finally, on September 23, the senator from Chiapas asked for the floor to read a declaration into the record. The chair, notified in advance of the nature of the statement, refused permission for an open reading but did allow the declaration to be entered into the record. The attack was emotional but eloquent and the clearest indication yet that Domínguez had become, in effect, the Mexico City spokesman for the Constitutionalist revolution. With more valor than good sense he chided his cohorts for their timidity:

> . . . during the rule of Mr. Victoriano Huerta, not only has nothing been gained in favor of the pacification of the country, but the present conditions in the Mexican Republic are infinitely worse than ever before; credit is in the throes of agony; the whole press of the Republic muzzled shamefully . . . our fields are abandoned; many towns have been destroyed, and lastly famine and misery in all its forms threaten to spread out on all the surface of our unfortunate country . . . .
>
> Peace, cost what it may, Mr. Victoriano Huerta has said. Fellow senators, have you studied the terrible meaning of those words . . . ? It seems as if our ruin were unavoidable . . . . Nevertheless, gentlemen, a supreme effort could save everything. Let the national assembly fulfill its duty and the country will be saved . . . . The national assembly has the duty of deposing Mr. Victoriano Huerta from the presidency. He is the one against whom our brothers in the north protest with so much reason, and consequently he is the one who is least able to carry out the pacification which is the supreme desire of all Mexicans.
>
> You will tell me gentlemen, that the attempt is dangerous; for Mr. Victoriano Huerta is a bloody and ferocious soldier who assassinates without hesitation anyone who is an obstacle to his wishes; this does not matter, gentlemen! The country exacts from you the fulfillment of a duty, even with risk, indeed the assurance, that you are to lose your lives. If in your anxiety to see peace reign again in the republic you have made a mistake and have placed faith in the words of a man who promised to pacify the country in sixty days; and you named him president of the republic, today when you see clearly that this man is an imposter, inept and wicked, who is rapidly bringing the country to ruin, will you for fear of death permit such a man to remain in power?

36. Miguel Alessio Robles, "La Figura de D. Belisario Domínguez," *El Universal*, October 10, 1930.

What would be said of the crew of a great vessel which during the most violent storm in a tempestuous sea would appoint as pilot a butcher who has no nautical knowledge, who was on his first trip, and who has no other recommendation but that of having betrayed and assassinated the captain of the vessel?

Your duty is clear gentlemen, and the country expects you to fulfill it . . . . The country hopes that you will honor her before the world, saving her from the shame of having as chief executive a TRAITOR AND AN ASSASSIN.[37]

A week later Domínguez asked the Senate to give him a commission to go to the presidential office and demand Huerta's resignation.[38] When the Senate refused, he renewed his vitriolic attacks on the regime. But early on the morning of October 8, four Mexico City policemen (Alberto Quiros, one of Huerta's sons-in-law, Gabriel Huerta, Gilberto Martínez, and José Hernández) burst into Domínguez's room at the Hotel del Jardín, forced him into an awaiting car, and drove him to a nearby cemetery. A grave site had already been prepared. Martínez and Quiros apparently did the shooting and the body was immediately interred. The following day the morally outraged Senate passed a resolution requesting full information on Domínguez's whereabouts and resolved to remain in permanent session until the information was received. Two days later Huerta dissolved both houses of Congress.

But the wave of assassinations had scarcely begun. Although the number of political homicides in 1913 and 1914 will never be determined precisely, no fewer than thirty-five cases can be documented with reasonable surety. In addition to the murders of Francisco Madero and Pino Suárez, Abraham González and Belisario Domínguez, four other congressmen, Adolfo G. Gurrión, Serapio Rendón, Edmundo Pastelín, and Néstor E. Monroy, were killed as were journalist Alfredo Campos Martínez and Nicaraguan poet Solón Argüello.[39] Army officers critical of the regime held no special immunity and the list of assassinated includes General Gabriel Hernández, Colonel Alfonso Zaragosa, Major Aurelio Saldaña, and Major Isidro López Neico.

37. The text of the speech can be found in Jesús Acuña, ed., *Memoria de la Secretaría de Gobernación Correspondiente al Período Revolucionario* (Mexico: Talleres Linotipográficos de "Revista de Revistas," 1916), pp. 157-58; and in Carlos Román Celis, *Belisario Domínguez: Legislador sin Miedo* (Mexico: Publicaciones Mañana, 1963), pp. xxxii-xxxv.

38. Marcos López Jiménez, "Los Mártires de la Revolución: D. Belisario Domínguez," *El Nacional*, October 8, 1934.

39. Argüello's poem "Viva Madero" was a scathing denunciation of Huerta. A copy is found in AM, Roll 17, fols. 141-48.

Professional men foolish enough to disparage the administration met a similar fate as did a number of minor bureaucrats who openly manifested their discontent.[40] It was a rare instance when the assassinations were preceded by the formality of a trial. In the large majority of cases the regime simply invoked *ley fuga*.

Because the exact details of the individual killings have never been brought to light, Huerta's personal involvement is virtually impossible to establish. But the impact of the terrorism is perhaps more significant. Whether or not the president ordered the killings himself, a substantial portion of the population held him accountable, and, as a result, the violence bolstered the rebels' cause. While the majority of Mexican governments since independence could scarcely be distinguished for either their scrupulous regard for constitutional guarantees or their general bonhomie, never before, not even during the grossest suppressions of the Díaz regime, had political assassination become so institutionalized and intimidation so endemic. The murder of prominent and widely respected government critics created fear and irresolution on the part of some and produced demands for revenge in kind on the part of others. Huerta's pleas for good will and the return of reason, made on occasion after occasion, cannot be viewed as other than the most ludicrous kind of duplicity. As the roster continued to mount and it became increasingly difficult to explain away or rationalize government involvement, many distinguished supporters disassociated themselves from the regime. A few went over to the Constitutionalists (fewer to the Zapatistas) while the majority opted for quiet retirement or, when fearful for their own lives, for self-imposed exile.

In spite of the blatant nature of the dictatorship, Huerta, in typical

40. The total number of murders attributed to the Huerta regime approaches one hundred if one simply computes names with no thought of independent verification. Some of these undoubtedly belong on the list, whereas others appear to be figments of the Constitutionalist imagination. In addition to those names cited above, the catalog of those assassinated definitely must include: Gustavo Madero, brother of the president; Adolfo Bassó; Licenciado Pablo Castañón Campoverde; Juan Izábal; Juan Pedro Didapp; José Llanes Abrego; Juan González Antillón; Mariano Duque; Licenciado Emilio Palomino; José María Ramos; Francisco José Menocal; Alfonso Pareda; Ing. Daniel Hubert; Carlos Rangel; Manuel H. Torres; Artemio Herrera; Licenciado Miguel Cervantes Carrillo; Ing. Carlos Villa; Javier Robles Espinosa; and Rafael Tapia. Further information can be gleaned from a critical reading of Meléndez, *Historia de la Revolución*, p. 154; Blancas, *Ensayo Histórico Sobre la Revolución*, p. 73; Mellado, *Crímenes del Huertismo*, passim; "Francisco Chávez Revela al Procurador de la República como se Cometieron los Asesinatos Ordenados por Huerta," *El Universal*, November 17, 1921; Valadés, *Historia de la Revolución*, 3:134-37; and "Memorias del Coronel Joaquín Pita," *El Universal*, July 6, 1948.

caudillo fashion, sought to perpetuate at least the facade of democracy. The Constitution of 1857 specified that the president was to govern with the advice and consent of a cabinet and Huerta did maintain this sham. But largely as a result of his own vanity his relationship with his cabinet ministers was impossible. His entire personality demanded that he be surrounded by sycophants, not advisors. During his seventeen months in office the nine cabinet positions were headed by thirty-two different ministers.[41] The most important position, the ministry of foreign relations, was directed by five different ministers: Francisco León de la Barra (February to July, 1913); Federico Gamboa (July to September, 1913); Querido Moheno (October, 1913, to February, 1914); José López Portillo y Rojas (February to May, 1914); and Francisco S. Carbajal (July, 1914). Officials were changed from ministry to ministry with such rapidity that they did not have sufficient time to learn even the fundamental operating principles of their positions. For example, Huerta named Manuel Garza Aldape secretary of education in June, 1913, secretary of fomento in August, and secretary of gobernación in September. Changes at the number two position in the cabinet, the undersecretaryships, were just as chaotic and, in fact, the number of undersecretaries during the seventeen month period even exceeded the number of secretaries.[42]

The original cabinet designated by the Pact of the Embassy provided Huerta with some of the most talented and experienced men in Mexico. John Lind's salty characterization of this group ("a worse pack of wolves never invested any community")[43] reveals much more about Lind than about the cabinet. Francisco León de la Barra had served Porfirio Díaz as ambassador to Washington and as secretary of foreign relations; after Díaz's overthrow he became interim president of the republic. Alberto García Granados, the new minister of gobernación, had held the same position in the de la Barra government. The new secretary of education, Jorge Vera Estañol, had also served in the same capacity under de la Barra. Secretary of Hacienda Toribio Esquivel Obregón, once seriously considered by Madero as his vice-presidential running mate, had served as a peace envoy when Díaz's federal army was defeated at Ciudad Juárez in May, 1911; he

41. For a complete listing of the changes, see Appendix C, pp. 237-238.
42. The dates of appointment of all secretaries and undersecretaries can be traced in the *Diario Oficial* for 1913 and 1914.
43. Lind to Bryan, November 13, 1913, RDS, 812.00/9704.

enjoyed the reputation of being one of Mexico's most distinguished scholars. General Manuel Mondragón, a Felicista and an experienced artillery officer who had authored several texts on military tactics, was the choice for secretary of war, while young and talented Rodolfo Reyes, the son of the general, became minister of justice. Secretary of Fomento Alberto Robles Gil, the only person in the cabinet without a national reputation, had served as governor of the state of Jalisco.[44] All men of integrity and experience, the cabinet could have been used effectively, but Huerta, unwilling to delegate even a modicum of responsibility, tyrannized over his ministers.

Difficulties first arose between the president and the cabinet in the spring of 1913. Although the president dismissed rumors of a cabinet crisis as unfounded, and instructed his government officials to deny them,[45] astute political observers realized by April that all was not well within the ranks of the new government.[46] Either Huerta could not work with his new ministers or they could not work with him. They often complained to one another that he gave them no latitude whatsoever in which to operate.[47] His decisions not only were irrevocable, they were not even debatable, and he often spoke to the ministers as an officer would speak to soldiers on the military trail.

Analysis of the resignations which occurred in the spring and summer of 1913 reveals two prime causes. In the first place Huerta could not tolerate anybody who would question the wisdom of his own judgment on any subject, no matter how miniscule. Of greater significance, however, the president wanted to break the Pact of the Embassy which provided that he share governmental powers with the Felicistas, his cohorts in the overthrow of Francisco Madero.[48]

44. An excellent contemporary analysis of the original cabinet can be found in Memorandum, prepared by Mr. Hohler (undated), F.O. 115/1738, fols. 46-51.

45. J. A. Fernández, Mexican consul general to various consuls, March 31, 1913, AREM, L-E 773, Leg. 9, fol. 1.

46. *El País*, April 18, 1913.

47. Querido Moheno to León de la Barra, March 9, 1914, Condumex/FLB, Notas Oficiales, Nombramientos y Renuncias, 1913-20.

48. Many of Huerta's ministers put their thoughts to paper after retiring from public life. These memoirs, together with several suggestive secondary analyses, are invaluable in determining the relationship between the presidency and the cabinet. See García Naranjo, *Memorias*, 7:30, 134; Querido Moheno, "Mi Actuación Después de la Decena Trágica (1913-1914)," *Hoy* 55 (March 12, 1938): 29-30; Vera Estañol, *La Revolución Mexicana*, pp. 318-30; Gabriel Ferrer Mendiola, "Los Ministros de Huerta," *El Nacional*, May 12, 1953, pp. 3, 6; Rubén Salido Orcillo, "El Primer Gabinete de Huerta," *Excelsior*, August 24, 1954, p. 6; and Miguel Alessio Robles, "Las Renuncias de los Ministros de Huerta," *El Universal*, December 20, 1937, pp. 3, 8.

Secretary of Gobernación Alberto García Granados, an independent thinker, was the first casualty. The dispute centered on Huerta's decision to deploy certain contingents of rurales (then under the jurisdiction of the ministry of gobernación) in areas deemed inadvisable by García Granados; the president's subsequent appointment of Joaquín Pita, judged incompetent by the secretary, as inspector general of police, also contributed to the disagreement. García Granados resigned on April 23, alleging poor health as his reason.[49] Significantly, Félix Díaz was not consulted when Huerta named the replacement (Aureliano Urrutia), although the Pact of the Embassy clearly stipulated that changes in the cabinet were to be made only with the consultation of the Felicistas.[50] A delegation of Felicistas led by Licenciado Gumersindo Enríquez protested passionately to the president but to no avail.[51]

Within two months after the resignation of García Granados, two Felicistas, Secretary of War Mondragón and Secretary of Education Jorge Vera Estañol, followed his example. Mondragón was the most bitter and, while waiting for the boat to carry him into exile, he drafted a long letter to Félix Díaz. Interestingly, his wrath was directed not against Huerta, whom he believed owed him nothing, but rather against Díaz who stood by idly and allowed him to be forced out of office without lifting a finger in his behalf.[52] But Díaz was in a position to do little as Huerta continued consolidating his position by purging the cabinet. One by one the president forced his ministers to submit their resignations. Secretary of Finance Toribio Esquivel Obregón left the government in midsummer, his disagreements with Huerta being prompted by differences on political appointments and certain irregularities in the operation of the treasury.[53] Rodolfo Reyes, possibly because of Huerta's affection for his father, was one of the last to go. But by September 13, 1913, the entire first cabinet had been replaced. Most of the fired ministers chose exile but a few stayed in Mexico. Francisco León de la Barra alone continued to serve the government. Because of his prominence and be-

49. H. L. Wilson to Bryan, April 24, 1913, RDS, 812.00/7250; Stronge to Grey, April 1913, F.O. 115/1739, fols. 51-52.
50. See Article II of the Pact of the Embassy, Appendix A, pp. 233-234.
51. Miguel Alessio Robles, "El General Huerta y el Doctor Urrutia," *El Universal*, June 13, 1938, pp. 3, 5.
52. Manuel Mondragón to Félix Díaz, June 26, 1913, *DHRM*, 1:92-95.
53. The specifics are treated in Genaro María González, *Toribio Esquivel Obregón: Actitud e Ideario Político* (Mexico: Editorial Libros de México, 1967), pp. 49-57.

cause his dispute with the administration was relatively minor, he received an appointment as envoy extraordinary and minister plenipotentiary to France and Great Britain.[54]

The cabinet shuffling in most cases was accompanied by crude attempts at face-saving. When he accepted the resignation of Foreign Secretary de la Barra, Huerta announced that the departure from the cabinet was prompted by the "urgent need of utilizing de la Barra's services in Europe."[55] The urgent mission, as it turned out, consisted of a diplomatic initiative to negotiate a treaty with Great Britain concerning free navigation for ships of the two countries in waters off Quintana Roo and British Honduras.[56] For replacements the president chose men whom he believed were loyal Huertistas. A few, such as Secretary of Foreign Relations José López Portillo y Rojas, had served honorably in the ranks of the Reyista movement during the late Díaz regime.[57] Others, such as Dr. Aureliano Urrutia, a famous surgeon, were personal friends of the dictator. José María Lozano's outstanding credential was his avid hatred of Félix Díaz. Nemesio García Naranjo and Querido Moheno had made national reputations for themselves with their steadfast congressional opposition to Madero during the summer and fall of 1912. But the new cabinet ministers, all personal choices of Huerta, fared little better than the first. The turnover continued unchecked, making continuity of policy almost impossible.

If Huerta's dealings with his cabinet were bad, his relationship with the national Congress was even worse. The Twenty-Sixth Mexican Congress had been elected in the summer of 1912 during the Madero presidency. Madero's supporters had gained a precarious majority in the lower house, the Chamber of Deputies, but his opponents had gained control of the Senate.[58] Huerta, as a result, would encounter little difficulty with the upper house but would be in constant conflict with the Maderistas and other opponents in the chamber.

54. Francisco León de la Barra, July 31, 1913, AGN/RSG, Varios Autógrafos de Gobernadores.
55. Carlos Pereyra to de la Barra, July 8, 1913, Condumex/FLB, Notas Oficiales, Nombramientos y Renuncias, 1913-20.
56. Nombramiento, El General de División Victoriano Huerta, Presidente Interino Constitucional de los Estados Unidos Mexicanos, Condumex/FLB, Notas Oficiales, Nombramientos y Renuncias, 1913-20.
57. Comité Central Directivo to Presidente del H. Club Central Reyista, August 28, 1909, AEM, vol. IV, fol. 233.
58. For a careful analysis of the 1912 congressional elections see Ross, *Madero*, pp. 225-27.

The anti-Huertista group in the Chamber of Deputies, led by the "Bloque Renovador," began to organize soon after the regular session of Congress began on April 1, 1913.[59] The ranks of the Maderistas were somewhat depleted in these early sessions as some of the deputies elected in June, 1912, decided after the events of February, 1913, to cast their lot with the Constitutionalists in the north rather than to return to their seats in the chamber. But other anti-Huertista elements soon joined the Maderistas. The opposition was by no means entirely liberal. As the cabinet crisis exacerbated the schism between the original signers of the Pact of the Embassy, a number of Felicista congressmen joined the opposition. By the late spring Huerta realized that he had a formidable foe in the lower house. The "Bloque Renovador" resolved to weaken the regime internally by trying to defeat all of the major legislation which Huerta introduced.[60]

Initially Huerta took no steps to quell his enemies in Congress. The Senate constituted no real threat and he believed that he had sufficient support even in the chamber to gain approval for his legislative program. Four articulate deputies, the *cuadrilatero*,[61] assumed the legislative initiative for the regime in the lower house. A little vocal opposition in the legislative branch helped to perpetuate the democratic charade. But the first major dispute was not long in coming. In the middle of April the administration sought to secure congressional authorization for negotiating a new loan abroad. The opposi-

59. The leaders of the group included Serapio Rendón, Luis Manuel Rojas, Félix Palavicini, and Manuel Puig Cassauranc.

60. Maderista congressmen who retained their positions after the coup of 1913 have been castigated mercilessly by the pro-Revolutionary school for serving the Huerta regime. José Valadés (*Historia de la Revolución*, 3:121-23), suggests that their opposition to the government was more feigned than real and that the entire idea was devised subsequently to justify their participation in the illegal administration of the usurper. Félix Palavicini, one of the leaders of the opposition faction, insists that Carranza knew of the plan and approved of it at the time. He even sent an envoy Eliseo Arredondo to Mexico City to encourage the "Bloque Renovador" in its efforts. Alberto Morales Jiménez goes still further and suggests that Carranza had given instructions to his supporters in Congress to provoke Huerta to such a degree that he could be forced to dissolve the Congress (see Morales Jiménez, "Huerta Disuelve la XXVI Legislatura," *El Nacional*, October 10, 1940). Mrs. O'Shaughnessy's entry for October 14, 1913, "If you scratch a Maderista Deputy you are sure to find a revolutionary of some sort," does not miss the mark by much (*A Diplomat's Wife in Mexico*, p. 15).

61. The group consisted of Francisco M. Olaguíbel (Mexico), José María Lozano (Jalisco), Nemesio García Naranjo (Nuevo León), and Querido Moheno (Chiapas). As all of these men were pulled out of the chamber subsequently to occupy secretaryships or undersecretaryships, Huerta's influence in the lower house declined.

tion initiated a series of delaying tactics and subjected cabinet officials sent to defend the proposal to hostile questioning.[62] When it appeared that the authorization might not be forthcoming, Huerta went directly to the public and, through the press, made an impassioned plea for support. "The present loan has for its purpose the reconquering of peace, the elevation of our prestige as a people, the salvation of society from anarchy."[63] The administration finally had its way as a begrudging chamber extended its authorization a few days before the regular session terminated on May 31, 1913.

Because the debate over the proposed loan had been quite time consuming, many other pressing issues had not been resolved in the regular session and in early June Huerta decided to call the Congress back into special session.[64] The permanent congressional committee which remained in session between regular sessions (the Diputación Permanente) was charged by the Constitution of 1857 with determining the need of any special session; this group, dominated by opposition deputies, refused to endorse the presidential request.[65] Huerta had experienced his first congressional defeat and the stage was set for a showdown when the entire Congress reconvened in general session on September 1.

The issue which brought the executive and legislative branches into open conflict was, at least in part, a bogus one. On September 17 Huerta named Eduardo Tamariz, a deputy from the state of Tlaxcala, as minister of education. Article 58 of the constitution specified that the chamber had to give its approval before a duly elected member of the body could accept a position in the executive branch. The request was received in the chamber on September 17 but not acted upon until the following day. Expecting no problem with the routine request for permission, the administration swore Tamariz into office on the morning of September 18 before the subject had been brought up before the chamber. The opposition now had an issue and they readily seized it. Huerta had violated the constitution and the debate was hot. The attacks on the administration were indirect and often couched in witticisms. Deputy Alardín quipped that with the violation of Article 58 only two articles of the constitution remained in force: thirty-three with respect to foreigners and 30-30

62. See especially *Diario de los Debates,* May 21, 1913, pp. 26-28.
63. *Mexican Herald,* May 9, 1913.
64. *Diario de los Debates,* June 6, 1913.
65. Ibid., July 4, 1913.

for the Mexicans.[66] But the debate did bring out at least one substantive issue. Tamariz was a member of the Catholic party and the
liberals opposed him on these grounds. Deputy Sarabia directed the
frontal assault:

> We liberals can accept the appointment of a member of the
> Catholic party as minister of gobernación, as minister of finance
> or for any other ministerial post; but it is profoundly significant,
> given the political orientation of this government, that this nomi-
> nation is for minister of education. It offers the most patent proof
> that the government is marching decisively . . . along the road
> of clericalism, the handmaiden of praetorianism . . . . Is the
> chamber going to give its approval to clericalism and praetorian-
> ism? Is the chamber going to accept the nomination of Licenciado
> Tamariz?[67]

Members of the Catholic party tried to fend off the attack appeal-
ing to the patriotism of their colleagues in a time of national emergency, but they were unsuccessful. The coalition of liberals, Reno-
vators, and some Felicistas, combined with those incensed at the
violation of the constitution, massed 108 votes against Tamariz. Only
20 votes were cast in his favor.[68]

The dispute over Eduardo Tamariz portended much more serious
difficulties between the executive and legislative branches. Emboldened by their victory, many opposition deputies began attacking the
regime directly in late September and early October. The witticisms
and assaults by innuendo were abandoned in favor of a new offensive directed against the person of the president. The speeches of
Belisario Domínguez were the harshest but other deputies and senators joined in the barrage. When Domínguez disappeared on October
8, the chamber sent a commission (Jesús Martínez Rojas, Adolfo E.
Grajales, Manuel Novelo Argüello, César Castellanos, and Eduardo
Neri) to the office of Secretary of Gobernación Manuel Garza Aldape
to determine what had happened to the senator and vowed to stay
in permanent session until an adequate answer was received. When
the delegation returned to the chamber with the news that Secretary
Garza Aldape could provide no information, Felicista Deputies Armando Z. Ostos and Miguel Hernández Jáuregui introduced a five-
point resolution: (1) a three member commission would be appointed

66. Ibid., September 18, 1913.
67. Ibid.
68. Ibid.

to determine the exact circumstances of Domínguez's disappearance; (2) the Senate was invited to establish a similar commission; (3) the commission would make appropriate recommendations based on its findings; (4) Huerta would be informed of the action and would be reminded that the executive branch of government had the responsibility to respect the rights and protect the lives of all civil functionaries; and (5) if another incident occurred, the Congress would be forced to move its deliberations to a place where the guarantees of the constitution would be observed.

The resolution, clearly complying executive complicity in the Domínguez case, passed and the commission was established. By the late afternoon of October 9 rumors began to circulate in Mexico City that Belisario Domínguez had indeed been assassinated for his attacks on the regime. Huerta was fully aware that the "Bloque Renovador," the liberals, the Felicistas, and other enemies of the government might try to capitalize on the psychological mood of the country at this critical juncture and either withdraw recognition of his administration or demand his resignation the following day. Tired of jousting, he called an emergency session of the cabinet that evening. Garza Aldape, supported by Minister of War Aureliano Blanquet, made the suggestion that the administration dissolve the Congress before it could assume the initiative. Secretary of Foreign Relations Querido Moheno and Secretary of Justice Enrique Gorostieta argued that this plan was much too harsh, but the hard line, favored by the president himself, carried the session. Early the following morning at Garza Aldape's prompting, and over the protests of Querido Moheno and Gorostieta, Huerta made an even more momentous decision. All those deputies judged to be enemies of the government would be arrested![69] The selection of the enemies was made on the spot and in a most arbitrary manner. Included on the list were Deputies Jorge Vera Estañol and Rodolfo Reyes, both of whom had served in Huerta's original cabinet and who had returned to the chamber after their resignations.

When the deputies arrived for their afternoon session at 3:00 on October 10, they found police milling inside the chamber building and army personnel outside. Troops from General Blanquet's crack

69. The cabinet meetings are discussed in Querido Moheno, "Revelaciones de Moheno," *Hoy* 54 (March 5, 1938): 28-29; Querido Moheno, "El Golpe de Estado de Victoriano Huerta," *El Universal*, September 4, 1920, p. 3; García Naranjo, *Memorias*, 7:172; Miguel Alessio Robles, "El Golpe de Estado de Octubre," *El Universal*, April 25, 1938, p. 1.

Twenty-ninth Battalion were in charge. The secretary of foreign relations had been assigned the unenviable task of announcing the decision reached by the administration. Shortly after the session was called to order, Secretary Moheno, visibly shaken, asked the deputies there assembled to rescind the five-point resolution that they had adopted the day before. This act, he explained, constituted an invasion of the rights of the judicial branch of government. The deputies, in turn, demanded that the police and troops be withdrawn from the chamber, as a deliberative body could not be expected to function intimidated by revolvers and Mauser rifles. The secretary refused to withdraw the troops and the deputies refused to invalidate the resolution of the previous day. Moheno then read the decree which had been prepared in the morning. "The Chamber of Deputies," he intoned in a nervous voice, "are from this moment declared dissolved . . . consequently any acts and regulations of the aforesaid legislative body shall be null and void, and shall not receive the sanction of the executive power. The Mexican people are hereby convoked for extraordinary elections of deputies and senators . . . on the twenty-sixth day of October." As the deputies got up to leave the chamber, the police and army troops moved in and began the mass arrests.[70] Eighty-four were apprehended on the spot and within twenty-four hours had been joined in the federal penitentiary by 26 additional colleagues. Of the 110 arrested deputies, only 1 represented the Catholic party. The list of enemies of the government did not include the Catholics except for the deputy from Chiapas who was a personal friend of Belisario Domínguez and expressed himself in no uncertain terms about the assassination of his fellow Chiapaneco.

When the news of the dissolution of the chamber reached the Senate, the upper house voluntarily voted to dissolve itself in protest. Huerta would have to worry no longer about a disruptive legislature. He explained his decision to the Mexican people as follows:

> When I assumed charge of the interim presidency . . . under circumstances with which you are acquainted, my only aim, my most fervent desire was, has been, and continues to be, the establishment of peace in the republic . . . . Unfortunately I have

70. A careful contemporary description of the dissolution of the Congress and the arrest of the deputies is contained in Carden to Grey, October 15, 1913, F.O. 115/1742, fols. 54-57. The reports of the United States chargé are neither as comprehensive nor as accurate; see O'Shaughnessy to Bryan, October 10, 1913, RDS, 812.00/9168. A subsequent analysis with the advantage of years of perspective is contained in Vera Estañol, *La Revolución Mexicana*, pp. 339-40.

failed in this supreme desire because the Chamber of Deputies has shown a systematic and implacable hostility toward each and every act of my government. I appointed the honorable citizen Eduardo Tamariz secretary of education and fine arts and the Chamber, on the specious pretext that he was a Catholic, denied him the corresponding leave . . . . Several executive bills have been introduced for the organization and reorganization of public services, and the Chamber, intransigent, has not taken action on these questions which are of such transcendental importance for the future of the nation . . . . The legislative branch did not stop here. Many, protected by their exemption from arrest, conspire in this very city . . . . The president of the republic has seen himself alluded to in a way profoundly offensive and calumnious committees have been appointed to investigate hypothetical offenses . . . . Such a situation can bring forth nothing but chaos and anarchy . . . . I was forced to decide upon the dissolution of the legislative branch, in order that the voting public, satiated with the anguish of a long civil struggle, may send to the national representative body, citizens whose only zeal, whose only ideal, is the reconstruction of the fatherland on a solid foundation of peace.[71]

The dissolution of Congress and the arrest of the deputies played into the hands of Huerta's enemies much as did his highhanded treatment of the cabinet and his scant regard for human life. Yet he still wanted to play one more political game with the hope that it would somehow pull him out of the morass in which he was mired. With all that had occurred since February, a vote of confidence from the people, he believed, would not only undermine the strength of the Constitutionalists in the north and the Zapatistas in the south, but would also serve notice on the enemy in the White House that his efforts were for naught.

The Pact of the Embassy did not stipulate any specific time for presidential elections but an early date was implicit in Félix Díaz's refusal to accept a cabinet position in the new government. Díaz contended that the only purpose of the interim regime was to sponsor elections. Huerta's first cabinet, dominated by the Felicistas, urged the interim president to schedule elections immediately but Huerta refused, indicating that pacification was the number one priority. In early March, 1913, before a specific date was set, Díaz announced his candidacy. His supporters, even in the face of Huerta's growing

71. Meléndez, *Historia de la Revolución,* 1:171-72.

hostility, were by no means united themselves. While the Felicistas could agree on Díaz's candidacy for the presidency, they were split into opposing factions on the number two spot on the ticket. One group favored General Manuel Mondragón, arguing that a distinguished military figure would instill confidence in a time of domestic crisis. Another group championed the cause of Rodolfo Reyes for the vice-presidency, suggesting that he could attract the old Reyista political machine to the Felicista cause. Neither side was prepared to give in and they finally had to settle on a compromise candidate. In March, José Luis Requena, the chairman of the Partido Liberal Democrático, announced a ticket of Félix Díaz and Francisco León de la Barra.

The Felicistas announced their platform on April 16. The planks were vague, disappointing, and committed the candidate to nothing concrete. Díaz called for effective suffrage, honesty in government, religious toleration, and respect for the rights of the states and territories. The only crucial issue raised by the candidate was the need to resolve the agrarian question but even here his philosophy of agrarian reform was not revealed to the public. The agrarian plank merely promised "to solve the agrarian question by prudent and adequate means, always preserving due respect for legitimate property rights." [72]

Late in April Huerta publicly promised elections within two months, but when Congress postponed the elections indefinitely, Díaz and de la Barra withdrew from the race in disgust. Díaz, however, cleverly allowed the door to remain ajar so that he could reenter if events so warranted. On May 1 the regime announced that the elections would be held on the last Sunday of October.[73] As Díaz began considering his rather precipitate withdrawal, he received an appointment from Huerta as special ambassador to Japan. His delicate task was to thank the emperor for Japan's participation in Mexico's centennial celebrations three years earlier. The contrived mission had as its only purpose disrupting the electoral activities of the Felicistas. If Díaz could be detained beyond October 26, his election would be null and void as the Constitution of 1857 provided that candidates had to be present in the country on election day.[74]

72. *Mexican Herald,* April 15, 1913.
73. *El País,* May 1, 1913; Wilson to Bryan, May 1, 1913, RDS, 812.00/7335.
74. Díaz's reasons for accepting the appointment have never been adequately explained. His biographer, Luis Licéaga, can do no better than to suggest weakly that he had to accept the appointment because he was an army officer following orders (*Félix Díaz,* p. 302).

Shortly after Díaz's departure for the Orient, a widely based political organization founded the Junta Unificadora Nacional. It comprised Maderistas, anti-Maderistas, some Constitutionalist sympathizers, and even a few members of the conservative Catholic party. The group believed that if it could find a strong and popular candidate to carry the elections, the Constitutionalists might be persuaded to accept the outcome. The junta was a distinct threat to Huerta's plans, however, and he crushed the group before it could get underway.[75] During the late summer and early fall, other candidates announced for the office. A group of independent liberals sponsored the candidacy of Manuel Calero and Jesús Flores Magón. David de la Fuente, just retired from the ministry of communications and public works, declared himself in the race with Andrés Molina Enríquez as vice-presidential candidate, their bid for office being sponsored by the Gran Partido Liberal Republicano. The Catholic party, after having been turned down by General Joaquín Maas and General José María Mier, shocked the Mexican political world by offering its presidential candidacy to Federico Gamboa, a Mason, and the vice-presidency to General Eugenio Rascón.[76] Gamboa resigned his position as secretary of foreign relations to accept the offer. Finally, the Anti-reelectionist party nominated Francisco Vásquez Gómez and Luis Cabrera.[77] With the proliferation of parties and candidates Huerta, shrewdly analyzing the political realities of the day, allowed Félix Díaz to return to Mexico to participate in the campaign. Another active candidate could only help his cause. It was extremely unlikely that all of the requirements for a legal election could be met. The electoral law then in force provided that a candidate, to be elected, had to receive a majority of the votes, and, at least 51 percent of the electoral districts in the country had to submit returns.[78] In addition, the constitution stipulated that one-third of the eligible voters in the country must cast ballots to meet the legal requirement.

By the time Díaz returned to Mexico in October, vice-presidential candidate de la Barra had convinced himself of the futility of the effort and obliged the party to choose a new running mate. Party

75. Huerta's political repressions during the summer of 1913 are discussed in Summary of Military Events, July 15 to July 23, Burnside Reports, July 22, 1913. The activities of the junta are traced in Vera Estañol, *La Revolución Mexicana*, pp. 331-32.

76. *El Independiente*, September 22, 23, 24, 1913.

77. Hohler to Grey, September 30, 1913, F.O. 115/1742, fols. 241-43.

78. Mexico, Secretaría de Estado y del Despacho de Gobernación, *Ley Electoral de los Estados Unidos Mexicanos* (Mexico: Imprenta del Gobierno Federal, 1913), passim.

Chairman José Luis Requena agreed to run himself but the Felicista campaign was lackluster. Given the state of the pacification program and the ever-increasing hostility of Washington, the only campaign promises that made sense were those of David de la Fuente and Andrés Molina Enríquez. They offered little in the way of reform and admitted frankly that if elected they would govern dictatorially until some semblance of order was attained. Arguing that free and meaningful elections were impossible under Huerta, they submitted that the only purpose of their administration would be to prepare the country for new elections. They hoped that these elections could take place within a year after which time they would step down.[79] Why substitute one dictatorial interim regime for another? The Constitutionalists were long on record as opposing the outcome of any election under Huerta's sponsorship and the United States followed suit after the dissolution of Congress. A new interim regime would not be so burdened and with a little good will on all sides, the country could return to normal.

By early October Huerta realized that none of the declared candidates were going to captivate the imagination of the voting public. There was insufficient time to conduct a campaign properly, most of the parties had only meager funds available to them, and the president was especially pleased that no concerted effort was being made to get the people to the polls. With the election two weeks away Huerta and his advisors knew that all of the legal requirements could not be met and that as a result, the interim president would remain in office. But Huerta wanted a little icing on the cake. In the middle of October he informed his confidants that he would respond favorably should the electorate give him a mandate to remain in office. The message was promptly communicated to the *jefes políticos* of the states in an effort to muster all governmental employees; army commanders were informed to turn out the military vote for Victoriano Huerta and Aureliano Blanquet.[80] Purposefully misinforming the public, Huerta, at approximately the same time, announced that he had no interest in continuing in office.[81]

Election day, October 26, 1913, found a very confused and apathetic

79. Manifiesto que los Señores Gral. Ing. David de la Fuente y Lic. Andrés Molina Enríquez . . . Dirigen a sus Conciudadanos, October 19, 1913, AEM, vol. 5.

80. Lind to Bryan, October 21, 1913, RDS, 812.00/9302; William P. Blocker, consul, Piedras Negras, to Bryan, October 25, 1913, RDS, 812.00/9385.

81. O'Shaughnessy to Bryan, October 23, 1913, RDS, 812.00/9341.

Mexican citizenry. For a week the newspapers had been contradicting one another with regard to Huerta's intentions and desires. At the very same time that Huerta denied his candidacy, placards proclaiming his candidacy were posted in public places. Francisco Vásquez Gómez and his Anti-reelectionist party had withdrawn from the race a few days before charging that the elections were going to be fraudulent.[82] A special congressional election, also scheduled for the same day, listed twenty-six different parties on the ballot.[83] There was little to recommend any of the presidential hopefuls. Few substantive issues had been raised and ideological commitment was noticeably absent. The public responded as Huerta knew they would, by failing to respond. In city after city, town after town, the turnout was embarrassingly small. In the state of Chihuahua the polls opened only in Ciudad Juárez and less than 5 percent of the registered voters appeared.[84] The pattern was similar throughout the republic. American consuls reported the voting in Nuevo León as "very light"; in Ensenada, as representing "less than seven percent of the voter's list"; in Acapulco, "little interest was shown"; and in Tampico, "no interest."[85] The calculated plot to divide the opposition, to confuse the voters, and at the same time to maintain the sham of trying to meet all legal technicalities worked perfectly.

The degree to which the election of October, 1913, was rigged is difficult to determine. John Lind reported to the secretary of state that he had seen private instructions given to General Joaquín Maas, military governor of Puebla; these instructions indicated that the election would be fraudulent and that Huerta and his running mate, Aureliano Blanquet, would come out on top.[86] The methods employed, Lind revealed sardonically, "would make a Tammany chieftain green with envy."[87] Certainly the soldiers and the government employees

82. Renuncia del Doctor Francisco Vásquez Gómez a su Candidatura, October 20, 1913, AEM, Vol. 2, follows fol. 18.
83. *Diario Oficial*, October 1, 1913, p. 325.
84. Thomas B. Edwards, consul, Ciudad Juárez, to Bryan, October 26, 1913, RDS, 812.00/9398.
85. Garret, consul, Nuevo Laredo, to Bryan, October 26, 1913, RDS, 812.00/9394; Claude E. Guyant, consul, Ensenada, to Bryan, October 27, 1913, RDS, 812.00/9409; Clement Edwards, Consul, Acapulco, to Bryan, October 27, 1913, RDS, 812.00/9430; W. W. Canada, consul, Veracruz, to Bryan, October 27, 1913, RDS, 812.00/9429.
86. Lind to Bryan, October 26, 1913, RDS, 812.00/9392. United States chargé Nelson O'Shaughnessy believed that the instructions seen by Lind were authentic. O'Shaughnessy to Bryan, October 27, 1913, RDS, 812.00/9416.
87. Lind to Bryan, October 25, 1913, RDS, 812.00/9401.

were instructed how to cast their ballots. With the small turnout, this alone could have made the difference. When the secretary of gobernación announced that Huerta had carried the day, the Felicistas charged that the votes had not been fairly counted, but there is little evidence to back up the charge. The official pressure had been exerted prior to the vote and there is little reason to assume that manipulations were necessary at the time of the counting.[88] Much more important, however, the election had not met the requirements of the electoral law and the constitution and, accordingly, was declared null and void. Huerta would remain in office and, at the same time, could state to friend and foe alike that he had received more votes than any of the opposition candidates even though he had not formally entered the race.[89]

Huerta's electoral farce, his dissolution of Congress, his browbeating of cabinet ministers, and his intemperate use of alcohol can be explained but not explained away. Even viewed most magnanimously they scarcely reveal the portrait of a statesman. As a historical figure Huerta will never instill pride in a generation of Mexican students or evoke passionate admiration. But these factors alone are insufficient to render intelligible the position which he occupies in the total historiographical scheme of things. More significant than any or all of these repulsive political and personal characteristics is the fact that the man is tinged and the regime totally discolored by the series of political murders. One will search in vain for any evidence that Huerta ever showed emotion or remorse when confronted with the facts. Hardly a product of his intransigent Huichol stoicism, his reaction, or lack of it, was conditioned by his own personality and by his own yardstick of human values.

Does Victoriano Huerta's scant regard for human life, as evidenced by the wave of assassination, not then justify the censure and abuse to which he has been subjected? If the historian is to exercise absolute moral judgments, any administration which had ordered man to kill his fellow man (irrespective of the presumed righteousness of the

88. Luis Licéaga in *Félix Díaz* (pp. 330-31) maintains that the Felicistas actually won the election but offers precious little in the way of substantive evidence. Both United States and British consular reports from the towns in which the votes were cast indicate a landslide victory for the Huerta-Blanquet ticket.

89. There is no evidence to support John Lind's contention that Huerta's plans for the October election had been prompted by British Ambassador Lionel Carden. See Lind to Bryan, October 23, 1913, RDS, 812.00/9355. Lind saw Carden's hand behind all manner of conspiracies against the United States but certainly Huerta needed no instruction in the inner workings of Mexican politics.

cause) must be censured. But few would argue that the value judgment can be that absolute. In his attempt to understand the nature of past societies the historian becomes to some degree a moral relativist. Alternative courses of action, relationship of means to ends, and the nature of the threat to the body politic or the state all weigh heavily in any reasonable determination. Certainly political assassination cannot be equated to the killing of soldiers in open combat; but neither should it be equated, even by implication, to calculated genocide. The distinctions in these cases are qualitative rather than quantitative. But the fact that previous Mexican administrations, as well as subsequent ones, used assassination as a political weapon more sparingly than did Huerta is simply a difference in degree, not in substance.[90]

Huerta was a cruel dictator who did not hesitate to eliminate his opposition by murder. The regime was misanthropic and repressive. But if other Revolutionary regimes employed the same weapons, albeit with more restraint, why is it that Huerta alone is held up for opprobrium? Why is it that his name exclusively is anathema in his own country? Is it simply that he was more excessive in his use of force and the list of assassinated is considerably longer? The explanation is not that simple. Huerta's record offers no long catalog of material accomplishments which historians often find redemptive even in the most dictatorial regimes. Antonio Guzmán Blanco in Venezuela, Manuel Rosas in Argentina, and indeed Porfirio Díaz in Mexico were perhaps no less tyrannical than Huerta but the internal development of their respective countries during their long tenures makes them somehow redeemable. Even more important, however, Huerta's assassinations are considered more odious than those of other military dictators since the Revolution of 1910 because of the commonly understood ideological posture of the regime. In twentieth-century Mexican historiography murder ostensibly committed in the name of a counterrevolution is judged infinitely worse than the same act committed in the name of the Revolution. Given the prevalence of this frame of reference it is interesting that the position of the Huerta regime on the major social issues of the day has never been deeply probed.

90. The list of Revolutionary assassinations during other regimes is indeed long. Some of the most famous cases include the assassination of Emiliano Zapata (by order of Venustiano Carranza?), of Felipe Carrillo Puerto (by order of Adolfo de la Huerta?), of Senator Francisco Field Jurado and Ramón Treviño (by order of Alvaro Obregón?), of Pancho Villa, Father Miguel Pro, presidential candidate Francisco Serrano, José Villa Arce, Daniel and Miguel Peralta, and Governor Carlos Vidal (by order of Plutarco Calles?).

CHAPTER 8

Revolution or Counterrevolution?

THE HUERTA REGIME traditionally has been portrayed as a classic representation of counterrevolution. Francisco I. Madero, having engineered the overthrow of a conservative dictatorship which had clouded the Mexican political horizon for over three decades, in turn fell victim to a military coup which was reactionary in orientation. The soldiers and politicians who consolidated their position in February, 1913, and maintained a rather tenuous control of the government for the next seventeen months, had as their prime motivation the reincarnation of the old stereotype system of nineteenth-century privilege and abuse. Hostile to all notions of twentieth-century

156

liberalism, this aristocratic elite feared that the social revolutionary seeds planted by Madero were about to reap a radical harvest. The movement, therefore, had to be nipped in the bud. Does this type of analysis meet the test of historical scholarship, however? Or are the Ten Tragic Days and the resulting Huerta dictatorship better explained in other terms?

It is necessary to begin with a consideration so seemingly insignificant that it could easily be misconstrued as mere pedantry. Yet its power to bemuse the issues is immense. Since the year 1910 Mexicanists have found it necessary to distinguish between *revolution* and *Revolution*. The basis for this distinction is simple enough. The social upheaval which began in the early twentieth century (the Revolution) is to be distinguished from the many *golpes de estado* (the revolts or revolutions) of the nineteenth century. The goal of the revolution is to change the government—that of the Revolution is to change the fabric of society which sustains that government. If one accepts that distinction (and most Mexican historians do), then it logically follows that a given political or military leader can be revolutionary without being Revolutionary, and more significant to the task at hand, can be counterrevolutionary without being counter-Revolutionary.

Historical myths generally are not fabricated out of the thin air. Most often they result from the misinterpretation and misrepresentation of a body of fact which, at least on the surface, seems to support the allegations and contentions. The reactionary and counter-Revolutionary orientation of the Huerta regime is no exception. In study after study the reactionary nature of the seventeen months is imputed from the composition of the various cabinets. Many of the individual members had served the Díaz regime in one capacity or another. Arbitrarily rejecting all possible mitigating considerations (such as men often change with the times), one can inductively construct an entire series of counter-Revolutionary propositions based solely on the composition of the cabinets. If the Huerta regime had lasted only one week, and if one wished to offer conjecture on what the nature of the regime might have been, this type of inductive reasoning, properly qualified, and in lieu of other data, might be considered tenable. But the Huerta government lasted for a year and a half. Yet virtually nobody has consented to let the record speak for itself.

The most basic goals of the Mexican Revolution were effected gradually in the 1920s and 1930s by a series of reforms which essentially altered the relationship of government and society. Agrarian reform sought to change traditional patterns of land tenure, a new philosophy of education broke with the elitest tradition of the Científicos, and economic nationalism seriously challenged the position of foreign, capital. For the first time in Mexican history the urban proletariat was given a genuine stake in society as protective legislation was put on the books and enforced. Mexico's Indian heritage was rescued from decades of derogation as conscientious efforts were made to inculcate pride in the nation's autochthonous past. And finally a new philosophy of international relations was predicated upon the concept of nonintervention in the internal affairs of other countries. All of these measures to a greater or lesser degree distinguished the Revolution from the Díaz regime. But they did not begin with Madero to be abandoned by Huerta only to be reinstituted by Carranza.

Having approached the task of analyzing Huerta's social program with a set of fairly conventional preconceptions, I was led to question seriously the posture of the regime by James W. Wilkie's landmark study, *The Mexican Revolution: Federal Expenditure and Social Change since 1910.* Wilkie examined projected and actual per capita budgetary expenditures administration by administration from 1910 to 1963. He broke the federal budgets down into three main categories —economic, social, and administrative expenditures. Included within social expenditures were outlays for education, Indian affairs, public health, welfare, potable water, sewage disposal, labor, housing, and various social security and government insurance programs. Wilkie's data reveal that the Huerta regime projected a slightly higher percentage of the per capita budget for social expenditure than Madero before him and a considerably higher percentage than Carranza after him.[1] His regime was the only one between 1910 and 1922 that earmarked more than 10 percent of the annual budget for social expenditures. Huerta's actual expenditure for social programs is not known. This information was either purposely or inadvertently destroyed when the Constitutionalists captured Mexico City in the summer of 1914.[2] But as Wilkie indicates, even though actual expenditures in the early Revolutionary period are generally slightly less than projected expenditures, the projections themselves indicate "how each

1. James W. Wilkie, *The Mexican Revolution: Federal Expenditure and Social Change since 1910* (Berkeley: University of California Press, 1967), p. 158.
2. It is interesting that the actual social expenditures of the Huerta administration are the only figures not available for the entire Revolutionary period. My attempt to follow this matter up during several research trips to Mexico City between 1967 and 1970 was no more successful than that of Wilkie.

president wanted to spend the federal purse" and how he might have spent it "had conditions been normal." [3] But the data on the Huerta period in the Wilkie study, while strongly suggestive, are by no means conclusive. The attitude of the regime on the specific measures which have come to embody the essence of the Revolution itself need to be examined.

Mexican education during the Díaz regime found its philosophical inspiration in the elitest views of the Científicos—especially Gabino Barreda. Díaz's ministers of education—Protasio Tagle, Joaquín Barranda, and even Justo Sierra—dictated that school construction in the last quarter of the nineteenth century should favor the large cities where the whites, not the Indians, lived. The curriculum was heavily weighted toward the natural sciences and mathematics, almost to the complete exclusion of the social sciences and humanities.[4] In the presidential elections of 1911, Francisco Madero had promised to widen the educational base. But his annual budget for 1911-12 revealed that he allocated only 7.8 percent for educational purposes as opposed to 7.2 percent in Díaz's last budget.[5] With clearly inadequate funds Madero did construct some fifty new schools in the rural areas and several evening and weekend instructional programs were initiated in the Federal District. The government also began to sponsor a modest program of school lunches for the underprivileged.[6] But Madero's educational program is more notable for what it did not do, or even attempt to do. No dramatic increase in expenditures was requested, nor was any program for revising the Científico curriculum advanced.

When Huerta prepared his first annual budget for 1913-14, he projected 9.9 percent for education, a figure larger than any Mexican administration until 1922.[7] The educational budget clearly was not designed to mollify the regime's conservative supporters. Huerta's

3. Wilkie, *The Mexican Revolution,* pp. xxii and 25.

4. See for example Eusebio Castro, "Trayectoria Idealógica de la Educación en México," *Historia Mexicana* 5 (July 1954-June 1955): 198-217; Victor Gallo M., "La Educación Preescolar y Primaria," in *México: 50 Años de Revolución,* vol. 4, *La Cultura,* pp. 43-78; and Francisco Larroyo, "La Educación Media," in *México: 50 Años de Revolución,* vol. 4, *La Cultura,* pp. 81-103.

5. Wilkie, *The Mexican Revolution,* p. 160.

6. Ross, *Madero,* pp. 247-48.

7. Huerta's second budget (1914-15), prepared during the height of the Constitutionalist revolution, reduced the amount to 6.9 percent. Nevertheless, the average for the two budgets is higher than the two budgets prepared by Madero and completely dwarfs Carranza's highest projection for the period 1917-20. The First Chief never projected an educational figure larger than 1.4 per cent and never actually spent even that. See Wilkie, *The Mexican Revolution,* p. 160.

actual plans for education were first revealed in the spring of 1913, when Secretary of Public Instruction and Fine Arts Jorge Vera Estañol went before the Congress. In an eloquent address the secretary denounced an educational system which left eleven million Mexicans, mostly those in the rural areas, untouched. Even the educational program in the cities catered to the very rich and contributed practically nothing to the needs of the larger community. As an example Vera Estañol chided the deputies about the kindergarten system in Mexico City which cost the government over one hundred thousand pesos for one thousand children; and worse, he continued, "because of their organization, they are utilized, if not exclusively, almost exclusively, by the well-to-do class, that is to say those who need them least." [8] As a corrective measure he proposed a kindergarten system to be located "not in the aristocratic center of the capital but in the outlying areas." [9] But the redefinition of priorities for preschool children was appurtenant to the paramount objectives of the ministry of education. As the deputies relaxed in their chairs they were treated to an impassioned plea for the rights of the rural Mexican, especially the Indian:

> If this honorable Chamber approves a request to spend 4,500,000 pesos, we can build *5,000 schools* throughout the entire country. In these schools if only the Spanish language were taught this would be worthwhile because it would awaken a sleeping civilization. But in addition we will teach reading, writing, and arithmetic, and when the schools are well-established, accepted and recognized . . . then the government will be in a position to slowly but surely transform these schools into something still more important. They will be schools with practical and decisive objectives. Once the transformation occurs the students can be taught, in addition to reading and writing, local geography, and above all national history and the principles of world civilization. That is to say we will develop the potential of the future citizen and contribute toward democracy in this country . . . . In other words these elementary schools will constitute the roots of a tree, the tree of society that will someday bear rich fruit for the country . . . . I wish, gentlemen, that I had at this moment the necessary eloquence to convey to you how deeply I feel about this matter so that you would be sure to approve this measure. Unfortunately I do not have these kinds of persuasive qualities

8. *Diario de los Debates,* May 12, 1913.
9. Ibid.

. . . but in the name of the Indians whom we cannot destroy or extinguish or condemn to death when we have so many evidences of their strength of character, I implore you, members of the Chamber, consider the budget request of the ministry of education for elementary schools and approve it.[10]

Vera Estañol's proposal for a vast new program of rural education was approved almost unanimously and at the same time the Chamber approved a 25 percent increase in salary for primary and secondary teachers.[11] The education ministry immediately set to work on the implementation of the rural education plan. Mexico was divided into thirty-six educational zones containing a total of five hundred school districts. Each district was to receive 10 new rural schools. The plan enjoyed wide support from a broad spectrum of the community. Private citizens made donations to supplement the governmental budget and many Indian communities provided the labor for construction.[12] Once the administration received approval from Congress, the program was initiated with funds that had been appropriated but not spent by President Madero. But when the summer cabinet shake-up forced Vera Estañol out of the ministry of public instruction less than three dozen of the 5,000 projected schools had been completed. The program continued into the fall and by late September Mexico could count 131 new rural schools with room for ten thousand new students.[13] However, when Nemesio García Naranjo became minister of education the emphasis changed.

García Naranjo's interest, unlike that of Vera Estañol, was in reforming the pattern of secondary education in the country. Greatly impressed with Henri Bergson's masterpiece *L'Evolution Créatrice* (1907), García Naranjo saw the opportunity to apply the Frenchman's philosophical assault on Comtian positivism and materialism in a major revision of the curriculum at the National Preparatory School. The course of study had not been seriously revised since the school was founded by Gabino Barreda during the Juárez period. Mathematics formed the core of the first year's training so that the student

10. Ibid.
11. After the Huerta regime was overthrown, the salary of the teachers was reduced by 25 percent because the increase had been given them by "an illegal regime," as Félix Palavicini noted in his memoirs, "Se aprovechó un pretexto revolucionario para aplicar un criterio reaccionario" (*Mi Vida Revolucionaria* [Mexico: Ediciones Botas, 1937], p. 167).
12. Vera Estañol, *Historia de la Revolución Mexicana*, pp. 321-22.
13. *Diario de los Debates*, September 16, 1913.

could then progress in order to cosmography, physics, chemistry, mineralogy, botany, geography, zoology, anatomy, human physiology, and finally in the fifth or last year to philosophy, logic, and history. García Naranjo was neither a romantic nor antiscientific, but he believed that the scientific thinking of the day, and its resultant determinism, neglected many equally important aspects of the human experience. The scientific curriculum produced a mechanistic view of the universe which stultified all spontaneous creativity. He could not accept the científico hypothesis that mathematics and the physical sciences formed the necessary foundations for philosophy and history. Those students who did not finish the last year (and there were many who dropped out) received a distorted view of the universe and those who did finish were cheated along the way.[14]

In December, 1913, García Naranjo and Licenciado Genaro García, the director of the National Preparatory School, initiated a new curriculum which broke abruptly with the positivist traditions of the past. The course of study for the first three years was amended to make room for literature, history, and philosophy. The sciences were not abandoned, but neither were the other branches of learning sacrificed to them. By striking a reasonable balance between the arts and the sciences at the National Preparatory School, García Naranjo struck an important first blow at the entire científico philosophical formulation of education. Within a decade the curriculum tried and tested at the National Preparatory School would be spread out to the entire nation.[15]

The reforms of both Vera Estañol and García Naranjo had a lasting impact on the course of the Revolution, but in the last analysis, because of the direction which the Revolution would move in the 1920s and 1930s, those of the former were more significant than those of the latter. Vera Estañol clearly linked the future of the Mexican nation with the future of the Mexican Indian. Invoking the name of Benito Juárez whenever possible, and alluding to the inherent

14. García Naranjo's educational philosophy is best articulated in his own *Memorias,* 7:178-96. A brief analysis is also contained in Manuel A. Quintana, "La Educación en la Epoca de Victoriano Huerta," *El Nacional,* October 29, 1945, pp. 3, 8, and in Querido Moheno, *Sobre el Ara Sangrienta* (Mexico: Editorial Andrés Botas e Hijo, 1922), pp. 218-19.

15. Historians have had a difficult time fitting García Naranjo's educational reforms into the counter-Revolutionary hypothesis of the Huerta regime. The overwhelming majority of studies ignore them completely. Those which do mention them simply offer that they were significant in spite of the fact that he was a minister under Victoriano Huerta. See, for example, Larroyo, "La Educación Media," p. 83.

qualities of the "bronze race," [16] he was really grasping for a new definition of Mexican nationalism—a nationalism rooted deeply in *indigenista* soil. National unity, he realized, was no more than an illusion when millions of Indians were so far removed from the rest of the community by language, customs, diet, and life expectancy. The administration, headed by a president whose Indian background was obvious to everyone who even glimpsed his picture,[17] did not initiate a well-defined program of incorporating the Indian into the mainstream of society, but neither was the Indian systematically denegrated and scorned as he had been in the past. Small steps were taken as when the government dignified an indigenista celebration honoring Cuauhtemoc by sending the Federal District police band to participate.[18] The regime was responsible for the foundation of the Instituto Etnográfico, the first government-sponsored agency dedicated to the development and protection of Indian arts and crafts.[19] At least one full-blooded Indian, Aureliano Urrutia, was brought into the cabinet as minister of gobernación. He was not given this position because he was an Indian (he was Huerta's personal friend and physician), nor was he brought in to work solely on Indian affairs, but on the other hand his Indian blood did not constitute an automatic disclaimer for a position of trust. During his brief tenure Urrutia began sending teams of government consultants into Indian villages with the purpose of organizing community projects which could make small but meaningful changes in daily life patterns. Mobilizing the Indian communities to work on sanitation facilities, roads, improved water supply systems, and school construction, he was able to make a discernible dent in the existing structure. When he left the cabinet in September, 1913, the program was not abandoned and, in fact, was still operating when Huerta was driven from office ten months later.[20]

Agrarian reform undoubtedly is the most pervasive theme of the

16. *Diario de los Debates,* May 12, 1913.

17. He often remarked publically, "Yo soy indio huichol" (see Molina Enríquez, *La Revolución Agraria,* 5:133). On one occasion, explaining Mexico's internal problems, he told Nelson O'Shaughnessy that the gachupines had spoiled a good race (O'Shaughnessy, *A Diplomat's Wife in Mexico,* p. 31).

18. *El Independiente,* August 22, 1913.

19. Andrés Molina Enríquez, "Huerta, el Presidente que Menos Sangre Derramó," *Todo* 176 (January 19, 1937): 19.

20. Secretaría de Gobernación to Secretaría de Estado y del Despacho de Comunicaciones y Obras Públicas, June 14, 1914, AGN/RSG, Gobernadores de Estados, Asuntos Varios, 1913-14; David Laúcher, presidente de la municipalidad de Milpa Alta, to Secretaría de Estado y del Despacho de Gobernación, June 10, 1914, ibid.

Latin American social revolution of the twentieth century. Mexico is far from being an exception. For an entire complex of historical reasons, land ownership during the latter stages of the Díaz dictatorship was highly concentrated in the hands of a few extremely wealthy hacendados. Less than 1 percent of the population owned about 85 percent of the land, while nine million peons barely eked out a living on the remainder. But the exaggerated land concentration had ramifications that went much beyond the grossly inequitable distribution of wealth. It created a social pattern in the rural areas in which the landless peon was a virtual slave in everything but name.

Francisco Madero's revolution against Porfirio Díaz was not an agrarian revolution, although it attracted many ardent agrarianists to the cause. Madero was not in the presidency long before he found himself caught between those advocating rapid rural change and those moralizing upon the virtues of the status quo. The president moved cautiously when he established a National Agrarian Commission under the chairmanship of Rafael Hernández, his minister of development. The commission studied the agrarian question and recommended that an agrarian executive committee be instituted to begin purchasing private estates for subdivision and sale to small farmers. The funding would be administered by the Caja de Préstamos de Irrigación y Fomento de Agricultura, an agency established during the waning years of the Díaz regime by José Ives Limantour. The capital available to the Caja was a sparce ten million pesos and the hacendados demanded such high prices for their land that the plan had to be laid aside; the commission instead concentrated its efforts on restoring the ejido lands which had been seized illegally by the land companies during the late Díaz period. A few of these cases were settled before Madero was driven from office in February, 1913, but little in the way of concrete progress had been made.[21]

Victoriano Huerta began his agrarian program by skirting the main issue—the redistribution of land. Instead he decided to follow Madero's cautious steps and utilize the institutions established during the administrations of his predecessors to improve the agrarian picture without attacking the structure of land tenure itself. At the end of February the administration announced that the National Agrarian

21. Madero's agrarian program and the problems he encountered are discussed in Ross, *Madero,* pp. 240-44; José C. Valadés, *Imaginación y Realidad de Francisco I. Madero,* 2 vols. (Mexico: Antigua Librería Robredo, 1960), 2:230-34.

Commission was prepared to distribute free seed to anyone who asked for it. By March 1 the program was underway with corn seed being passed out at no cost.[22] A few weeks later Secretary of Development Alberto Robles Gil announced that the activities of the agricultural school in Mexico City would be expanded so that a branch of the school would be opened in each climatic zone in the country.[23] The administration also continued Madero's program of restoring ejido lands and in the month of April granted permission for the reoccupation of seventy-eight ejidos seized from the Yaqui and Mayo Indians of Sonora during the late Díaz regime.[24] A few months later the government announced a plan for dividing some government owned lands into plots for subsequent distribution to the small farmer.[25]

Expanding the inadequate programs of the Madero administration whetted appetites but resolved little. Huerta took a much more dramatic step in the late spring. He decided to abolish Madero's National Agrarian Commission and in its place created a new cabinet ministry. The old ministry of development became the ministry of industry and commerce, whereas the agrarian commission, previously under the jurisdiction of the development ministry, was given independent cabinet status with as much autonomy as any ministry enjoyed during the Huerta regime.[26] To indicate that he was serious about resolving the agrarian question Huerta had his Congress double the funds available to the Caja de Préstamos.[27] But the figure of twenty million pesos to resolve the endemic problems of land concentration was almost as unrealistic as ten million. Huerta needed a completely new approach, and because he contended that the problem was basically an economic one (a questionable premise at the best), he asked his Secretary of Finance Toribio Esquivel Obregón to develop a new proposal.

Esquivel Obregón, once considered by Madero as a vice-presidential

22. *El País,* February 28, 1913, and March 3, 1913.
23. Ibid., March 22, 1913.
24. Ricardo Delgado Román, *Aspecto Agrario del Gobierno del General Victoriano Huerta* (Guadalarjara: Imprenta Gráfica, 1951), p. 11.
25. *Diario de los Debates,* September 16, 1913.
26. Because of problems with Congress, a minister of agriculture was not finally approved until February, 1914. Carranza's reaction to the new ministry of agriculture was exactly the same as his reaction to Huerta's educational reforms. When he came to power he abolished the agriculture ministry and moved a step backward to Madero's agrarian commission. See Delgado Román, *Aspecto Agrario,* p. 48.
27. *Diario de los Debates,* April 23, 1913.

candidate, had a long-standing interest in the agrarian question. A fiscal conservative, he believed that the government simply could not shoulder all of the costs. Although he recognized that subdivision of land was mandatory, he believed that the state should not move directly to expropriate property. He argued that the function of the state was to create a proper set of circumstances so that a major subdivision could occur on the basis of individual initiative. Many of the large haciendas were not productive and were heavily mortgaged, thus constituting a financial drain on the hacendados. They wanted to sell them, he contended, but the lower classes who wanted to purchase them were living outside the monetary economy. The solution which he envisioned was for the government to extend credit to the landless peon through the emission of guaranteed government bonds. It would then be performing a legitimate function —serving as an intermediary between those who wanted to sell and those who wanted to buy.[28]

Monetarily, Esquivel Obregón's program was sound, but as a practical matter it was unrealistic. The entire plan was predicated on the very questionable thesis that the hacendados wanted to rid themselves of their mortgaged estates. It failed to take note of the fact that the hacendados purchased land for speculative purposes and therefore the mortgages, although real, were not considered a genuine liability. In addition, the social status of the hacendados was inexorably intertwined with the amount of acreage they accumulated. It was extremely unlikely that they would voluntarily rid themselves of their estates.[29] Perhaps the Congress realized the impracticality of the suggestions, or perhaps it was motivated by other considerations. At any rate, Congress turned the plan down.

When Eduardo Tamariz became Mexico's first minister of agriculture, the agrarian reformers were not pleased. The Tamariz family were large landowners and Eduardo, a talented lawyer, bore all the marks of the well-bred, conservative, Catholic politician. But shortly after assuming office he surprised many by initiating a legislative proposal more advanced than anything that had yet been introduced before the Chamber of Deputies. Secretary Tamariz believed that the government was not empowered to expropriate property. He could find nothing in the Constitution of 1857 which even implied this

28. Toribio Esquivel Obregón, "La Cuestión Agraria y la Conciliación de los Intereses," *Excélsior*, November 5, 1928, pp. 5, 10.
29. An excellent analysis of the proposal is contained in Fernando González Roa, *El Aspecto Agrario de la Revolución Mexicana* (Mexico: Dirección de Talleres Gráficos, 1919), pp. 245-48.

right. But he realized that the Esquivel Obregón approach was impractical. His problem, therefore, was to devise a scheme of coercing the hacendados without exceeding the authority of the state. He found his solution in the taxation provisions of the constitution. The Congress, he urged, should increase taxes on the large estates markedly. As taxes were increased, the land would be less valuable for speculation and the hacendados would at least have to consider sale. As a corollary, he believed that taxes òn the small farms should be lowered or eliminated entirely.[30]

The Tamariz proposal fared no better in Congress than had the Esquivel Obregón plan. Yet it is significant that the administration was not opposed to the subdivision of the large estates. And in the case of Eduardo Tamariz one can detect a few hesitant steps toward income redistribution. Both plans were timid, neither would be enthusiastically endorsed by the ardent agrarianist, but the Huerta administration was thinking in terms quite different from that of the Díaz regime.[31] The landowners themselves recognized the change and slowly began to desert the regime in the late summer.[32]

Still another of the counter-Revolutionary propositions is predicated upon the administration's alleged relationship with the Roman Catholic church. In this matter, perhaps more than any other, the important issues have been clouded by the emotion which all too often typifies discussion of religious institutions. Rejecting the *modus vivendi* which Díaz had reached with the church, the Revolution, after 1915, became increasingly anticlerical, so much so that until about 1940 a Revolutionary's credentials were not considered impeccable unless they demonstrated, in one form or another, some hostility toward that venerable institution. Because Huerta was not anticlerical, he has been cast in the role of a neo-Porfirian. But the logic is no more persuasive than labeling José de San Martín a Bolivarian because he shared the liberator's desire to drive the Spanish off the South American continent. In reality Huerta never defined the administration's position vis-à-vis the church. He simply allowed his enemies in the north to do that for him.

The evidence linking the administration to the church in a

30. Ibid., pp. 251-52.
31. Neither plan is given a fair hearing in Lucio Mendieta y Núñez's widely cited *El Problema Agrario de México* (Mexico: Editorial Porrua, 1960).
32. The hacendados may well have been just as concerned with Huerta's inability to keep the peace as they were with his timid threats of land reform. It is significant, however, that the regime lost their support. See Leebeus R. Wilfrey to General Leonard Wood, July 29, 1913, RDS, 812.00/8498.

counter-Revolutionary partnership is spotty and inconclusive: Archbishop Mora y del Rio of Mexico City offered a solemn *Te Deum* in Huerta's honor at the conclusion of the Decena Trágica; the church contributed twenty-five million pesos to Huerta's coffers; not only did priests serve the government as spies but, armed with Mauser rifles, actually led government troops into battle; and Huerta allowed the church to dedicate the country to the Sacred Heart of Jesus in January, 1914. Most of these allegations are at best half-truths and at worst fabrications. The *Te Deum* of February, 1913, could not have been more natural in a Roman Catholic country. Not sung to honor Huerta, it was offered to celebrate the restoration of peace in Mexico City after a ten-day battle that had claimed hundreds of civilian lives. Church money, it is true, was used to help replenish an empty treasury but the amount was closer to twenty-five thousand pesos than to twenty-five million. Moreover, the church did not volunteer it; it was collected as a forced loan under the threat of coercion. The archbishop feared, perhaps with justification and perhaps without, that unless Huerta received the money to pay his troops their back salary, they would begin to sack the churches.[33] It is not impossible that a few isolated parish priests took up arms against the Constitutionalists, but one looks in vain for supporting evidence in the military archives or in the military histories of the Revolution and must rely solely on contemporary Constitutionalist allegations and subsequent studies based on them.

The most convincing suggestion that Huerta was in league with the church is the ceremony which took place in cathedrals throughout the country on January 6, 1914. He could certainly have stopped the dedication had he desired to do so. But even this event should be viewed in its own historical context. From February to October, 1913, Huerta's relationship with the church was proper but cool. The church hierarchy did not automatically respond favorably to requests for aid in the pacification efforts.[34] And above all, Huerta was no more prepared to accept criticism from Catholics than from anyone else. When P. Alfredo Méndez Medina's Círculo de Estudios Sociales León XIII founded a Catholic action newspaper, *La Unión Popular*,

33. For a brief but perceptive discussion of Huerta's relationship with the church see Robert E. Quirk, "The Mexican Revolution and the Catholic Church, 1910-1929: An Ideological Study," (Ph.D. diss., Harvard University, 1950), pp. 45-66.

34. Manuel Mondragón to Illmo. y Rev. D. Manuel Fulcheri [bishop of Cuernavaca], March 15, 1913, Condumex/AJA, Carpeta 2.

which was critical of the government, Huerta closed it down, much as he had a number of secular dailies.[35] The relationship between church and state was further strained by the dissolution of Congress in which the Catholic party was well represented. Certainly the fraudulent presidential elections in October, 1913, did not further good feelings between the government and the hierarchy of the church. The Catholic party candidates Federico Gamboa and General Eugenio Rascón, realizing that the party had run strongly in the state and local elections of 1912, believed that they stood a good chance. But Huerta's political manipulations ended their political careers and came close to finishing off the party. And as a final blow Huerta arrested Gabriel Fernández Somellera, the president of the Catholic party, and shipped him off to Veracruz.[36]

The Constitutionalists adopted an anticlerical posture from the outset of their movement. Carranza unjustifiably charged the church with supporting Huerta's reactionary dictatorship and individual Constitutionalist commanders took it upon themselves to retaliate, not only by adopting a patronizing attitude, but by baiting priests, desecrating churches, appropriating church funds, and, in general, by making life as miserable as possible for both the parish priest and the hierarchy.[37] But not even these repressions brought about a monolithic Catholic response with regard to the government in Mexico City. When *El País,* the Catholic daily in the capital, criticized the administration for dissolving the Congress, the bishops of Aguascalientes, Zamora, and Zacatecas disavowed the disavowal.[38] But in the winter of 1913-14 intensified Constitutionalist attacks against the institution and its personnel, and in some cases against religion itself, produced the classic self-fulfilling prophecy. The church did draw itself closer and closer to the regime and did begin to support it more and more; Huerta finally embraced it by authorizing the dedication ceremonies of January. The president believed that the church could be a useful and powerful ally as long as there was no question con-

---

35. Alicia Olivera Sedano, *Aspectos del Conflicto Religioso de 1926 a 1929: Sus Antecedentes y Consecuencias* (Mexico: Instituto Nacional de Antropología e Historia, 1966), p. 39.

36. Alfonso J. Junco, "Madero, Huerta y los Católicos," in Mena Brito, *Carranza,* p. 85.

37. Examples of Constitutionalist abuse of church officials are numerous. As an example see O'Shaughnessy, *A Diplomat's Wife in Mexico,* pp. 28-29.

38. *El País,* October 18, 1913, October 19, 1913; *El Independiente,* October 18, 1913.

cerning who was in authority.[39]

Huerta's relationship with foreign capital was determined much more by political exigencies than by a clearly defined philosophy of economic nationalism, yet on this issue again the regime broke sharply with the past. The two largest sources of capital investment in the country, the United States and Great Britain, had been engaged in a spirited competition for control of the Mexican petroleum reserves since the late Díaz period. It was in this industry that Huerta was forced by circumstances to outline the Mexican position. The British interests, dominated by Weetman Pearson (Lord Cowdray) had a much closer working relationship with the government of Prime Minister Herbert Asquith than did American investors Edward Doheny and Henry Clay Pierce with the Wilson administration. In July, 1913, Winston Churchill, the first lord of the admiralty, announced that the Royal Navy was being converted from coal to oil; Lord Cowdray's Anglo-Mexican Petroleum Company (El Aguila) would be expected to supply a substantial proportion of the British needs.[40] The British had supported Huerta almost from the outset and, as a result, the Mexican president had no intention of treating British and American petroleum investors in the same manner. Policy formulations, therefore, had to allow the chief executive considerable latitude.

During the spring and summer of 1913 when the administration still held out some hope for a rapprochement with Washington, Huerta promised foreign investors of all nationalities that their interests would be protected. Understanding Woodrow Wilson no better than the American president understood him, Huerta hoped that the United States business community could dissuade his American antagonist from a hostile attitude. As the diplomatic climate continued to deteriorate, however, the Huerta administration performed a clever *volte-face*. First announcing a contemplated tax increase of three centavos a barrel on all oil produced, Huerta then called upon his supporters in Congress to draft a proposal for nationalizing the industry. In September, Deputy Querido Moheno presented in Congress, the first comprehensive, administration-supported call for economic emancipation to be heard in the Mexican Revolution. Arguing persuasively that there was nothing novel in a country's

39. An interesting account of anticlericalism during the Constitutionalist revolution is contained in David C. Bailey, "Alvaro Obregón and Anti-Clericalism in the 1910 Revolution," *The Americas* 36 (October 1969): 183-98.
40. Calvert, *The Mexican Revolution,* p. 173.

taking steps to protect its resources, he cited as examples Germany's and France's nationalization of the railroads, France's nationalization of the salt and tobacco industries, and England's nationalization of its coal deposits. Lamenting the fact that such a large percentage of Mexico's petroleum wealth was leaving the country with no benefit to the Mexicans, he declared that it was time to take a new bold step; to counteract this alarming trend, he was submitting to the proper chamber committee a plan for the nationalization of the petroleum industry.[41] But according to executive wishes, Moheno's plan gave the president tremendous flexibility. Nationalization could be applied against United States interests but not against British interests if Huerta determined this course of action to be advisable.[42] But the British government was worried and the United States ambassador in London noted a marked cooling in attitude toward Huerta after the nationalization plan was announced.[43]

To indicate that the threat of nationalization enjoyed presidential support and was no idle bluff, Huerta appointed Querido Moheno secretary of foreign relations two days after the latter made his speech in Congress. The United States and Great Britain would be dealing directly with the most articulate spokesman of the plan. At the time of his new appointment Querido Moheno told the press that he felt so strongly about nationalization, he would leave the cabinet and return to Congress, if necessary to lead the bill through.[44] The following week, with the nationalization bill still in committee, the Belisario Domínguez case broke and as a result Huerta dissolved the legislature. When the new Congress convened following the electoral farce of late October, the matter was taken up once again, but by then, with an entire series of new pressures upon the government, other matters seemed more urgent and the nationalization scheme was never submitted to a final vote.

In the early spring of 1914 the administration considered still another plan for taking charge of the petroleum industry—controlling

41. *El Independiente,* September 29, 1913, and September 30, 1913; Taracena, *La Verdadera Revolución,* 2:97.

42. The proposal was made public in November. See *El Imparcial,* November 4, 1913. The needed flexibility was provided by Article III which empowered the president to enter into contracts with certain companies for exploitation of the petroleum reserves after having declared them the property of the nation.

43. Walter Hines Page to Bryan, November 13, 1913, RDS, 812.00/9703. The British minister in Mexico began to change his attitude as well when expropriation was seriously debated within the ranks of the government. O'Shaughnessy to Bryan, November 13, 1913, RDS, 812.00/9719.

44. *El Independiente,* October 1, 1913.

the oil tankers and pipelines. If the transportation of crude oil were solely in government hands, the American and English companies would be subjected indirectly to Mexican government direction. This scheme, extremely mild in comparison with the idea of nationalizing the industry, was being considered carefully in April when the United States intervened in Veracruz disrupting all domestic programs.[45]

If Huerta's thoughts of controlling foreign capital are but a faint shadow of the comprehensive sentiments of economic nationalism so evident in the country during the 1930s, his government's definition of nonintervention is so close to the so-called Carranza doctrine as to bring into serious question the propriety of that term. Whether one choses as his example Secretary of Foreign Relations Federico Gamboa's correspondence with John Lind;[46] Francisco León de la Barra's conferences with Boaz W. Long and his public pronouncements while in the United States;[47] Huerta's complaints against the United States for showing favoritism toward the Constitutionalists;[48] Manuel Garza Aldape's rejection of Wilson's demands;[49] or the bellicose protests of Secretary of Foreign Relations José López Portillo y Rojas or Undersecretary Roberto A. Esteva Ruiz at the time of the invasion of Veracruz,[50] there is little of substance to distinguish Huerta's attitudes on intervention and nonintervention from those of his Constitutionalist successors. While it is true that the principle of nonintervention was never expressed with great precision, nor promoted as a principle of international law during the Huerta regime, nevertheless the propositions of the government are abundantly clear to those who would read and consider the diplomatic correspondence. For example in November, 1913, in answer to Woodrow Wilson's

45. The idea of taking over the petroleum transportation industry rather than the petroleum itself was suggested to the administration by the German Minister von Hintze. He hoped that some of the shares would be put up for sale in Berlin, thus giving the German government a lever in the Mexican petroleum industry. See García Naranjo, *Memorias,* 7:239-52.

46. Lind to Bryan, August 29, 1913, RDS, 812.00/8593.

47. De la Barra to Secretaría de Relaciones Exteriores, August 9, 1913, and August 13, 1913, Condumex/FLB, Correspondencia Interesante, Actividades Alemanes.

48. J. B. Moore to A. Algara R. de Terrenos, May 9, 1913, AREM, L-E 771, Leg. 1, fol. 112.

49. In November Garza Aldape specifically rejected the right of any foreign power to intervene in the domestic affairs of the Mexican nation. O'Shaughnessy to Bryan, November 15, 1913, RDS, 812.00/9757.

50. The regime's reaction to the Veracruz invasion will be discussed in Chapter 10.

demand that Huerta resign and name a provisional government acceptable to the United States, the Mexican president responded, "We cannot accept the intervention of any foreign power, no matter how high and respectable it may be in the matter of domestic questions which are solely of the competence of the Mexican people." [51] The regime held that intervention in the internal affairs of another nation constituted a hostile act, violated sovereignty, and could not be countenanced. This is the essence of the "Carranza doctrine."

Finally Huerta's labor policy should be considered. A year prior to Francisco Madero's overthrow, he had initiated a National Labor Office and subsequently placed it under the jurisdiction of the ministry of fomento. This semi-independent agency contributed to the settlement of a number of strikes and encouraged the formulation of minimum wage and maximum hour legislation. Of equal importance was the Casa del Obrero Mundial which came into existence during the Madero presidency. Not properly a union itself, the Casa served as a place where labor leaders could come together, exchange views, and disseminate propaganda favorable to the cause. If Huerta had desired to return to the Díaz policy of labor repression, he could easily have abolished the labor department and immediately crushed the nascent union movement. To the contrary, for a time the president considered giving the labor department independent ministerial status[52], and although the plan was never brought to fruition, he did expand the department's functions. Within a month after the new regime took office agents of the department began inspection tours of factories where women were employed with the purpose of improving wages, hours, and working conditions.[53] If certain minimal conditions were not met factory owners were threatened with shut down.[54] Factory owners who arbitrarily increased hours or lowered wages were forced to back down.[55]

Before military exigencies raised the draft calls Huerta also established a special agency of the labor department to help find work for the unemployed. Industrialists, miners, and landowners were

51. O'Shaughnessy to Bryan, November 15, 1913, RDS, 812.00/9757.
52. *El País,* April 5, 1913.
53. Ibid., March 7, 1913.
54. Ibid., April 22, 1913; April 27, 1913; May 5, 1913.
55. For example when the workers of the Santa Elena Factory in Tlaxcala complained to the department that the owner of the plant had added one working hour a day to their schedule, the department forced him to rescind the order. See *El País,* March 2, 1913.

encouraged to submit notice of vacancies to the department so that these vacancies could be matched with the available labor force.[56] Realizing that the federal government could not itself hope to attack the endemic needs of the Mexican worker, the president encouraged the state governments to institute labor departments similar to the federal one in order "to improve the economic, judicial, and social position of the working classes."[57] And to focus public attention on the labor problem Adalberto Esteva, the head of the National Labor Office, began publication of a monthly labor bulletin outlining conditions in various areas of the country. Contrary to popular belief Huerta did not suppress strikes. The contemporary newspapers reveal that walk outs were a weekly occurrence with the administration serving as mediator. Some of the strikes were resolved in favor of labor, others in favor of management.

But in assessments of his administration these actions are overlooked and the Huerta regime is associated only with crushing the Casa del Obrero Mundial and thus manifesting a reactionary labor policy. It is true that the regime arrested a number of labor leaders but this action was a political rather than a social maneuver. On May 1, 1913, the Huerta administration allowed the Casa del Obrero Mundial to sponsor the first May Day celebration in Mexican history. Twenty-five thousand workers representing stone masons, carpenters, tailors, shoemakers, textile workers, mechanics, and painters demonstrated at the *zócalo* for an eight-hour day and a six-day week. The government did nothing to interfere with the proceedings.[58] Several weeks later, however, another meeting was held in which the speakers began to attack the regime directly. The most outspoken leader, Antonio Díaz Soto y Gama, attacked Huerta viciously, charging him among other things with Madero's assassination.[59] Huerta would not accept this type of abuse from anyone whether liberal or conservative, Catholic or atheist. The leaders were arrested; the foreigners among them expelled from the country. But Huerta did not shut down the Casa at this time as is so often implied. He allowed it to operate for more than another year; in fact he gave it considerably more latitude than

56. Ibid., March 6, 1913.
57. Secretaría de Gobernación to Gobernador de Hidalgo, July 24, 1913, AGN/RSG, Varios Autógrafos de Gobernadores.
58. Marjorie Ruth Clark, *Organized Labor in Mexico* (Chapel Hill: University of North Carolina Press, 1934), p. 24.
59. Luis Araiza, *Historia del Movimiento Obrero Mexicano*, 4 vols. (Mexico: Talleres de la Editorial Cuauhtemoc, 1964-65), 3:42.

he gave to most of his critics. But in the winter of 1913-14 the Casa intensified its attacks against the administration and at the same time allied itself more closely with the Constitutionalists. Huerta held off until the spring when he finally closed down the Casa and arrested much of the leadership. But had his decision been predicated on an antilabor social philosophy, he most certainly would not have waited for fifteen months to take this decisive step. He might have been suspicious of labor's motives but he was not hostile to it as a means of ameliorating the conditions of the working class.

In summation two questions should be raised. Is it possible to draw conclusions about Huerta's personal attitudes toward social reform from proposals and actions which must be attributed fairly to his ministers? And does the program of the regime constitute a social revolution? Because of the nature of the evidence, the answer to the first question must be inferential and to the second, cautiously speculative.

During his seventeen months in office, Huerta made numerous speeches and issued countless presidential pronouncements supporting almost all of the domestic programs and projected courses of action. But it is dangerous to draw conclusions from these public statements because of the strong possibility that they were motivated more by political expedience than by personal conviction. It is likely that the group of intellectuals in the various cabinets, in spite of the conservative reputation that many of them enjoyed, envisioned the need for constructive change much more clearly than did the president himself. But as one examines the reasons (publicly stated at the time and subsequently revealed in memoirs and private correspondence) for the cabinet resignations and dismissals, the sensitive questions revolving around the need for social change are uniquely absent. It would appear that on most of the reform proposals Huerta did not assume the initiative but, in fact, was led by the cabinet. But neither did he resist their constant prodding on these matters. In spite of his inability to stem the Constitutionalist rebellion and the Zapatista uprising, there was never any question of who controlled the processes of government in Mexico City. He most certainly could have vetoed any of the proposals had he desired to do so. Concerned as he was with the military and diplomatic engagements, he failed to clearly perceive the potential significance of the series of measures emanating from within his government.

The central question introduced by this chapter (Does the Huerta regime constitute a Revolution or a counter-Revolution?) deserves special consideration because of the historical and historiographical factors posited at the outset. It must be answered within the context of definition. Reduced to its most basic ingredient the Revolution is a struggle for a better life for the masses. But the struggle is not won by good intentions, good will, or even specific programs designed to assuage specific miseries. The Revolution is an integrated and coordinated assault on the sustaining structure. It has clearly definable goals and interdependent programs are designed to attain these goals. The social programs of the Huerta regime fell conspicuously short of meeting this definition. The prime goal—increasing social mobility through a series of carefully plotted reforms—was never defined and the reforms themselves bore little demonstrable relationship to one another. There was no attempt at syncretization. At best Huerta's cabinets allowed themselves to be tossed around by the winds of twentieth-century change when they could have secured themselves tightly on a series of nineteenth-century pegs. Many of the ministers spotted the critical areas for reform but none of them were thinking in terms of a fundamental social upheaval designed to alter the nature of society from the top to the bottom. The steps they did take were pre-emptive, designed to mollify those more genuinely interested in refashioning the contours of society. But the point need not be over-stressed since no historian has yet suggested that the Huerta regime represents a genuine social revolution.

But even less is it a counter-Revolution in the social sense. In the first place Huerta's administration can be no more counter-Revolutionary than Madero's government was Revolutionary. Although Madero's biographers correctly point to a number of significant breaks with the past, his program for change was both timid and hesitant. His failure to accomplish more, or even to propose more, is explained largely in terms of an impossible internal situation which forced him to expend the energy of his office fighting civil wars on many fronts. But if the basis for the argument is sound for Madero (and it well might be), why then has it never been applied to Huerta as well? Not a single day in his seventeen-month presidency passed without armed insurrection against him. He was certainly forced to expend just as much time and energy battling opponents as did his predecessor. And yet, as the thesis of this chapter suggests, many of the reforms introduced or proposed between February, 1913, and July, 1914, were more advanced and more farsighted than those of Madero.

Politically, to be sure, the Huerta regime represents a counter-revolution as it manifested a reaction against the government which resulted from the overthrow of Díaz. But Huerta and his advisors both realized that the days of Díaz were gone forever and the advisors recognized the need for reform. They did not attempt to stem the new energies and forces unleashed in 1910; rather they attempted to moderate them. Except for the obvious and censurable abuses of political power, there is simply no evidence to support the contention, repeated in study after study, that the Huerta regime represents an attempted reincarnation of the Age of Díaz.

CHAPTER 9

Financing a Regime

Huerta's failures on the diplomatic front had repercussions which must have astounded all but the most astute political observors of the day. The sustaining foundations of the regime began to buckle under the weight of a series of interrelated military and diplomatic pressures. These, in turn, served to choke off vital financial support from at home and abroad. Huerta's failure to attain recognition encouraged the Constitutionalists to continue the fight. As the war spread, it became more costly, but simultaneously as the chaos increased, normal revenues declined. The administration turned to foreign loans for relief, but European bankers and investors were hesitant to advance funds in large amounts as long as the United States refused to recognize the regime.

Victoriano Huerta inherited a treasury almost empty in February, 1913,[1] and with the gradual extension of the war in the summer and fall the entire economic structure of the country was severely tested. By relying on the *leva* to fill the ranks of the federal army, the government depleted the work force in the rural areas and the cities. Cotton rotted in the fields, coffee beans fell off the trees, and sugar cane stood unharvested on the large plantations of the Gulf Coast.[2] As food, manufactured goods, and cash became scarce, a black market began to flourish in the larger urban areas. The disruption by the Constitutionalists of the country's rail facilities and rolling stock also exacted a heavy economic toll.[3] The small amount of railroad expansion underway when Huerta assumed the presidency came to a rapid halt as crews were pulled off new projects to work full time on track repair in the major zones of conflict. But even when the tracks were repaired and secured many trains did not run regularly for lack of fuel. Those that did often found it necessary to use circuitous routes to avoid possible danger spots. In the summer of 1913 service on over half of the nation's railways was either interrupted or irregular.[4] Unsure of the transportation system shippers refused to take chances on large consignments. Unable to count on the necessary flow of raw materials, factories and smelters closed their doors, and many mine owners, finding no way to transport or sell their ore, shut down operations.[5] By the end of the year mining stocks on the Mexico City exchange had fallen off from 20 percent to 50 percent of their

1. Testimony of Walter Flavius McCaleb, *Fall Committee Hearings,* 1:737; Walter Flavius McCaleb, *Present and Past Banking in Mexico* (New York: Harper and Brothers, 1920), p. 207. While there is little doubt that the treasury was near empty in February, 1913, there is no justification for the charge voiced in some studies that the Maderos had looted it.

2. Lind to Bryan, October 23, 1913, RDS, 812.00/9355.

3. The destruction of track was reduced to a science. By the use of wrecking cranes and heavy steel cables the locomotive engine could be used to destroy the track over which it passed. For a description of Constitutionalist ingenuity in this field one can consult Fred Wilbur Powell, *The Railroads of Mexico* (Boston: Stratford Co., 1921), pp. 13-16.

4. Summary of Military Events, July 1-8, 1913, Burnside Reports, July 8, 1913.

5. Wilbert Bonney, consul, San Luis Potosí, to Bryan, December 18, 1913, RDS, 812.00/10466; Stronge to Grey, August 29, 1913, F.O. 115/1741, fol. 37; *El País,* January 21, 1914.

1910 averages.[6] Cattlemen in the north lost thousands of head to the rebels, and many of the smaller ranchers were forced out of business altogether.[7] Fruit growers on coastal plantations, realizing that their perishable products were vulnerable to delays in shipment and also cognizant that the potential market had shrunk, cut back on production. The most important lumber mills in Chihuahua suspended operations. Even the large oil companies did a minimum amount of exploratory drilling in 1913 and 1914 because of the unsettled conditions.[8]

Visably shaken by the dangerous lack of vitality in the economy, the banking community initiated a series of emergency measures which in many cases aggravated the problems they were seeking to relieve. During the summer the banks throughout the country raised interest rates and tightened credit, even for the oldest and most established commercial houses. When the Mexico City bankers announced that they would no longer redeem bank notes with silver, almost all of the gold and silver specie disappeared from circulation.[9] Short of funds themselves, many of the leading banks stopped paying interest on deposits.[10] A few smaller banks failed and closed their doors in the faces of depositors. With the deterioration of public confidence in the banking structure, domestic capital began to flee the country in search of more secure financial institutions in Europe or the United States. The regime responded by decreeing a 10 percent tax on all gold exports but the measure was virtually impossible to enforce and failed to stem the outflow.[11]

If the breakdown of transportation, a tight money policy, high interest rates, shortage of specie, and general unstable business climate were not enough by themselves to discourage foreign trade, a rapidly

6. Marvin D. Bernstein, *The Mexican Mining Industry, 1890-1950: A Study of the Interaction of Politics, Economics, and Technology* (Albany: State University of New York Press, 1964), p. 97.

7. The "requisitioning" of beef on the hoof was not undertaken simply to feed a hungry rebel army. Much of the cattle was butchered and sold in the United States and even sent to Europe as a source of revenue for the Constitutionalists. See J. C. Peyton to A. B. Fall, January 9, 1914, ABFC, Group P; Walthall and Gamble, attorneys to A. B. Fall, January 18, 1914, ABFC, Group W.

8. Testimony of Edward L. Doheny, *Fall Committee Hearings,* 1:233.

9. Bonney to Bryan, December 18, 1913, RDS, 812.00/10466.

10. Testimony of Walter Flavius McCaleb, *Fall Committee Hearings,* 1:735.

11. McCaleb, *Present and Past Banking in Mexico,* p. 209. A follow-up decree in August prohibited the export of all silver and gold coin from Mexico, but this measure as well was circumvented by various kinds of subterfuge, including contraband traffic. See Ricardo Torres Gaitán, *Política Monetaria Mexicana* (Mexico: n.p., 1944), p. 105.

depreciating currency provided the finishing touch. From its par value of 49.5 centavos to the dollar in February, 1913, the peso slipped to 42 in the summer and then to 36 by the fall. And the bottom had not yet been reached. As the cost of imports rose, so did prices for the consumer, and before the summer was out a serious inflation was added to the country's other economic woes. The cost of local products rose almost at the same rate as the imports. As so often the case, the lower income families in the cities were most directly affected as the prices of food staples and other basic commodities soared and the purchasing power of the peso declined.[12]

The financial paralysis manifested itself in small but poignant ways. A number of federally supported schools were closed for lack of funds. Patriotic demonstrations, traditionally subsidized by the ministry of gobernación, were cancelled or drastically reduced in size as the government repeatedly responded negatively to requests for financial aid.[13] The refusals invariably specified "the critical position of the treasury" as the grounds for denial. More important yet, many government employees were not paid on time. The consular staff in Laredo, Texas, on one occasion waited a hundred days for their monthly salary check.[14] Similarly the consul in Marfa, Texas, unable to pay the rent on the consulate offices, suggested that the foreign ministry close the operation down.[15] S. Pearson and Son, a famous English construction firm, could not obtain payment for harbor works and terminal facilities built at Coatzacoalcos (Puerto México),[16] and many other business concerns simply refused to contract their services to a government increasingly reticent about its financial obligations. But the economic strain hit the small man too. Food supplies to the villages dwindled as fields lay abandoned. These shortages in the north combined with the other ravages of war to induce a substantial emigration of rural Mexican poor to the United States.[17]

12. H. L. Wilson to Bryan, April 19, 1913, RDS, 812.00/7205.

13. Secretaría de Gobernación to Clemente Hernández, Secretario del Comité Patriótico, Hidalgo, July 16, 1914, AGN/RSG, Varios, Recuerdos del Ministro. Secretaría de Gobernación to Presidente del Comité Patriótico Morelos, December 6, 1913, ibid.; Secretaría de Gobernación to Comité Patriótico Liberal Permanente, June 24, 1914, ibid.

14. Secretaría de Relaciones Exteriores to Secretaría de Gobernación, July 29, 1914, AGN/RSG, Varios.

15. Francisco Serrano to Secretaría de Relaciones Exteriores, May 7, 1914, AREM, Francisco Serrano, Su Expediente Personal, L-E 1340, Leg. 1.

16. Stronge to Grey, July 22, 1913, F.O. 115/1740, fol. 282.

17. Arturo M. Elías, Consular Inspector San Antonio to Sec. de Relaciones Exteriores, October 5, 1913. AREM, L-E 758, Leg. 1.

Huerta initially took the easiest (and coincidentally the least effective) measure possible to solve the economic crisis, while placing the country on a wartime footing: he authorized the emission of new paper currency. The Ley General de Instituciones de Crédito specified that each 'peso issued had to be backed by at least fifty centavos of metallic reserves. Not only did the president decree that thirty-three centavos of metal were sufficient for each peso printed, but he also ordered that certificates of the Exchange and Currency Commission and state debts to the federal government be accepted as adequate guarantees.[18] Depositors immediately turned up at the banks with large canvas bags so that they could carry off their deposits in silver.[19] But they were disappointed: the banks could not possibly pay in specie their demands and the regime was obligated to suspend that particular section of the banking code.[20] Within a short time many of the states were authorized to print new paper money as well.

As the paper money began rolling off the government presses, the Constitutionalists decided that, not to be bested, they would also issue their own legal tender.[21] Disparagingly known as *bilimbique*,[22] the Constitutionalist paper was esthetically pleasing (featuring pictures of erupting volcanoes, attractive women, and *dobles cananas*) if well-nigh valueless. It was no accident that many of the signatures were illegible. Some of the rebel paper carried no date and no guarantor whatsoever. But the Constitutionalist command staff decreed that circulation and acceptance of the new currency was mandatory.[23] Others joined the game as well. Mining corporations, industrial concerns, and large agricultural enterprises began printing scrip. The famous Real del Monte Mining Company in Hidalgo alone

18. Antonio Manero, *¿Que es la Revolución?* (Veracruz: Tipografía la Heróica, 1915), p. 66.

19. O'Shaughnessy, *A Diplomat's Wife in Mexico*, p. 46.

20. O'Shaughnessy to Bryan, November 15, 1913, RDS, 812.00/9571.

21. It can be argued that Carranza's financing his movement with Constitutionalist paper rather than with bonds that would have to be repaid ultimately was better for the country.

22. The origin of the word is somewhat obscure. The most current etymological explanation is that an American miner in Sonora with his own *tienda de raya* paid his workers with slips of paper containing only his name—William Vicks. The hispanization of the name—*bilimbique*—came to refer to all valueless paper currency.

23. *El País*, January 20, 1914. The Constitutionalists minted a large number of poor quality coins as well. One of these, appropriately inscribed *Muera Huerta*, is today a collector's item. See Carlos Gaytán, *La Revolución Mexicana y sus Monedas* (Mexico: Editorial Diana, 1969), p. 66.

issued several hundred thousand pesos early in 1914.[24] Late in the year the American consul in Durango reported that there were twenty-five different kinds of paper currency in circulation in his district.[25] Counterfeiters, of course, had a field day, some of them operating with impunity in the United States. Not even experienced bankers could tell the good money from the bad. Fluctuating values of exchange between the various currencies constituted a banker's and tax collector's nightmare. Many persons traveled to Mexico City to exchange state paper for federal paper but the Banco Central refused to accept state notes not adequately guaranteed.[26] The federal paper was not worth much more than the state paper at any rate.

It is doubtful that the total amount of currency issued in 1913 and 1914 will ever be accurately computed. The federal government alone increased currency in circulation from about 110 million pesos during the late Díaz regime to almost 222 million by April, 1914.[27] By legislative decree the Constitutionalists authorized themselves to issue 5 million pesos in April, 1913 (Emisión de Monclova), and 25 million more nine months later (Emisión del Ejército Constitucionalista).[28] Unauthorized printing by other rebel chieftains was tremendous and by conservative estimate total currency in Mexico trebled or quadrupled. What is certain, however, is that the profusion of paper currency, not backed by metallic reserves, exacerbated the inflationary spiral already in evidence by the late summer of 1913.[29]

The printing of paper money, subjected to the most generous of analyses, was simply an expedient. The federal treasury still had to be shored up from either internal or external sources, or both. In the country itself the regime tapped every potential source that it could devise. The nation's banks provided the government with 46.5 million pesos,[30] the Banco Nacional and the Banco de Londres y México being the largest two contributors. There is some question concerning whether the loans were forced or were voluntary. Although William Bain Mitchell, general manager of the Banco de

24. Ibid., February 12, 1914.
25. Hamm to Bryan, December 16, 1913, RDS, 812.00/10406.
26. Torres Gaitán, *Política Monetaria Mexicana*, p. 106.
27. Ernesto Lobato López, *El Crédito en México: Esbozo Histórico Hasta 1925* (Mexico: Fondo de Cultura Económica, 1945), p. 255.
28. Torres Gaitán, *Política Monetaria Mexicana*, p. 109.
29. Raul Ortiz Mena, "Moneda y Crédito," in *México: 50 Años de Revolución*, 4:83-92. There is no indication that the administration ever considered price controls or other stringent government measures as a means of stemming inflation.
30. Lobato López, *El Crédito en Mexico*, p. 257.

Londres y México, testified many years later before a United States Senate hearing that the loans from his institution were coerced,[31] there is little contemporary evidence that the majority of banks objected strenuously.[32]

In addition to bank loans, Huerta broadened and deepened the tax structure to make up some of the gap between revenues and expenditures. He felt that this measure was necessary because some American corporations had stopped paying their taxes altogether once Woodrow Wilson's attitude toward the regime became clear.[33] To compensate Huerta raised the import tariff on most goods by 50 percent and doubled the stamp tax.[34] In addition, a few new export taxes were enacted, such as the 3 percent levy put on coffee in the winter of 1913-14.[35] A number of the states increased old taxes and instituted new property and real estate taxes so that by a transfer of funds they might be able to help the federal government out of its financial doldrums.[36] And in November, with the most dramatic tax measure of all, Huerta decreed a 15 percent tax on all bank deposits.[37] The new capital levy was less a symbol of changing social attitudes than a desperation measure to bring in funds.

The tax revenues were supplemented by a wide array of forced loans. Both Mexican corporations and foreign nationals felt the burden of these special assessments, first in small amounts, and then larger ones. The regime levied an assessment of 12,500 pesos against the American Smelting and Refining Company in Monterrey, 10,000 pesos against the Monterrey Steel Company, and 7,500 pesos against the Waters-Pierce Company.[38] The leading residents of Saltillo, after being held in the government palace for almost seven hours, decided that they could donate 100,000 pesos.[39] The merchants of Progreso, Yucatán, "contributed" 30,000 after being threatened with possible

31. Testimony of William Bain Mitchell, *Fall Committee Hearings*, 1:686.

32. Mitchell's position is corroborated in McCaleb, *Present and Past Banking in Mexico*, pp. 215-16.

33. Testimony of Edward L. Doheny, *Fall Committee Hearings*, 1:277.

34. Bernstein, *The Mexican Mining Industry*, p. 97.

35. Lind to Bryan, February 24, 1914, RDS, 812.00/10965.

36. Alberto Razgudo, governor of Sinaloa, to Secretaría de Gobernación, November 28, 1913, AGN/RSG, Gobernadores de Estados, Asuntos Varios.

37. Lind to Bryan, November 3, 1913, RDS, 812.00/10121. The large majority of depositors who had not yet taken their savings out of the country did so promptly after the November decree.

38. Bernstein, *The Mexican Mining Industry*, p. 97.

39. Sanford, vice-consul, to Wilson, consul, March 10, 1913, F.O. 115/1738, fol. 261.

damage to their businesses if they refused,[40] and Wells-Fargo was tapped for an enormous 750,000 late in the year.[41] Upon occasion the threats were less pre-emptive and more veiled. A local commander, pleading government bankruptcy, would merely suggest that his troops would have to be withdrawn, leaving the city to the mercy of the rebels, until a substantial subvention was made by the local businessmen. The persuasiveness of the argument was generally dependent on the reputation of the proximate rebel general. But the forced loans took their toll. As Captain W. A. Burnside noted in one of his frequent understatements, "the loans are not increasing the popularity of the Huerta government." [42]

More important than the internal efforts at raising funds were the long and complicated negotiations for securing foreign loans. Huerta initiated the procedure when he dispatched Minister of Finance Toribio Esquivel Obregón to Congress to plead the government case.[43] The request for authorization became a political football, the main issues being lost in the scrimmage between government supporters and opponents. The government, through the ministry of finance, argued that the money would be used for paying off previous debts, paying interest on loans, preserving building projects already initiated, subsidizing the railroads, initiating irrigation projects, and making port improvements.[44] But almost one-third of the amount requested was marked for prosecution of the war, and as a result Constitutionalist supporters and sympathizers put up a good fight on the floor of Congress. Seven weeks passed before a grudging legislature authorized the administration to secure a loan of 200 million pesos at an interest rate not exceeding 6 percent.

While the congressional debate was still hot, Huerta, anticipating ultimate victory, began to negotiate for the loan in France and England. Time, he realized, was crucial because a previous loan for almost 41 million pesos, negotiated by President Madero with Speyer and Company of New York, was coming due on June 10.[45] If the Mexican government defaulted on the repayment of the Speyer loan,

---

40. O'Shaughnessy to Bryan, January 20, 1914, RDS, 812.00/10618.
41. Lind to Bryan, December 15, 1913, RDS, 812.00/10205.
42. Summary of Military Events, November 27 to December 3, 1913, Burnside Reports, December 3, 1913.
43. Article 72 of the Constitution of 1857 stipulated the necessity of congressional approval for all loans.
44. *Diario de los Debates,* May 8, 1913.
45. James Speyer to John Bassett Moore, May 1, 1913, RDS, 812.00/7545.

the new loan would be almost impossible to secure.[46] Huerta's agent in Europe, Luis León de la Barra, the Mexican financial commissioner and brother of the minister of foreign relations, had a difficult time convincing potential European creditors to extend the loan. Carranza's confidential agent in Washington, Roberto V. Pesqueira, issued a public statement early in May declaring that the Constitutionalists did not recognize the validity of any loan negotiated by the usurping government and therefore would not feel obliged to repay it upon their seizure of the government.[47] At approximately the same time a young, articulate Constitutionalist spokesman José Vasconcelos was dispatched to London to propagandize against the loan.[48] Miguel Díaz Lombardo assumed a similar function in Paris.[49] But in the last analysis the lure of handsome profits won out over the polished rhetoric of the Constitutionalist spokesmen. The movement in northern Mexico was not yet strong and Luis de la Barra was willing to settle for a compromise: some of the money would be extended at once and the rest at the option of the creditors would flow later.

On June 8, 1913, the Mexican representative in Paris signed a loan for £20 million sterling with the Banque de Paris et du Pays Bas representing a group of French, German, English, and United States financiers.[50] Only £6 million sterling (approximately 60 million pesos) were to be advanced immediately, however, with the creditors holding the option on the remaining 14 million. The 6 million was extended for a ten-year period with 38 percent of Mexico's import duties pledged as security.[51] The option, if extended, would carry the same terms.[52]

46. The shaky status of the Mexican economy at this time is detailed most graphically in Toribio Esquivel Obregón's report to the Congress in April. See *Diario de los Debates,* April 3, 1914.

47. Circular de don Robert V. Pesqueira, May 9, 1913, *DHRM,* 1:27-28.

48. F. González Gante to Venustiano Carranza, May 11, 1913, *DHRM,* 1:31-32.

49. In May he wrote to Carranza soliciting financial support for his mission and arguing that "es pues casi tan importante en estos momentos la lucha contra el empréstito como la lucha contra los cañones" (Díaz Lombardo to Carranza, May 13, 1913, *DHRM,* 1:42).

50. The banking syndicate, in addition to the Banque de Paris et du Pays Bays, included Grenfel and Co., Henry Schroeder and Co. of London, Credit Lyonnaise, Societé General, Banque Francaise of Paris, and the New York firms— J. P. Morgan and Co., Kuhn and Co., National City Bank, First National Bank, and Guaranty Trust Co. of New York.

51. Rafael Nieto, "La Deuda de Huerta," *El Universal,* April 4, 1921, p. 3.

52. At the time the loan was made, it was rumored that José Ives Limantour, Díaz's famous minister of finance then residing in Paris, had been influential in helping to secure the loan for Huerta. Although the government in Mexico City promptly denied that Limantour had assisted in any way, the Constitutionalists

President Huerta advertised the loan as a great victory for his government. It was clear evidence, he argued somewhat theatrically, that in spite of the continued hostility of the United States, the leading powers in Europe had full confidence in his regime and he would shortly be able to prove them correct in this assessment. But in purely economic terms the loan meant little. Forty-one million pesos were paid immediately to Speyer and Company[53] and another 4 million were used to retire a note to the Banco Nacional de México. Of the remaining 15 million pesos, 7.5 million were owed to the National Railroad and a tremendous 6 million went to pay the commissions of various parties who had served as intermediaries during the negotiations.[54] The 1.5 million which actually went into the treasury scarcely sufficed to shore up the economy with troop payments alone taking 3.5 million pesos a month.[55] The government's monthly deficit by August had reached some 6 million pesos.[56]

In the late summer and early fall Huerta began campaigning hard for the next installment of the loan—50 million pesos to be extended by the end of the year. But at the same time the Constitutionalist representatives in Europe intensified their campaign, and on this occasion the series of military victories in northern Mexico gave added substance to the arguments which they offered.[57] With the dissolution of Congress and the ever-increasing hostility of the United States, the European bankers listened to their exhortations carefully. Huerta dispatched a new minister of finance Adolfo de la Lama to Paris to press the government case but his powers of persuasion were severely circumscribed by the problematic political and military

---

were apparently convinced otherwise because upon their victory Limantour's name appeared on the list of those who were to be tried under the law of January, 1862. See Salvador Alvarado to C. General Subsecretario Encargado del Despacho de Guerra y Marina, November 12, 1914, AHDN, Cancelados, Exp. XI/III/104-1. I have been unable to confirm Limantour's participation in the loan negotiations, but it is not unlikely that because of the great respect he enjoyed in European financial circles, he was consulted by the bankers before the loan was extended.

53. The 41 million pesos were never actually extended to Huerta as the European bankers had agreed with James Speyer that this portion of the loan would pass directly to him.

54. García Naranjo, *Memorias*, 7:133.

55. Summary of Military Events from July 15 to July 22, 1913, Burnside Reports, July 22, 1913.

56. Stronge to Grey, August 29, 1913, F.O. 115/1741, fol. 34.

57. Vasconcelos to Carranza, August 29, 1913, *DHRM*, 1:118-22. Minister of Finance Toribio Esquivel Obregón believed that the efforts of the Constitutionalists in Europe were decisive in the final decision of the bankers. See O'Shaughnessy to Bryan, transmitting report of Esquivel Obregón, October 13, 1913, RDS, 812.51/95.

situation at home. In addition, the French government, anticipating a default, urged the bankers not to advance any additional funds.[58] While awaiting a decision Huerta once again was reduced to expedients to keep his government afloat. General Ignacio Morelos Zaragoza, the military governor of Tamaulipas, sent Mexico City 50,000 pesos from revenues he collected in his state.[59] A government concession to the Mexican Express Company yielded a quick 100,000 pesos and a discount on tobacco stamps to El Buentono Cigar Company brought in 500,000 pesos.[60] Huerta also made the decision to purchase all government operating supplies on credit whenever credit could be obtained. But he still missed a military payroll in December, and rumors of army defections spread through the capital.

At the end of the year the European bankers informed the government in Mexico City that they had decided not to exercise their option on the remainder of the loan. Huerta, in a monumental decision, retaliated by suspending payment on the interest on the national debt for a period of six months. The president believed that he really had no choice. His position was remarkably similar to that of Benito Juárez fifty-two years earlier. He could not pay his army nor his civil servants. Private creditors within the country, both domestic and foreign, were clamoring for repayment. As the treasury was drained for arms and ammunition shipments, public works projects and plans for reform had to be laid aside. If the remainder of the loan was not going to be extended anyway, why worry about the interest payments for the time being? The Mexico City press supported the moratorium as a life or death measure.[61] But the decision, announced to the world in January, 1914, was far-reaching indeed. Politically it marked the beginning of Huerta's isolation from his former staunch supporters in Europe. They realized that Huerta would be no more able to pay his debts in June than he was in January. Even some of Huerta's own diplomatic staff in Europe began to desert him. Miguel Covarrubias, for example, who had served Huerta in London for six months, offered his services to Juan Sánchez Azcona, the new Constitutionalist representative on the Continent.[62] The Constitutionalists accepted

58. Myron T. Herrick, minister in Paris, to Bryan, December 17, 1913, RDS, 812.51/100.
59. *El País*, January 31, 1914.
60. Canada to Bryan, December 12, 1913, RDS, 812.51/99.
61. *El País*, January 17, 1914.
62. G. Fernández MacGregor to Secretaría de Relaciones Exteriores, January 21, 1914, AREM, Miguel Covarrubias, Su Expediente Personal, L-E 375, Leg. 6; Circular de don Venustiano Carranza, January 6, 1914, AREM, Juan Sánchez Azcona, Su Expediente Personal, L-E 1002, Leg. 1.

Covarrubias and sent him back to London to work for the rebel cause.[63]

At the same time, the decision of the European bankers strengthened the hand of the United States. Woodrow Wilson had been trying to isolate Huerta for months, and although Wilsonian diplomacy in Europe had failed on this score, Mexico's financial dilemma effected the same end. Finally, there simply was no place else to turn for financial help. All measures to strengthen the economy had faltered under the strain of war. The government presses in Mexico City worked overtime churning out more and more paper money, and early in 1914 more and more of the states followed suit, printing scrip with which local officials paid federal troops stationed in their territory.[64] But financial collapse was imminent and the panic set in. The peso exchange rate was down to thirty-four cents in January and two months later had reached twenty-nine cents. Arms manufacturers who previously had demanded payment on delivery now asked for cash before the shipment left their factories.[65]

Huerta had enjoyed the support of the business and banking communities when he assumed office in February, 1913, because they believed that he would be able to restore order and financial stability. Foreign investors, hoping for commercial advantages, also had pledged their cooperation. But a year later, Huerta had lost the support of the business community, the industrialists, and the land-owners because he could not provide them with the guarantees they believed they had the right to expect.[66] The regime did not collapse because of its failure to obtain the remainder of the loan in January, 1914, but the economic crises meshed with the diplomatic and military ones during the next six months. By the spring the administration was sinking into a decline from which there could be no return.

63. Carranza to Covarrubias, February 28, 1914, AREM, Miguel Covarrubias, Su Expediente Personal, L-E 375, Leg. 6.

64. Lind to Bryan, January 26, 1914, RDS, 812.00/10965.

65. Robert Lansing to Gregory, July 2, 1914, Records of the Department of Justice, File 157013-a-7 (hereafter cited as RDJ with appropriate information).

66. As early as late summer reports from Mexico City indicated that Huerta had lost the support of the monied elements in the country. Leebeus R. Wilfrey to General Leonard Wood, July 29, 1913, RDS, 812.00/8498.

CHAPTER 10

The Collapse of a Regime

VICTORIANO HUERTA AND HIS FAMILY spent New Year's Day, 1914, in Popotla with a few close friends. There was little to celebrate, however, as the wars on both the military and diplomatic fronts were going badly for the government in Mexico City; moreover just a few weeks before the bankers in Europe had made their decision not to extend the remainder of the loan. The regime somehow managed to hold on for another six and a half months but there were few moments for government optimism between January and July. It was a period of cumulative decline and decay during which the country seemed to drift aimlessly into anarchy.

190

Constitutionalist strategy early in 1914 called for a concerted three-pronged drive to Mexico City. With the northern tier of Mexican states secure, Torreón, captured earlier by Pancho Villa but subsequently lost, carried top military priority. The city was not only an important railroad center in the middle of the cotton belt, but was the logical stop on the way to Zacatecas and eventually Mexico City. Villa began his drive south from Chihuahua on March 16, surrounded by a command staff including some of the most famous guerrilla leaders of the Revolution: Felipe Angeles, José Trinidad Rodríguez, Maclovio Herrera, Tomás Urbina, and Eugenio Aguirre Benavides. His 8,200 men had ample arms and ammunition and twenty-nine cannon,[1] for a month earlier President Wilson, at the constant prodding of John Lind, William Bayard Hale, Secretary Bryan, and Venustiano Carranza, had lifted the United States arms embargo.[2] Almost immediately the Constitutionalist command staff were flooded with offers of more arms and ammunition than they could profitably use or possibly pay for.[3] The diplomatic and military wars had merged to Villa's advantage at a propitious time, but the city of Torreón would not be an easy prize as General José Refugio Velasco had been preparing his defenses for months. Preliminary skirmishes occurred on March 20 and 21 at two federal outposts—Mapimí and Tlahualilo. In both cases the federals were forced to retreat back into the more protected environs of Torreón itself. A similar precursory engagement at Gómez Palacio, slightly to the northwest of the city, turned out differently as it was Villa who was forced to pull back; he was able to retake it the next day, however. The jousting continued for three more days with each side testing the other. It was not until the evening of the twenty-sixth that Villa's troops entered the city itself.

The Battle of Torreón lasted for five days and not since the Decena Trágica had such a large population center been witness to such ravages of war. The house-to-house fighting exposed noncombatants

1. R. González Garza, P. Ramos Romero, and J. Pérez Rul, *La Batalla de Torreón* (Mexico: Secretaría de Educación Pública [1964?]), p. 50.
2. Bryan to Wilson, August 13, 1913, Wilson-Bryan Correspondence; Hale to Bryan, November 12, 1913, RDS, 812.00/9685; Carranza to Henry Allen Tupper, October 31, 1913, *DHRM*, 1:144-45.
3. General Merifield to Villa, February 5, 1914, AREM, L-E 760; Ernesto Fernández Artéaga to General E. Aguirre Benavides, February 5, 1914, ibid.; J. F. Sepúlveda to General Pablo González, February 6, 1914, ibid.; Venustiano Carranza to Gil Herrera [Hopkins], February 8, 1914, ibid.; Félix Sommerfeld to Pancho Villa, February 18, 1914, ibid.

to cross fire. Mortars leveled sections of the city and scores of burning buildings lit up the night skies. On the afternoon of April 1, Villa withdrew his troops from the city temporarily. Federal burial details had to cover their faces with handkerchiefs to protect themselves from the stench. But just before dusk Villa had Felipe Angeles lay down a heavy artillery barrage. The result was more devastating than he knew at the time because the same night General Velasco began making plans to withdraw. The following afternoon, in the middle of a heavy dust storm, Velasco and his troops executed their retreat and Villa moved into the city a few hours later.[4] The toll on both sides was high. The government troops suffered 1,000 deaths, 2,200 wounded, and lost another 1,500 through desertions and 300 taken prisoner. Constitutionalist losses were less but nevertheless substantial: 550 deaths and 1,150 wounded.[5] Because Velasco's retreat was well planned and well executed few arms and little ammunition were left behind. However, 150,000 bales of cotton remained in Torreón after the evacuation, much to the chagrin of the textile manufacturers throughout the country. Many of them were forced to cease operations in the spring as a result. But more importantly Villa's victory graphically exposed the vulnerabilities of the federal war machine.

If diplomatic, economic, and military pressures all coalesced to the advantage of the Constitutionalists with the capture of Torreón on April 2, 1914, this was but a faint shadow of what the regime in Mexico City had to look forward to one week later. The stage for the next drama was not the north central region, where Villa became temporarily bogged down because of difficulties with his First Chief, but the northeast, where the Constitutionalists were also driving toward the capital. After a disappointing first year the rebels under General Pablo González, Francisco Murguía, and Jesús Carranza, brother of the First Chief, began to give a better accounting of themselves in early 1914. Late in March, at the same time that Villa had laid seige to Torreón, the rebels of General Luis Caballeros began to march on the city of Tampico, Mexico's second-ranking port.[6] During the last

4. Guzmán, *Memorias de Pancho Villa*, pp. 341-52.
5. González Garza, Romero, and Rul, *La Batalla de Torreón*, p. 52.
6. The following summation of the Tampico incident, except when other references are cited, is based on Robert E. Quirk, *An Affair of Honor: Woodrow Wilson and the Occupation of Veracruz* (New York: W. W. Norton and Co., 1967), pp. 1-33. Pertinent documentation in the foreign relations ministry, not available to Quirk when the research for the book was completed, has subsequently been made available and offers basis for a more detailed evaluation of the Mexican position.

few days of the month federals and rebels began to probe each other's outer defenses with mortar and shrapnel. Residents and merchants in the city initiated preparations for the impending battle and United States naval officers stationed in the harbor offered to evacuate foreign nationals if they decided to leave. The rebel attack began in earnest on April 5. General Ignacio Morelos Zaragoza, in charge of the city's defenses, utilized two government gunboats—the *Veracruz* and the *Zaragoza*—to good advantage, firing shrapnel shells on the enemy positions in the hills surrounding the port. Two days later the rebels tried to enter the city at the Iturbide Bridge but were driven back. A second attempt at the same location on April 8 was similarly unsuccessful as Morelos Zaragoza had received reinforcements from Veracruz and drove the attackers off.

On the morning of April 9, Captain Ralph T. Earle of the U.S.S. *Dolphin,* stationed in the harbor, ordered his assistant paymaster, Ensign Charles Copp, to take a whaleboat into the canal to a warehouse where gasoline could be secured. The warehouse was within a hundred yards of the Iturbide Bridge, the point at which the rebels twice had attempted to enter the city. The small landing party reached the warehouse dock without incident, but as they were loading the gasoline aboard the whaleboat they were accosted by a small detachment of Mexican soldiers of the Tamaulipas state guard under the command of Colonel Ramón H. Hinojosa. After being briefly detained, the sailors were ordered to march through the streets to Hinojosa's headquarters where they were reprimanded about being in a restricted area without a special pass; but they were then released and allowed to finish loading the gasoline and return to their ship.

Rear Admiral Henry T. Mayo, commander of the United States naval forces at Tampico, was on board the *Dolphin* when Captain Earle was informed of the incident. Not knowing that the sailors had already been released, Mayo ordered Captain Earle to proceed to the office of United States Consul Clarence Miller and with him to go to the headquarters of General Morelos Zaragoza for the purpose of lodging a strong protest. General Morelos Zaragoza had no knowledge of the incident until the Americans arrived, but immediately apologized, attributing the incident to the stupidity of Colonel Hinojosa. He further promised that Hinojosa would be punished and immediately issued an order for his arrest.[7] Consul Miller and Captain

7. Aureliano Blanquet to Secretaría de Relaciones Exteriores, April 10, 1914, transmitting report of Morelos Zaragoza, AREM, L-E 796, Leg. 13.

Earle believed that the incident had been closed but Admiral Mayo decided to press for advantage. Several of the arrested sailors had been removed from the whaleboat which, Mayo contended, was flying the American flag.[8] This incident was of sufficient magnitude to warrant a more official and elaborate apology. Accordingly, later in the afternoon of April 9, Mayo, without first clearing his plan with Washington or with Veracruz (where his commanding officer, Admiral Frank F. Fletcher, was stationed), submitted a list of demands to the Mexican commander:

> I do not need to tell you that taking men from a boat flying the American flag is a hostile act not to be excused. I have already received your verbal message of regret that this event has happened and your statement that it was committed by an ignorant officer. But the responsibility for hostile acts cannot be avoided by the plea of ignorance.[9]

The demands which accompanied the note included a formal disavowal of the action brought personally to the admiral by suitable members of the general's staff, assurance that Colonel Hinojosa would receive severe punishment, and, most importantly, the hoisting of the American flag at some prominent place on shore and the firing of a twenty-one gun salute to it. All of the demands were to be met within twenty-four hours. General Morelos Zaragosa informed Mayo that he was without power to act on such matters without specific instructions, reminded the admiral that he had already ordered the punishment of Hinojosa, and sent the list of demands to his superiors in Mexico City.[10]

President Wilson's receipt of the news from Tampico occasioned no great alarm; Admiral Mayo's demands were deemed reasonable and would receive White House endorsement. The president asked Secretary Bryan to make strong representations to the Huerta government through Chargé Nelson O'Shaughnessy.[11] In Mexico City, however, the news resulted in much consternation with Huerta receiving contradictory advice from his ministers. Because of a delay in the original communication from Morelos Zaragoza, subsequent

8. Daniels to Bryan, transmitting report of Mayo, April 14, 1914, RDS, 812.00/11510.

9. Ibid.

10. Aureliano Blanquet to Secretaría de Relaciones Exteriores, April 10, 1914, transmitting report of Morelos Zaragoza, AREM, L-E 796, Leg. 13.

11. Wilson to Bryan, April 10, 1914, RDS, 812.00/11483.

delays in decoding the message, and still further delays in forwarding the dispatch from the ministry of war to the ministry of foreign relations, the twenty-four-hour period had almost expired when Huerta first heard of the arrest of the American sailors.[12] In addition, there was a major inconsistency in the story as interpreted by Admiral Mayo and by General Morelos Zaragoza. The former maintained that the whaleboat had been flying the United States flag while the latter categorically denied it.[13] Huerta would make no major decision until he had all of the facts.

Chargé O'Shaughnessy was first informed of the Tampico incident by Undersecretary of Foreign Relations Roberto A. Esteva Ruiz.[14] Esteva Ruiz wrote him that after the brief detention of the sailors, the commander in Tampico had extended every courtesy, to the point of arresting the offending officer, but he added that the error should be completely understandable to reasonable men. "It is perfectly explicable that a military officer who sees uniformed individuals arrive at a place he is guarding should detain them until he determines whether or not the presence of those individuals is justified."[15] Consequently, the undersecretary asked O'Shaughnessy to telegraph Tampico asking that the ultimatum be withdrawn.[16] Still without official instructions from Washington, O'Shaughnessy proceeded to call on Huerta. The Mexican president was even more adamant than Esteva Ruiz had been. He insisted that no offense to the United States flag had been committed. He would not accede to the demands but did agree that since the United States contended that the whaleboat was flying the American flag, a full investigation should be made. O'Shaughnessy forwarded the account of his meeting with Huerta to the secretary of state and felt constrained to add: "I do not understand such an ultimatum being issued without superior authority in view of the tense situation now existing."[17]

The situation remained static for the several days. The only flexibility demonstrated by either side was Washington's agreement

12. Secretaría de Relaciones Exteriores to Secretaría de Guerra y Marina, April 10, 1914, AREM, L-E 796, Leg. 13.
13. Aureliano Blanquet to Secretaría de Relaciones Exteriores, April 10, 1914, transmitting report of Morelos Zaragoza, AREM, L-E 796, Leg. 13.
14. The Secretary of Foreign Relations José López Portillo y Rojas was not in the capital when the news arrived. He had gone to Guadalajara for Holy Week.
15. Esteva Ruiz to O'Shaughnessy, April 10, 1914, AREM, Desocupación, III/252(73:72)-353.
16. Ibid.
17. O'Shaughnessy to Bryan, April 10, 1914, RDS, 812.00/11484.

to extend the deadline. But the Mexican position remained firm. To give in to the demands, the foreign ministry declared, would be tantamount to accepting the sovereignty of another nation over Mexican territory.[18] As the regime's military power continued to evaporate it became increasingly sensitive to matters of national honor. But privately many of Huerta's advisors were becoming jittery. On April 11, the Mexican chargé in Washington, Angel Algara, urged Huerta to salute the American flag as a means of avoiding still greater difficulty.[19] Two days later he reiterated his pleas, adding that the United States had already ordered a large fleet to Tampico.[20] The Mexican military attaché in Washington agreed with Algara and also urged the government in Mexico City to submit to the demands.[21] The first secretary of the Mexican embassy advised that a salute to the American flag would avoid serious injuries for both countries.[22] The British chargé in Mexico, at the request of the United States government, reminded Huerta that the United States government had saluted the flags of France, Brazil, and Spain in instances of a breach of international law by low-ranking officials.[23] But Huerta would hear none of it. He would not allow that the United States had the right to intervene in Mexico's internal affairs in such a blatant manner. But he also had something else in mind.[24]

Huerta found in the bellicosity of the United States a chance to salvage some of what his army had lost on the battlefields of Torreón. His entire reaction to the constant pressure of the United States stemmed from this military defeat. As the days passed he became increasingly intransigent. He had convinced himself that his only chance was to play on Mexican nationalism. If he could appeal properly to the Mexican sense of honor, he might be able to shore up public support for his steadily weakening regime. Meanwhile, he decided to wait for the most opportune moment. For the time he would keep news of the Tampico incident out of the press so that

18. López Portillo to Angel Algara, April 12, 1914, AREM, L-E 796, Leg. 13.
19. Algara to Secretaría de Relaciones Exteriores, April 11, 1914, AREM, L-E 796, Leg. 13.
20. Algara to Sec. de Relaciones Exteriores, April 14, 1914, AREM, L-E 796, Leg. 13.
21. Avalos to Secretaría de Guerra y Marina, no date, AREM, L-E 796, Leg. 13.
22. José Castellot to Huerta, no date, *DHRM*, 2:18.
23. Sir Cecil Spring Rice to Grey, April 27, 1914, F.O. 115/1793, fol. 250.
24. O'Shaughnessy to Bryan, April 12, 1914, RDS, 812.00/11485. Among the proposals considered were simultaneous salutes by both countries and, if that were not acceptable, a written guarantee on the part of the United States that the Mexican salute would be returned properly.

his enemies in the north could not capitalize on the news themselves. On April 16 he told O'Shaughnessy that he had done everything he felt obliged to do in connection with the Tampico incident.[25] He continued to base his refusal to do more on the grounds that the whaleboat carrying the sailors was not flying the American flag.[26] But the time to make the public announcement was approaching much more rapidly than Huerta himself imagined.

In Washington President Wilson, after conferring with his cabinet and ranking members of Congress in both parties, was preparing a drastic action. On the afternoon of April 14, the Atlantic fleet was ordered into Mexican waters to reinforce the vessels already there under the command of Admiral Mayo at Tampico and Admiral Fletcher at Veracruz. For the next several days the diplomatic correspondence between the two capitals kept the telegraphers occupied but accomplished nothing of substance. As Huerta was informed of the military preparations being undertaken by the United States, he ordered his federal army to begin bracing themselves for a naval assault on Tampico.[27] But a seemingly unrelated event changed the site of the operation south to Veracruz.

In the late fall of 1913, when the United States arms embargo was still in effect, Huerta decided to try to circumvent the regulations by engaging a team of smugglers north of the Río Grande. One of these, León Raast, the Russian vice-consul in Mexico City, traveled to New York in November, purchased a cargo of arms from the Colt Automatic Arms Company in Hartford, Connecticut, and arranged for the shipment of these and some additional arms which had already been secured by other means. In order to avoid the embargo restrictions the arms were not sent directly to Mexico but went first to Odessa, Russia, and then to Hamburg, Germany, where they were placed aboard the S.S. *Ypiranga*, a steamer of the Hamburg-American line.[28] In early April the *Ypiranga* lifted anchor for Veracruz with a huge cargo of arms and ammunition in its hold.[29]

25. O'Shaughnessy to Bryan, April 17, 1914, RDS, 812.00/11540.
26. *Diario de los Debates,* April 21, 1914.
27. Secretaría de Guerra y Marina to Secretaría de Relaciones Exteriores, April 20, 1914, AREM, L-E 796, Leg. 13.
28. The story of the purchase and shipment of this controversial cargo is contained in Michael C. Meyer, "The Arms of the *Ypiranga*," *Hispanic American Historical Review* 50 (August 1970): 543-56.
29. The cargo manifest revealed 10,000 cases of .30-caliber (central fire) cartridges; 4,000 cases of seven-millimeter cartridges; 250 cases of .44-caliber cartridges; 500 cases of carbines (50 in each case); 1,000 cases of 14/30 carbines; 20 rapid-fire machine guns; 717 cases of shrapnel; 1,333 cases of rifle ammunition; 78 cases of miscellaneous ammunition, and one battery lunette.

On April 18, William W. Canada, the American consul in Veracruz, reported to the secretary of state that the *Ypiranga*, with arms for Huerta, was scheduled to arrive in Veracruz three days later.[30] In a more urgent message on April 20, the consul advised that the ship would arrive the following morning and would begin discharging its huge cargo at Pier 4. The arms and ammunition, he continued, would immediately be loaded aboard three trains of ten cars each and rushed to Mexico City. The astute consular agent tried to buy a little additional time for his superiors in Washington by urging the captain of the Ward Line steamer, *Mexico,* then berthed at Pier 4, to remain in dock as long as possible.[31]

In the early morning of April 21, Secretary Bryan telephoned the White House, informed the president of the impending crisis, and received his instructions. Secretary of the Navy Josephus Daniels was to order Rear Admiral Frank Fletcher to seize the Veracruz customhouse to prevent the landing of the arms from the *Ypiranga*. The invasion of Veracruz began shortly after 11:00 A.M. on April 21. Marines and bluejackets from the *Utah,* the *Prairie,* and the *Florida* approached the shore in small landing craft. At the same time Consul Canada telephoned General Gustavo Maass, commander of the federal forces in Veracruz, informing him of the impending attack and requesting his cooperation. Maass answered that he was bound to repel the American forces if they attempted to make a landing.[32] But General Maass's position was almost hopeless. Many of the troops under his command had already been sent north to reinforce the federal garrison of General Morelos Zaragoza at Tampico and those that remained at his disposal were untrained and haphazardly armed. Some of them had been pulled out of prison only a few days before to fill in for the more experienced troops sent to Tampico.[33] Within the hour the Americans had taken possession of the customhouse, the telegraph office, the post office, and the railroad terminal. President Wilson had been led to believe, by John Lind and others, that the city could be turned over to him without resistance, but the Mexicans, including many civilians fought and many died. Noncombatants of

30. Canada to Bryan, April 18, 1914, RDS, 812.00/11547.
31. Canada to Bryan, April 20, 1914, RDS, 812.00/11564.
32. Maass to Secretaría de Relaciones Exteriores, April 24, 1914, AREM, Desocupación, III/252(73:72)/353. The full report of General Maass, prepared almost a month later, is contained in Maass to Secretaría de Guerra y Marina, May 17, 1914, AHDN, XI/481.5/315.
33. Quirk, *An Affair of Honor,* p. 90.

both sexes and young cadets from the naval academy were among the casualties. General Maass was forced to pull back to the more defensible confines of Tijería, a few miles inland, where he laid plans to try to forestall any American march on Mexico City.[34]

President Huerta may have been surprised at the place of the American assault but he most certainly was not surprised by the fact of intervention. He was ready to try to turn the intervention against the invaders and immediately set out to secure both international and domestic support. Secretary of Foreign Relations López Portillo y Rojas did not need a team of international jurists to advise him that the United States had just flagrantly violated Article XXI of the Treaty of Guadalupe-Hidalgo (1848), which provided for the pacific settlement of all future disputes between the two countries without resort to arms. He at once ordered the Mexican chargé in Washington to make the most strenuous representations at the State Department.[35] At the same time the Mexican charges from both Tampico and Veracruz were disclosed to the world press, replete with all the details of the fight for control of the latter port city. Huerta also ordered that circular telegrams be sent to all of the governments with whom his regime maintained diplomatic relations briefly outlining the Mexican position.[36] But Huerta knew that mere exhortation and appeal to the sanctity of treaty obligations would, by themselves, accomplish little. He concentrated on obtaining domestic support, allowing his Congress to speak for him.

The deputies in Congress needed little prompting to go on record with some of the most scathing denunciations ever noted in the *Diario de los Debates*. The attitude expressed by Deputy Múzquiz Blanco was not atypical:

> Gentlemen, at this time I have only curses on my lips, rage in my heart, and blows on my fists for the blond thieves who struck at Veracruz with a cowardly naval assault. One feels

34. There is only slight evidence that the Americans ever planned to move on the capital. Lind had discussed it several times but apparently the idea was not seriously entertained in Washington. The Mexican government did not know this, however, and both military and consular reports indicated a genuine concern. See as examples, Secretaría de Guerra y Marina to Espinosa de los Monteros, April 8, 1914, AEM, vol. 2, fol. 7; and Oficial Mayor de Relaciones Exteriores to Secretaría de Guerra y Marina, April 28, 1914, *DHRM*, 3:15-16.

35. Subsecretaría de Relaciones Exteriores to Encargado de Negocios, Washington, April 21, 1914, AREM, Desocupación, III/252(73:72)/353.

36. Circular a los Enviados Extraordinarios y Ministros Plenipotenciarios, April 21, 1914, *DHRM*, 2:36-37.

nausea at seeing the beaches of Veracruz stained with Yankee blood. And no matter how much was let, it would not repay a single drop of the blood of the Niños Héroes of Chapultepec . . . . Who are these [Yankees]? The same ones, always the same ones, the eternal highwaymen, the eternal thieves; they are the same as those who blew up the *Maine,* the same that committed the crime of the Philippines; the same that committed the crime of Nicaragua; the same that committed the crime of Cuba; they are guilty of all of those crimes and today they begin the crime of Mexico.

(*A voice interrupts from the floor:* Death to the thieves of 1848!)[37]

The exhortations struck a responsive chord in the hearts of many Mexican nationalists. The newspapers in the capital contributed to the hysteria by reporting that the United States had already crossed the border in the north and had attacked other Mexican towns. Speakers throughout the country vied with one another in damnation of the United States and in praise of the tough and courageous stand that Huerta had taken. On street corners and in front of national monuments they urged retaliatory action. Mexican businessmen, to distinguish themselves from their American counterparts, began adorning their shops with the Mexican flag. As indignation swelled crowds took to the streets in the larger cities.[38] The George Washington statue in Mexico City, dedicated only two years earlier, was torn from its pedestal and dragged through the streets. A small bust of Father Hidalgo was put in its place. Shops owned by United States business-men were targets for brick throwing and occasional looting.[39] In Monterrey an angry mob ripped the American flag off of the consulate and burned it on the spot, but the Stars and Stripes, over which such furor had been raised in Tampico, suffered still greater indignities in Mexico City. Tied to the tail of a donkey it was used to sweep the streets at the *zócalo*. In Progreso and Mazatlán the crowds moved into the American residential areas, prompting great alarm but doing relatively little damage. United States citizens residing in rural areas began moving their families to the larger cities and a number were arrested by local authorities along the way.[40] But nowhere was the hysteria greater than in Tampico. When the United States navy pulled

37. *Diario de los Debates,* April 21, 1914.
38. Hohler to Grey, April 22, 1914, F.O. 115/1793, fols. 111-12.
39. Calero, *Un Decenio de Política Mexicana,* p. 148.
40. Burnside to Bryan, April 26, 1914, RDS, 812.00/11784.

out to join the invading fleet in Veracruz, distraught American citizens, fearing for their lives, took refuge in the Southern Hotel.[41] One bard among them took the opportunity to jot down some doggerel in his notebook:

> We were crowded in the Southern
>   Like a flock of frightened sheep.
> We had heard the news from Vera Cruz
>   And no one thought of sleep.
> For a crowd of fish-eyed Mexicans
>   Was thirsting for our gore
> And brickbats, stones and epithets
>   Were hurling against the door.
>   . . . .
> Our pickets on the Southern roof
>   Strove with distended ears
> To catch some sign of Mayo's men
>   Or hear the Jackies' cheers;
> But Daniels slept in Washington
>   And Bryan lectured peace.
> No hope for us that Uncle Sam
>   Would aid in our release.[42]

Within a few days after the invasion, student groups organized and offered their services to the government in defense of the fatherland,[43] as did a number of Mexican exiles in the United States.[44] Red Cross units were organized in the capital and the leadership of the Unión Obrera Mexicana asked its members to lay aside their differences with Huerta and come to the aid of the country. The railroads promised the government 150,000 men if it wanted them.[45] Factory workers began military drilling during their lunch hours. For the first time since he came to power Huerta had more recruits than he could actually use in the ranks of the federal army. But by far the most important private initiative was the formation of the Comité Civil de la Defensa

41. Statement of Facts Given to the People of the United States by 372 Tampico Refugees Aboard the S.S. *Esperanza* Lying in Quarantine in Galveston Harbor, no date, ABFC, Group T.

42. The Seige of Fort Fouts, Southern Hotel, Tampico, April 21, 1914, ABFC, Group T.

43. Miguel O. de Mendizabal to Subsecretaría de Relaciones Exteriores, April 23, 1914, AREM, L-E 797, Leg. 16.

44. Miguel E. Diebold to Secretaría de Guerra y Marina, April 21, 1914, AREM, L-E 784, Leg. 2.

45. *El Independiente*, April 22, 1914.

Nacional, organized by old Reyista party leader Samuel Espinosa de los Monteros. Shortly after the invasion, the committee began publication of a bulletin which urged all Mexicans to lay aside their internal differences and present a united front against the foreign aggressor.[46] The committee also notified the ministry of war that its full services were available to the government and offered specifically to send men to Mexico City to assume routine military jobs so that all available soldiers could be sent into the field.[47] Although the war ministry informed Espinosa de los Monteros that the Guardia Civil of Mexico City was already performing that particular function, he did agree to receive a group of civilian committee members for training in dynamite and sabotage should the Americans decide to move from the coast to the capital.[48] Throughout May new groups were organized and by the end of the month the organization had operations underway in the states of Veracruz, Michoacán, Puebla, Tlaxcala, Oaxaca, Chiapas, Mexico, Querétaro, and San Luis Potosí. The Veracruz group, understandably the most active, served the government as an intelligence network. The committee in that state was given free use of the National Telegraph to send their dispatches to Mexico City.[49] But the contributions of the Comité Civil de la· Defensa Nacional was negligible in the military sense. It served its most useful function as a molder of public opinion. Throughout May it saturated the country with propaganda sheets, stirring up support for the government.

With more public enthusiasm than he had ever previously enjoyed, Huerta moved into action to unify the country. He first asked his Congress for extraordinary powers in all matters of war, finance, and communications, and in the emotion charged atmosphere of April 21, the request was granted without serious debate.[50] With his expanded powers the president decreed a new amnesty law for all rebels who would lay down their arms within fifteen days and dispatched two confidants to carry the message, urging compliance, to the Constitutionalist headquarters in the north and the Zapatista headquarters

46. Boletín del Comité Civil de la Defensa Nacional, April 27, 1914, AEM, vol. 2, follows fol. 57.

47. Secretaría de Guerra y Marina to Espinosa de los Monteros, April 24, 1914, AEM, vol. 2, fol. 6.

48. Secretaría de Guerra y Marina to Espinosa de los Monteros, May 8, 1914, AEM, vol. 2, fol. 7.

49. Joaquín Beltrán, governor of Veracruz, to Espinosa de los Monteros, May 1, 1914, AEM, vol. 2, fol. 24.

50. *Diario de los Debates,* April 21, 1914.

in the south.[51] At the prompting of Querido Moheno, Huerta also agreed to release those few remaining congressmen still in jail from the mass arrests of the previous October.[52] Throughout the country military officers, following the president's lead, asked their rebel counterparts to join forces with them to expel the intruder from Mexican soil.[53] And as a final measure, Chargé Nelson O'Shaughnessy was handed his passports on April 22 and asked to leave the country as soon as possible.

Neither the Huerta government nor the Wilson government knew exactly what the Constitutionalist reaction to Veracruz would be. Both hoped for more than they ultimately received as the First Chief walked a miraculously narrow path between the two opposing factions. Carranza showed himself at his best in late April and early May. His approach was a clever one—he blamed Huerta for having deliberately provoked the assault at Veracruz but at the same time he vowed to fight to the end against the Americans if they persisted in their aggression.[54] Some of Carranza's commanders, however, were not so astute. With more bravado than common sense Constitutionalist General Pánfilo Natera answered General Medina Barrón's request for cooperation by arguing that the rebels themselves were strong enough to eject the Americans without allying themselves with the traitors in Mexico City.[55] Emiliano Zapata seemed to vacillate first moving in one direction and then the other. But Pancho Villa, perhaps because of a steadily growing schism with Venustiano Carranza or perhaps because he simply was not politically perceptive, refused to criticize the invasion at all.[56]

President Wilson had some fairly good evidence which he could have used to predict the Constitutionalist response to his invasion. When he toyed with the idea of sending troops into Mexico to cooperate with Carranza the previous fall, the First Chief's response

51. Subsecretaría de Relaciones Exteriores to Mendizabal, April 23, 1914, AREM, L-E 797, Leg. 16; Fernando Saldaña Galván and Luis Padilla Nervo to Secretaría de Relaciones Exteriores, May 7, 1914, AREM, L-E 797, Leg. 16; Womack, *Zapata*, pp. 185-86.

52. García Naranjo, *Memorias*, 7:282-83.

53. Joaquín Téllez to Alvaro Obregón, April 22, 1914, *DHRM*, 2:41; Luis Medina Barrón to Pánfilo Natera, April 23, 1914, *DHRM*, 2:53-54; T. Quintana to Pablo González, April 29, 1914, *DHRM*, 2:78.

54. Obregón to Téllez, April 22, 1914, *DHRM*, 2:42; Carranza to Huerta, no date, AREM, Desocupación, III/252(73:72)/353.

55. Natera to Medina Barrón, April 30, 1914, *DHRM*, 2:54-55.

56. Villa to Wilson, April 25, 1914, RDS, 812.00/12282.

had been firmly negative.[57] But it is possible that Wilson reckoned that
Carranza would assume a different posture when actually confronted
with the fact of intervention. He immediately asked George Carothers,
the American consul at Torreón, to determine the Constitutionalist
response.[58] Carranza's answer to the United States was not dissimilar
to his answer to Huerta. After listing for the American president his
well-known complaints against the regime in Mexico City, he concluded by charging that the military occupation of Veracruz was a
violation of Mexican sovereignty and, in addition, was an act completely disproportionate to the problem it was attempting to resolve.
As a consequence he demanded the immediate withdrawal of
American forces from Mexican territory.[59] In spite of Wilson's repeated
protestations that the occupation of Veracruz was an act against
Victoriano Huerta and not against the Mexican people, Carranza
refused to accept the subtle differentiation. The Constitutionalist position was most clearly articulated by Alvaro Obregón, who argued that
if the United States bombarded Mexican ports it was the nation that
suffered, not Huerta.[60]

The invasion of Veracruz by the United States created a situation
of immense complexity for all concerned. Huerta remained in power,
but the United States, in the face of an outraged Mexican public, a
cool reaction at home, and a less than friendly attitude from the
supposed beneficiaries in northern Mexico, was not of a mind to
pursue the military venture any further. But a precipitate withdrawal
would be a tantamount admission of error and Wilson was unwilling
to consider such action. Huerta, on the other hand, recognizing the
futility of any attempt to eject the Americans by force, also realized
that the public support engendered by the attack could quickly prove
ephemeral should he become engaged in a second war of attrition.
Because neither side found in the status quo any real hope of military
or diplomatic advantage, they agreed to sit down at the conference
table.[61]

57. Wilson to Bryan, September 13, 1913, Wilson-Bryan Correspondence;
Carranza to Pesqueira, January 30, 1914, AREM, L-E 760, Leg. 2.
58. Carothers to Carranza, April 22, 1914, AREM, Desocupación, III/
252(73:72)/353.
59. Carranza to Carothers, April 22, 1914, AREM, Desocupación, III/
252(73:721)/914.1.
60. Obregón to Carranza, April 21, 1914, *DHRM*, 2:38-39.
61. For months Huerta had considered an international mediation as a way
out of his difficulties with the United States and had even discussed the

Four days after the invasion the ministers of Argentina, Brazil, and Chile offered to mediate the dispute. They extended an invitation to Carranza to attend the sessions as well, and the First Chief agreed in principle to send a representative after he determined to his satisfaction the precise purpose of the conference.[62] After some initial haggling the contending parties agreed that the meeting should be held on neutral territory, at Niagara Falls on the Canadian side of the border. The three mediators—Domicio da Gama from Brazil, Rómulo S. Naón from Argentina, and Eduardo Suárez Mújica from Chile— argued that the conference should treat only the outstanding difficulties between the United States and Mexico; President Wilson, however, wanted the agenda enlarged to include a mediation of Mexico's internal struggle as well and the mediators agreed to expand the agenda. Wilson's sole purpose was made clear when, in a confidential dispatch to the mediators, he warned that no settlement would be acceptable which did not provide "for the entire elimination of Huerta."[63] Huerta's instructions to his delegation (Emilio Rabasa, chief of delegation, Agustín Rodríguez, and Luis Elguero) specified that the negotiations were to be confined only to the controversy between the United States and Mexico.[64] Interestingly, Carranza took basically the same position, positing that the international conference had no right to meddle in the internal affairs of the Mexican nation.[65] Therefore, when the conference convened on May 20, 1914, there was no agreement even on what matters should be discussed. Because the domestic questions had not been explicitly proscribed beforehand, Carranza decided not to appoint an official delegation.

In the early sessions of the conference it became patently evident that it was impossible to divorce the United States—Mexican imbroglio

---

possibility of British mediation with Sir Lionel Carden. See Carden to Grey, F.O. 115/1742, fols. 312-14. For detailed accounts of the A.B.C. mediation one can consult Grieb, *The United States and Huerta*, pp. 159-77; Eduardo Luquín, *La Política Internacional de la Revolución Constitucionalista* (Mexico: Biblioteca del Instituto Nacional de Estudios Históricos de la Revolución Mexicana, 1957), pp. 77-141; James L. Slayden, "The A.B.C. Mediation," *American Journal of International Law* 9 (1915): 147-52; and José Gaxiola, *La Frontera de la Raza* (Madrid: Tipografía Artística, 1917), pp. 104-63.

62. Carranza to Pesqueira, May 2, 1914, *DHRM*, 3:28.
63. Quoted in Link, *Wilson and the Progressive Era*, p. 126 n. 42.
64. Pliego de Instrucciones Giradas por el Licenciado Roberto A. Esteva Ruiz . . . a los Licenciados Emilio Rabasa, Agustín Rodríguez, y Luis Elguero, no date, *DHRM,* 3:63-73.
65. Isidro Fabela to Roberto V. Pesqueira, May 4, 1914, *DHRM*, 3:36-37.

from the civil war; Huerta's delegation, as a result, did not insist on its earlier position that only the international dispute be considered. In fact when the mediators, following the United States lead, suggested to Mexico City that the only way out of the present difficulties might be Huerta's resignation, the Mexican president replied that if he were shown that his separation from power would lead to peace he would resign. Considering the statement a major concession on Huerta's part, the delegates launched into a protracted debate on the make-up of the provisional government which was to succeed him. But in reality Huerta had conceded little. The schism in the Constitutionalist leadership was growing wider by the day. It was well known to all the governments represented at Niagara Falls as well as to the world press.[66] How then could anyone give reasonable guarantees that Huerta's resignation would result in peace? All attempts to arrange for a cease fire in Mexico failed as Carranza maintained that such an arrangement would work to Huerta's advantage.[67] So while the mediators vied with the delegates and their respective governments, the war in Mexico continued. The issues would once again have to be resolved on the field of battle.

Victoriano Huerta's plan to capitalize upon the invasion was good, but Carranza's response was still better. He refused to allow the government to appropriate all nationalist sentiment by showing quite clearly how a loyal Mexican could continue being a loyal Mexican without giving his support to the Huerta regime. A few anti-government forces suspended the fight against Huerta to fight the gringo[68] but the overwhelming majority did not. The enthusiastic support which Huerta enjoyed for the first week quickly began to dissipate when the Americans did not move on Mexico City but contented themselves with the occupation of the port city. Within three weeks after the invasion the rebels and the government were back to business as usual.

In at least one important respect the government position had deteriorated. Immediately following the invasion of Veracruz, Huerta,

66. After being informed of the difficulties among the rebels in early June, Secretary Bryan urged George Carothers: "Do not overlook any opportunity to advise Carranza and Villa against falling out. It is essential to the cause of the Constitutionalists that they work harmoniously together" (Bryan to Carothers, June 24, 1914, RDS, 812.00/12737).

67. Carranza to Ministros Plenipotenciarios de Argentina, Brazil y Chile, May 1, 1914, *DHRM*, 3:22-23.

68. Charles C. Cumberland, "Huerta y Carranza ante la Ocupación de Veracruz," *Historia Mexicana* 6 (April-June 1957): 539.

fearful that the Americans might march on Mexico City, began to call his troops back to defend the capital. The rebels quickly moved into the military vacuums. In Morelos the Zapatistas captured four district capitals as the federals withdrew,[69] and in the north the Constitutionalists took Tampico and Tepic in the middle of May and then poised themselves for an attack on Zacatecas. Villa had the strength to capture Zacatecas late in the month but the First Chief, timorous that his rebel general would move on to Mexico City before Alvaro Obregón to the west and Pablo González to the east could catch up with him, entrusted Zacatecas to Pánfilo Natera. At the same time he ordered Villa north to help with the campaigns against Saltillo— obviously a political rather than a military expedient.

Pánfilo Natera, never adept in any large military engagement requiring planning, coordination, and genuine leadership, was forced to give up after his assaults on Zacatecas were repelled for three days.[70] He withdrew north to Fresnillo. Villa, once having taken Saltillo, on his own initiative, in fact in defiance of Carranza's explicit orders, decided to move on Zacatecas himself. The First Chief tried his best to remove Villa from command of the famous Division of the North but he found out, much to his discomfiture, that Villa's men, especially his officer staff, considered themselves Villistas first and Constitutionalists second.

Villa's troops approached Zacatecas on June 19 and Felipe Angeles directed the emplacement of his fifty artillery pieces on the hills north of the city. The federal army of General Luis Medina Barrón was well entrenched and was awaiting the arrival of 3,000 reinforcements under the command of Pascual Orozco. The federals, without the reinforcements could count on about 12,500 troops, eleven heavy artillery pieces, and about ninety machine guns,[71] but they were badly out-manned as Pánfilo Natera joined Pancho Villa on the outskirts of the city bringing the rebel total to over 21,000 men. Villa began his attack in earnest on the morning of June 23 and by the midafternoon he had overrun two of the strongest federal outposts—La Bufa, the site of the famous colonial silver discoveries, and Guadalupe. The federals in both of these positions withdrew to the city in panic. Orozco's troops

69. Womack, *Zapata*, p. 185.

70. The previous January, Natera had been placed in charge of the rebel offensive at Ojinaga and had been unable to dislodge the federal force there until Villa himself arrived and assumed command.

71. Carothers to Bryan, July 5, 1914, RDS, 812.00/12473.

had not yet arrived. As the Villistas poured into the city from three directions they took heavy losses but their sheer force of numbers overwhelmed the federal positions. Late in the afternoon General Medina Barrón issued his evacuation order, first dynamiting the federal arsenal and the state office building, killing a number of civilians in the process.[72] The battle for Zacatecas had claimed thousands of federal lives, had wounded thousands more, and caused several hundred soldiers to fall into enemy hands as prisoners. Rebel losses were high as well but at least were compensated by the capture of the city. Those federals who escaped headed south toward Aguascalientes. On the way they met Pascual Orozco and his 3,000 reinforcements moving north to help; Orozco had received his orders too late.[73]

The loss of Zacatecas was catastrophic for Huerta. The door to Mexico City, if not wide open, was very much ajar. The continued occupation of Veracruz by the United States not only hurt Mexican pride but had more tangible effects as well. The occupation was perhaps not as significant militarily as it was economically. Military supplies could be secured through other ports. The controversial arms shipment aboard the *Ypiranga,* for example, reached the federal arsenal in Mexico City after being unloaded south of Veracruz at Puerto México. But American control of the customhouse meant that normal import revenues were going to be stopped before they reached the federal treasury and the regime obviously did not have any financial cushion to fall back on. The military, diplomatic, and economic pressures had all merged and the alliance was too formidable to overcome.

Huerta made his decision to resign on July 8, but he had been thinking about it seriously for a week. To provide for an orderly succession he named Francisco S. Carbajal as secretary of foreign relations. With the resignations of Huerta and Aureliano Blanquet, Carbajal would assume the office until the Constitutionalists reached the capital. For the next week Huerta and Doña Emilia made preparations for a period of extended exile in Europe. The actual letter of resignation, submitted to Congress on July 15, 1914, showed a bitter and defeated man but not one without pride. He began by

72. Ibid.
73. The official military report on the battle, a fifty-page document, is found in Batalla de Zacatecas, June-July, 1914, AHDN, Exp. XI/481.5/334, vol. 2, fols. 251-302.

reminding the Congress that in his first message he had promised to reestablish peace—cost what it may. He realized now that the cost was his own resignation so he was giving it to them. Contending that an army adequate to the task had been created, he continued: "You all know the immense obstacles placed in my path by the shortage of funds as well as by the manifest and decided protection given to the rebels by a great power on this continent. . . . There are those," he went on, "who argue that I remained in power only for personal satisfaction, and not for the best interests of the country. This letter of resignation gives them their answer as well. In conclusion let me say that I leave the presidency taking with me one of the greatest of human riches, and I have deposited it in the Bank of Universal Conscience. I am referring to the honor of a Puritan."[74]

74. *Diario de los Debates,* July 15, 1914.

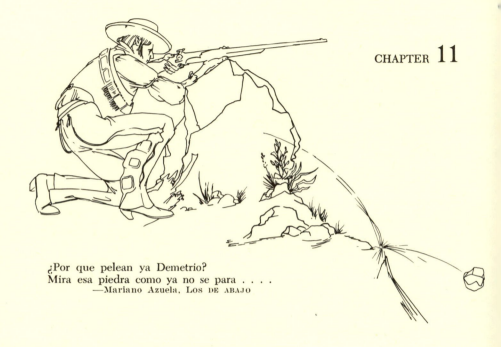

¿Por que pelean ya Demetrio?
Mira esa piedra como ya no se para . . . .
      —Mariano Azuela, Los de Abajo

The Revolt of the Exiles

ON THE MORNING of the day that Huerta submitted his letter of resignation his family left the capital for the coast. Veracruz, of course, was out of the question since it remained in United States hands and Tampico was even less thinkable as it was held by the Constitutionalists. Remembering the ease with which the arms from the *Ypiranga* had reached Mexico City after having been unloaded at Puerto México, south of Veracruz, Huerta sent his family off to that small port. The wives and children of David de la Fuente and Aureliano Blanquet were in the entourage as well when the president bid them farewell at the train station. He promised to join them in a day or so. After personally supervising the loading of personal belongings onto the train, he returned to the National Palace, put the finishing touches on his letter of resignation, calmly cleared out his desk and asked General Blanquet, who would go into exile with him, to make preparations for a sufficiently large armed escort to accompany them. The two generals left the capital late the same afternoon. After passing through Puebla, the train headed south to Tierra Blanca where it stopped until morning. Both men passed a restless night, fearing a possible Constitutionalist assault and not really knowing whether to trust one another.[1]

Reunited with their families in Puerto México the following afternoon, the suspicions seemed to dissipate. The plans had been carefully laid beforehand. The exiles would be taken to Jamaica on the German cruiser *Dresden*. Leaving Puerto México on July 20, they arrived in Kingston four days later[2] and spent several days relaxing in the sun before chartering a United Fruit Company steamer, the *Patia*, for the voyage to Europe.[3] The ten-day journey to Bristol occurred without incident. After a few days of sight-seeing in London, the Huertas returned to the port city for the short cruise to Spain where they had decided the family should take up permanent residence. After docking in Santander the Huertas traveled to Barcelona, their home for the next seven months.[4]

The small hotel where the Huerta family resided in Barcelona quickly became a focal point of interest for Spanish journalists. The "Aztec General," as they dubbed him, was good copy. As they clustered in his hotel lobby, they solicited his opinion on everything from the European war, just begun, to the beauty of Spanish womanhood. They tended to forgive his occasional insults about Spanish cognac or the *gachupines* themselves.[5] Many Spanish nationalists were still smarting from the loss of Cuba at the conclusion of the Spanish-American War and Huerta too was considered a victim of Yankee aggression. For a time the former president seemed to enjoy himself,

1. [Piña], *Memorias de Victoriano Huerta*, pp. 126-27.
2. Bundy, consul, Kingston, to Bryan, July 24, 1914, RDS, 812.001 H 87/3.
3. Bundy to Bryan, July 29, 1914, RDS, 812.001 H 87/4; Bundy to Bryan, July 30, 1914, RDS, 812.001 H 87/5.
4. George Rausch, "The Exile and Death of Victoriano Huerta," *Hispanic American Historical Review* 42 (May 1962): 134.
5. González-Blanco, *Carranza y la Revolución*, pp. 548-50; [Piña], *Memorias de Victoriano Huerta*, p. 130.

traveling to Guipúzcoa, the birthplace of Doña Emilia's grandfather, and visiting Granada for a tour of the Alhambra. A number of Mexican army officers, also exiles, came to visit him.[6] On one occasion he even shared a bottle of cognac and an hour of conversation with Juan Belmonte, the most famous Spanish bullfighter of the day. But before long the retired warrior began to get a little restless. One reporter pictured him pacing nervously in the lobby of his hotel, as if he had something serious in the back of his mind.[7] The observation was a shrewd one; the former president had already begun thinking of attempting a come back and took the initial hesitant step in early December when he called at the British embassy in Madrid.

After exchanging pleasantries with British Ambassador A. H. Hardinge, Huerta complained to the diplomat that he found the Spanish winter very harsh. He had enjoyed his brief stay in Jamaica, he confided, and wondered if His Majesty's government would have any objection to his returning to that island or one of the other British possessions in the West Indies. Hardinge wrote home to Foreign Secretary Grey and then passed on his answer: "Sir Edward Grey has asked me, in view of the still disturbed state of Mexico and of the probability that Your Excellency's presence so near that country might possibly give rise to political misconceptions and complications, to suggest to Your Excellency as an alternative, the Cape Verde or Canary Islands where the climate is very similar to Jamaica." Hardinge, picking up the all too obvious cue, offered gratuitously that Madeira was also warm and pleasant and suggested that Huerta might consider that island as well.[8]

Not wanting to isolate himself even more than he was already, Huerta never entertained the notion of wintering in the Cape Verdes, Canaries, or Madeira. As he shivered through the bleak Spanish winter of 1914-15, he kept himself occupied by reading as much as he could about the deteriorating conditions at home. The victors, as he could have assuredly predicted, had begun to fight among themselves for the spoils. The names of the opposing factions had changed (now it was Conventionists vs. Constitutionalists) but the Revolutionary rhetoric and vituperations remained amazingly constant. Each side

6. Hurst, consul, Barcelona, to Bryan, September 17, 1914, RDS, 812.001 H 87/6.

7. González-Blanco, *Carranza y la Revolución*, p. 549.

8. Hardinge to Huerta, December 9, 1914, F.O. 115/1803, fols. 131-32; Hardinge to Huerta, December 9, 1914, F.O. 115/1803, fol. 133.

impugned the patriotism and the masculinity of the other. Neither Villa nor Carranza demonstrated either the ability or the desire to compromise with one another. A few solicitous Mexican exiles visited Barcelona in January asking Huerta to commit himself to doing something about the chaotic conditions in the fatherland, but, as much as the idea may have appealed to him, he realized that the scheme was foolhardy without massive financial support and a closely knit revolutionary organization to work with. In February, however, he received two important visitors and they provided him with the assurances that he demanded.

The first visitor was sent to Barcelona by the intelligence division of the German General Staff (Abteilung III B). Captain Franz von Rintelen had served in both the United States and Mexico during the waning years of the Díaz dictatorship and the early years of the Revolution. Familiar with the reaction in Mexico to Woodrow Wilson's constant badgering of Huerta, he was assigned the delicate task of negotiating a cooperative agreement between his government and the former Mexican president.[9] The German reasoning was basically sound. The eventual entry of the United States into World War I, even in the spring of 1915, was a strong possibility. A friendly government in Mexico could give Germany a base of operations in the Western Hemisphere and, at the same time, would keep the Wilson government occupied with matters closer to home. If United States arms and ammunition could be diverted from the Allies because of the threat of a hostile government to the immediate south, this would constitute an added benefit. With these purposes in mind Rintelen, on behalf of Kaiser Wilhelm II, offered Huerta financial support if he desired to make a comeback. Huerta was interested but refused to make a definite commitment at that time. When Rintelen left Barcelona, Huerta promised to keep in contact.

Huerta's second visitor a few weeks later brought equally interesting news. A group of Mexican exiles in the United States were planning to launch an anti-Constitutionalist movement from Texas. Huerta's friend and supporter Pascual Orozco would assume the military leadership of the movement but the exiles needed a strong political figure to rally around. With this purpose in mind the exiles dispatched

9. Prior to the Rintelen mission the General Staff had entrusted its Mexican operations to Captain Horst von der Goltz, another German officer with Mexican experience. His mission had been a failure, however. See Michael C. Meyer, "The Mexican-German Conspiracy of 1915," *The Americas* 23 (July 1966): 80-81.

Enrique Creel, a former governor of Chihuahua and secretary of foreign relations, to elicit Huerta's cooperation. Creel undoubtedly informed Huerta of the long list of names that Carranza had gathered to try for treason under the law of 1862 and probably told him that many of these men had fled to the United States in order to avoid the death sentence or a long prison term.[10] Never before had so many prominent Mexicans gone into exile at the same time.

The names on the list of proscription have never been matched with those known to have gone into exile in the United States but it can be established, at a minimum, that the following well-known civilian and military officials from the proscribed list crossed over into the United States shortly after the Carrancista victory: Civilians Enrique Creel, Félix Díaz, Toribio Esquivel Obregón, Querido Moheno, José María Luján, Francisco S. Carbajal, Federico Gamboa, Jorge Vera Estañol, Luis Fernández Castellot, Miguel Bolaños Cacho, Aureliano Urrutia, Ricardo Gómez Robelo, Nemesio García Naranjo, José María Lozano, Eduardo Tamariz, Eduardo Iturbide, Jesús Flores Magón, José Elguero, Manuel Calero, and Enrique Gorostieta and Generals Pascual Orozco, Rómulo Cuellar, Juan A. Hernández, Joaquín Téllez, Jesús González Garza, Luis Medina Barrón, Ignacio Bravo, José Delgado, José Refugio Velasco, Joaquín Maass, and Gustavo Maass.[11] But the list of exiles was even more impressive. The number

10. A few stayed in Mexico and some, such as Alberto García Granados, were shot without ceremony by a Constitutionalist firing squad. Others, such as Francisco Olaguíbel, were thrown into prison. The excesses committed by the Constitutionalists were not limited to prominent Huertistas in Mexico City, however. In Hermosillo, for example, Antonio Caballero and Roberto Montano Llave were shot for having attended a banquet celebrating Madero's fall from power. In Mazatlán an old apolitical businessman Francisco de Sevilla was executed because he had sent a telegram of condolence to the family of José Riveroll, an officer shot during the arrest of Madero. See Valadés, *Historia de la Revolución,* 5:70-71.

11. My calculations are based on a comparison of the proscription list with a number of individual documents from United States and Mexican archives and from several newspapers from the border region. Salvador Alvarado to General Subsecretario Encargado del Despacho de Guerra y Marina, November 12, 1914, AHDN, Cancelados, Exp. XI/III/1-104; Hugh Obear to Charles Warren, assistant attorney general, July 6, 1915, RDJ, Straight Numerical File 90755-U-25; R. E. Muzquiz to Carranza, May 5, 1915, Condumex/AC, Documentos, 1915; Juan Gutiérrez, chief of reserve police Brownsville, to José Z. Garza, consul, Brownsville, October 12, 1914, AREM, L-E 788, Leg. 16; Pan American News Service to R. D. De Negri, February 6, 1915, AREM, L-E 836, Leg. 1; José Z. Garza to Secretaría de Relaciones Exteriores, September 19, 1914, AREM, L-E 788, Leg. 16; *San Antonio Express,* May 2, 1915; *El Paso Morning Times,* September 14, 18, and November 3, 27, 1914.

of nonprominent exiles from the list of proscription was still greater and, in addition, many persons not on the list, fearing retaliation for Huertista sympathies, voluntarily exiled themselves. Uncounted scores sought the shelter of the United States border just to escape the ravages of the continuing war. And a few well-known political figures, although not actually proscribed, believed that they would be more comfortable in the United States than in Carranza's or Villa's Mexico. In this category one must include Francisco Vásquez Gómez, Emilio Vásquez Gómez, and Pedro Lascuráin. Envoy Creel did not have to remind Huerta that the list could be expanded still further by the Mexican exiles in Europe and other Latin American countries: David de la Fuente, Francisco León de la Barra, Manuel Mondragón, Aureliano Blanquet, Francisco Bulness, and Rodolfo Reyes to name only a few. Not everyone on the exile rolls could be counted as a Huertista by any means, but they were all anti-Constitutionalists and none relished the thought of spending the rest of their lives away from home.

Creel also informed the former president that he believed the rebellion could count on the support of the much abused Mexican-American population of Texas. The idea of an alliance between the exiles and Mexican-Americans had its roots in an obscure political document dated November 26, 1914, and signed by Francisco Alvarez Tostado. Addressed to "Los Hijos de Cuauhtemoc, Hidalgo y Juárez en Tejas," the document called on the Mexican-Americans to throw off their political and social shackles, establish an independent republic, and when Mexicans began living according to the principles of the Constitution of 1857 to request annexation.[12] By the time Creel arrived in Spain the idea had developed further; a group of Mexican-Americans with Huertista sympathies had promulgated the better known Plan de San Diego [Texas].[13] More radical than its predecessor this plan called for the restoration to Mexico of all lands lost at the end of the Mexican War. Militantly irredentist and completely uncompromising, the signers called for the execution of all adult North American males and vowed not to except Mexican-Americans who refused to join the cause (Article 7).[14]

12. A los Hijos de Cuauhtemoc, Hidalgo y Juárez en Tejas, November 26, 1914, Condumex/AC, Documentos, 1915 *[sic]* (Mayo 7 a 30).

13. A manuscript copy is contained in AEM, vol. 2, following fol. 60.

14. In an interesting move to broaden the movement, the Plan de San Diego also called for a restoration of Indian lands stolen by the gringo and the creation of six southern states for the American Negro (Articles 8 and 11).

Creel talked; Huerta listened; and finally the envoy convinced Huerta that his participation was essential to the repatriation of all those who had supported him in one way or another during his presidency. Huerta agreed to assume political leadership of the movement and having made the commitment informed Creel of the visit of Franz von Rintelen. As subsequent events clearly demonstrate, the two men decided to accept German financial assistance. Huerta and Creel left Spain together in late March aboard the Spanish steamer *López*. Traveling with them were José Delgado, who had become Huerta's personal secretary and alter ego, and Abraham Ratner,[15] a New York based businessman who had been active in securing arms for Huerta in the United States during the period of President Wilson's arms embargo.[16] The departure of the exiles for the United States was well publicized in the press; and even before their scheduled arrival in New York City on April 12, 1915, Francisco Elías, the Constitutionalist consul general in Washington, and Enrique Llorente, Pancho Villa's confidential agent in the same city, protested that because of the exile activity in the border states Huerta should not be permitted to land. Mexican consuls all over the country followed suit.[17] Huerta did land, however, and passed through customs as a transient alien after having declared under oath that he would do nothing to violate the neutrality laws of the country he was entering. The reporters were waiting for him as he cleared customs and, in response to their questions, he stated that he had come on a combination business and pleasure trip during which time he hoped to do some traveling.[18]

Shortly after his arrival Huerta was interviewed by Mexican journalist Luis Lara Pardo who found him

> still very erect, without any traces of remorse or fatigue and without any of the outward signs of alcoholism. His face was very

15. Hurst to Bryan, April 16, 1915, RDS, 812.001 H 87/9.
16. Ratner had been involved in the *Ypiranga* arms cargo. See Meyer, "The Arms of the *Ypiranga*," p. 547.
17. U. S. Department of State, *Papers Relating to the Foreign Relations of the United States, 1915* (Washington, D. C.: Government Printing Office, 1924), pp. 827-28; Llorente to Bryan, April 10, 1915, RDS, 812.001 H 87/11; Ives G. Lelevier, consul, Naco, to Wilson, April 13, 1915, RDS, 812.001 H 87/13; Enrique Schreck, consul, Port Arthur, to Wilson, April 24, 1915, RDS, 812.001 H 87/13; E. A. González, consul, San Diego, to Wilson, April 14, 1915, RDS, 812.001 H 87/13; E. Osuna, consul, Albuquerque, to Wilson, April 16, 1915, RDS, 812.001 H 87/13.
18. *New York Times,* April 13, 1915.

tan and quite wrinkled around the eyes and lips . . . . His eyes, partially hidden behind dark glasses, were sunken. The gruff voice had lost the impetuous tone so familiar to those who had surrounded him during the height of his power.[19]

Within a week Huerta began to hold conferences with German embassy personnel and German secret service agents in New York City. In addition to reestablishing contact with Rintelen, who had preceded him to the United States, the former president also held several meetings with German Naval Attaché Karl Boy-Ed and Military Attaché Franz von Papen, both of whom had already made trips to the Mexican border to confer with some of the leaders in exile and to arrange for the storage of supplies and ammunition.[20] He told Rintelen as much as he dared about the hopes and desires of his compatriots in exile and indicated that they needed money and arms.[21] The details were all worked out by May. Huerta's German patrons deposited $895,000 in various bank accounts, secured eight million rounds of ammunition, ordered an additional three million rounds, and promised to supply ten thousand rifles which would be dropped off along the Mexican coast by German U-boats.[22]

Huerta was understandably concerned about his allies on the border. Some were Felicistas, others he had dismissed from cabinet posts and other positions of trust, and a few, although anti-Constitutionalist, he could number among his personal enemies. Could

19. Lara Pardo, *Matchs de Dictadores,* pp. 160-61.

20. John Price Jones and Paul Merrick Hollister, *The German Secret Service in America* (Boston: Small, Maynard and Co., 1918), p. 291.

21. Franz Rintelen von Kleist, *The Dark Invader: Wartime Reminiscences of a German Naval Intelligence Officer* (New York: Macmillan Co., 1933), p. 176.

22. The extent of the German involvement and the role of the various officials is treated in Meyer, "The Mexican-German Conspiracy of 1915," pp. 83-85; Rausch, "The Exile and Death of Victoriano Huerta," pp. 136-37; and Friedrich Katz, *Deutschland, Diaz und die Mexicanische Revolution: Die Deutsche Politik in Mexiko, 1870-1920* (Berlin: Veb Deutscher Verlag der Wissenochaften, 1964), pp. 339-49. A somewhat cautious, but carefully conceived, evaluation is found in Grieb, *The United States and Huerta,* pp. 183-86. The evidence indicates to me that Huerta discussed the Mexican-American–exile movement on the border with his German backers. The lines of progression to the famous Zimmermann telegram seem to begin with the declaration of November, 1914, and run through the Plan de San Diego. At a minimum the idea of restoring the lands lost during the Mexican War was a Mexican-American and Mexican exile idea which the Germans subsequently picked up. A recent article by Allen Gerlach corroborates these conclusions, although Gerlach was not aware of the Alvarez Tostado document of 1914. See his "Conditions Along the Border—1915: The Plan de San Diego," *New Mexico Historical Review* 43 (July 1968): 195-212.

this jumble of political dissidents possibly be molded into a cohesive force with which to strike out against those in power in Mexico? He needed reassurance; so his aides, Delgado, Ratner, and son-in-law Luis Fuentes began inviting exiles to New York City to confer with him. Generals Eduardo Cauz and Prisciliano Cortés, former governors of Veracruz and Yucatán respectively, were among the first to pay their respects and solicit his support. Next came Pascual Orozco with some interesting news. Two of his lieutenants, José Inés Salazar and Emilio Campa, had already launched a small rebellion in northern Chihuahua which was going much better than expected.[23] They were ready to join forces with the exiles when the time came. Northern Mexico was vulnerable Orozco informed Huerta. In addition, the Chihuahua rebel reported that he had been purchasing arms and ammunition and storing them at conveniently located sites along the border. He and his men were ready to move whenever Huerta gave the order.

Other exiles visited the former president in New York as well. They informed him that the San Diego movement was well underway. Basilio Ramos (one of the signers of the plan), his father, and three brothers had organized raiding bands and had attacked rural settlements along the lower Rio Grande valley.[24] Messages of encouragement and personal visits continued all through May. Huertista exiles had organized in California and were especially active in the Los Angeles area.[25] The Mexican community in Europe was shaken from its lethargy when Manuel Garza Aldape and David de la Fuente left London and made their way to San Antonio and El Paso.[26] Aureliano Blanquet followed their example a few weeks later.[27]

23. Tomás Ornelas to Gobernador Militar de Chihuahua, December 24, 1914, STC, Correspondence and Papers. This rebellion is discussed in Meyer, *Mexican Rebel,* pp. 118-21.

24. Charles C. Cumberland, "Border Raids in the Lower Rio Grande Valley—1915," *Southwestern Historical Quarterly* 57 (October 1953): 285-311. When Basilio Ramos was arrested and brought to trial, the judge in Brownsville, not realizing that the far-fetched objectives of the Plan de San Diego were simply a spoke in a much bigger wheel, informed the defendant that he ought to be tried for lunacy rather than for conspiracy against the United States. He then dismissed the charges. See William H. Hager, "The Plan of San Diego: Unrest on the Texas Border in 1915," *Arizona and the West* 5 (Winter 1963): 331.

25. Adolfo Carrillo to Carranza, May 11, 1915, Condumex/AC, Documentos, 1915 (Mayo 7 a 30); R. D. De Negri, consul general, San Francisco, to Secretaría de Relaciones Exteriores, April 15, 1915, AREM, L-E 835, Leg. 1.

26. J. G. Nava to Carranza, April 5, 1915, Condumex/AC, Documentos, 1915 (April 1 a 15).

27. *San Antonio Express,* May 7, 1915.

The growing support was comforting but Huerta still needed a reading on the political climate of the exile movement on the border and the nature of its organization. Visitors in late May and early June briefed him on the Mexican Peace Assembly with headquarters in San Antonio. Founded in the middle of January, 1915, by Querido Moheno, Eliseo Ruiz, Miguel Bolaños Cacho, and Ismael Zúñiga, its stated purpose was to bring an end to the civil war which had ravaged the country for four and a half years. The president of the Directive Council, Federico Gamboa, sent letters to all of the leading military chieftains urging them to stop the madness of killing their fellow Mexicans. Francisco Villa, Venustiano Carranza, Alvaro Obregón, Felipe Angeles, José M. Maytorena, Emiliano Zapata, Eulalio Gutiérrez, and Esteban Cantú all were implored to lay down their arms and begin talking. Only Villa, Obregón, and Angeles bothered to answer and they all rejected the urgency of the plea.[28] By the spring the leaders of the peace assembly realized that they could hope to accomplish little by their appeal to reason. Peace could be restored, they concluded, only by a little bit more war—this time a gigantic military onslaught from the north which would sweep Mexico clean of its scores of revolutionary factions. Were they reactionaries as both the Carrancistas and the Villistas contended? They were the same men who had initiated the moderately progressive reform programs of the Huerta presidency. And they went on record again as favoring the redistribution of land and the establishment of credit institutions for the small farmer.[29] But the civil war and their own exile experience had polarized their attitudes and pushed them to the right. Their call for reform in the spring of 1915 has a very hollow ring. The revolt of the exiles was, in reality, much more counterrevolutionary than the Huerta presidency itself.

Huerta had only one final doubt. His old nemesis Félix Díaz had recently moved from Havana to New Orleans and rumors filled the exile circles that he too was contemplating a comeback. Among the exiles generally, and even in the Mexican Peace Assembly, one could count many Felicistas. Did they belong to Huerta or to Félix Díaz? Huerta's body of advisors, and the continuing flow of visitors from the Southwest, slowly convinced him that the San Antonio group, as

28. Antimaco Sax, *Los Mexicanos en el Destierro* (San Antonio: International Printing Co., 1916), pp. 17-20.
29. Toribio Esquivel Obregón to Woodrow Wilson, March 8, 1915, RDS, 812.00/14576.

well as its local affiliates all along the common border, was his for the asking. They did not tell him that the organization was rampant with division, fear, and mistrust,[30] nor did they inform him that the peace assembly had earlier considered giving their endorsement to Félix Díaz.[31] They told him only what they believed he wanted to hear and thus secured his commitment. Convinced at last, Huerta chose June 28 as the target date for his rebellion. He confided a bit of his military and political strategy to Nemesio García Naranjo, who visited him in early June in Abraham Ratner's New York City office. His exile army would move first on Chihuahua City and once the city was in rebel hands Huerta would make it his provisional capital.[32] From this point he hoped the movement would gather momentum and move on to Mexico City.

On June 24 Huerta left New York on a westbound train, telling reporters that he planned to visit San Francisco, California. At approximately the same time Mexican exiles from all over the southwestern states and the West Coast began to converge on El Paso, Texas.[33] Carranza's agents in the United States, witnessing these events, became more and more nervous and urged the State Department to take meaningful action against Huerta and his fellow conspirators.[34] Huerta must have been aware that United States Department of Justice agents had been following his activities for weeks, for he arranged to meet his contact man in Texas, Pascual Orozco, not in El Paso proper, but rather in Newman, New Mexico, about twenty miles north of the border city. The two men would then cross into Mexico at Bosque Bonito, near Sierra Blanca, Texas. Huerta's train arrived at the Newman station early on Sunday morning, June 27. Orozco and Huerta's son-in-law Luis Fuentes met him and had a car all ready to whisk him off to the border. Before the Mexicans could leave the station, however, they were apprehended

30. Moheno, *Sobre el Ara Sangrienta*, p. 23.
31. Folsom Pan American News Service to De Negri, February 7, 1915, AREM, L-E 836, Leg. 1.
32. García Naranjo, *Memorias*, 8:133. García Naranjo refused to commit himself definitely at the June meeting. Remembering Napoleon's Hundred Days and Agustín de Iturbide's ill-fated attempt at returning to power, he simply put Huerta off, promising to talk to him again in El Paso.
33. Adolfo Carrillo, consul, Los Angeles, to Enrique A. González, consul, San Diego, July 2, 1915, AREM, L-E 817, Leg. 1; González to Carrillo, June 30, 1915, AREM, L-E 817, Leg. 1.
34. Eliseo Arrendondo to Robert Lansing, June 26, 1915, AREM, Expediente Personal de Venustiano Carranza, L-E 1441, Leg. 3.

by Justice Department officials and federal troops who had been informed by railroad officials of Huerta's plans to leave the train at Newman.[35]

Huerta had given much thought to his relationship with the German government and even more to his position in the exile community. But he had given insufficient consideration to the reaction that his visit to the United States had provoked at the White House and the State Department. He believed incorrectly that the war in Europe had pre-empted the energies of his old foes Wilson and Bryan. Far from being unconcerned, Secretary Bryan notified officials along the border of Huerta's return only a few days after the former president landed in New York City. He mentioned to Zachary Cobb, the collector of customs in El Paso, that Huerta's arrival in the United States disturbed him deeply.[36] Special agents of the Justice Department were assigned to watch Huerta's every step and even the War Department was ordered to keep the attorney general apprised of any new developments.[37] When the State Department learned that in all likelihood Huerta would soon be making a trip to Texas, the secretary of state asked the attorney general to take all steps necessary to assure that the general did not cross over into Mexico. The message was relayed to the United States district attorney in San Antonio who promised Washington that he would exert himself most forcefully: "I will resort to every means known to the law to prevent him from setting on foot another revolution in Mexico, and, if evidence cannot be obtained against him sufficient to institute prosecution for violation of neutrality laws of the United States, in all probability we can hold him for investigation for deportation."[38]

When Huerta got off the train in Newman, border officials, Justice Department agents, soldiers, and police were all ready. Huerta and Orozco were both taken to El Paso and formally charged with conspiracy to violate the neutrality laws of the United States. The news of the arrests circulated rapidly among the Mexican-American

35. Bielaski, agent in Department of Justice, to Robert L. Barnes, June 26, 1915, RDJ, 90755-U-11.

36. Bryan to Cobb, April 26, 1915, RDS, 812.00/14928.

37. J. A. Ryan to Engineer Officer, Southern Department, April 28, 1915, Records of the Adjutant General's Office, National Archives, No. 2284054 (hereafter cited as AGO); Lindley M. Garrison to Attorney General, May 6, 1915, AGO, No. 2284054.

38. Report of Conditions along the Border, April 25, 1915, RDS, 812.00/14971; J. L. Camp to Attorney General [Thomas W. Gregory], May 21, 1915, RDJ, 90755-U-4.

and exile population of the city and a huge crowd assembled outside
the federal building. They carried pictures of Huerta and placards
denouncing the criminal revolutionists who were currently governing
the Mexican nation.[39] Fearing violence, or perhaps even an attempt
to free the prisoners,[40] Thomas Lea, the mayor of El Paso, asked
federal officials to detain the two Mexicans at Fort Bliss, rather than
in the city itself.[41] The federal authorities were delighted to make the
change because they did not have much confidence in Lea who,
although mayor, had agreed to serve as Huerta's attorney.

Tom Lea called on the prisoners as soon as they were transferred
to Fort Bliss and immediately set to work arranging a bond. It did
not take him long to ascertain that the attorney general's office had
asked for the highest bail possible.[42] But in spite of a specific
admonition to the United States District Attorney J. L. Camp that
the president of the United States desired "every effort made to
prevent entrance [of] Huerta [and] Orozco into Mexico,"[43] Lea
secured a relatively modest bond of $15,000 for Huerta and $7,500
for Orozco.[44] After posting bond, the prisoners were released the same
evening, but because of the proximity of the Mexican border both
men were placed under house arrest in El Paso. Official Washington,
and not least the president, was upset with the way the case had been
handled and an entire series of dispatches debated the feasibility of
raising the bond. But this was scarcely practical once the prisoners
had been set free. Telegrams from El Paso assured the president that
the two Mexicans were being closely guarded and would be arrested
if they attempted to cross the border.[45] But in spite of the precautions,
on the evening of July 3, Pascual Orozco jumped through a rear
window in his home, eluded his guards, and escaped from his house
arrest.[46] As soon as the news reached the attorney general, he wired

39. Cobb to Bryan, June 28, 1915, RDS, 812.001 H 87/22.
40. The exiles had already staged one spectacular jailbreak. The previous
November they overpowered the guards at the Bernalillo County Jail in Albuquerque, New Mexico, and freed prisoner José Inés Salazar. *Albuquerque Morning
Journal,* November 21, 1914.
41. Cobb to Bryan, June 27, 1915, RDS, 812.001 H 87/18.
42. Charles Warren, assistant attorney general, to Woodrow Wilson, June 28,
1915, RDJ, 90755-U-8.
43. Ibid.
44. They were prepared to post as much as $300,000. Cobb to Lansing, June
28, 1915, RDS, 812.001 H 87/22.
45. T. W. Gregory to Woodrow Wilson, June 30, 1915, RDJ, 90755-U-15.
46. Frederick Funston to Adjutant General, July 4, 1915, AGO, No. 2303485.

his El Paso staff to "spare no effort or expense to apprehend Orozco
. . . use additional precautions as to Huerta." [47] The only feasible
response was to cancel Huerta's bond and rearrest him. In addition,
five of his colleagues were placed in jail at the same time: Generals
José Delgado, Eduardo Cauz, Ignacio Bravo, and José Ratner and
Enrique Gorostieta.

Huerta evidenced considerable bad humor on his second trip to
jail. On the first occasion he had been treated more like a celebrity
than a prisoner, even dining at the home of the commander of Fort
Bliss.[48] But this time the former president was placed in a cramped
cell in the El Paso jail like any common criminal. Observers who a
week earlier had described him as suave, courteous, and self-reliant
noted that he was badly shaken by his second arrest.[49] Perhaps he was
beginning to realize that his days of molding events, shaping the
destinies of men, and exerting his own character forcefully were
drawing to an end. For the last six months of his life Huerta would
be a passive object rather than a dynamic subject of the events which
engulfed him. The exiles wanted him to lead a revolution, the Villistas
and the Carrancistas wanted to extradite him,[50] and the United States
wanted to convict him for the violation of neutrality laws. In confine-
ment, of course, he was unable to directly affect the outcome of these
opposing pressures.

Huerta remained in his El Paso jail cell for the next six days.
Subsequent events suggest that during this period Justice Department
agents either intimidated him or struck an agreement with him. For
on July 9 his bond was once again set at a modest $15,000, but on
this occasion, for some unexplained reason, he declined to meet it
and agreed to remain a prisoner if transferred to Fort Bliss. His own
explanation to the press was that the first time he was released on bond
he was guarded as a prisoner in his own house and since he was

47. Thomas W. Gregory to R. E. Crawford, July 3, 1915, RDJ, 90755-U-23 ½.
48. Customs Inspector Cobb had asked that Huerta be provided with meals
and comforts "in keeping with his station" in order that the Mexican population of
El Paso should not be further angered. Cobb to Lansing, June 27, 1915, RDS,
812.001 H 87/19; Colonel H. Morgan to Commanding General, Southern Department, June 29, 1915, AGO, No. 2284054.
49. Cobb to Lansing, June 27, 1915, RDS, 812.001 H 87/21; Cobb to Lansing,
July 3, 1915, RDS, 812.001 H 87/36.
50. Venustiano Carranza to Pablo González, July 5, 1915, Condumex/AC,
Telegramas de V. Carranza a Estado de México; James E. Ferguson, governor of
Texas, to Secretary of State, June 30, 1915, RDS, 812.001 H 87/21; Fidel Avila,
governor of Chihuahua, to Ferguson, June 29, 1915, RDS, 812.001 H 87/24.

unable to receive any assurance that this would not again be the case, he preferred not to subject himself to that indignity.[51] It is possible that the decision merely reflected the convictions of a proud man. But all indications point to the fact that neither Huerta nor the exiles had yet given up hope of launching their movement from Texas soil. The exiles remained in El Paso and according to reports from the border the movement continued to grow in intensity.[52] Certainly Huerta could not hope to coordinate the activities of the exiles from the confines of Fort Bliss. The quarters he was promised at the army base were obviously an improvement over his cramped cell in El Paso, but they still denied him the freedom of movement he would have enjoyed in his residence on Stanton Street in the city itself. Firm evidence of coercion does not exist but it is difficult to explain certain correspondence without resort to this possibility.

On July 6 United States District Attorney Camp, after a conference with Huerta's attorneys, had reason to report to the attorney general that he was "confident that Huerta will *now* gladly accept detention by military."[53] He did not venture any specifics. But something obviously occurred at that meeting which, when relayed to Huerta by his attorneys, convinced him that it was better to remain in jail than to accept bail and be set free. It is doubtful that even an ill-advised federal attorney would have threatened Huerta or his family with possible harm to their persons. But the message was questionable enough to be kept a secret. There is no evidence that the attorney general was ever apprised of the exact nature of the agreement or even inquired about it. District Attorney Camp might well have acted completely on his own after the embarrassing incident of Orozco's escape. Did he suggest that if Huerta accepted bond the United States might well honor Mexican requests for his extradition? One can only conjecture.[54] It can be determined that extradition was at least considered by the Department of State. On July 6 Secretary Robert

51. The explanation is accepted by George Rausch, "The Exile and Death of Huerta," pp. 146-47; and Kenneth Grieb, *The United States and Huerta*, pp. 189-90.

52. Cobb to Lansing, July 1, 1915, RDS, 812.001 H 87/27; Cobb to Lansing, July 5, 1915, RDS, 812.001 H 87/37.

53. Camp to Gregory, July 6, 1915, RDJ, 90755-U-58. Emphasis added.

54. The pertinent documentation possibly has been destroyed. At the beginning of the special Huerta file in the records of the Department of State relating to Mexican affairs, one reads that "the red ink papers filed under this number and dated prior to January 1, 1924 have been destroyed under authorization of Congress" (RDS, 812.001 H 87/——).

Lansing drafted a telegram to the governor of Texas in which he stated that "in view of the disturbed conditions in Mexico and in the absence of a recognized government there, Department could not recognize as binding on itself obligations of extradition treaty between the United States and Mexico." But the message was too strong and the telegram was cancelled before it was sent.[55] In order to leave his options open the secretary of state, following the advice of the office of the solicitor, settled for a much less binding response to Texas Governor James E. Ferguson's request for information. He stated simply that Huerta's extradition would be unwise at this time.[56] Camp may have only suggested the possibility of future extradition to Huerta's attorneys. He did feel very strongly about the case and indicated in one dispatch that he believed it "urgently necessary" that Huerta not be set free.[57]

It is possible, of course, that the threat to Huerta may have been of a different kind but there seems little doubt that some kind of itimidation occurred. Several months later, when Huerta's health was failing badly, his attorneys threatened Camp with exposing the agreement if Huerta were not released. They warned: "Do not force us to a habeas corpus. We believe you understand our position thoroughly. We are convinced that this old man should not be longer held when he can give bond."[58] Short of something as drastic as extradition Huerta would not have given up so easily. He would have gladly died on the northern deserts leading his fellow exiles in the conquest of Chihuahua, but he did not relish the thought of meeting his end before a Villista or Carrancista firing squad.

Huerta's trial was set for January, 1916, at the federal district court in San Antonio. As he began contemplating his defense, he received some news that disturbed him greatly. Mrs. Huerta and the children had followed the general from Spain to New York City and, after his arrest, decided to move to El Paso to be near him. Once they were settled in their house Huerta was given special permission to visit them. Accompanied by guards, he arrived at the house on the afternoon of July 26 and was informed by a distraught wife that two Department of Justice agents, without her permission, searched the

55. Lansing to Ferguson, July 6, 1915, RDS, 812.001 H 87/30.
56. Lansing to Ferguson, July 6, 1915, RDS, 812.001 H 87/24.
57. Cobb to Lansing, July 5, 1915, RDS, 812.001 H 87/37.
58. Thomas Lea, McGrady, and Thomason to Camp, November 1, 1915, RDJ, 90755-U-58.

entire house early in the morning and had treated her and the children very discourteously.[59] Huerta immediately sent a telegram to the attorney general protesting vigorously. Asking nothing for himself, he called on the "Chief of American Justice" to give him some indication that his family would be able to live in the United States with all of the normal guarantees provided by law.[60] He waited two days for an answer. None came. As he pondered the situation, it must have occurred to him that Germany was at least in part responsible for his current predicament. He then decided to send another telegram, this time to Count Johann von Bernstorff, the German ambassador in Washington. Complaining that members of his family were not accorded any guarantees, he added: "I write to know whether the government of His Imperial Majesty, that you so worthily represent in Washington, can do me the favor of protecting my wife and children as the officers of the Federal American Justice [Department] do not let them sleep or eat and search my house at will." [61] But the Germans had already given up on Huerta and Bernstorff did not bother to respond either. Instead he turned the telegram over to Secretary of State Lansing, who, in turn, gave a copy to President Wilson. Huerta was being shunned and he knew it. But at least he could take some comfort in the fact that the incidents in his El Paso house were not repeated.

Not long after the distasteful episode with his wife and family worse news reached him. On September 1 an orderly brought him a copy the the *El Paso Morning Times.* The lead story on the front page detailed the death of his old companion in arms Pascual Orozco and four other Mexican exiles. Since his escape from house arrest in El Paso, Orozco had managed to keep one step ahead of local, state, and national law enforcement officials. On the morning of August 30, Orozco, Andrés Sandoval, Crisóforo Caballero, Miguel Terrazas, and José Delgado (who had been arrested with Huerta but subsequently released) were reported to be in the Big Bend area of Culberson County, Texas. A posse made up of federal marshals, deputy sheriffs, Texas Rangers, and army troops from the Thirteenth Cavalry was quickly formed and moved into the area. The Mexicans were spotted late in the afternoon camped in Green River Canyon, approximately

59. R. E. Crawford to T. W. Gregory, July 28, 1915, RDJ, 90755-U-45 ½.
60. Huerta to T. W. Gregory, July 26, 1915, RDJ, 90755-U-44.
61. J. Bernstorff to Lansing, July 28, 1915, transmitting telegram of Huerta, RDS, 812.001 H 87/52.

twenty-five miles east of Sierra Blanca. The posse manned the ridges on both sides of the canyon and opened fire on the unsuspecting Mexicans. By dusk all five had been killed.[62]

Huerta never really recovered from the despondency which engulfed him on receiving this news. Not only had five of his close associates been gunned down but the revolt of the exiles had been killed with them. Huerta now found hypocrisy everywhere. The death of Orozco and his colleagues was explained to the United States public as the ultimate justice for a group of Mexican cattle thieves. Huerta's "Puritan in the White House" could moralize about the wave of assassinations that had occurred while he was president of Mexico, but five of his friends had been assassinated just as surely. The government version of what had happened (the cattle thieves were killed in a fair fight) was just about as convincing as the official explanation of Madero's death had been two and a half years earlier.

The exiles who had converged on El Paso with such anticipation a few months earlier now began to disperse. Huerta once again found his solace in the bottle. His health deteriorated rapidly as he began drinking to excess daily. He became more and more introspective. There is no report of his reaction to the news that Woodrow Wilson extended *de facto* recognition to Carranza in the middle of October. But it is obvious that he had become fatalistic about Mexico and about himself. Despite his declining health, he refused to go to the military hospital at Fort Bliss when its facilities were offered to him.[63] His attorneys took it upon themselves to try to secure his release. They argued that he was old and sick and that the conditions along the border which prompted his arrest were no longer applicable since most of the exiles had already left and since the White House had recognized the Carranza regime.[64] The argument was persuasive enough that the attorney general allowed the prisoner to be taken to his home on November 5. He remained with his family for about a month, refusing to leave the house or talk to anyone but a few very close friends. But the rumors of the impending revolt picked up once again and on the basis of these rumors United States Marshal for the Western District of Texas J. W. Rogers decided to move the prisoner

62. I have examined the circumstances surrounding Orozco's death in greater detail in *Mexican Rebel*, pp. 131-35.

63. Crawford to Gregory, November 4, 1915, RDJ, 90755-U-54.

64. Lea, McGrady, and Thomason to J. J. Camp, November 1, 1915, RDJ, 90755-U-58.

back to Fort Bliss.[65] For two weeks Huerta scarcely moved from his bed. At the end of the year the army doctors reported that he was dangerously ill and that he had but the slightest chance to recover.[66] He expressed to one of his jailers that he would like to die at home and this last request was honored.[67] Two weeks later, after two operations, he was dead.

Not even the news of Huerta's death could be handled dispassionately. The contemporary press fashioned a legend which was readily seized and elaborated upon by subsequent chroniclers. He died, according to some, because he had been denied his daily supply of alcohol;[68] others found that President Wilson ordered his assassination and invented the medical story to cover it up;[69] still others held that some mysterious Mexican with a long black beard, posing as a surgeon, entered his house, cut him open, and did not sew him back up.[70] Only slightly more moderate was that the man who performed the operation was indeed a surgeon but an incompetent one.[71] And finally rumors that Huerta had been poisoned were widely circulated.[72]

In spite of the controversies, the circumstances surrounding Huerta's death are clear. In late December he developed jaundice. His physician, Dr. M. P. Schuster, suspecting that an inflamed gall bladder was preventing bile from reaching the intestine, prevailed upon him to agree to surgery. The operation occurred in an El Paso hospital on January 1, 1916. Dr. Schuster removed several gall stones but reported to the press that the operation had revealed more serious complications.[73] While Huerta was on the operating table, Dr. Schuster detected a serious degenerative disease of the liver, most likely toxic cirrhosis, common in chronic alcoholics. Two days later Huerta underwent surgery again, a simple tapping procedure to remove excess fluid from the intestinal tract. But nothing was done about the cirrhosis. For

65. Rogers to Gregory, December 11, 1915, RDJ, 90755-U-61.
66. Gregory to Rogers, December 28, 1915, RDJ, 90755-U-64.
67. Camp to Gregory, January 3, 1916, RDJ, 90755-U-72.
68. Mena Brito, *Felipe Angeles*, p. 120.
69. Ignacio Muñoz, *Verdad y Mito de la Revolución Mexicana*, 4 vols. (Mexico: Companía de Ediciones Populares, 1960-65), 1:367. It seems obvious that had President Wilson wanted to kill Huerta for some reason the easiest and cleanest way of doing so would have been to honor either Villa's or Carranza's requests for extradition.
70. Lara Pardo, *Matchs de Dictadores*, p. 164.
71. Miguel Alessio Robles, "La Muerte de los Gobernantes Mexicanos," *El Universal*, July 11, 1938.
72. Angel Peral, *Diccionario Biográfico Mexicano*, 1:399.
73. *New York Times*, January 3, 1916.

about a week he seemed to improve and was taken home, but then he began to fail badly. On January 12 his doctors called his family and his priest, Father Francis Joyce, the Fort Bliss chaplin, to his bedside.[74] A short supplementary will was prepared leaving his small estate to Doña Emilia, except for a box of private papers hidden in Mexico City. These Huerta willed to Father Joyce with the understanding that the American clergyman would try to get them out of Mexico and then turn them over to the family which would arrange for their publication.[75] Huerta was already too weak to sign the document but did manage to mark an X on the appropriate line.[76] The will prepared, Father Joyce administered the last rites of the church. Huerta, at ease with himself, died quietly in his own bed the following day.[77] He was buried at Concordia Cemetery in an unpretentious grave site next to that of Pascual Orozco.

With the death of Orozco and the illness and death of Huerta, the revolt of the exiles all but collapsed. A few stout souls rallied around Félix Díaz in New Orleans and with him attempted an invasion of Mexico in February, 1916. But the planning, the coordination, and the execution were all faulty and the movement was easily crushed. Huerta and Orozco might have done better, at least in the northern part of Mexico where they enjoyed some measure of support, but the movement ultimately would have failed for the same reason that the Constitutionalist revolution, after winning a military victory, failed to unite a war-torn country. The personalism inherent in the exile community had already bred jealousies which, in turn, bred factionalism and internal dissent. Huerta to his last moment had not fully recognized the pitfalls of trying to satisfy a wide spectrum of political tastes.

Victoriano Huerta's position in the social movement unleashed by Francisco I. Madero in November, 1910, has been misrepresented for years. And it is useless to try to understand it without appreciating the immense and hopeless bitterness which divided the opposing factions

74. Cobb to Lansing, January 12, 1916, RDS, 812.001 H 87/56.
75. Father Joyce tried for four years to persuade the United States government to help him secure the family papers. Knowing that the Mexican government would not easily let them out of the country, he asked that he be allowed to send them in the diplomatic mail pouch. His request was passed around from one agency to another from 1916 to 1920 with absolutely no resolution of the problem. As Huerta's widow became quickly destitute, Father Joyce also tried to secure for her some of the bond money which Huerta had posted for his friends. He was equally unsuccessful in this venture.
76. *New York Times*, January 13, 1916.
77. Ibid., January 14, 1916.

of that first revolutionary decade. Each revolutionary group developed its own unique personality and distinct character. Hatreds ran so deep, passions were so intense, that contending parties of all ideological persuasions committed excesses of the first order in the political arena as well as on the field of battle. The most scathing epithets—traitor, assassin, maniac—even embellished with the most potent adjectival profanities, became so commonplace that they lost their impact. To the general hostility of the new order to the old was added the enmity of moderates to radicals, generals to civilians, and nationalists to the United States. But the conflicts were by no means entirely a product of reasoned ideological dispute. All ideology aside there were profiteers and political opportunists who simply availed themselves to the golden opportunities afforded by an agonizing and destructive civil war. Hasty changes in allegiance following a change in government at the local, state, or national level attest to the fact that ideological commitment was often in short supply.

Huerta became a symbol around which groups with differing motivations could agree. Many were genuinely outraged by the murder of Madero and Pino Suárez and the numerous political assassinations that followed. Many believed that social reform was so long overdue that the moderate and pre-emptive program of the administration was clearly inadequate. Others contended that military dictatorship was anachronistic in early twentieth century Mexico and that the country should now proceed along an admittedly tortuous path toward political democracy. On grounds ranging from moral revulsion to humanitarianism it is easy to identify with these sentiments so often eloquently and courageously expressed. But what the pro-Revolutionary school of Mexican historians has neglected is that in addition some of the most vociferous opposition to the regime came from the politically ambitious, from victims of the spoils system, from those who wanted United States intervention, and from those who trafficked illicitly in supplies of war, both north and south of the United States border. Working from diametrically opposed principles, the two groups of allies not only embraced one another but engaged one another in a spirited competition. The game was one of vituperation and invective. The strategy unfortunately capitalized upon the utter despair of the great masses of Mexicans. And the object was to turn the anti-Huerta movement into a point of Revolutionary faith. Between them the two groups succeeded and for generations Mexicans have worshipped with sacerdotal piety at the Revolutionary font, believing that it was erected on the ashes of a counter-Revolutionary regime.

That Mexico desperately needed a fundamental social transformation is scarcely at issue. While new scholarship may yet show that there was more opportunity in Porfirian Mexico than is commonly supposed, nevertheless, society was predominately stagnant. The possibility of social mobility was nonexistent except for the select few. What is at issue is precisely when and how that social transformation was spawned. The answer is embodied in an analysis of the universal historical problem of continuity and change. The orthodox representation of the early Revolution is that the change came with Madero, that the Huerta regime embodied a belated attempt at reestablishing Porfirian continuity, and that Carranza methodically began to sow the revolutionary seeds first thrown into the winds by Madero. But one can embrace this interpretation only if he does not allow the historical data to get in his way. What clearly emerges is an undulating line of progression from the late Díaz period to the Madero presidency, through the Huerta regime to Venustiano Carranza and the Constitution of 1917. And even more inescapable is the fact that the downward undulations are not more prominent from 1913 to 1914 than in any other period circumscribed by the fall of Díaz and the promulgation of the new constitution.

If one dare transgress historical tradition by concluding with a personal anecdote, I would like to relate an incident which occurred on a research trip to Mexico City during the fall of 1967. A Mexican friend, familiar with the outlines of my project, asked me pointedly who I would have chosen as a personal friend—Madero or Huerta? I answered that although I personally preferred a steak and a glass of cognac to a dinner of wheat germ and carrot juice, nevertheless, I would have been more comfortable sharing a table with Madero than with Huerta. He then pressed further and asked why I was determined to write an anti-Madero account of the Revolution. I informed him that this was not my intention, but I felt it desirable to give a fresh look to a very complicated and misunderstood period of Mexican history. Nurtured on the pabulum of the survey textbook, he insisted that I could not present the Huerta regime any differently without maligning Madero. Not at all able to convince him that it was possible to view the Huerta dictatorship more objectively without impugning the motives of the administration which preceded it, I fell back on a revealing phrase which I discovered in the memoirs of Nemesio García Naranjo. And I commend it good-naturedly to those who would judge my unconventional interpretations too harshly: *Soy adversario del maderismo pero no de la primavera!*

Appendix A

VICTORIANO HUERTA'S MILITARY SERVICE RECORD
ASSIGNMENTS, PROMOTIONS, AND SPECIAL HONORS

January 4, 1872	Matriculated at Colegio Militar de Chapultepec
December 14, 1874	Commissioned as a student corporal at Colegio Militar de Chapultepec
December 4, 1875	Commissioned as a student sublieutenant at Colegio Militar de Chapultepec
April 7, 1877	Commissioned a lieutenant in the Corps of Engineers on his graduation
September 26, 1878	Assigned as an adjutant of the General Staff
January 25, 1879	Promoted to first captain of the Special Corps, General Staff
September 17, 1879	Assigned to the Geographic Exploratory Commission in Puebla
December 18, 1879	Served in the Campaign of the West (Sinaloa and Tepic)
April 27, 1882	Appointed commander of the Geographic Exploratory Commission
July 1, 1884	Promoted to lieutenant colonel of the Special General Staff
October 6, 1887	Served as a highway engineer with a special commission to Veracruz
August 2, 1890	Promoted to colonel of the Special General Staff
November 16, 1895	Appointed commander of the federal forces in Chilpancingo
May 12, 1897	Awarded the Cross of Military Merit, Third Class

233

April 12, 1901	Chosen to command the Third Infantry Battalion in the Guerrero campaign
May 6, 1901	Promoted to temporary brigadier general, Special General Staff
October 23, 1901	Served in the Yucatán campaign
January 11, 1902	Promoted to permanent brigadier general
July 29, 1902	Awarded Special Decoration of Military Merit
May 5, 1903	Awarded Special Decoration of Service, State of Yucatán
August 15, 1903	Appointed a magistrate on the Military Supreme Court
May 5, 1909	Awarded the Cross of Honor, First Class
April, 1910	Commanded federal forces in the Morelos campaign
April 1, 1912	Commissioned commander in the Campaign of the North (Orozquista)
July 30, 1912	Promoted to general of division
February 9, 1913	Appointed commander of the federal forces in Mexico City
May 5, 1913	Awarded the Cross of Military Merit, First Class
March 4, 1914	Promoted to general of the army

Appendix B

PACT OF THE CIUDADELA[1]

In the city of Mexico, at nine-thirty in the evening on February 18, 1913, Generals Félix Díaz and Victoriano Huerta met in conference, the former assisted by Licenciados Fidencio Hernández and Rodolfo Reyes, the latter by Lieutenant Colonel Joaquín Maass and Ingeniero Enrique Cepeda. General Huerta stated that because of the unbearable situation created by the government of Mr. Madero, he had, in order to prevent the further shedding of blood and to safeguard national unity, placed the said Madero, several members of his cabinet, and various other persons under arrest. He expressed to General Díaz his sincere wish that the [political] elements General Díaz represented join with him and that all parties reunited put an end to the current deplorable situation. General Díaz stated that his only reason for raising the standard of revolt was a desire on his part to protect the national welfare, and in that light he was ready to make any sacrifice that would prove beneficial to the country.

After a discussion in which the above mentioned gentlemen took part, the following resolutions were agreed upon:

FIRST. From this time forward the former chief executive is not to be recognized. The [political] elements represented by Generals Díaz and Huerta are united in opposing all efforts to restore him to power.

SECOND. The present situation will be settled with the least possible delay and by the most convenient lawful means. Generals Díaz and Huerta will do all in their power to enable the latter to assume, within seventy-two hours, the provisional presidency of the republic with the following cabinet:

1. The Pact of the Ciudadela can be found in many printed sources. A convenient reference is DHRM, 9:147-48.

235

Foreign Affairs: Licenciado Francisco León de la Barra
Finance: Licenciado Toribio Esquivel Obregón
War: General Manuel Mondragón
Public Works: Ingeniero Alberto Robles Gil
Interior: Ingeniero Alberto García Granados
Justice: Licenciado Rodolfo Reyes
Education: Licenciado Jorge Vera Estañol
Communications: Ingeniero David de la Fuente

A new department to be known as the Department of Agriculture will be created for the purpose of resolving the agrarian question and related matters. The portfolio of this department is to be held by Manuel Garza Aldape.

Whatever changes may be necessary in the proposed cabinet will be agreed upon in the same way that the cabinet itself was agreed upon.

THIRD. Until such time as the legal situation is settled, Generals Huerta and Díaz will remain the depositaries of all authority that is necessary to give full protection to all interests.

FOURTH. General Díaz declines the offer of being a member of the provisional cabinet when General Huerta assumes the provisional presidency so that he can retain his freedom of action in fostering the interests of his party during the next elections. He wishes to make this point very clear to everyone and to indicate that the undersigned are in full agreement.

FIFTH. Official notification shall be sent immediately to the representatives of foreign nations, mentioning solely that the incumbent chief executive has been removed, that steps will be taken at once to select his successor, and that in the meantime Generals Díaz and Huerta shall exert all their authority to assure full protection to all foreign nationals.

SIXTH. All rebels are invited to cease hostilities at once. Each case will be settled individually.

GENERAL VICTORIANO HUERTA
GENERAL FELIX DIAZ

Appendix C

Ministers of Foreign Relations
Francisco León de la Barra — February to July, 1913
Federico Gamboa — July to September, 1913
Querido Moheno — October, 1913, to February, 1914
José López Portillo y Rojas — February to May, 1914
Francisco S. Carbajal — July, 1914

Ministers of Gobernación
Alberto García Granados — February to April, 1913
Aureliano Urrutia — June to September, 1913
Manuel Garza Aldape — September to November, 1913
Ignacio Alocer — February, 1914, to July, 1914

Ministers of Justice
Rodolfo Reyes — February to September, 1913
Adolfo de la Lama — September, 1913
Enrique Gorostieta — September, 1913, to July, 1914

Ministers of Instrucción Pública y Bellas Artes
Jorge Vera Estañol — February to June, 1913
Manuel Garza Aldape — June to August, 1913
José María Lozano — August to September, 1913
Eduardo Tamariz — (appointed but not confirmed, September, 1913)
Nemesio García Naranjo — October, 1913, to July, 1914

237

Ministers of Fomento (Industria y Comercio after February, 1914)
  Alberto Robles Gil   February to July, 1913
  Manuel Garza Aldape   August to September, 1913
  Leopoldo Rebollar   September, 1913
  Querido Moheno   February, 1914, to July, 1914
  Salomé Botello   July, 1914

Ministers of Comunicaciones y Obras Públicas
  David de la Fuente   February to September, 1913
  José María Lozano   September, 1913, to July, 1914
  Arturo Alvaradejo   July, 1914

Ministers of Hacienda
  Toribio Esquivel Obregón   February to July, 1913
  Enrique Gorostieta   August to September, 1913
  Adolfo de la Lama   September, 1913, to July, 1914

Ministers of Guerra y Marina
  Manuel Mondragón   February to June, 1913
  Aureliano Blanquet   June, 1913, to July, 1914

Ministers of Agricultura y Colonización
  Eduardo Tamariz   February, 1914, to July, 1914
  . Carlos Rincón Gallardo   July, 1914

Bibliographical Essay

Because of the abundance and general availability of bibliographical material on the Mexican Revolution, a simple listing of archives and books consulted would serve little purpose except perhaps to reassure the reader that my project was undertaken with suitable diligence. I have chosen instead to include a selective and critical bibliographical essay in which I can provide some indication of the use to which specific items have been put. The critical statements on the secondary works will alert the reader to my own historiographical prejudices and allow him to accept or reject the interpretive information in the text accordingly, whereas the descriptive commentary on the archives perhaps will suggest possibilities for others working in the early Revolutionary period. Except for the items included under Bibliographies, Guides, and Aids, only the documentary collections, books, and articles cited in the footnotes are included. For purposes of standardization English rules for capitalization have been followed throughout.

Key to the Bibliographical Essay
  I. Bibliographies, Guides, and Aids
 II. Primary Sources
     A. Manuscript Collections
     B. Published Documents
     C. Memoirs, Diaries, and Contemporary Accounts
III. Secondary Works
     A. Biographies
     B. General Accounts of the Revolution
     C. Diplomatic and Military Histories
     D. Institutional and Legal Studies
     E. State and Local Histories
     F. Miscellaneous Articles
 IV. Newspapers

I. Bibliographies, Guides, and Aids

For years the basic bibliographical guide to Mexican Revolutionary history has been Roberto Ramos, *Bibliografía de la Revolución Mexicana*, 3 vols. (Mexico: Biblioteca del Instituto Nacional de Estudios Históricos de la Revolución Mexicana, 1959-60). Originally published between 1931 and 1940 the bibliography was praised for its thoroughness (over 5,000 titles), but a poor organization and absence of a genuinely useful index greatly limited its utility. Recently it has been rendered almost obsolete by the more complete and better organized *Fuentes de la Historia Contemporánea de México*, 5 vols. (Mexico: El Colegio de México, 1961-66). The first three volumes, under the editorship of Luis González, are devoted to *Libros y Folletos*, whereas the fourth and fifth, subtitled *Periódicos y Revistas*, were prepared under the editorship of Stanley Ross. The González volumes overshadowed the earlier Ramos effort in every regard, while the Ross volumes made possible for the first time the most expeditious use of Mexico's fine collection of newspapers and periodicals at the Hemeroteca Nacional. Of more value to Mexican than to United States historians is the recent compilation by Charles W. Johnson entitled *México en el Siglo XX: Bibliografía Política y Social de Publicaciones Extranjeras* (Mexico: Universidad Nacional Autónoma de México, Instituto de Investigaciones Sociales, 1969), containing over 2,600 references published in languages other than Spanish.

Dated and of more limited value, but still worth the trouble, are Helen L. Clagett, *A Guide to the Law and Legal Literature of the Mexican States* (Washington, D. C.: Library of Congress, 1947), and Annita M. Ker, *Mexican Government Publications* (Washington, D. C.: Government Printing Office, 1940). For the subject it covers the bibliography of the Comisión de Estudios Militares of the Secretaría de Guerra y Marina, *Apuntes para una Bibliografía Militar de México, 1536-1936* (Mexico: Secretaría de Guerra y Marina, 1937) is helpful, as is Ignacio B. del Castillo's *Bibliografía de la Revolución Mexicana de 1910 a 1916* (Mexico: Talleres Gráficos de la Secretaría de Comunicaciones y Obras Públicas, 1918). To keep current on historical scholarship one should, of course, review the appropriate sections of the annual *Handbook of Latin American Studies* (Cambridge, Mass., and Gainesville, Florida, 1936-), prepared by the Hispanic Foundation of the Library of Congress, and the annual volumes published by El Colegio de México under the title of *Bibliografía Histórica Mexicana*, 3 vols. (Mexico: El Colegio de México, 1967-69). Both annotate a large number of articles and books and in addition the *Handbook* contains useful interpretive summaries of the yearly production.

For the diplomacy of the Revolution two extensive works complement one another: Daniel Cosío Villegas, *Cuestiones Internaciones de México, Una Bibliografía* (Mexico: Secretaría de Relaciones Exteriores, 1966), and David Trask, Michael C. Meyer, and Roger R. Trask, *A Bibliography of United States Latin American Relations Since 1810: A Selected List of Eleven Thousand Published References* (Lincoln: University of Nebraska Press, 1968). Both works are organized for maximum efficiency and contain detailed indexes. The Trask, Meyer, and Trask guide contains some descriptive annotations. And finally for references which are not available anywhere else, the highly useful guide to the literature of the border region, Charles C. Cumberland's "The United States–Mexican Border: A Selective Guide to the Literature of the Region," Supplement to *Rural Sociology* 25 (June 1960) is invaluable.

Published guides to archival collections are still at a premium for the Revolutionary period. Most useful is Berta Ulloa's excellent *Revolución Mexicana, 1910-1920* (Mexico: Secretaría de Relaciones Exteriores, 1963). A descriptive guide to the 259 bound volumes of documents in the Foreign Relations Archive, the work can save the researcher days of time if he uses it carefully before he enters the archive itself. In addition to the extensive descriptions, the name index is a valuable tool. At the present time there is no comparable volume for the Archivo Histórico de la Defensa Nacional, although one is under preparation under the direction of Professor Luis Muro of El Colegio de México. Not of the same magnitude, a pamphlet entitled *Centro de Estudio de Historia de México* (Mexico: Fundación Cultural de Condumex, 1969) discusses the nature of the holdings of the Condumex Archive but does not attempt a description of the archival collections themselves. John P. Harrison's *Guide to Materials on Latin America in the National Archives* (Washington: General Services Administration, 1961) is useful as far as it goes but does not pretend to be definitive. Michael C. Meyer's "Albert Bacon Fall's Mexican Papers: A Preliminary Investigation," *New Mexico Historical Review* 40 (April 1965): 165-74, is simply an introduction to the collection, not a detailed description.

The biographical dictionary is an invaluable tool for the historian of the Revolutionary period because of the large number of relatively obscure personages whose names appear repeatedly, without any identification, in the manuscripts and secondary works. By far the best is the *Diccionario Porrua: Historia, Biografía e Geografía de México* (Mexico: Editorial Porrua, 1964) for which a supplement appeared two years after the initial volume. Having the *Diccionario Porrua* close at hand can save many hours of frustrating search in other volumes not designed to answer the kinds of specific queries to which it directs itself. Not nearly as complete but still useful are Miguel Angel Peral, *Diccionario Biográfico Mexicano,* 2 vols. (Mexico: Editorial P.A.C., 1944); Francisco Naranjo, *Diccionario Biográfico Revolucionario* (Mexico: Imprenta Editorial "Cosmos," 1935); and Manuel García Purón, *México y sus Gobernantes: Biografías* (Mexico: Librería de Manuel Porrua, 1964). Two additional biographical guides are designed more for the student and general reader than for the research scholar: Daniel Moreno, *Los Hombres de la Revolución* (Mexico: Libro Mex Editores, 1960), and Alberto Jiménez Morales, *Hombres de la Revolución Mexicana: 50 Semblanzas Biográficas* (Mexico: Biblioteca del Instituto Nacional de Estudios Históricos de la Revolución Mexicana, 1960).

Mexican historians have yet to produce a major historiographical work on all of the important literature of the Revolution, but a number of limited ones are useful for their interpretive insights into the nature of the historical production. Daniel Cosío Villegas, *Nueva Historiografía Política del México Moderno* (Mexico: Editorial del Colegio Nacional, 1965) treats a few studies of the early Revolutionary period but is concerned primarily with books and articles covering the period from the end of the French intervention through the Díaz dictatorship, the same period studied in his multivolume *Historia Moderna de México.* A recent Mexican appraisal of United States contributions to Mexican Revolutionary historiography is Eugenia Meyer, *Conciencia Histórica Norteamericana Sobre la Revolución de 1910* (Mexico: Instituto Nacional de Antropología e Historia, 1970). Periodical literature of an interpretive nature which treats both United States and Mexican contributions to revolutionary historiography includes Robert A. Potash, "Historiografía del México Independiente," *Historia Mexicana* 10 (July 1960-June 1961): 363-412; Stanley R. Ross, "Aportación Norteamericana de la Revolución Mexicana," *Historia Mexicana* 10 (July 1960-June 1961): 282-308; Stanley R. Ross, "El Historiador y el Periodismo Mexicano," *Historia Mexicana* 14 (July 1964-June 1965): 347-83; and Michael C. Meyer, "Perspectives on Mexican Revolutionary Historiography," *New Mexico Historical Review* 44 (April 1969): 167-80.

II. Primary Sources

A. *Manuscript Collections*

The historian interested in the early Revolutionary period is fortunate indeed to have extant a relatively large number of manuscript collections. Most of them are well preserved and accessible if not always conveniently organized. The most important single source of manuscripts for this study was the Archivo de la Secretaría de Relaciones Exteriores de México. ·Located in the basement of a handsome new building in Mexico City's Ciudad Tlaltelolco, the collection contains almost as many documents pertinent to Mexico's internal history during the period as to its international relations. The entire collection is cataloged, and although the individual investigator is not allowed to use the huge subject index (because of the classified nature of some of the references), staff personnel are helpful in assuming the task themselves and securing the requested information. The most valuable single set of documents in the collection are grouped under the title Revolución Mexicana Durante los Años de 1910 a 1920: Informaciones Diversas de la República y de las Oficinas de México en el Exterior, L-E 610 to L-E 868. It is for this collection that the researcher can prepare himself with the previously mentioned Berta Ulloa guide (see p. 240). In addition to the 259 bound volumes in this collection, I found extremely useful the collection organized under the general title Mensajes Relativos a la Evacuación del Puerto de Veracruz por los Americanos, III/252 (73:72)/353. In spite of the title, the collection contains innumerable documents pertaining to the occupation as well as the evacuation and, in fact, is valuable for the general history of the period covered by the occupation. Finally in using the Foreign Relations Archive one should not overlook the large number of personal *expedientes* of government officials during the period of his interest. These files often contain documentation not elsewhere available. Those which I consulted include Victoriano Huerta, L-E 1579; Venustiano Carranza, L-E 373-376; Francisco Serrano, L-E 1340; Juan Sánchez Azcona, L-E 1002-1003; Roberto A. Esteva Ruiz, L-E 1343; Enrique C. Llorente, L-E 1289-1290; Antonio V. Lomelí, L-E 1186-1189; and Miguel Covarrubias, L-E 373-376.

The Archivo General de la Nación contains the records of the secretaría de gobernación and a series of Francisco Madero copybooks. The ministry of gobernación was charged by Huerta with maintaining all coordination between the national government and the states and, throughout much of the regime, was also the government agency which exercised command over the rurales. The documentation therefore is of both a civilian and military nature. Unfortunately there is no available catalog to the gobernación records and one must merely request that the documents be brought for inspection. The legajos which I found most helpful were those labeled: 4° Cuerpo Rural, Armamento y Municiones; 4° Cuerpo Rural, Armas, Diversas, 1913-14; Cuerpos Rurales de la Federación, 1912-13; Policía, Gobierno del Distrito, 1912-13; Imprenta del Gobierno, 1914; Inspección General de Policía, 1913; Decretos, 1913; Gobernadores de Estados, Asuntos Varios, 1913-14; Varios Autógrafos de Gobernadores; and Diversas Secretarías, Gobierno del Distrito, Cuerpos Rurales, Relaciones con los Estados, 1913-14.

The Madero copybooks, four bound volumes of correspondence, are somewhat mysteriously numbered 1, 2, 3, and 12. Arranged chronologically, they consist of Madero's outgoing correspondence during his presidency. Madero wrote the letters himself during the first nine months, taking the time not only to answer specific queries but also to volunteer his opinions on a wide array of topics. After that time, however, his personal secretary, Juan Sánchez Azcona, began answering the correspondence for him and the utility of the letters for historical purposes declines markedly.

The most extensive body of military documentation is that located in the Archivo Histórico de la Defensa Nacional. Not an easy collection to gain access to, the groundwork must be laid carefully in advance if one is to secure admittance. The effort can be most rewarding, however, if one's requests for permission are in the end honored. The largest collection of pertinent documentation for the early Revolutionary period is the huge body of correspondence located under File Series XI/481.5. This group consists of the reports of the military commanders of the states, dispatches of various subaltern officers, battle reports, personnel and equipment requests, and a wide variety of other military documentation. When I worked in the National Defense Archives, I was denied permission to consult Huerta's personal military record in the Cancelados section. Subsequently, however, the file was opened, a copy secured by Professor Eugenia Meyer, and graciously made available to me.

A relatively new archive with three important manuscript collections for the early Revolutionary period is that of the Fundación Cultural de Condumex. Located in Mexico City's industrial zone of Vallejo, Condumex has established a Center of Historical Studies with an excellent library and archive. The three collections which I used were the Correspondencia Personal y Oficial de Francisco León de la Barra como Embajador de México y Presidente de la República, Adquisición X; the Archivo Carranza, Documentos Pertenecientes al Archivo del Primer Jefe del Ejército Constitucionalista de México, don Venustiano Carranza, Adquisición XXI; and the Archivo Particular del General Jenaro Amezcua sobre la Revolución Zapatista, Adquisición VIII.

Certainly not to be overlooked is the Archivo de don Francisco I. Madero, a microfilm copy of which is available for consultation in the new Museo Nacional de Antropología e Historia. The collection is extensive, some sixty thousand sheets of correspondence, public and private documents, pamphlets, and newspaper clippings. Two smaller collections which can be rewarding are the Archivo Particular de Bernardo Reyes and the Archivo Espinosa de los Monteros. The Reyes archive, held by the family in the Capilla Alfonsina, is comprised of approximately seventy boxes and folders touching upon all aspects of the general's career. The Espinosa de los Monteros Archive, located at the Historical Annex to Chapultepec Castle, consists of nine bound volumes which have been catalogued by Josefina González de Arrellano. Because Samuel Espinosa de los Monteros was the secretary of the Reyista party, the collection is rich on the political history of the period 1909 to 1913, but it also contains interesting documentation on the Mexican reaction to the United States invasion of Veracruz in April, 1914.

The most extensive collection of manuscript materials on Revolutionary Mexico in the United States is the Records of the Department of State Relating to the Internal Affairs of Mexico, 1910-29, Microcopy 274. This collection of documents contains the correspondence of the secretary of state, American ambassador and chargé in Mexico, consular officials throughout the country, and special agents dispatched to that country by President Wilson. The index to the huge collection is of little value and one must consult the documents themselves to use the archive advantageously.

From the National Archives in Washington I secured microfilm copies of records from a number of government agencies which were interested in Mexico generally and Huerta specifically during the early Revolutionary period. Of greatest value were the following collections: War Department and General and Special Staff, Military Intelligence Division File 5761, Reports of Captain Burnside, 1912-13, Record Group 165; Records of the Adjutant General's Office,

Consolidated File 2284054, Record Group 94; Records of the Department of Justice, Straight Numerical File 90755-U-, Record Group 60; and Department of State, Correspondence of Secretary of State Bryan with President Wilson, 1913-15, Microcopy T 841.

Senator Albert Bacon Fall of New Mexico, long interested in Mexican affairs maintained an extensive file of Mexican correspondence, newspaper clippings, books, and pamphlets. The original documents are now housed in the Huntington Library. Microfilm copies are available at the University of New Mexico and the University of Nebraska under the title: Albert Bacon Fall Collection, Papers from the Senate Office Files of Senator Albert Bacon Fall Relating to Mexican Affairs. The extensive Silvestre Terrazas Collection, Correspondence and Papers, held by the Bancroft Library at Berkeley was of limited value for this particular topic but should not be overlooked for its store of information on the late Díaz period and early Revolution.

Finally, from the British Public Record Office, I obtained the foreign papers pertaining to Mexico during the years 1913 and 1914. The British embassy personnel and consular agents were on the whole much more astute than their United States counterparts and, as a result, the British records are generally superior to the Department of State records. Microfilm copies are available under the title, Foreign Office Records: Embassy and Consular Archives, America, F.O. 115.

B. *Published Documents*

Without question the most valuable set of published Revolutionary documents for any historical topic is the *Documentos Históricos de la Revolución Mexicana,* 21 vols. to date (Mexico: Fondo de Cultura Económica and Editorial Jus, 1960-70). The project was initiated by the late Isidro Fabela and after his death carried forward by his widow, Josefina E. de Fabela, and the Comisión de Investigaciones Históricas de la Revolución Mexicana, comprised of Roberto V. Ramos, Luis G. Ceballos, Miguel Saldaña, Baldomero Segura García, and Humberto Tejera. With two volumes still to be published at the time of this writing the *Documentos Históricos* are a veritable storehouse of valuable information. Documents have been selected from the private collection of Fabela as well as most of the important public archives in Mexico City. While this set should not be considered a substitute for archival research, it will yield many a thesis, dissertation, and article in the next ten years. The volumes have been reviewed individually in the *Hispanic American Historical Review* but the reviews can do no more than offer a brief summation of the documentation contained therein. Although each volume contains a summary index, the student willing to turn each page will be amply rewarded.

Three other works of lesser magnitude are valuable because they contain all of the most important political plans, constitutions, public speeches, letters of leading figures, and legislation: Manuel González Ramírez, ed., *Fuentes para la Historia de la Revolución Mexicana, vol. 1, Planes Políticos y Otros Documentos* (Mexico: Fondo de Cultura Económica, 1954), covering the period 1906 to 1940; Felipe Tena Ramírez, *Leyes Fundamentales de México, 1808-1957* (Mexico: Editorial Porrua, 1957); and Ernesto de la Torre Villar, Moisés González Navarro, and Stanley Ross, *Historia Documental de México,* 2 vols. (Mexico: Universidad Nacional Autónoma de México, 1962-64). The last mentioned work will be published shortly in an English edition by the University of Nebraska Press.

Unique in Mexican Revolutionary historiography is Gustavo Casasola, ed., *Historia Gráfica de la Revolución Mexicana,* 6 vols. (Mexico: Archivo Casasola, n.d.; new ed., 4 vols., Mexico: Editorial F. Trillas, 1965). A photographic history of the Revolution interspersed with text and documentary extracts, it is a delightful experience for the Mexico buff as well as the scholar. A critical eye can glean almost as much from the pictures of the Decena Trágica and the Battle of Torreón as from a dispatch of a witness. The new edition, printed on quality paper, is much superior to the old.

Official Mexican government documents have not been adequately utilized in many studies of the early Revolutionary period, not even the congressional debates. Although tedious to use they provide information which simply cannot be obtained elsewhere. Those which I found most helpful were: Mexico, Congreso, *Diario de los Debates de la Cámara de Diputados del Congreso de los Estados Unidos Mexicanos* (Mexico: Imprenta de la Cámara de Diputados, 1922); Mexico, *Diario Oficial* (Mexico: Imprenta del Gobierno Federal, 1913-14); Mexico, Secretaría de Estado y del Despacho de Gobernación, *Ley Electoral de los Estados Unidos Mexicanos* (Mexico: Imprenta del Gobierno Federal, 1913), which provides the legal basis for the October, 1913, elections; and Mexico, Secretaría de Relaciones Exteriores, *Labor Internacional de la Revolución Constitucionalista de México* (Mexico: Imprenta de la Secretaría de Gobernación, n.d.), which contains important diplomatic dispatches of the period February, 1913, to September, 1918.

The published documents from United States agencies I found most helpful include the widely used U. S., Department of State, *Papers Relating to the Foreign Relations of the United States*, for the years 1911, 1912, 1913, 1914, and 1915 (Washington, D. C., Government Printing Office, 1918-24); U. S., Senate, *Investigation of Mexican Affairs. Report and Hearing before a Subcommittee on Foreign Relations, Senator Albert Bacon Fall, Presiding, Pursuant to Senate Resolution 106,* Senate Document no. 285, 66th Cong., 2d sess., 2 vols. (Washington, D. C., 1919-20); and Albert Bacon Fall, *Affairs in Mexico* (Washington: Government Printing Office, 1914).

Miscellaneous documentary publications treating the period are Alfredo Alvarez, ed., *Madero y su Obra: Documentos para la Historia* (Mexico: Talleres Gráficos de la Nación, 1935), containing a short selection of Madero's correspondence with Zapata, Reyes, and de la Barra; Jesús Acuña, ed., *Memoria de la Secretaría de Gobernación Correspondiente al Período Revolucionario* (Mexico: Talleres Linotipográficos de "Revista de Revistas," 1916), comprising government documents put together by the Constitutionalists after Huerta's overthrow but covering the period February, 1913, to November, 1916; Rafael Alducín, ed., *La Revolución Constitucionalista, los Estados Unidos, y el A.B.C.* (Mexico: Talleres Linotipográficos de "Revista de Revistas," 1916), which is a compilation treating Mexico's international relations with the United States including contemporary periodical selections and editorial opinion; and Calixto Maldonado R., ed., *Los Asesinatos de los Señores Madero y Pino Suárez: Recopilación de Datos Históricos* (Mexico: n.p., 1922), a valuable collection containing results of the official and nonofficial investigations of the assassinations.

C. *Memoirs, Diaries, and Contemporary Accounts*

Mexican Revolutionary historiography is rich in memoirs, diaries, and other contemporary accounts. Certainly they must be used critically because of the intense partiality of the age and the general tendency of self-glorification and exculpation. But the possible pitfalls should not discourage the use of these sources because of their valuable insight into motivation, historical settings, and personal responses to historical stimuli.

The most controversial of all the memoirs is the apocryphal *Memorias de Victoriano Huerta* (Mexico: Ediciones Vertice, 1957). Originally published in El Paso, Texas, in 1915 and subsequently republished many times, they most assuredly were not written by Huerta but rather by someone who knew him well. The favorite suggestion is Mexican journalist Joaquín Piña. For years scholars have held that in spite of the apocryphal nature, Huerta's memoirs are very useful because of their insights into the man. With a few exceptions I did not find them to be of much value. They scarcely compare to the genuine memoirs of other persons in the government.

The most detailed set of memoirs from the period are Nemesio García Naranjo's *Memorias de Nemesio García Naranjo,* 10 vols. (Monterrey: Talleres de "El Porvenir," n.d.). The seventh volume, entitled *Mis Andanzas con el General Huerta,* is devoted exclusively to the regime with heavy emphasis on the author's role in the ministry of education. Other Huerta officials who recorded their recollections include Querido Moheno, *Mi Actuación Política Después de la Decena Trágica* (Mexico: Ediciones Botas, 1939), and *Sobre el Ara Sangrienta* (Mexico: Editorial Andrés Botas e Hijo, 1922). The first of the Moheno volumes covers the period during which he was in the cabinet, whereas the second is devoted to his period of exile after the Constitutionalist victory. Two additional cabinet ministers recorded their thoughts as well: Toribio Esquivel Obregón, *Mi Labor en Servicio de México* (Mexico: Ediciones Botas, 1934), and Rodolfo Reyes, *De mi Vida: Memorias Políticas,* 2 vols. (Madrid: Biblioteca Nueva, 1929-30). Finally Joaquín Pita, the chief of police in Mexico City from February to September, 1913, published his memoirs in a series of newspaper articles in 1948. See "Memorias del Coronel Joaquín Pita," *El Universal,* July 1-6, 1948.

Those personages outside the government offer an altogether different view. The military campaigns can be traced in the famous Martín Luis Guzmán, *Memorias de Pancho Villa* (Mexico: Compañía General de Ediciones, 1960; English ed., Austin: University of Texas Press, 1965), and Alvaro Obregón, *Ocho Mil Kilómetros en Campaña* (Mexico: Fondo de Cultura Económica, 1960). More politically oriented are Manuel Calero, *Un Decenio de Política Mexicana* (New York: Middleditch Co., 1920); Alfredo Breceda, *México Revolucionario, 1913-17,* 2 vols. (Madrid: n.p., 1920; Mexico: Ediciones Botas, 1941); Federico González Garza, *La Revolución Mexicana: Mi Contribución Político-Literaria* (Mexico: A. del Bosque Impresor, 1936); and Alberto J. Pani, *Mi Contribución al Nuevo Régimen, 1910-1933* (Mexico: Editorial Cultura, 1936). Salvador Alvarado's *Mi Actuación Revolucionaria en Yucatán* (Mexico: Librería de la Vda. de Ch. Bouret, 1920) contains useful commentary on social conditions prevailing in Yucatán during the Constitutionalist revolution, while Félix F. Palavicini affords a view of the opposition in Congress in his *Mi Vida Revolucionaria* (Mexico: Ediciones Botas, 1937). The interpretations of Juan Andreu Almazán were serialized in *El Universal* in the fall of 1957.

Of the memoirs of foreign observers, those in the diplomatic circle are most revealing. The American ambassador's impressions of the assassination of Madero and the early months of the Huerta regime are recorded in Henry Lane Wilson, *Diplomatic Episodes in Mexico, Belgium, and Chile* (New York: Doubleday Page, 1927). The Cuban ambassador, a staunch supporter of Francisco Madero, offers a valuable impressionistic account in his M. Márquez Sterling, *Los Ultimos Días del Presidente Madero: Mi Gestión Diplomática en México* (Havana: Imprenta el Siglo, XX, 1917). Edith O'Shaughnessy, the wife of the American chargé, records much capital city gossip in her *A Diplomat's Wife in Mexico* (New York: Harper and Brothers, 1916). The volume is comprised of letters written to her mother and evidences a pro-Huerta bias.

Farther from the locus of power, but nevertheless perceptive, are the memoirs of Rosa King, I. Thord-Grey, and Franz Rintelen von Kleist. Mrs. King, an English subject, owned a hotel in Cuernavaca where Huerta once stayed during the Zapatista campaigns. Her *Tempest Over Mexico: A Personal Chronicle* (Boston: Little, Brown and Co., 1935) contains interesting commentary on the brutality of the war in the south. General I. Thord-Grey, a Swedish born citizen of the United States, fought in Villa's ranks as an artillery officer and published his experiences under the title *Gringo Rebel* (Coral Gables, Fla: University of Miami Press, 1960). The memoirs of Franz Rintelen von Kleist, *The Dark Invader: Wartime Reminiscences of a German Naval Intelligence Officer* (New York: Macmillan Co., 1933) are useful for Huerta's intrigues with Germany after his ouster.

The contemporary accounts written by Mexicans almost all reflect either a pro-Constitutionalist or pro-Huerta bias. In the first category one should include Alfredo Aragón, *El Desarme del Ejército Federal por la Revolución de 1913* (Paris: n.p., 1915), which is dedicated to Carranza and is a bitter indictment of the army for having supported Huerta during the Decena Trágica; Edmundo González-Blanco, *Carranza y la Revolución de México* (Madrid: Imprenta Helénica, 1916), and Pedro González-Blanco, *De Porfirio Díaz a Carranza* (Madrid: Imprenta Helénica, 1916) are both part of a series entitled Biblioteca Constitucionalista; Antonio Manero, *Por el Honor y por la Gloria* (Mexico: Imprenta T. Escalante, 1916), a collection of fifty newspaper editorials written in Veracruz during the Constitutionalist Revolution, and by the same author *¿Que Es la Revolución?* (Veracruz: Tipografía la Heróica, 1915), an exaggerated analysis of the social content of Constitutionalist doctrine; and finally Guillermo N. Mellado, *Crímenes del Huertismo* (Mexico: n.p., 1914), which details thirty-four assassinations, all attributed to Huerta.

Contemporary accounts by admirers of the regime are equally uncritical. Topping the list is Manuel Doblado's *El Presidente Huerta y su Gobierno* (Mexico: Imprenta de Antonio Enríquez, 1913), a total apologia. Equally eulogistic, but at least containing some useful documentary reproductions, is Gregorio Ponce de León, *La Paz y sus Colaboradores* (Mexico: Imprenta y Fototipia de la Secretaría de Fomento, 1914). In the same category one should include G. Núñez del Prado, *Revolución de México: La Decena Trágica* (Barcelona: F. Granados y Co., 1914?); José Fernández Rojas, *La Revolución Mexicana de Porfirio Díaz a Victoriano Huerta, 1910-1913* (Mexico: Editores F. P. Rojas y Cía, 1913); and Gonzalo N. Espinosa, Joaquín Piña, and Carlos B. Ortiz, *La Decena Roja* (Mexico: n.p., 1913) all of which accept the defection of Huerta and the army as the only means of preventing further loss of life and restoring order in the capital.

Between these extremes are two additional contemporary works by Mexicans, noteworthy because of the documentary extracts included: Antimaco Sax, *Los Mexicanos en el Destierro* (San Antonio: International Printing Co., 1916), containing newspaper articles from Nemesio García Naranjo's *La Revista Mexicana* and *La Prensa* of San Antonio; and Fortunato Hernández, *Mas Allá del Desastre* (Mexico: n.p., 1913), containing part of Huerta's service record.

Many foreigners prepared contemporary accounts during brief trips and extended periods of residence in Mexico. Those which I consulted and found instructive include Edward I. Bell, *The Political Shame of Mexico* (New York: McBride, Nast and Co., 1914); [Jan Leander De Bekker], *De Como Vino Huerta y Como se Fué: Apuntes para la Historia de un Régimen Militar* (Mexico: Librería General, 1914); Chilean resident Emigdio S. Paniagua, *El Combate de la Ciudadela Narrado por un Extranjero* (Mexico: Tipografía Artística, 1913); United States journalist John Reed's very readable *Insurgent Mexico* (New York: International Publishers, 1969); Louis Simonds "Victoriano Huerta: A Sketch from Life," *Atlantic Monthly* 113 (June 1914):721-32; and John Kenneth Turner, *Barbarous Mexico* (Austin: University of Texas Press, 1969).

III. SECONDARY WORKS

A. *Biographies*

The very nature of the Mexican Revolution seems to lend itself to biography more readily than to any other single historical genre. Some of the worst and some of the best studies of the Revolutionary period fall within a broadly conceived biographical classification. Interestingly, however, the Porfirio Díaz has not yet found a scholarly biographer and the regime must be studied in the indispensable multivolume *Historia Moderna,* edited by Daniel Cosío Villegas, for the Seminar on Modern Mexican History of El Colegio de México. Francisco Bulnes's *El Verdadero Díaz y la Revolución* (Mexico: Editorial Nacional, 1960) is helpful but scarcely meets the rigors of serious biographical scholarship. Bernardo Reyes, a figure whose public career spans the old regime and the new has been studied in two excellent doctoral dissertations solidly researched in the Reyes archives: Anthony T. Bryan, "Mexican Politics in Transition, 1910-1913: The Role of General Bernardo Reyes," (Ph.D. diss., University of Nebraska, 1969), and Victor Eberhardt Niemeyer, "The Public Career of General Bernardo Reyes," (Ph.D. diss., University of Texas, 1958). The latter dissertation has been published in Spanish under the title *El General Bernardo Reyes* (Monterrey: Universidad de Nuevo León, 1966).

The disparate nature of the biographical enterprise is nowhere better illustrated than in the studies of Francisco Madero. Three superior studies, all based on the pertinent archival sources, are available to the serious student: Stanley R. Ross, *Francisco I. Madero: Apostle of Mexican Democracy* (New York: Columbia University Press, 1955); Charles Curtis Cumberland, *Mexican Revolution: Genesis under Madero* (Austin: University of Texas Press, 1952); and José C. Valadés, *Imaginación y Realidad de Francisco I. Madero,* 2 vols. (Mexico: Antigua Librería Robredo, 1960). Poor quality studies of the martyred president abound. By no means the worst, but nevertheless several steps below the aforementioned titles, are Alfonso Taracena, *Madero: Vida del Hombre y del Político* (Mexico: Ediciones Botas, 1937), and by the same author, *La Labor Social del Presidente Madero* (Saltillo: n.p., n.d.); as well as Rafael Martínez and Eduardo Guerra, *Madero: Su Vida, su Obra* (Monterrey: n.p., 1914), a simple exercise in hero worship.

Huerta himself has been studied twice in English. George J. Rausch, Jr., prepared a competent dissertation, "Victoriano Huerta: A Political Biography," (Ph.D. diss., University of Illinois, 1960), which subsequently yielded two important articles: "The Early Career of Victoriano Huerta," *The Americas* 21 (October 1964): 136-45; and "The Exile and Death of Victoriano Huerta," *Hispanic American Historical Review* 42 (May 1962): 133-51. First pointing up the need for a fresh look at the Mexican dictator were William L. Sherman and Richard E. Greenleaf in *Victoriano Huerta: A Reappraisal* (Mexico: Mexico City College Press, 1960). Although based entirely on printed materials, the study is useful for its commentaries into the nature of the secondary works on the early Revolutionary period.

Of Huerta's supporters only three have received careful study. Genaro María González has written a significant intellectual biography of the first minister of hacienda, *Toribio Esquivel Obregón: Actitud e Ideario Político* (Mexico: Editorial Libros de México, 1967). The career of General Pascual Orozco is studied in my *Mexican Rebel: Pascual Orozco and the Mexican Revolution, 1910-1915* (Lincoln: University of Nebraska Press, 1967). And finally Luis Liceaga's *Félix Díaz* (Mexico: Editorial Jus, 1958) is a sympathetic but solid biography based upon documentary research.

As should be expected, the opposition camp has attracted the interest of many more biographers. Amazingly there is no first-rate biography of Venustiano Carranza and therefore, one must rely in the interim on Ignacio G. Suárez's less than critical *Carranza: Forjador del México Actual* (Mexico: B. Costa-Amic, Editor, 1965); Alfonso Taracena's subjective *Venustiano Carranza* (Mexico:

Editorial Jus, 1963); and Bernardo Mena Brito, ed., *Carranza: Sus Amigos, sus Enemigos* (Mexico: Ediciones Botas, 1935), a series of articles and contemporary documents. Biographies of other Constitutionalists which I found helpful include Armando de María y Campos, *Múgica: Crónica Biográfica* (Mexico: Compañía de Ediciones Populares, 1939), and Bernardo Mena Brito, *Felipe Angeles, Federal* (Mexico: Publicaciones Herrería, 1936).

Constitutionalist sympathizer Abraham González has been carefully studied twice. The best published account is by Chihuahua historian Francisco Almada, *Vida, Proceso y Muerte de Abraham González* (Mexico: Biblioteca del Instituto Nacional de Estudios Históricos de la Revolución Mexicana, 1967). A much more balanced treatment, however, is rendered in William H. Beezley, "Revolutionary Governor: Abraham González and the Mexican Revolution in Chihuahua, 1909-1913" (Ph.D. diss., University of Nebraska, 1968). Congressman Belisario Domínguez has received biographical treatment of sorts in Carlos Román Celis, *Belisario Domínguez: Legislador sin Miedo* (Mexico: Publicaciones Mañana, 1963), which consists of a series of memorial essays and selections from his congressional speeches.

John Womack, Jr., has produced a much celebrated study of Emiliano Zapata and the agrarian movement in Morelos. His *Zapata and the Mexican Revolution* (New York: Alfred A. Knopf, 1969) is meticulously researched, well written, and certainly must be considered one of the most valuable pieces of historical scholarship on the Revolution written during the last two decades. Older but still valuable for the great wealth of detail it contains is Zapatista Gildardo Magaña's *Emiliano Zapata y el Agrarismo en México*, 5 vols. (Mexico: Editorial Ruta, 1951-52), the last two volumes of which were completed by Carlos Pérez Guerrero. Less satisfactory than either of these works are Porfirio Palacios, *Emiliano Zapata: Datos Biográficos-Históricos* (Mexico: Libro Mex Editores, 1960), and Baltasar Dromundo, *Emiliano Zapata* (Mexico: Imprenta Mundial, 1934).

Woodrow Wilson has received biographical treatment in literally hundreds of accounts. The best are the series of works by Arthur S. Link, and of these his *Woodrow Wilson and the Progressive Era, 1910-1917* (New York: Harper and Row, 1963) contains extensive sections on Wilson's Mexican policy. Parts of this work combined with other Link studies have appeared in Spanish under the title *La Política de los Estados Unidos en América Latina, 1913-1916* (Mexico: Fondo de Cultura Económica, 1960). Wilson's most important special agent is treated sympathetically in George M. Stephenson, *John Lind of Minnesota* (Minneapolis: University of Minnesota Press, 1935). The Lind mission is reconstructed entirely from English sources.

B. *General Accounts of the Revolution*

The best general history of the Revolution is José C. Valadés, *Historia General de la Revolución Mexicana*, 5 vols. (Mexico: Manuel Quesada Brandi, Editores, 1963-65). More interpretive and more controversial is Andrés Molina Enríquez's *La Revolución Agraria de México*, 5 vols. (Mexico: Talleres Gráficos del Museo Nacional de Arqueología, Historia y Etnografía, 1933-37). Molina Enríquez views Mexico's entire history within the context of the struggle for land. A four-volume cooperative project sponsored by the Mexican government to celebrate the fiftieth anniversary of the Revolution appeared under the title *México: 50 Años de Revolución*, vol. 1, *La Economía;* vol. 2, *La Vida Social;* vol. 3, *La Política;* vol. 4, *La Cultura* (Mexico: Fondo de Cultura Económica, 1960-62). Although the essays are of uneven quality, the compendium is a handy reference for many diverse subjects. The overwhelming majority of survey accounts offer a rather standard pro-Revolutionary interpretation. They differ only on minor details, emphasis, and scope of coverage. Most of them contain pages which could be used intact by Partido Revolucionario Institucional candidates running for political office. Among the pro-Revolutionary accounts which I consulted are the following: Miguel Alessio Robles, *Historia Política de la Revolución* (Mexico: Ediciones Botas, 1946); Juan Gualberto Amaya, *Madero y los Auténticos Revolucionarios de 1910 Hasta la Decena Trágica y Fin del General Pascual Orozco* (Mexico: n.p., 1946), and a follow-up volume by the same author under the title *Venustiano Carranza: Caudillo Constitucionalista* (Mexico: n.p., 1947); Diego Arenas Guzmán, *Del Maderismo a los Tratados de Teoloyucan* (Mexico: Talleres Gráficos de la Nación, 1955); Luis Bello Hidalgo, *Antropología de la Revolución: De Porfirio Díaz a Gustavo Díaz Ordaz* (Mexico: B. Costa Amic Editor, 1966); Roberto Blanco Moheno, *Crónica de la Revolución: De la Decena Trágica a los Campos de Celaya* (Mexico: Libro Mex Editores, 1958); José T. Meléndez, *Historia de la Revolución Mexicana* (Mexico: Talleres Gráficos de la Nación, 1938); Alberto Jiménez Morales, *Historia de la Revolución Mexicana* (Mexico: Instituto de Investigaciones Políticas, Económicas, y Sociales del Partido Revolucionario Institucional, 1951); Jesús Romero Flores, *Del Porfirismo a la Revolución Constitucionalista* (Mexico: Libro Mex Editores, 1960); Juan Sánchez Azcona, *La Etapa Maderista de la Revolución* (Mexico: Biblioteca del Instituto Nacional de Estudios Históricos de la Revolución Mexicana, 1960), and by the same author *Apuntes para la Historia de la Revolución Mexicana* (Mexico: Biblioteca del Instituto Nacional de Estudios Históricos de la Revolución Mexicana, 1961); and Jesús Silva Herzog, *Breve Historia de la Revolución Mexicana,* 2 vols. (Mexico: Fondo de Cultura Económica, 1960).

A few general studies view the Mexican Revolution in terms of the classical Marxist class struggle, and even fewer from a decidedly conservative point of view. In the first category one can include José Mancisidor, *Historia de la Revolución Mexicana* (Mexico: Libro Mex Editores, 1959); Benito R. Blancas, *Ensayo Histórico Sobre la Revolución Mexicana* (Mexico: Talleres de Publicaciones Mexicanas, S.C.L., 1963); and Rafael Ramos Pedrueza, *La Lucha de Clases a Traves de la Historia de México* (Mexico: Talleres Gráficos de la Nación, 1941). The best conservative account is Jorge Vera Estañol, *Historia de la Revolución Mexicana* (Mexico: Editorial Porrua, 1967). Also within the conservative category is Ricardo García Granados, *Historia de Mexico Desde la Restauración de la República en 1867 Hasta la Caída de Huerta,* 2 vols. (Mexico: Editorial Jus, 1956).

Personal and highly partisan interpretations are found in José Vasconcelos, *Breve Historia de México,* 3rd ed. (Mexico: Ediciones Botas, 1937); Francisco Ramírez Plancarte, *La Revolución Mexicana: Interpretación Independiente* (Mexico: Editorial B. Costa Amic Editor, 1948); and Emilio Portes Gil, *Autobiografía de la Revolución Mexicana* (Mexico: Instituto Mexicano de Cultura, 1964). Ignacio Muñoz's *Verdad y Mito de la Revolución Mexicana,* 4 vols. (Mexico: Compañía de Ediciones Populares, 1960-65) is strongly impressionistic and anecdotal but scarcely judicious enough to be much value to the scholar.

General accounts by United States scholars include two older but still valuable works: Ernest Gruening, *Mexico and its Heritage* (New York: D. Appleton-Century, Co., 1934), and Frank Tannenbaum, *Peace by Revolution: Mexico After 1910,* 2nd ed. (New York: Columbia University Press, 1966). Of all of the recent survey accounts by nonhistorians by far the best is William Weber Johnson, *Heroic Mexico: The Violent Emergence of a Modern Nation* (Garden City, N. Y.: Doubleday and Co., 1968). Finally the landmark study of James W. Wilkie, *The Mexican Revolution: Federal Expenditure and Social Change since 1910* (Berkeley: University of California Press, 1967) is in a category by itself for having broken new ground and introduced new methodology.

C. *Diplomatic and Military Histories*

For the student interested in the general history of the diplomatic relations between the United States and Mexico two works are highly recommended: Howard F. Cline, *The United States and Mexico* (New York: Atheneum, 1963), and Samuel Flagg Bemis, *The Latin American Policy of the United States: An Historical Interpretation* (New York: W. W. Norton Co., 1967). Covering a more specific topic but over a long period of time is Sheldon B. Liss's careful study entitled *A Century of Disagreement: The Chamizal Controversy, 1864-1964* (Washington, D. C.: University Press, 1965).

Works treating the diplomacy of the specific period under consideration are numerous but only a few of them are noteworthy for their research and objectivity. Two well-researched and carefully presented studies of Huerta's relations with Great Britain are available: Peter Calvert, *The Mexican Revolution, 1910-1914: The Diplomacy of Anglo-American Conflict* (Cambridge: Cambridge University Press, 1968); and William Sidney Coker, "United States-British Diplomacy over Mexico, 1913" (Ph.D. diss., University of Oklahoma, 1965). Similarly Huerta's German policy can be examined in Friedrich Katz's scholarly exposition of *Deutschland, Diaz und die Mexicanishe Revolution: Die Deutsche Politik in Mexiko, 1870-1920* (Berlin: Veb Deutscher Verlag der Wissenochaften, 1964).

The most detailed work treating the diplomatic conflict between Huerta and Wilson, based on research in both countries, is Kenneth J. Grieb, *The United States and Huerta* (Lincoln: University of Nebraska Press, 1969). The diplomacy of the period 1913 to 1916 is covered in three other works: Eduardo Luquín, *La Política Internacional de la Revolución Constitucionalista* (Mexico: Biblioteca del Instituto Nacional de Estudios Históricos de la Revolución Mexicana, 1957), which demonstrates a good, but not excellent familiarity with the documents; Arthur S. Link, *La Política de los Estados Unidos en América Latina, 1913-1916* (Mexico: Fondo de Cultura Económica, 1960), which in spite of the title is heavily weighted toward Mexico; and Louis M. Teitelbaum, *Woodrow Wilson and the Mexican Revolution, 1913-1916* (New York: Exposition Press, 1967), a not altogether satisfactory venture into diplomatic history by a practicing lawyer.

The Veracruz invasion illustrates the best and the worst in diplomatic historiography. In the former category is Robert E. Quirk's award winning *An Affair of Honor: Woodrow Wilson and the Occupation of Veracruz* (New York: W. W. Norton Co., 1967). Contrasted with the Quirk study is Justino N. Palomares's violently polemical *La Invasión Yanqui en 1914* (Mexico: n.p., 1940). While one can appreciate the sense of outrage, nevertheless, the Palomares study has little to recommend it.

Highly interpretive accounts of the diplomacy of the Huerta regime are found in three studies. José Gaxiola's *La Frontera de la Raza* (Madrid: Tipografía Artística, 1917) is unique in that it offers a pan-Hispanist account of the relations between Woodrow Wilson and Mexico. Luis Lara Pardo's *Matchs de Dictadores* (Mexico: A. P. Márquez, 1942) demonstrates familiarity with the documents but neglects to consider dispatches which conflict with the argumentation being developed. An economic determinist, Lara Pardo argues, not very persuasively, that Woodrow Wilson was controlled by the business community. Finally, a pro-Huerta account of the diplomatic entanglements with the United States is found in Rafael de Zayas Enríquez, *The Case of Mexico and the Policy of President Wilson* (New York: Albert and Charles Boni, 1914).

Works which can only be labeled polemics include Ramón Prida's *La Culpa de Lane Wilson, Embajador en la Tragedia Mexicana de 1913* (Mexico: Ediciones Botas, 1962, and M. S. Alperovich and B. T. Rudenko's *La Revolución Mexicana de 1910-1917 y la Política de los Estados Unidos* (Mexico: Fondo de Cultura

Popular, 1966). The former presents inferential statements as scientific fact and accepts all manner of charges against the American ambassador as inviolable truths. The work by the two Soviet historians is a typical Marxist stricture of the United States. Not very imaginative, the gratuitous remarks made in passing leave no doubt as to the underlying assumptions of the book.

Periodical literature on the diplomatic questions is rich and as a rule is much more reasoned and less partisan than many of the books. Two early studies on the subject are Robert H. Murray, "Huerta and the Two Wilsons," *Harper's Weekly* 62 (March 25-April 29, 1916): 301-3; 341-42; 364-65; 402-4; 434-36; and 466-69; and James L. Slayden, "The A.B.C. Mediation," *American Journal of International Law* 9 (1915), 147-52. The latter work is an essay on the meaning of mediation to future United States-Latin American relations rather than a catalog of the agreements and failures of the conference. More recent studies which I found useful include Lowell L. Blaisdell, "Henry Lane Wilson and the Overthrow of Madero," *Southwestern Social Science Quarterly* 43 (September 1962): 126-35; Charles C. Cumberland, "Huerta y Carranza ante la Ocupación de Veracruz," *Historia Mexicana* 6 (April-June 1957), 534-47: Martín Luis Guzmán, "Henry Lane Wilson: Un Embajador Malvado," *Cuadernos Americanos* 129 (July-August 1963): 203-8; John P. Harrison, "Henry Lane Wilson, el Trágico de la Decena," *Historia Mexicana* 6 (January-March 1957): 374-405; Victor Niemeyer, "Frustrated Invasion: The Revolutionary Attempt of General Bernardo Reyes from San Antonio in 1911," *Southwestern Historical Quarterly* 67 (July 1963-June 1964): 213-25; Frederick C. Turner, "Anti-Americanism in Mexico, 1910-1913," *Hispanic American Historical Review* 47 (November 1967): 502-18.

Conditions along the common border are treated in one book and four articles: Clarence C. Clendenen, *Blood on the Border: The United States Army and the Mexican Irregulars* (New York: Macmillan Co., 1969); Michael C. Meyer, "The Mexican-German Conspiracy of 1915," *The Americas* 23 (July 1966): 76-89; Michael C. Meyer, "The Arms of the *Ypiranga*," *Hispanic American Historical Review* 50 (August 1970): 543-56; Allen Gerlach, "Conditions Along the Border— 1915: The Plan de San Diego," *New Mexico Historical Review* 43 (July 1968): 195-212; and William H. Hager, "The Plan of San Diego: Unrest on the Texas Border in 1915," *Arizona and the West* 5 (Winter 1963): 327-36.

The three standard military histories of the early Revolution are Daniel Gutiérrez Santos, *Historia Militar de México, 1876-1914* (Mexico: Ediciones Ateneo, 1955); Miguel A. Sánchez Lamego, *Historia Militar de la Revolución Constitucionalista*, 2 vols. (Mexico: Talleres Gráficos de la Nación, 1956); and Juan Barragán Rodríguez, *Historia del Ejército y de la Revolución Constitu-cionalista*, 2 vols. (Mexico: Talleres de la Editorial Stylo, 1946). Works focusing on the military campaigns in the north include Adolfo Calzadíaz Barrera, *Hechos Reales de la Revolución*, 2 vols. (Chihuahua: Editorial Occidental, 1959-60), and Justino N. Palomares and Francisco Muzquiz, *Las Campañas del Norte: Sangre y Héroes* (Mexico: Andrés Botas, Editor, n.d.). For detailed coverage of important battles one can consult José G. Escobedo, *La Batalla de Zacatecas* (Mexico: n.p., 1946), and R. González Garza, P. Ramos Romero, and J. Pérez Rul, *La Batalla de Torreón* (Mexico: Secretaría de Educación Pública [1964?]).

D. *Institutional and Legal Studies*

With relatively few exceptions the studies treating Mexican institutions and other special topics during the early Revolutionary period are not very satisfactory for the Huerta period. Often the period is passed over altogether; if something positive is determined it is reported with a sense of embarrassment. Agrarianism is a point in question. Lucio Mendieta y Núñez's standard survey, *El Problema Agrario de México* (Mexico: Editorial Porrua, 1966) covers the topic from the preconquest time through 1962 but has nothing on the Huerta regime. The same can be said of José S. Noriega, *Diversos Aspectos del Problema Agrario* (Mexico: n.p., 1931). More useful are Fernando González Roa, *El Aspecto Agrario de la Revolución Mexicana* (Mexico: Dirección de Talleres Gráficos, 1919), and Ricardo Delgado Román, *Aspecto Agrario del Gobierno del General Victoriano Huerta* (Guadalajara: Imprenta Gráfica, 1951). The latter work suggests that Huerta actually initiated the agrarian reform legislation of the Revolution. The philosophy of Toribio Esquivel Obregón on the land question is best revealed in his own "La Cuestión Agraria y la Conciliación de los Intereses," *Excélsior,* November 28, 1928, pp. 5, 10.

The standard sources on the labor movement devote little time to the Huerta regime. General coverage is provided in Luis Araiza, *Historia del Movimiento Obrero Mexicano,* 4 vols. (Mexico: Talleres de la Editorial Cuauhtemoc, 1964-65); and Marjorie Ruth Clark, *Organized Labor in Mexico* (Chapel Hill: University of North Carolina Press, 1934). The regimes relationship to the church is best studied in the long background section of Alicia Olivera Sedano's forcefully presented *Aspectos del Conflicto Religioso de 1926 a 1929* (Mexico: Instituto Nacional de Antropología e Historia, 1966). Olivera offers an unbiased study of this emotion-laden topic. Her study can be supplemented by appropriate sections of Robert E. Quirk, "The Mexican Revolution and the Catholic Church, 1910-1929: An Ideological Study" (Ph.D. diss., Harvard University, 1950), and David C. Bailey, "Alvaro Obregón and Anti-Clericalism in the 1910 Revolution," *The Americas* 36 (October 1969): 183-98.

The most exhaustive treatment of the role of the military and the curbing of militarism is Edwin Lieuwen, *Mexican Militarism: The Political Rise and Fall of the Revolutionary Army* (Albuquerque: University of New Mexico Press, 1968). Less interpretive and generally less satisfactory is Rosendo Salazar, *Del Militarismo al Civilismo en Nuestra Revolución* (Mexico: Libro Mex Editores, 1958), which covers the period through 1946. The new study by Jorge Alberto Lozoya, *El Ejército Mexicano (1911-1965)* (Mexico: El Colegio de México, 1970), appeared too late to be consulted for this work.

Mexico's economic institutions have been the subject of more perceptive studies for the late Revolutionary period than for the early period. Three notable exceptions are Walter F. McCaleb, *Present and Past Banking in Mexico* (New York: Harper and Brothers, 1920); Marvin D. Bernstein, *The Mexican Mining Industry, 1890-1950: A Study of the Interaction of Politics, Economics, and Technology* (Albany: State University of New York, 1964); and Ernesto Lobato López, *El Crédito en México: Esbozo Histórico Hasta 1925* (Mexico: Fondo de Cultura Económica, 1945). The Bernstein study is a painstaking analysis of a difficult topic. Lobato López's study on Mexican credit contains a highly useful chapter on the financial collapse of 1913. Also see Ricardo Torres Gaitán, *Política Monetaria Mexicana* (Mexico: n.p., 1944), and Fred W. Powell, *The Railroads of Mexico* (Boston: Stratford Co., 1921).

The legal status of the Huerta regime has been studied in three scholarly works. Felipe Tena Ramírez argues in his *Derecho Constitucional de México* (Mexico: Editorial Porrua, 1955) that the government emanating from the coup of February, 1913, met all of the legal requirements and therefore should not be considered an illegal usurpation. The opposite point of view is presented in Gabino Fraga, *Derecho Administrativo* (Mexico: Editorial Porrua, 1956), and Arturo Amaya Morán, *Examen Histórico-Jurídico del Gobierno de Huerta* (Mexico: Universidad Nacional Autónoma de México, 1952).

E. *State and Local Histories*

The cultivation of state and local history is still in its infancy in Mexican

Revolutionary historiography, although it is beginning to attract the interest of a young generation of scholars. In addition to the biographies mentioned on pp. 247-249, many of which focus on state and local leaders, a number of state histories have been produced in the last decade. Within Mexico the group most active in this field is the Instituto Nacional de Estudios Históricos de la Revolución Mexicana. Some of the volumes published by the instituto are considerably better than others. Those which I found most informative are Francisco R. Almada, *La Revolución en el Estado de Chihuahua*, 2 vols. (Mexico, 1964-65); Edmundo Bolio, *Yucatán en la Dictadura y la Revolución* (Mexico, 1967); Jesús Romero Flores, *Historia de la Revolución en Michoacán* (Mexico, 1964); and José G. Zuno, *Historia de la Revolución en el Estado de Jalisco* (Mexico, 1964).

In addition to the state histories published by the instituto, other recent works include Nelson Reed, *The Caste War of Yucatán* (Stanford, Calif.: Stanford University Press, 1964), a competent and interesting treatment by a nonprofessional; Claudio Dabdoub, *Historia de el Valle del Yaqui* (Mexico: Librería de Manuel Porrua, 1964), the most authoritative account of the campaigns against the Yaqui's; Vicente Fuentes Díaz, *La Revolución de 1910 en el Estado de Guerrero* (Mexico: Nacional Impresora, Fresno 30, 1960), which contains much useful information; and José Luis Melgarejo Vivanco, *Breve Historia de Veracruz* (Xalapa: Universidad Veracruzana, 1960), a rather pedestrian survey.

The most illuminating of the older works is Francisco Ramírez Plancarte, *La Ciudad de México Durante la Revolución Constitucionalista*, 2nd ed. (Mexico: Ediciones Botas, 1941), the first chapter of which is devoted to the capital during the Huerta presidency. Less satisfactory are Sergio Valverde, *Apuntes para la Historia de la Revolución y de la Política del Estado de Morelos* (Mexico: n.p., 1933), and Eduardo W. Villa, *Compendio de Historia del Estado de Sonora* (Mexico: Editorial Patria Nueva, 1937).

F. Miscellaneous Articles

The occasional historical article appearing in Mexican newspapers or other nonprofessional journals affords the historian of the Revolution a source of information which has often been overlooked. With the new Ross guide to periodicals and newspapers (see p. 240), however, the citations are easily traceable in the Hemeroteca Nacional and the short articles should be utilized. Weekly or biweekly historical series often never appear in more extensive monographic works, and, therefore, if they are to be consulted and evaluated one must go to the newspaper in which they originally appeared in serial form.

Brief biographical sketches of Huerta include the following: Sandalio Mejía Castelán, "El Verdadero Huerta," *Excélsior,* August 30, 1951, pp. 6, 12; Andrés Molina Enríquez, "Huerta, el Presidente que Menos Sangre Derramó," *Todo* 176 (January 19, 1937): 18-19; Héctor R. Olea, "El Indio Victoriano," *El Nacional*, February 17, 1955, p. 11; Joaquín Piña, "Triunfo y Calvario del Presidente Huerta," *Así* 275 (March 23, 1946): 48-52; Hernán Rosales, "Huerta: Los Azares de su Destino," *Todo* 254 (July 21, 1938): 40-41, 62; Rubén Salido Orcillo, "El Coronel Ahumada y Huerta," *Excélsior*, April 5, 1954, p. 6; and Oswaldo Sánchez, "Para los Depositarios de la Verdad Histórica: D. Victoriano Huerta, Cuartelacista por Temperamento," *El Nacional,* June 25, 1930, pp. 3, 7.

Similar sketches of cabinet members and other officials who surrounded the dictator are traced in: Miguel Alessio Robles, "Las Renuncias de los Ministros de Huerta," *El Universal*, December 20, 1937, pp. 3, 8; and by the same author, "El General Huerta y el Doctor Urrutia," *El Universal*, June 13, 1938, pp. 3, 5; Gabriel Ferrer Mendiola, "Los Ministros de Huerta," *El Nacional*, May 12, 1953, pp. 3, 6; Rubén Salido Orcillo, "El Primer Gabinete de Huerta," *Excélsior,* August

24, 1954, p. 6; Armando de María y Campos, "Los Ministros de Huerta Explican su Actuación," *A.B.C.* 66 (December 6, 1952): 44-47; and Alberto Morales Jiménez, "Gente del Cuartelazo: Victoriano Huerta," *El Nacional,* September 25, 1943, pp. 3, 7.

Periodical treatment of the Decena Trágica and the subsequent assassinations of Madero and Pino Suárez is immense but most of it contains little that is original or refreshing. Those articles which do reveal new data include: Isaac Díaz Araiza, "Preliminares Revolucionarios," *Hoy* 353 (November 27, 1943): 22-23, 81; Agustín Haró y T., "Guatemala Vengó a Madero y Pino Suárez," *Crisol* 36 (December 1931): 410-14; Armando de María y Campos, "Renuncia de Lascuráin y Protesta de Huerta," *A.B.C.* 64 (November 22, 1952): 38-40; Armando de María y Campos, "El Asesinato de Madero y Pino Suárez," *A.B.C.* 67 (December 13, 1952): 30-33; and [Rafael Martínez], "La Verdad en la Muerte de Fcs. I. Madero," *Excélsior,* February 22, 1927, p. 6.

Valuable material on the Huerta presidency itself is as scarce in the periodical literature as in the monographic literature. Only a few articles are worthy of note: Miguel Alessio Robles, "El Golpe de Estado de Octubre," *El Universal,* April 25, 1938, p. 1; Alberto Morales Jiménez, "Huerta Disuelve la XXVI Legislatura," *El Nacional,* October 10, 1940, p. 8; Rafael Nieto, "La Deuda de Huerta," *El Universal,* April 4, 1921, p. 3; Miguel A. Quintana, "La Educación en la Epoca de Huerta," *El Nacional,* October 29, 1945, pp. 3, 8; and Rubén Salido Orcillo, "Huerta y el Ejército Federal," *Excélsior,* June 5, 1954, pp. 6, 9.

IV. NEWSPAPERS

The Mexican government maintains one of the best newspaper archives in Latin America. The Hemeroteca Nacional not only houses all of the most important local, state, and national newspapers, but also a respectable sampling of the world press. A good card catalog and a competent and cooperative staff greatly facilitates use of the newspaper holdings.

The Mexican newspapers which I consulted during the course of this project were examined not merely for the store of information they contained but also to determine the regime's relationship with the press. In most cases they were revealing more for their distortion of fact than for their elucidation of it. The following newspapers from Mexico City were useful: *El Diario, El Diario del Hogar, El Heraldo Mexicano* and its English edition *The Mexican Herald, El Imparcial, El Independiente, La Nueva Era, El País, El Sol, El Universal,* and *La Verdad.*

Provincial newspapers were consulted only when a local item was of special interest or when I was led to it by another source. Those used included: *El Caustico* (Jalapa); *El Correo* (Chihuahua); *El Eco de la Frontera* (Ciudad Juárez); *El Legalista* (Hidalgo del Parral); *El Noticiero* (Monterrey); and *La Voz de Sonora* (Hermosillo).

The most valuable foreign newspaper for its general coverage was the *New York Times.* But for specific information on the border region and on exile problems newspapers from Texas and New Mexico were of considerably more utility. Especially helpful were the *Albuquerque Morning Journal, El Paso Morning Times, San Antonio Express, San Antonio Light,* and *El Presente* (San Antonio).

Finally, while tracing the activities of Francisco Cárdenas in Guatemala, I consulted three Guatemalan newspapers in the Archivo General de Centro América: *El Diario de Centro América, Diario Nuevo,* and *Excélsior: Diario Independiente de la Tarde.*

Index

A

257

C

Caballero, Antonio, 214 n
Caballero, Crisóforo, 226
Caballeros, Luis (constitutionalist general), 192
Cabinet: alleged role of Huerta's in assassinations, 80-81; Huerta's discusses disposition of Madero and Pino Suárez, 70; Madero's appoints Huerta to command troops during Decena Trágica, 49; Madero's appoints Huerta to engage Orozco, 34-35; as provided in Pact of the Ciudadela, 60, 66; relationship to Huerta, 100, 140-43, 147, 157. *See also names of individual cabinet officials*
Cabrera, Luis, and election of 1913, 151
Cadets, 49, 100. *See also* Colegio Militar de Chapultepec; Escuela Militar de Aspirantes; National Naval Academy
Caja de Préstamos de Irrigación, 164, 165
Calero, Manuel: and election of 1913, 151; exile of, 214; as secretary of foreign relations, 34
California, 122, 218, 220
Calles, Plutarco Elías, 85, 155 n
Calvert, Peter, 20 n
Camarena, Benjamín (federal officer), 135, 136
Camargo, Chihuahua, 90, 94
Camp, U.S. District Attorney J. L., 222, 224, 225
Campa, Emilio (Orozquista officer), 218
Campos Martínez, Alfredo (journalist), assassination of, 138
Canada, William W. (consular agent, Veracruz), 118, 198
Cananea, Sonora, 89
Cantú, Esteban, 219
Carbajal, Francisco S.: exile of, 214; interim president of Mexico, 77, 208; as president of Supreme Court, 44; as secretary of foreign relations, 140, 208
Carden, Sir Lionel (British ambassador), 120, 154 n
Cárdenas, Francisco (major of rurales): confession of, 77-79; exile and death

of, 79 n, promotion of, 82; role of in assassinations, 72-73, 74, 76
Carothers, George (U.S. consular agent, Torreón), 204, 206 n
Carranza, Jesús, 192
Carranza, Venustiano: and A. B. C. mediation, 205-6; attitude toward Huerta government, 68, 69, 82, 84; and exiles, 219, 220; difficulties with Villa, 192; as First Chief, 90, 92, 93-94, 105, 107, 113, 144 n; as governor of Coahuila, 50 n; as president of Mexico, 155 n, 158, 159 n, 165 n, 231; proscription list of, 214-15; receives *de facto* recognition from U.S., 227; relations with U.S., 119, 121-26, 191; and Veracruz invasion, 203-5; withdraws recognition of Huerta, 84. *See also* Constitutionalists
Carrillo Puerto, Felipe, assassination of, 155 n
Casa del Obrero Mundial, 173, 174-75
Caso López, Arnoldo (federal officer), 29
Castañón Campoverde, Lic. Pablo, assassination of, 139 n
Castellanos, Congressman César, 146
Castillo Calderón, Rafael del: candidate for governor of Guerrero, 8; rebellion of, 8-10
Castro, Jesús Agustín, 90
Catholic party, 146, 148, 151, 169. *See also* Church, Roman Catholic
Cattle industry, 180
Cauz, Eduardo (federal general in exile), 218, 223
Cedillo, Saturnino, 91
Censorship. *See* Newspapers; Press
Cepeda, Enrique, 56
Cepeda, Rafael (governor of San Luis Potosí), 83, 86; as peace envoy to Carranza, 91-92
Cervantes Carrillo, Miguel, assassination of, 139 n
Chamber of Deputies: dissolved by Huerta, 147-49; during Huerta's presidency, 145; during Madero's presidency, 143; on Madero's resignation, 55, 62. *See also* Congress; Senate
Chamizal controversy, 112 n
Chan Santa Cruz, Yucatán, 11, 13
Chao, Manuel (constitutionalist offi-